Praise for *The Wre*

"Thomas Frank is back with another hunk of dynamite. *The Wrecking Crew* should monopolize political conversation this year. It's the first book to effectively tie the ruin and corruption of conservative governance to the conservative 'movement building' of the 1970s, and, before that, the business crusade against good government going back at least to the 1890s." —Salon.com

"Tom Frank has hold of something real. *The Wrecking Crew* can be good, spirited fun. Frank captures a quality of exuberant bullying in those of his conservative subjects he knows well enough to identify individually, rather than categorically."

—*The New Yorker*

"Compelling." —*The Baltimore Sun*

"Frank's new book is a more determined work of exposé, in the muckraking tradition of Lincoln Steffens and Ida Tarbell. Frank writes with the delighted outrage of an authentic satirist. The book repays reading just for its portrait of Abramoff. . . . Entertaining."

—*The New Republic*

"Readers entranced by the vivid prose and sweeping themes of *Kansas* won't be disappointed."

—*The American Prospect*

"Entertaining and engaging." —*The Nation*

"Hard-hitting . . . Frank's sentences inhale and unfurl with a wit and verve." —*The New York Observer*

"Conservatives in office have made their share of blunders and mistakes, and Frank is at his finest in depicting some of the stunning instances of hypocrisy and idiocy in the period of Republican rule."
—*The New York Post*

"*The Wrecking Crew* eviscerates the cynical governing strategy that dominates 'market-based' government. Frank does so with graceful prose and an acerbic, charmingly old-timey wit that reads like it was ripped from the notebook of a crusading 1930s muckraker."
—*In These Times*

"Smart, thoroughly researched, and written with wit and panache."
—*The Wichita Eagle*

"A welcome read. There is no doubt that Frank is helping to restore the journalistic and literary standards to political books. Elegant . . . *The Wrecking Crew* has the rhetorical power to illustrate the dire consequences of a government sold off piece by piece to the highest bidder. One finishes the book feeling as if one's political vision has been brought into focus."
—*The Courier-Journal*

"A superb follow-up to *What's the Matter with Kansas?* . . . Thorough reporting and incisive historical analysis. With genuine outrage and blasts of polemic, but Frank never allows *The Wrecking Crew* to become just another seething right- or left-wing political tract preaching to the choir." —*The Oregonian*

Also by Thomas Frank

What's the Matter with Kansas?

One Market Under God

The Conquest of Cool

THE WRECKING CREW

THOMAS FRANK

THE WRECKING CREW

How Conservatives Ruined Government, Enriched Themselves, and Beggared the Nation

A HOLT PAPERBACK

Metropolitan Books / Henry Holt and Company

New York

Holt Paperbacks
Henry Holt and Company, LLC
Publishers since 1866
175 Fifth Avenue
New York, New York 10010
www.henryholt.com

A Holt Paperback® and ® are registered trademarks of
Henry Holt and Company, LLC.

Distributed in Canada by H. B. Fenn and Company Ltd.

Library of Congress Cataloging-in-Publication Data

Frank, Thomas, 1965–
The wrecking crew : how conservatives ruined government, enriched themselves, and beggared the nation / Thomas Frank.—1st ed.
p. cm.
Includes bibliographical references and index.
ISBN-13: 978-0-8050-9090-1
ISBN-10: 0-8050-9090-8
1. Republican Party (U.S.: 1854–) 2. Conservatives—United States. 3. Politics, Practical—United States. 4. United States—Politics and government. I. Title.
JK2356.F72 2008
973.92—dc22 2008015802

Henry Holt books are available for special promotions and premiums. For details contact: Director, Special Markets.

Originally published in hardcover in 2008 by Metropolitan Books
First Holt Paperbacks Edition 2009

"Then" and "Now" by Benjamin Edwards
Designed by Meryl Sussman Levavi

Printed in the United States of America
1 3 5 7 9 10 8 6 4 2

"If we did any of these things alone the papers and the public could concentrate on it, get the facts, and fight. But we reasoned that if we poured them all out fast and furious, one, two, three—one after the other—the papers couldn't handle them all and the public would be stunned and—give up. Too much."

We sat there, he amused, I as stunned as his public.

"Well, you Pennsylvania politicians know something even Tammany doesn't know."

He nodded. "Yes," he said. "We know a lot they don't know. We know that public despair is possible and that that is good politics."

—*The Autobiography of Lincoln Steffens,* 1931

Contents

THE WRECKING CREW

INTRODUCTION

Follow This Dime

Washington is the city where the scandals happen. Every American knows this, but we also believe, if only vaguely, that the really monumental scandals are a thing of the past; that the golden age of misgovernment-for-profit ended with the cavalry charge and the robber barons, at about the same time presidents stopped wearing beards.

I moved to Washington in 2003, just in time for the comeback, for the hundred-year flood. At first it was only a trickle in the basement, a little stream released accidentally by President George W. Bush's friends at Enron. Before long, though, the levees were failing all over town, and the city was inundated with a muddy torrent of graft.

How are we to dissect a deluge like this one? We might begin by categorizing the earmarks handed out in those days by Congress, sorting the foolish earmarks from the costly earmarks from the earmarks made strictly on a cash basis. We could try a similar approach to the Bush administration's contracting practices: the no-bid contracts, the no-oversight contracts, the no-experience contracts, the contracts handed out to friends of the vice president. We might consider the shoplifting career of one of Dubya's former domestic policy advisers or the habitual plagiarism of the president's liaison to the Christian right. And we would certainly have to find some way to parse the extraordinary incompetence of the executive branch, incompetence so fulsome and steady and reliable that at some point in those years Americans stopped being surprised and began simply to count on it, to think of incompetence as the way government works.

But the onrushing flow swamped all taxonomies. Mass firing of federal prosecutors; bribing of newspaper columnists; pallets of shrinkwrapped cash "misplaced" in Iraq; inexperienced kids running the Baghdad stock exchange; the discovery that many of Alaska's leading politicians were on the take—our heads spun. We climbed to the rooftops, but we could not find the heights of irony from which we might laugh off the blend of thug and pharisee that was Tom DeLay—or dispel the nauseating suspicion, quickly becoming a certainty, that the government of our nation deliberately fibbed us into a pointless, catastrophic war.

So let us begin on the solid ground of basic historical fact: this spectacular episode of misrule coincided with the political triumph of the right. Other times and other lands have seen misgovernment by other political persuasions, of course, but if we wish to understand the specific dynamics of the period just ended we must look to American conservatism, and in particular to that movement's ideas about the state.

We must also look to Washington itself. During the era that is our subject here, the capital region became one of the wealthiest metropolitan areas in America.[1] Through this enchanted city, the gentlemen of the right rolled like lords of creation. Every spigot was open, and every indulgence slopped out for their gleeful wallowing. All the clichés roared at full, unembarrassed volume: the wines gurgled, the T-bones roasted, the golf courses beckoned, the Learjets zoomed, the contractors' glass buildings sprouted from the earth, and the lobbyists' mansions grew like brick-colonial mushrooms on the hills of northern Virginia.

Democrats, for their part, tried to explain the flood of misgovernment as part of a "culture of corruption," a phrase at once obviously true and yet so amorphous as to be quite worthless. Republicans have an even simpler answer: government failed, they tell us, because it is the nature of government enterprises to fail. As for the great corruption cases of those years, they cluck, each was merely a one-of-a-kind moral lapse unconnected to any particular ideology—an individual bad apple with no effect on the larger barrel.

Which leaves us to marvel helplessly at what appears to have been a spectacular run of lousy luck. My, what a lot of bad apples they were growing back then!

Corruption is uniquely reprehensible in a democracy because it violates the system's first principle, which we all learned back in the sunshiny days of elementary school: that the government exists to serve the public, not particular companies or individuals or even elected officials. *We Are the Government,* insisted the title of a civics primer published in the earnest year of 1945. "The White House belongs to you," its dust jacket told us. "So do all the other splendid buildings in Washington, D.C. For you are a citizen of the United States." For you, young citizen, does the Post Office carry letters to every hamlet in the nation. For you does the Department of Agriculture research better plowing methods and the Bureau of Labor Statistics add up long columns of numbers.[2]

The government and its vast workforce serve the people: The idea is so deep in the American grain that we can't bring ourselves to question it, even in this disillusioned age. Republicans and Democrats may fight over how big government should be and exactly what it should do, but almost everyone shares those baseline good intentions, we believe, that devotion to the public interest.

We continue to believe this in even the most improbable circumstances. Take the worst apple of them all, lobbyist Jack Abramoff, whose astonishing career as a corruptionist unreeled in newspaper and congressional investigations in 2005 and 2006. Abramoff started out as a great political success story, a protégé and then a confidant of the leaders of the conservative faction of the Republican Party. But his career disintegrated on news of the inventive ways he ripped off his clients and the luxury meals and lavish trips with which he bribed legislators. Journalistic coverage of the Abramoff affair has stuck closely to the "bad apple" thesis, always taking pains to separate the conservative movement from its onetime superstar. What Abramoff represented was "greed gone wild," asserts the most authoritative account on the subject. He "went native," say others. Above all, he was "sui generis," a one-of-a-kind con man, "engaged in bizarre antics that your average Zegna-clad Washington lobbyist would never have dreamed of."[3]

In which case, we can all relax: Jack Abramoff went to jail. The system worked; the bad apple was plucked; the wild greed and the undreamed-of antics ceased.

But the truth is almost exactly the opposite, whether we are discussing Abramoff or the wider tsunami of corruption. The truth is as obvious as a slab of sirloin and yet so obscured by decades of pettifoggery that we find it almost impossible to apprehend clearly.

The truth is just this: Fantastic misgovernment of the kind we saw during the Bush era was not an accident, nor was it the work of a few bad individuals. It was made possible by the triumph of a particular philosophy of government, of a movement that understands the liberal state as a perversion and considers the market the ideal nexus of human society. This movement is always friendly to industry not just by force of campaign contributions but by conviction; it believes in entrepreneurship not merely in commerce but in politics; and the inevitable results of its ascendance were, first, the capture of the state by business and, second, all that followed: incompetence, graft, and all the other wretched flotsam that we came to expect from Washington.

The correct diagnosis is the "bad apple" thesis turned upside down. There are plenty of good conservative individuals, honorable folks who would never participate in the sort of corruption we have watched unfold over the last few years. Hang around with grassroots conservative voters in Kansas, and in the main you will find them to be honest, hardworking people. Even our story's worst villains can be personally virtuous. Jack Abramoff, for example, is known to his friends as a pious, polite, and generous fellow.

But put conservatism in charge of the state, and it behaves very differently. Now the "values" that rightist politicians eulogize on the stump disappear, and in their place we can discern an entirely different set of priorities—priorities that reveal more about the unchanging historical essence of American conservatism than do its fleeting campaigns against gay marriage or secular humanism. The conservatism that speaks to us through its actions in Washington is institutionally opposed to those baseline good intentions we learned about in elementary school. Its leaders laugh off the idea of the public interest as airy-fairy nonsense; they caution against bringing top-notch talent into government service; they declare war on public workers.[4] Indeed, during their years in power, they made a cult of outsourcing and privatizing, they wrecked established federal operations because they disagreed with them, and they deliberately piled up an Everest of debt in order to force the government into crisis. The ruination they wrought was thorough; it was a professional job. Repairing it will require years of political action.

There have been many calls for official investigations of the graft and misrule of the Bush years. It is unlikely that such inquiries will ever be made, however, and it is even less likely that, were they actually to take place, they would delve into the role of ideology in conservative-era corruption.

What follows is not a discussion of conservatives as individuals, and it is most certainly not an ethnography of conservatives as a political tribe. It is about the very particular, very predictable things that happened when the faction that calls itself "conservative" managed to squeeze behind the controls of the state. They were "predictable" because conservatism-in-power attends far more closely to the needs of the business community than does its street-level cousin. While the conservatism you meet on best-seller lists is concerned largely with cultural questions, the Beltway version is given almost obsessively to free-market theory—which it then proceeds to abandon quietly whenever the requirements of business demand it. And it is to this Washington form of conservatism, not the academic or culture-war varieties, that we must look to understand the many public failures of recent years.

Conservatives do not hold some kind of monopoly on corruption and misgovernment, of course. But they do go crooked from time to time. And when they do, their corruption tends to take a distinctive form. While liberal turpitude is something we know well from endless radio rants against "big government," the particular kind of corruption associated with conservatism has been left relatively unexamined and untheorized. Yet it is this species of misgovernment, not liberal pandering to interest groups, that was responsible for remaking Washington over the last three decades, for redrawing the social structure of the nation, and for plunging the world economy into catastrophe.

It might seem that the group I have chosen to describe here is just a collection of cranks, people so far removed from the main currents of American thought that they aren't worth considering. And it is indeed true that my characters' views are often bizarre and unpopular. But that, too, is consistent with the movement's essence. By and large, what conservatism did in its decades at the seat of power *was* fundamentally unpopular, and a large percentage of its leaders *were* men of eccentric ideas. While they believed things that would get them laughed out of the American Sociological Association, that only made them more typical of the movement. And for all their peculiarity, these people—Grover Norquist, Tom DeLay, Jack Abramoff, Newt Gingrich, and the whole troupe of activists, lobbyists, and corporatrons who got their start back in the Reagan years—were, for the last three decades, among the most powerful individuals in America. Their wave of misgovernment was brought to you by ideology, not incompetence.[5]

Yes, these conservatives disgraced themselves, but they did not stray from the teaching of their forefathers or the great ideas of their movement. On the contrary: both the Bush and the Reagan administrations were filled with idealists, with true believers, with people who wanted to sound the trumpets of free-market democracy in every corner of the globe. And yet the very same individuals sat and watched as spectacular episodes of corruption, fraud, and misgovernment played out all around them.

The paradox is easily resolved, however. When conservatives appointed the opponents of government agencies to head those government agencies; when they auctioned their official services to the purveyor of the most lavish "golf weekend"; when they mulcted millions from groups with business before Congress; when they dynamited the Treasury and sabotaged the regulatory process and forced government shutdowns—in short, when they treated government with contempt—they were running true to free-market form. They did not do these awful things because they were bad conservatives; they did them because they were *good* conservatives, because these unsavory deeds followed naturally from the core doctrines of the conservative tradition.

And, yes, there was greed involved in the effort—a great deal of greed. Every tax cut, every cleverly engineered regulatory snafu saved industry millions and perhaps even billions of dollars, and so naturally securing those tax cuts and engineering those snafus became a booming business here in Washington. Conservative rule made the capital region rich, a showplace of the plutocratic order. But this greed cannot be dismissed as some personal failing of lobbyist or congressman, some badness-of-apple that could easily have been contained. Conservatism, as we have seen it, is a movement that is *about* greed, about the "virtue of selfishness" when it acts in the marketplace. In right-wing Washington, you could be a man of principle and a boodler at the same time.

One of the instructive stories *We Are the Government* brought before generations of schoolkids was the tale of a smiling dime whose wanderings were meant to introduce us to the government and all that it does for us: the miner who digs the ore for the dime has his "health and safety" supervised by one branch of the government; the bank in which the dime is stored enjoys the protection of a different branch, which "sees that [banks] are safe places for people to keep their money"; the dime gets paid in tax on a gasoline sale; it then lands in the pocket of a Coast Guard lieutenant, who takes it overseas and spends it on a parrot, which is "quarantined for ninety days" when the lieutenant brings it home. All of which is related with the blithest innocence, as though taxes on gasoline and quarantines on parrots were so obviously beneficial that they required little further explanation.

Clearly, a more up-to-date version is required. So let us follow the fortunes of the dime in a capital governed by conservatives. Its story, we will find, is the reverse of what it was in 1945. That old dime was all about service, about the things government could do for us. But the new dime is about profit—about the superiority of private enterprise, about the huge sums that can be squeezed out of federal operations. Instead of symbolizing good government, the conservative-era dime shows us the wrecking crew in full swing.

This dime first comes to Washington as part of some good citizen's taxes, and it leaves the U.S. Treasury in a payment to a company that has been hired to do work on the nation's ports. Back in 1945, the government would have done the work itself, but under conservatism it used contractors for such things. This particular contractor knows how to win a bid, but it doesn't know how to do the work, so it subcontracts the job to another outfit. The dime follows, and it eventually makes up a worker's salary, who incorporates it into his monthly car payment. From there it travels into the coffers of an auto industry trade association, which happens to be very upset about a rule proposed by a federal agency that would require cars to notify drivers when their tire pressure is low.

So the trade association gives the dime to a Washington consultant who specializes in fighting federal agencies, and this man launches challenge after challenge to the studies that the federal agency is using in the tire-pressure matter. It takes many years for the agency to make its way through the flak thrown up by this clever fellow. Meanwhile, with his well-earned dime, he buys himself a big house with nice white columns in front.

But this is only the beginning of the story. As we make our study of the late conservative Washington, we shall begin to glimpse something much greater than single acts of incompetence or obstruction. We shall see a vast machinery built for our protection reengineered into a device for our exploitation. We shall behold the majestic workings of the free market itself, boring ever deeper into the tissues of the state. Ultimately, we shall gaze upon one of the true marvels of history: democracy buried beneath an avalanche of money.

PART I

Insurgents

CHAPTER 1

Golconda on the Potomac

The richest county in America isn't in Silicon Valley or some sugarland preserve of Houston's oil kings; it is Loudoun County, Virginia, a fast-growing suburb of Washington, D.C., that is known for swollen suburban homes and white rail fences of the kind that denote "horse country." The second richest county is Fairfax, Virginia, the next suburb over from Loudoun; the third, sixth, and seventh richest counties are also suburbs of the capital.[1] The Washington area has six different Morton's steakhouses to choose from, seven BMW dealerships,[2] six Ritz-Carlton installations,[3] three luxury lifestyle magazines, and a Capital Beltway that is essentially an all-hours Mercedes speedway.

There are malcontents all over America with a ready explanation for why this is so: Washington is rich because those overpaid federal bureaucrats are battening on the hard work of people like us, gorging themselves on the bounty that the IRS extracts out of the vast heartland. In blog and barbershop alike they rail against big government like it's 1979, moaning about meddling feds and cursing the income tax as a crime against nature.

As a way of explaining the stratospheric prosperity of Washington today, however, this old, familiar plaint makes as much sense as attributing the price of stocks to the coming and going of sunspots. After all, it isn't FTC paper pushers who buy the six-thousand-square-foot "estate homes" of Loudoun County, and even the highest-ranking members of Congress drool to behold the fine cars and the vacation chateaus of the people sent to lobby them by, say, the pharmaceutical industry.

The reason our barbershop grumblers don't get it is that their myths don't account for the swarming, thriving fauna that has come to populate the capital. Even though conservatives dominated the city for years, conservative Washington was always unknown territory. The private offices to which it delegated the nation's public business were never included on the tourist's map. Its monuments were not marked. Its operations were not well understood outside the city. But Washington's opulence gives us our first clue as to what those operations entailed.

Washington is a strange place under any circumstances. If you happen to come here from the urban Midwest, as I did, the city seems alien and hopelessly unreal. The blue-collar workers who make up a good portion of the population elsewhere in America are a minority in Washington, with lawyers outnumbering machinists, to choose one example, by a factor of twenty-seven to one. There are few rusting factories or empty warehouses in Washington—and few busy factories or well-stocked warehouses either. The largest manufacturing outfit in town, at least as of the early 1980s, was the Government Printing Office.[4] The neighborhood taverns one finds on nearly every street corner in Chicago are almost completely absent, as are the three-flats that house much of that midwestern metropolis.

While the capital has desperately poor people in abundance, members of the political class have almost no reason to mingle with them. If you stay within the boundaries of the federal colony, you will meet only people like your tidy white-collar self: college graduates wearing ID badges and speaking correct American English. In one residential neighborhood I visited, a full 50 percent of the adult population possess advanced degrees.

The city is a perfect realization of the upper-bracket dream of a white-collar universe, where economies run on the information juggling of the "creative class" and where manufacturing is something done by filthy brutes in far-off lands. In the hard-hit heartland this fantasy seems so risible as to not require attention. In Washington and its suburbs, however—where there are hundreds of corporate offices but little manufacturing—it is thought to be such an apt description of reality, such a pearly pearl of wisdom, that the city's big thinkers return to it again and again. The malls and offices and housing developments of northern Virginia so overwhelmed Joel Garreau, the man on the "cultural revolution" beat at the *Washington Post*, that in describing them he slipped into the past-tense profundo: the region's "private-enterprise, high-information, high-education, post–Industrial Revolution economy," he raved in 1991, "made it a model of what American urban areas would be in the twenty-first century."[5]

Washington has boomed before, and it's even been proclaimed a model for the world before—most famously during the thirties and forties, when the federal government looked like the savior of the nation and maybe even of the planet. The city was occupied then by an army of "New Dealers" who were idealistic about the possibilities of government, talented, and young—far younger than the gray old gentlemen who had previously run the place. Today we naturally think of Washington as a young person's town, thanks to all the fresh-faced interns and aides and paralegals who fill its offices. But in the thirties this was a novel development, made possible by the stock market crash and the Depression, which closed other doors and utterly destroyed the traditional American faith in limited government and benevolent business.

Disabused of the old myths, and unable to get a job, the class of 1933 went to Washington instead of Wall Street. They lived in group houses, drank hard, and threw themselves into building the new regulatory state. It's not a calling that anyone associates with glamour anymore, but excitement and high patriotism are constant themes in the literature of the New Deal period. One account from 1935, for example, described the city's "mood of adventure, the exhilaration of exciting living which the humblest office-holders share with the Brain Trust [the president's close advisers] as co-workers in the great experimental laboratory set up in their city."[6]

The stories of that period always seemed to follow the same pattern: how the bright young man arrived in the city, fresh from law school, where he was put to work immediately on business of the utmost urgency; how he went for days without sleep; how he marveled at the awesome abilities of the people the administration had brought to Washington. I know of none in which the young man came to Washington to get rich. When the New Dealers grew older, of course, they found ample opportunity to pile up the coin, often by guiding business interests through the bureaucracies that they themselves had created.[7] But in those early years, when business had failed so spectacularly and when the country looked desperately to Washington for relief, public service became the object of a sort of cult.[8]

Liberalism was something strong and bold in those days, and making government work was at the very heart of it. This was the period when the United States developed a first-rate bureaucracy, and the famous law professor Felix Frankfurter attributed its appearance to the epochal migration of idealistic youth to the capital (a movement for which Frankfurter was partially responsible). "The ablest of them—in striking contrast to what was true thirty years ago—are eager for service in government," he wrote in 1936. "They find satisfaction in work which aims at the public good and which presents problems that challenge the best ability and courage of man."[9]

Like all historical myths, the legend of the capable and selfless New Dealer is surely overdrawn. Even so, there were in those years enough genuine cases of honest public service delivered despite peril to the public servant's career to make the thirties and forties truly seem like some kind of bureaucratic golden age. The chairman of the Tennessee Valley Authority, for example, provoked the berserk, undying hostility of the senior senator from Tennessee by refusing to allow this worthy to pack the TVA with cronies and patronage hacks. The head of the Office of Price Administration, responsible for wartime rationing, fended off not only the spoilsmen of Congress but the profiteers of the private sector, earning the enmity of senators and industrialists alike. And when Franklin D. Roosevelt's nominee for chairman of the Federal Reserve was informed that the private sector would agree to his appointment if he would abandon his liberalism, he responded, "You can tell your banker friends to go to hell."[10]

True, Washington crawled with millionaires back then, just as it does today. There was a critical difference, however: in those days the millions almost always came from somewhere else. At the turn of the twentieth century, in the golden age of unregulated capitalism, the masters of the great fortunes had found it amusing to settle down among the diplomats and statesmen of the federal city, and so Massachusetts Avenue came to be lined with the grand palazzos of people who had made their pile—or, more accurately, whose parents had made their pile—in mining or manufacturing or railroads or steel or breakfast cereal. Occasionally these nabobs went in for politics themselves: A 1905 novel by David Graham Phillips is set in "one of the very finest of the houses that have been building since rich men began to buy into the Senate and Cabinet." But by the thirties their days in public service had ended. Now these patricians spent their time throwing dinner parties for ambassadors, publishing newspapers, settling back into comfortable alcoholic delirium, and, of course, raging against the New Dealers who had supplanted them.[11]

"Never before have such vast numbers of officials swarmed to the capital, and never before have so few of them been welcomed by the permanent dwellers," wrote one of these embittered Washington aristocrats in the *Saturday Evening Post* in 1936, the same year that Felix Frankfurter penned his homage to the visionary young bureaucrat. What Frankfurter saw as idealism was exactly what made the "hordes of New Dealers" so contemptible to the capital's highborn hostesses. The New Dealer "exists on a high spiritual plane; he, and he alone, is a good man," the aristocrat sneered. "He proves it by the violent sincerity of his intolerance." He gives further offense by showing up at dinner parties late or in business clothes, by his inexperience with servants, and by radiating "malice and envy toward the successful," meaning the tycoons this impudent nobody proposed to regulate. Fortunately, the aristocrat concluded, the New Dealer's persecution of bankers and captains of industry was inadvertently bringing to town numerous more suitable dinner guests; indeed, "the only attractive and able men who come to Washington today, are brought there by subpoenas."[12]

Those swarms of New Dealers changed the appearance of the city, too. The architectural hallmark of their Washington boom was the unassuming two-story, redbrick, colonial-style house, built by the thousands in a great residential arc around the city's

Then

core. These homes were for bureaucrats, not billionaires; they were made affordable by loans guaranteed by the New Deal's Federal Housing Administration; and they were constructed according to the FHA's vision of the ideal family dwelling. In Arlington Forest, a suburban neighborhood that opened up in 1939, the houses look like perfect cubes, almost identical, each one set back from the street exactly the same distance, with four windows spaced evenly on the square facade. For your $590 down payment, you got three bedrooms, a kitchen whose sink featured a double drain board, chrome-plated bathroom fixtures, and a basement suitable for remodeling into a rec room. No garage.[13]

I remember the first time I visited the capital as a college student and found myself in one of those brick-cube neighborhoods, with the rusting Buicks parked in the street and the aluminum bay windows bolted on the fronts of the houses in an effort to disguise their sameness. Surveying a row of them, stretching down the block like packing crates on a conveyor belt, was enough to make one an instant punk rocker, and I recall climbing back in the car, turning up the volume on Government Issue or Naked Raygun, and swearing to myself that I would never live this way.

Looking at them today, I can only think of the middle-class nation that we have left behind. To own a house made of bricks was something of a declaration in 1939, and what New Deal Washington was declaring was that everyone in the land was entitled to this: a safe place to raise kids, a good public school, an easy commute, and a shopping center nearby.

The model survived up into the seventies. A friend of mine who grew up in the suburb of McLean, Virginia, drove me around his old neighborhood, a typical development of that period, with brick split-levels and lots of houses with flimsy pillars out front. He pointed out for me the row house his family owned, the park he played in, the Safeway he walked to, the public schools he attended. No, he wasn't able to tee off from his patio if he wanted, but it was a pleasant way of life nevertheless. His mom stayed home, his dad worked on Capitol Hill, and the whole arrangement was affordable on a congressional aide's annual salary of $20,000. It was designed to be that way; that's what liberalism was all about.

The Washington boom that began in the eighties and that exploded under George W. Bush was of an entirely different character. This time the millionaires were homegrown, and the template for Washington housing was ostentatious, aristocratic, and gargantuan. Driving around McLean you get the impression that in those days the capital was minting tycoons the way it used to generate environmental regulations and amendments to the tax code. Every few miles you pass another castle, sometimes with stone posterns so large they are seemingly meant to serve as a defensive perimeter. Battlements are much in vogue; one house I saw had matching his 'n' hers turrets on either end. For those not so keen on martial architecture, there is the good old Washington colonial, only tripled in size, like three of the Arlington Forest cubes arranged in a flying wedge, with a three-car garage trailing along behind.

The one I visited in 2007, after reading an advertisement headlined "Celebrate Your Destiny," was a Grand Monet, a model in the "two to two-point-five" range. A more affluent destiny might conceivably lead you to other models, like the Grand Michelangelo, the Grand Cézanne, the Grand Rembrandt, or even the Grand Rembrandt Platinum. But the Grand Monet was good enough for me. It towered over the surrounding neighborhood of brick ranches and split-levels like an elephant in a herd of cows. Not to worry, though; this was a tear-down section of McLean, I was assured, where destruction was inevitable and everyone knew it. What would be left when the inevitable had come to pass was an entire neighborhood of houses like the Grand Monet: a billowing drywall circus tent, with granite countertops and beige carpets and fiberglass bathtubs and walk-in closets large enough by themselves to contain a bedroom from one of the New Deal colonials. There was space for a huge TV in the family room and for an even bigger TV in the basement "theater room," where a thick tangle of wires waited to deliver exceptional entertainment experiences to the discerning eyes and ears of the occupants.

This sort of grandiosity was typical of suburban development everywhere in America, but in northern Virginia the form was brought to a grotesque consummation—a *platinum* consummation in which the developer's worst instincts were permitted their full expression. At Evans Farm, a gated and walled-off subdivision built on the last green space in the area, the developers shoehorned in the luxe and the splendor so tightly that visitors might think they're actually in a city . . . a city where Beaux Arts and Tudor houses have been whimsically incorporated into blocks of Georgian Revivals. At the Reserve, the preeminent choice of local millionaires a few years ago, the houses run to "12,000 square feet of luxurious and innovative space," as a builder's Web site brags, but propping them up on the hilly terrain appears to require earthworks of such height and mass that they might have been borrowed from a medieval castle.

When you drive among these wonders, northern Virginia appears as a kind of technicolor vision of prosperity, American-style; a distillation of all that is mighty and righteous about the American imperium: the airport designed by Eero Saarinen; the shopping mall so vast it dwarfs other cities' downtowns; the finely tuned high-performance cars zooming along an immaculate private highway; the masses of flowers in perfectly edged beds; the gas stations with Colonial Williamsburg cupolas; the street names, even, recalling our cherished American values: Freedom, Market, Democracy, Tradition, and Signature drives; Heritage Lane; Founders Way; Enterprise, Prosperity, and Executive Park avenues; and a Chivalry Road that leads, of course, to Valor Court.

As you travel west into Loudoun County, the Washington affluence begins to mingle with the distinctive prosperity of the Virginia Hunt Country. Shops and restaurants bear the quaint monikers of long-dead British aristocrats; the suburban developments include some stretches of whitewashed wooden horse fence; all conversation is drawn by some occult force of linguistic gravity to the Civil War. There are also vineyards—less because this is a good place to make wine, I suspect, than because winemaking is something people are expected to do in a top-drawer place like this.

Loudoun also has the distinction of hosting the first suburban development on earth to bear the Ritz-Carlton brand name. It is presently under construction, so the precise level of excellence that it will attain remains a subject of anxious wonderment, like the vagaries of the stock market or the mysteries of space. Its promotional materials assure us, however, that it will be tops in privilege and exquisiteness. There will be

> 180 opulent homes—truly a limited edition opportunity for fine living . . . heirloom quality estate residences. . . . Where every day you can avail yourself of comprehensive five-star services. . . . The unlimited vistas, sophistication and élan of a truly unequalled club community, available as a limited edition for the most discerning homeowners.

There are to be gates and private security forces, I was assured, presumably to keep out the marauding hordes of Loudoun.*

***Who** are these people?* I asked everyone I met in these golden reaches of the federal metropolis. *Who lives in these houses,*

---

*Ritz-Carlton removed its name from the suburb when it was sold to a new developer in March, 2009, during the real estate collapse.

these estate homes, these gated reserves and Grand Rembrandts? Sometimes I would hear about the tech princes of the nearby Dulles Airport Corridor, a sort of Silicon Valley of the East; more frequently the answer had to do with the defense and homeland security contractors for whom the past decades have been a piñata laden with gold doubloons; but always the answer would include the phrase *and of course lobbyists,* sometimes added as something so obvious it hardly merited mention, sometimes spat out with contempt for the intelligence of anyone who didn't know this already. "Who do you *think* lives in these houses?"

Actually, the most accurate answer is more general: it's everyone who grabbed as the government handed off its essential responsibilities to the private sector over the last few decades, including weapons designers, "systems integrators," computer servicers, contract winners of every description, and, yes, the lobbyists who greased the wheels.

To solve the mystery of conservative Washington's prosperity, all you had to do was spend a day touring the suburbs of northern Virginia, duly noting the names proudly emblazoned on the region's new office buildings. In the Crystal City complex in Arlington, nestled comfortably between the Pentagon and Reagan Airport, you would have seen sleek glass buildings marked "Boeing," "SAIC," and, staring at one another across a patch of trophy greenery, the identical, featureless office buildings of General Dynamics and Kellogg Brown & Root, the former Halliburton subsidiary that did so well in Iraq.

The Crystal City shopping center, which runs underneath these bland towers, is possibly the only mall in the world with no mall rats; just army officers in camo and executives in suits, interfacing comfortably in eateries where the light of day never penetrates. Even the hamburgers sometimes come with a tiny American flag mounted on a toothpick. As I ate mine, I glanced through the latest issue of *Special Operations Technology*, one of those only-in-Washington publications that assumes you're in the market for a "remotely operated turreted weapons system" and that narrates the exciting quest for "advanced door breaching ammunition."

Looking for the main offices of CACI International, a company that provides job opportunities to former soldiers—known in the biz as people employed in "warfighter-related areas"—I went to a branch office by mistake, a blank box situated across the street from another tower marked "Boeing." Such mistakes are common when you're touring northern Virginia: There are in fact no fewer than eight Boeing offices in the region, seven Raytheon addresses, and six General Dynamics outposts, all of them occupying glass-and-steel office boxes thrown up over the last twenty years and distinguishable only to the true connoisseur of suburban blandness. The champion in this respect is Science Applications International Corporation (SAIC), a contractor-of-all-trades that not only boasts eight separate installations in northern Virginia, but which has its own "Science Applications Court" in Vienna and "SAIC Drive" in McLean—the latter of which soon intersects with "Solutions Drive."

Before the collapse of late 2008, the gushing profitability of it all was unmistakable. In the main General Dynamics building, I happened upon one of the most conspicuously luxurious restaurants I have ever entered, a place of truffle-tasting menus, elaborate displays of port and cognac, accents both French and British among the staff, and original art by Rodin and Dalí. An Edwardian fantasy of naked, delirious nymphs hung over the fireplace, and I imagined how the sight of them might soothe the souls of the gray-haired defense contractors who sat at the bar, the exact modern incarnations of the imperialist gentlemen for whose pleasure these swooning maidens were first committed to canvas.

George W. Bush's Washington, it should be clear by now, was an entirely different city from the haven for federal fat cats we know from the familiar talk-radio myths. Nor was it that New Deal beacon of liberalism where talented civil servants fend off spoils-minded congressmen. Yes, it is true that many of the region's inhabitants persist in their ancestral liberalism—in the District of Columbia proper, Dubya drew the support of only 9 percent of the electorate in 2004—but that is not the story I am telling here. Bush's Washington was a developers' city, a lobbyists' city, a defense contractors' city; a capital undone and remade by a thousand wild-eyed deregulators.

To get a sense of the inner workings of conservative Washington, we need only take a glimpse at the politics of suburban Loudoun County itself, where a nasty fight between business interests and, well, people has been going on for years. At the beginning of the decade, established residents of the county started looking for some kind of brake on the traffic problems, school crowding, and increasing tax burden that further growth would bring. Having won control of the county's Board of Supervisors, they reworked the zoning rules in order to slow Loudoun's high-speed development.

Instantly the developers and big landowners were in revolt. The battle cry was "property rights," the idea being that zoning constituted a particularly intolerable form of big-government tyranny. "We are molded and created by God to obey God," one *enragé* told the board. "If you take away people's private property, you'll have to answer to God as well as man." Another was even blunter: "It's terrorism, pure and simple."[14]

The forces arrayed against the "terrorism" of zoning uncorked first a deluge of lawsuits against the board and then a deluge of money into the bank accounts of the Loudoun Republican Party, who made sure that defenders of "property" took control of the

BOEING
NORTHROP GRUMMAN
LOCKHEED MARTIN
GENERAL DYNAMICS
CACI
Bearing Point
BOEING
SAIC
KBR
BECHTEL
ManTech
Raytheon

Now

county board in 2003. And then they rolled up their sleeves, spat on their hands, and proceeded to enact every last item on the wish list of the developer interests that had bankrolled their election. They approved developer-requested rezoning measures by the truckload. They opened vast new tracts of the county to construction. They settled several of the lawsuits that their developer patrons had filed against the previous board—basically by conceding to the developers.[15] They filled the county's various advisory committees with representatives of the real-estate industry. They got advice on running board meetings from developers' representatives. One of them even got advice on denying accusations of corruption from developer PR people.[16] And, of course, they leveled conflict-of-interest charges at their political opponents.[17]

The individuals who had sponsored Loudoun's revolt against "terrorism" made out particularly well. The landowning organizer of the Loudoun ring, who had invested heavily in electing the new board, saw her vast personal holdings rezoned a few months into the new regime; by the *Washington Post*'s estimation she was able to reap four times as much from their sale than she would have under the old board. A short while later, the new board decided to buy a piece of land for which the same woman was the agent, bringing her yet another handsome return on her political investment.[18]

But one doesn't become a champion of property rights without the prospect of raking in a little property oneself. The head of the county's Planning Commission, for example, approved one development scheme only after the developer had invested in a business deal of the commissioner's own. The leader of the Board of Supervisors, meanwhile, made it his business to push along one of the county's more grandiose projects, a "luxury destination spa" that is being constructed by a famous local billionaire. He conspicuously became this billionaire's friend, riding on her private jet, attending the games of her pro sports teams. He even began representing himself to developers in other states as her agent.[19]

The Loudoun ring, in case you haven't guessed by now, was made up of men and women of the right.* One of the staunchest members of the pro-development faction, for example, was board member Eugene Delgaudio, who once told the *Washington Post* that "builders would be his 'shadow board.' "[20] Delgaudio was even better known, though, as the zaniest of the Bill Clinton haters of the nineties, sending out mass-mailings begging for money so he could track down the murderer of Vince Foster. Later on, his morbid horror of Clinton morphed into a morbid horror of homosexuality.[21] His trademark tactic is to dramatize these views with public spectacles that are so juvenile and so thick-witted that one actually feels shame for the man. His Web site features photos of him and his cadre of young followers staging a "Kennedy Sobriety Checkpoint," traveling the country with signs reading "Unibombers 4 Gore," and, mysteriously, pretending to arrest Moses while wearing uniforms marked "Thought control police."[22]

Delgaudio is a queer bird even by the standards of the American right, with its long tradition of eccentric people and peculiar ideas. But the operations of the Loudoun County ring—from its outraged rhetoric to its steamrolling of opponents to its sordid self-serving to its backing by business interests and its generous handouts to same—were not deviant or extraordinary in any way. What the county's government did may well land some of its principals in trouble, but it is precisely what we should expect governments to do when they are controlled by business. Indeed, the activities of the Loudoun ring were an almost perfect expression,

---

*The "smart growth" faction reclaimed control of the Loudoun Board of Supervisors in elections held in November 2007, but the damage had already been done. In its busy term in office, the Loudoun ring approved enough rezonings to keep the developers working for years to come.

in miniature, of the principles that for decades guided the behavior of the far larger government situated thirty miles down the Dulles Corridor. We might even call this richest of American counties a laboratory of democracy—in which all the experiments were designed to see just how much public stuff private interests could grab before democracy does something to stop them.

This is what all of America looks like when conservatives run the machinery of the state.

CHAPTER 2

Their Enemy, the State

In the aftermath of the various scandals of Warren Harding's fabulously corrupt administration, it was discovered that many of the malefactors "felt morally justified" about their cronyism because that was simply the way business was done in the private sector.[1] And the Harding administration was all about business. "I speak for . . . the omission of unnecessary interference of Government with business," Harding had blustered in his 1921 inaugural address, "for an end to Government's experiment in business, and for more efficient business in Government administration."[2]

More business in government, less government in business. Harding mangled the phrase, but at the time this was a basic and well-known principle of American conservatism, an official slogan of no less an institution than the U.S. Chamber of Commerce.[3]

There was nothing mystifying or elusive about the concept of a conservative state in those days. Conservatism was the natural creed of American government, regardless of whether Republicans or Democrats controlled it. Conservatism was "normalcy," in Harding's famous description. Everyone knew what conservatism was, whom it answered to, what it did, and what it stood for: control of the state by the people who obviously should control it. The successful, the powerful, and the wealthy—men of means who had the most at stake. Conservatism knew the rules of God and of nature; it knew how society was meant to be organized; it knew the rightful role of bankers, industrialists, legislators, workers, and even intellectuals, whose job was to justify and explain, rather than question or criticize.[4]

In other lands and in other times, conservatism has meant traditionalism, an attitude of respect for institutions inherited from times past. In America, however, conservatism has always been an expression of business. Absorbing this fact is a condition to understanding the movement; it is anterior to everything else conservatism has been over the years. To try to understand conservatism without taking into account its grounding in business thought—to depict it as, say, the political style of an unusually pious nation or an extreme dedication to the principle of freedom—is like setting off to war with maps of the wrong country. Yes, there have been exceptions, and yes, the conservative coalition has changed over the years, but through it all a handful of characteristics have remained steadfast: a commitment to the ideal of *laissez-faire,* meaning minimal government interference in the marketplace, along with hostility to taxation, regulation, organized labor, state ownership, and all the business community's other enemies.[5] Laissez-faire has never described political reality all that well, since conservative governments have intervened in the economy with some regularity, subsidizing railroad construction, putting down strikes, adjusting tariffs, and propping up the gold standard. But as a theory of society, laissez-faire has always been highly persuasive to the business class. The free-market way is nature's way, conservatism has always held; the successful succeed because they damned well *deserve* to succeed.

One obvious weak point in all this was that, as the official doctrine of the American order, laissez-faire would be discredited should the business system ever suffer a catastrophic breakdown. Which is, of course, what eventually happened. Being the natural party of government in 1929 was like being pro-hurricane in New Orleans in 2005. And in the aftermath of the economic disaster, conservatism was repudiated so crushingly it looked like laissez-faire might go extinct altogether.

What emerged after World War II, in the United States and every industrialized nation, was a regulated economy and a truce between business and labor, the great warring parties of the preceding fifty years. Both sides gave up trying to win some sort of final triumph over the other: management accepted unions in the workplace, union leaders kept the peace, and even when Republicans controlled the government, they left Social Security alone and took pains to include representatives of labor in whatever agencies or commissions they set up. It was the age of the liberal consensus, a sort of domestic détente.

The conservatism that made such a huge comeback in the seventies and eighties was a mutation specifically adapted to survive a disaster of the 1929 variety. By which I do not mean that conservatism abandoned laissez-faire, its raison d'être, but that from now on it would present itself to the world as a form of opposition to the established order, changing its shape as circumstances required. From now on it would be a movement not of bankers and manufacturers but of outsiders, of rebels, of freedom fighters, even. It would recruit and mobilize the embittered and the aggrieved—blue-collar patriots worried about the Soviet threat, born-again Christians watching their culture fall apart—and form them into a vast grassroots insurgency. It would wallow in preposterous theories about the secret treason of the ruling liberals and encourage the darkest imaginable interpretation of the government's every deed. This was a movement defined by what it was *against*.

And the main thing it was against, as everyone knows, was *Big Government,* which is to say, the *liberal state* or, more commonly, just *Washington.* To this day, conservatives keep the volleys coming with remarkable consistency, denouncing the federal city and its works. Into this effort they pour all their ingenuity, their outrage, and their vast material resources. Their reasoning is so familiar by now that most Americans can recite it as they drift off to sleep. Government takes—steals—what you earn through taxation. This vast stream of dollars flooding into Washington, the story goes, is then diverted by the know-it-all government to people it deems worthier than you. And when Washington's bureaucrats aren't wasting your tax dollars on idiotic projects that they always bungle, they are telling you how to run your business, compiling regulation upon regulation into a bookshelf of legalese that no one can ever hope to understand or obey. "Every businessman has his own tale of harassment," thundered Ronald Reagan in 1964. "Our natural, inalienable rights are now considered to be a dispensation of government, and freedom has never been so fragile, so close to slipping from our grasp as it is at this moment."

It has been forty-five years now since Reagan's electrifying vision of homegrown tyranny fueled Barry Goldwater's run for the nation's highest office; it has been four decades since a diluted version of it propelled Richard Nixon to the presidency. If we adopt the conservatives' own time line and date their "revolution" to Reagan's election, it has been twenty-nine years. From that day to January 20, 2009, with only a few interruptions, conservatives held either executive or legislative power over the very state that it is their first article of faith to despise. The big government that they railed against was, by and large, *their* government.

For a political faction to represent itself as a rebellion against a government for which it is itself responsible may strike you as a supremely cynical maneuver. If so, you are beginning to understand conservative Washington. Cynicism is of this movement's essence. It is cynical not only in the way it wriggles about, denying everything, dumping its former heroes, endlessly repositioning itself; but more fundamentally, it is cynical about the very possibilities of improvement through government.

This attitude has been present, no doubt, since the first social Darwinist was moved to guffaw at the first tea-sipping do-gooder. But cynicism only really came into its own in the twentieth century—in the age of liberalism—when conservatives acquired a big, fat federal target at which to aim their poisoned darts. Today the movement's cynicism is simply reflexive. It sneers professionally, automatically, almost unthinkingly. Cynicism is the health of this state.

Now, I'm the kind of guy who believes there is a wholesome quality to cynicism. I think it's healthy to laugh at the powerful and at the rococo fantasies they dream up in order to rationalize their exalted place in the world. One of my favorite books is a 1931 compilation called *Oh Yeah?* made up entirely of optimistic quotations from the great economists and bankers of that era, interrupted every now and then with charts and headlines about the ongoing disaster in Wall Street.

Scoffing of this particular kind was a trademark of the left in our grandparents' time. Its classic expression was "The Treason of the Senate," a series of magazine articles written in 1906 by the novelist David Graham Phillips, in which the leading senators of the day were flayed for being servants and hirelings of various private corporations, chiefly railroads. Phillips used the term *traitors* to describe his subjects, he explained in perfect period style, because they served not the public but "interests as hostile to the American people as any invading army could be, and vastly more dangerous; interests that manipulate the prosperity produced by all, so that it heaps up riches for the few; interests whose growth and power can only mean the degradation of the people, of the educated into sycophants, of the masses toward serfdom."[6]

Phillips's contempt for Washington was as strong and as thorough as that of any present-day howler against "big government," but the difference between the cynicism of his time and the contemporary conservative variety is crucial: *Phillips thought government could be redeemed.* With the Senate occupied by big business, it naturally helped the rich to "despoil the masses"; but if it were reconfigured to meet "the real demand of the people," the Senate would just as naturally pass legislation regulating the railroads and the various other monopolies.[7]

David Graham Phillips was thus both a skeptic and an optimist, a product of the old "reform" tradition, which held that corruption—just like economic disaster, poverty, and a thousand other ailments—was subject to legislative remedy. This line of thought assumed that fairness and economic democracy were not just desirable but possible.

Conservative cynicism scoffs at even that. It is fiercer, more nihilistic stuff, and it assumes that talking about the public interest is just another trick politicians use to get into your pockets. For the right-wing cynic, "reform" is high-minded talk used to camouflage the despoliation of the successful by the many. Compared with the petty sins described by Phillips—the Vanderbilt family acquiring its own U.S. senator,* for example—"reform" is flatly obscene, an outrage.

Admittedly, cynicism seems like an unlikely quality to find in a movement whose rank and file get misty-eyed contemplating the

---

*According to progressive lore, the Vanderbilt family's personal public servant was Chauncey Depew, a senator from New York from 1899 to 1911. "Everyone knew he was the Vanderbilts' creature," wrote David Graham Phillips in *The Treason of the Senate,* pp. 72–73.

> Those who saw him in the presence of the members of the family to which he was soul-vassal, whether the elder members or the little children, half-pityingly

flag, the family, the founding fathers, and the Boy Scouts, and who can be moved to hold candlelight vigils to protect Ten Commandments monuments. Change the subject to government, though, and you will have opened the floodgates of sarcasm, disbelief, contempt, and ridicule. It was sunny Ronald Reagan who claimed to find terror in the phrase "I'm from the government and I'm here to help." And it was Reagan's economic adviser David Stockman who, in 1981, penned this bitter verdict on the Carter administration that he was preparing to terminate. "Much of the vast enterprise of American government was invalid, suspect, malodorous," he wrote with disgust. The "projects and ministrations" of liberalism "were not spawned from higher principles . . . ; they were simply the flotsam and jetsam of a flagrantly promiscuous politics, the booty and spoils of the organized thievery conducted within the desecrated halls of government."[8]

Conservative antigovernment cynicism can be found in many forms. It comes in a scientific version, in which cold economic reasoning is used to prove that politics is a form of extortion conducted at the expense of business.[9] It comes in a "realistic" version, in which conservatives charged with protecting the public interest laugh off the very idea of the public interest as so much liberal make-believe.[10] It even comes in a quasi-Marxist version, in which bureaucrats and intellectuals are said to be a class unto themselves, using government to exploit every other group in society. But most of all, it comes in a philosophical version, in which government is said to be an offense against nature, a force entirely at odds with civil society. While the market is an organic institution, the state is an artificial construct, a kind

---

despised him for his truckling, despised him the more that he was beyond question a man of unusual ability and mentality. The wife of one of the younger Vanderbilts refused to have him at her table.

"I do not let my butler sit down with me," she said to the head of the house; "Why should I let yours?"

of weapon used by the various elements of society to steal from one another.

Conservatives are even capable of being idealistic about their cynicism. Malcolm Wallop, a senator from Wyoming who used to say that "big Government has become our chief domestic enemy," gave a farewell speech to his colleagues in 1994 looking back over his public career and taking stock of his accomplishments. He had been against communism all those years, he reminded them, and now the Soviet Union had fallen. He had also opposed "big government and the culture of statism," and now it gave him great satisfaction to note that "illusions about the benevolence of government have well-nigh vanished among ordinary Americans." Nice going, Senator.[11]

It is true that public attitudes toward government conform ever more closely to the cynical views of the right; it is even true that the right's fortunes depend on robust public cynicism toward government. But no individual senator can rightly claim all the credit for this development. At least some of the thanks must go to our mass culture, whose typecast politicians are always on the take and even whose FBI agents are the pawns of a mysterious conspiracy. It is no coincidence that the movies to which Jack Abramoff and his team of right-wing lobbyists referred constantly were the *Godfather* series; these are classics of the disillusionment genre, in which the cops and the senators are always corrupt and only thieves have honor, secretly pulling the puppet strings of the visible world.*

Perhaps you think I'm being too cynical about cynicism. Perhaps you think I'm exaggerating its place in conservative thought.

---

*This romantic passion for the mafia makes a kind of cosmic sense for the antigovernment crowd, as the mafia's real-world power is greatest in those regions of Italy where government is worst and civic trust is feeblest. Nor is it limited to the confessed felon Abramoff; Rudy Giuliani is, oddly, a big fan of *The Godfather,* and according to John Podhoretz, all the young "Reaganites" in the eighties loved to quote from the movie. See "A Reaganite Reconsiders," *Weekly Standard*, February 5, 1996.

Let us turn again, then, to the cynics themselves. As it happens, conservative antigovernment crusaders have often taken up the question of what to do about government.

The utopian dream is to wreck it, an impossible goal that is nevertheless the frequent object of conservative reverie. "The mystery of government is not how Washington works," writes the humorist P. J. O'Rourke, "but how to make it stop."[12] There are silver-bullet theories for destroying the state: repeal the amendment that allowed for the income tax; bring back the gold standard and thus break the state's power over money; or—most ingeniously—interpret the eminent domain clause of the Constitution so as to invalidate almost the entire body of government regulation enacted in the twentieth century.[13]

Every now and then conservatives give it a try. "By the time we finish this poker game, there may not be a federal government left, which would suit me just fine," boasted Tom DeLay, the spiritual leader of the Republican Congress elected in 1994. Before long DeLay and his colleagues had parlayed a budget disagreement with President Clinton into a full-blown government shutdown, which some of them celebrated as a sweet taste of things to come, an overwhelming demonstration of their supreme ideological point.[14]

Unfortunately, the shutdown turned out to be a monumental political blunder that led ultimately to Bill Clinton's reelection. All of the movement's other direct frontal assaults come to the same end, running headlong into the solid brick wall of public sentiment. The brute fact reasserts itself every time: *people like the liberal state*. They like the prospect of a secure retirement, a guaranteed education for their kids, pure food, clean air, crash-free airplane trips, safe working conditions, and a minimum wage.[15]

Realizing that they will never get to dismantle big government in this direct way is, for some conservatives, cause for despair. For example, Albert Jay Nock's 1935 book, *Our Enemy, the State*—regarded as a "founding text" of the modern conservative movement[16]—ends by claiming that "simply nothing" can be done to stop the growth of the beast. But then, this man Nock was a born pessimist. He loved to muse about how the majority of mankind were a lesser species and the only beings that mattered were a "remnant" of civilized gentlemen who persisted through this fallen age—a daft idea that he saw fit to assert in the very middle of the 1930s, the so-called proletarian decade.

Nock's unsparing pessimism blinded him to the possibilities of his own material. Read *Our Enemy, the State* closely enough and it dawns on you that Nock's caustic version of history might well provide the ideological basis for conservative governance. The state, according to Nock, is an instrument for "the economic exploitation of one class by another." He was especially contemptuous of the New Deal, which he described as a "coup d'état" in which the shiftless "masses" rip off the hardworking few and indirectly "loot their own treasury" through such devices as Social Security.[17]

But Nock's cynicism encompassed far more than the Roosevelt administration. *All* states are built to steal and exploit, including the American state founded in 1776. On this Nock is most explicit. The United States, he declares, was set up as a "merchant state," a polity organized around the "fundamental doctrine that the primary function of government is not to maintain freedom and security but to 'help business.'" Our Constitution, Nock asserts, was constructed by financiers and other businessmen to allow them to suppress their rivals. This hero of conservatism then goes on to dismiss Abraham Lincoln as a clever propagandist, classify Patrick Henry as a ruthless speculator, and depict numerous champions of the early Republic as upper-class tyrants.[18]

"Wherever the state is, there is villainy," Nock has taught

generations of young conservatives: Governments are instituted among men in order to help one group in society exploit another; governments are then captured by some other class, which sets about exploiting some other group, and so on. David Graham Phillips, who accused the Senate of "treason" for carrying out such an operation, held out hope for the day things were run differently, when the People finally had the power instead of the Interests. Conservatives merely take away the hope. For them there is no conceivable instance in which the state might be reformed or function morally: only oppression succeeding oppression all the way to the far horizon.[19]

Albert Jay Nock didn't approve of any of this, but that was merely because his cynical nerve failed in the end. If we contemplate this thing with the nihilistic eye of the conservative warrior, the answer to the problem of the state becomes obvious. Since there is no possible moral difference between modes of government, it doesn't matter whether the beast is "big" or "small"; all that matters is whose interests it serves. The object of the political war is not to shrink the state or shut it down; it is to capture the thing and run it for your constituents' benefit.

Less government in business and more business in government. This, not the *Reader's Digest* utopia of "small government," is now and has always been the great goal of conservative administrations. How to achieve this end when the public expects the opposite has been a subject of the greatest urgency since the first glimmerings of the liberal state, encompassing not only cynical literary abstractions but also cynical political science. The Magna Carta of the new form was a letter written in 1892 by the railroad lawyer Richard Olney, whom Grover Cleveland (a Democrat, for what it's worth) had chosen to be his attorney general. Olney was a man so dedicated to his employer that, before accepting the post, he requested confirmation that taking the top law-enforcement job in the nation would be in "the true interest" of the railroad. But of course it would! Only a few years previously Olney had been part of a crack corporate legal team that had blown holes in the Sherman Anti-Trust Act; now he would be in charge of enforcing what remained of that very statute. Just before Olney took office, his former boss at the railroad wrote to him about abolishing the Interstate Commerce Commission, the very first American regulatory agency, which had been set up in 1887. Its arrival represented the birth of "big government," and the question put to Olney was whether to smother the ICC in its cradle. Olney's answer was no, and his reasoning, spelled out in a letter to his former boss, is justly famous.

> The Commission, as its functions have now been limited by the courts, is, or can be made, of great use to the railroads. It satisfies the popular clamor for a government supervision of the railroads, at the same time that that supervision is almost entirely nominal. Further, the older such a commission gets to be, the more inclined it will be found to take the business and railroad view of things. It thus becomes a sort of barrier between the railroad corporations and the people and a sort of protection against hasty and crude legislation hostile to railroad interests. . . . The part of wisdom is not to destroy the Commission, but to utilize it.[20]

By the 1920s, the Olney strategy of "utilizing" the regulatory state was standard conservative practice. A series of Republican presidents filled the boards of the nation's few regulatory agencies with men distinctly hostile to those agencies' very purpose. George Norris, a liberal senator from Nebraska (and also a Republican), raged against the technique in a famous 1925 essay called "Boring from Within."

> If the Federal Trade Commission, established for the purpose of protecting the small business man against the machinations of trusts and monopolies, is to be administered by men who believe that best results can be obtained by giving monopoly full sway, then why have the commission at all? If the men and corporations that are intended to be regulated by it are themselves to manage it and run it, then why not take the logical step—repeal the law and abolish the commission?[21]

This was sarcasm, touched with anger. As Norris and everyone else knew, the reason conservatives didn't abolish the FTC—then or now—was that such a move would be political suicide. People like to believe that someone in Washington is watching out for their well-being; to make it obvious that this is not taking place would be to trigger an explosion of public outrage.

The true cynic, however, when moved to comment on the tactical undermining of federal agencies, looks up from reading Albert Jay Nock and yawns, saying, *What did you expect?* This is the message of one of the great monuments of conservative political thought, the 1971 essay on regulation by the economist George Stigler that won him the Nobel Prize. According to Stigler, there was nothing strange or unusual about industries controlling the regulatory process—or the political process, for that matter. It was all a simple matter of buying and selling: "the industry which seeks political power," for example, must "go to the appropriate seller, the political party." Thus, liberal criticism of the Interstate Commerce Commission for acting on behalf of railroad interests, as the ICC had done more or less since Olney's day, was "exactly as appropriate as a criticism of the Great Atlantic and Pacific Tea Company [better known as A&P] for selling groceries, or as a criticism of a politician for currying popular support." In each case, they're just doing what comes naturally.[22]

When Stigler's essay appeared in 1971, however, Washington was heading in precisely the other direction. The liberal Congress was in the process of launching the greatest wave of regulatory endeavors in American history: the Environmental Protection Agency, the Occupational Safety and Health Administration, a series of Clean Air acts; all of them detested by the business community. The reason the liberal Congress did these things was simple: regulation worked. It reduced pollution, for example, when industry, left to its own devices, did not. In the 1890s or 1920s, maybe, undermining liberal reform had been a relatively simple matter. Not anymore. The country had embarked on a massive regulatory offensive, and reversing it would require conservative mobilization on an equally massive scale. Business would have to spend billions of dollars, enlist lobbyists, back political candidates, and launch an entire flotilla of right-wing Washington foundations—all to regain control over the regulatory state.

The modern-day versions of the Chamber of Commerce's demand for "less government in business" are sufficiently well known: deregulation, tax cuts, and privatization. It is in implementing the other half of the slogan—"and more business in government"—that the conservative movement has shown real genius.

A more businesslike government is, on the surface, a goal to which nearly everyone in Washington aspires. Greater efficiency and less waste are objectives with obvious appeal, and every few years it occurs to someone that there ought to be a study or hearings or a report on how government should be run more like a business. Each of these efforts has supposedly been politically neutral, just an innocent search for better results, but each one has in fact carried a powerful political charge arising from the basic fallacy that *government is not a business*. It does not seek profits; its employees cannot take tips; it answers to the people, not to a small clique of owners.

The granddaddy of all these efforts was the 1984 President's Private Sector Survey on Cost Control, usually called the "Grace Commission" after its chairman, the swaggering right-wing industrialist J. Peter Grace. What was meant by *Private Sector* was "top executives"; the Grace Commission included among its 161 members exactly one representative of organized labor. The commission was charged with rooting out waste and inefficiency in federal spending as a means to bring down the by-then enormous federal deficit. It proposed the mass privatization and outsourcing of federal operations, on the grounds that business was automatically and in almost every situation more efficient than government, but otherwise its deficit-reduction ideas were generally ignored.[23] As a political symbol, however, the Grace Commission's significance was enormous. For years, government had snooped around in the affairs of business, but now it was business's turn to investigate government, to deplore its incompetence and tell the bureaucrats how to put their own house in order.[24]

The softer, Democratic version of these ideas came in a 1992 book called *Reinventing Government*, which promised an "American Perestroika" through the exciting-sounding concept of "entrepreneurial government." Freedom had toppled the Communist dictatorships, and now "empowerment" would sweep through the bureaucracies of Washington, ushering in a new dawn of market-based solutions to every sort of problem. The book carried an endorsement from none other than Bill Clinton himself, and sure enough, the Democratic administration quickly embarked on its own "reinventing government" program, with Vice President Al Gore even writing a book of public-sector management theory that he called *Businesslike Government: Lessons Learned from America's Best Companies.*[25]

George W. Bush is famous for his stumbling speech, but this was one idea he nailed concisely: "Government should be market-based," he proclaimed upon taking office.[26] When Bush said this, he was referring specifically to outsourcing the federal workforce, but the utterance might just as well serve as the motto for his entire administration, which speaks of business as its "customer," which has tried to replace social insurance with private savings plans, jettison "adversarial" regulation for "partnerships" between business and government, and turn over government operations to the private sector.

It was Grover Norquist who showed me what "market-based" government really meant. A self-proclaimed " 'winger' from way back," Norquist has been for many years one of the most influential conservatives in the capital, the central organizer of the movement as well as an informal adviser first to Newt Gingrich and then to Karl Rove.[27] I met Norquist a few times in 2006 at the Palm, a favorite steakhouse of the power set where drawings of bygone politicians smile down on the room, frozen forever in whatever posture of bonhomie it was that voters found so endearing back in the sixties or seventies. From where we sat you could actually see Norquist's own caricature, jovial and beaming, on the restaurant's back wall.

Norquist is a small, well-dressed man with a squeaky nasal voice, a reddish beard, and a taste for bloody, boasting metaphors. He reportedly has no interests other than politics, and that subject he tackles with an unshakable confidence, rattling off well-defended, interlocking opinions on subject after subject. He also has a twinkling air of amusement; on the occasions we met I found him reasonable, even charming, and he led me to believe that all his infamous remarks over the years—like the time he raved about drowning government in a bathtub—had simply been misunderstood. Murder ol' Uncle Sam? Oh, no no no. Ha ha ha ha ha.

What we talked about was money in politics, a hardy Washington perennial that usually takes the form of the question *How are we to get money out of politics?* Norquist, however, is a Harvard-trained MBA who did a hitch at the Chamber of Commerce, and the way he talked about it, the problem was turned upside down: how to get money *into* politics in large enough amounts so that it starts to behave rationally. So that it starts to make, I thought, the same sort of demands that money makes everywhere else in the economy.*

People underinvest in politics, Norquist told me. When he speaks to business leaders, Norquist makes a point of informing them about the potential rate of return on a political expenditure. He referred me to an article in *Fortune* reporting that "the return on lobbying investments can be truly enormous." Numbers like 163,536 percent are thrown around.[28]

And then it struck me, sitting there in the Palm, surrounded by all those grinning gargoyles of power brokers past, that Norquist was hinting at something both ingenious and incredibly malevolent: a systematic connection between conservative politics and private profit. Consider what the liberal order had to offer, back in its heyday: affluence for most, civic peace, and a certain amount of social justice. When the liberal machine worked, it delivered 5 or 6 percent growth per year—a great deal for the nation, but a handful of crumbs when compared to the

---

*This way of looking at the issue is common on the right. "The problem is not that there is too much money spent in politics. The problem is that there isn't enough money spent in politics," writes Tom DeLay, the former House majority leader, in his memoirs. "We need to grow up as a country and realize that politics is something worthy of investment." (Tom DeLay with Stephen Mansfield, *No Retreat, No Surrender: One American's Fight* [New York: Sentinel, 2007], pp. 13, 142–43.)

return-on-investment that Norquist was talking about. Who will stand up for the liberal state when there are hundred-thousand-fold returns to be made from wrecking it? Money gravitates to right-wing pressure groups like Norquist's—as well as the Club for Growth, and the Chamber of Commerce—because *that is the rational thing for money to do*. That's how you deliver shareholder value.

And the conservative movement delivered. But in order to do so, it had to put itself through a remarkable metamorphosis.

CHAPTER 3

The World as War and Conspiracy

Of all the image makeovers in American politics, conservatism's rebranding from haughty orthodoxy to marginalized outsider must rank among the greatest. That this victimology persists today, after so many decades of conservatives in power, puts it beyond implausible. It is more on the order of a foundational myth, like the divine right of kings, a fiction that everyone involved must simply accept as fact.

The conservatives' sense of their own exclusion is fundamental; it predicates everything they do, say, and enact. The government is never theirs, no matter how much of it they happen to control. "Even when conservatives are in power they refuse to adopt the psychology of an establishment," marveled the journalist Sidney Blumenthal in the middle of the Reagan years, long after the liberals had been routed. George W. Bush, who grabbed more power for the executive branch than anyone since Nixon, actually saw himself as a "dissident in Washington." One of his more worshipful biographers called him the nation's

Rebel-in-Chief: he "operates in Washington like the head of a small occupying army of insurgents. . . . He's an alien in the realm of the governing class, given a green card by voters."[1]*

The hallucination is dazzling, awesome. For most of the last three decades these insurgents have controlled at least one branch of government; they were underwritten in their rule by the biggest of businesses; they were backed by a robust social movement with chapters across the radio dial. Still, however, they are the victims, the outsiders; they fight the power, the establishment, the snobs, the corrupt. In 2008, Republican presidential candidate John McCain railed against Washington as the "city of Satan"—which in any sober cosmology would have made him Lucifer's right-hand man. Fred Barnes, the author of *Rebel-in-Chief,* is such a well-known Washington fixture that he hosts a TV show called *The Beltway Boys.* In 2004 Karl Zinsmeister, the editor of a magazine published by the ultra-insiders at the American Enterprise Institute, reviled the people of the capital as "morally repugnant, cheating, shifty human beings." Soon afterward he was rewarded for his adherence to the fantasy by being appointed chief domestic policy adviser to President Bush.

Reaction-as-revolution was not always such a ridiculous idea. In the fifties and sixties, conservatism was widely regarded as a deluded relic of an earlier age. The Republican Party itself was dominated at that time by its moderate faction, which conservatives defeated only after a titanic struggle spanning many years. Then, in the seventies, right-wing insurgencies spread across the country: conservative cliques took control of the Southern Baptists and

---

*Insurgency is a perennial favorite of the right-wing imagination. In February of 2009, with Bush having departed the White House less than a month before, Representative Pete Sessions of Texas advised his fellow Republicans to think of themselves as "an insurgency" and even suggested that the tactics of the Taliban might offer useful hints in this new role.

the National Rifle Association, and in 1978 the first of a wave of tax revolts shook California. In 1981 came the turn of the College Republicans, where the right-wing takeover was led by none other than the future supercorruptionist Jack Abramoff. This uprising holds special significance for the historian, since it not only introduces us to the cast of characters who went on to dominate Washington during the Gingrich and Bush eras, but also provides a window into the conservative soul.

This particular story of conservative triumph starts as the story of a generation. *My* generation, as chance would have it. The traditional label for my cohort, dating to the early nineties, is swiped from Billy Idol's punk band, Generation X. But before the stereotype of the bepierced slacker became fixed in the public mind, there was a slightly different stereotype, one that might also have been lifted from the name of a punk band: Reagan youth.[2]

In 1980, the year of the Reagan Revolution, there appeared on the national scene a phenomenon that bewildered seasoned political observers: legions of politicized, energetic college students who were conservatives rather than liberals or radicals, as had been typical in the two decades previous.[3] And not only were their politics deeply square, but the idol of this unlikely youth craze was the oldest president ever. Reagan's entire Pennsylvania campaign, for example, was run by a lad of twenty. In 1984, the aged actor won 60 percent of the college-student vote.[4] The historical turnabout was irresistible, and Reagan youth became one of the great journalistic clichés of the period, powering hundreds of newspaper columns and at least one beloved TV sitcom.

These sons of Reagan had a strong sense of generational self-awareness and they loudly told the world how they had come by it. One account related how, in the midst of the interminable Iran hostage crisis, a crowd of college students were moved so profoundly by a showing of *Patton* that they demonstrated spontaneously in favor of a nuclear attack on that country, shaking the ivory towers with chants of "First strike now!"[5] Another well-known story of the era was how a bunch of privileged kids at Dartmouth College, a traditional fortress of privilege, decided that embracing the traditional politics of privilege and mimicking the traditional manners of the privileged were actually acts of great daring, exposing them to persecution by tyrannical liberals.[6] Then there was Jack Abramoff, a College Republican leader in the Boston area who gained a "reputation as one of the most innovative of the national Conservative youth leaders" after he mounted such a massive grassroots push for Reagan in 1980 that he single-handedly shifted Massachusetts into the Republican column.[7]

The inevitable comparison, of course, was to the sixties. The young conservatives were said to be a mirror image of the New Left, using the same outrageous tactics, and the heroic Abramoff, a burly fellow from Beverly Hills who came to Washington in 1981 to assume the chairmanship of the College Republican National Committee, encouraged the comparison. Back in the Vietnam days it had been leftists who fought the power, Abramoff mused, but in the eighties the tables had been turned. "Now *we're* the campus radicals," he told reporters, and his newly energized College Republicans (CRs) fanned out across the nation instructing clean-cut kids on how to use the tactics of the sixties left for their own causes.[8] A snapshot of Abramoff using a bullhorn to rally a conservative throng was proudly reproduced in the CRs' *Annual Report* for 1983, just across the page from another of Ralph Reed, the future Christian Coalition leader who was then Abramoff's right-hand man, waving his fist at the head of an angry swarm of sign-waving wingers.[9] In both instances the young men had gone into action wearing neckties.

It was Abramoff's friend Grover Norquist, then a recent graduate of the Harvard Business School, who came up with the plan for changing the very nature of the College Republicans.

The idea was to transform the organization from "a resume-padding social club," as one account puts it, "to an ideological, grassroots organization."[10] Abramoff made Norquist the College Republicans' executive director, and the two put his theory into action. They purged the "old guard." They amended the CRs' constitution,[11] establishing a structure that made the Washington office more powerful and that rewarded proselytizing on campus.*

What the new sensibility treasured above all other things was "confrontation" with the left. It called for a quasi-military victory over liberalism; it would have no truck with civility or fair play; and it made heroes out of outrage-courting lib fighters like Reagan's press secretary Pat Buchanan, the organizer and orator Howard Phillips, and the young Jack Abramoff.[12] Conservatives were no longer defenders of tradition but rebels from within. "We are different from previous generations of conservatives," winger chieftain Paul Weyrich once declared. "We are no longer working to preserve the status quo. We are radicals, working to overturn the present power structure of the country."[13]

The first and most noticeable characteristic of this new militancy was an air of swaggering truculence. There are, of course, bullies from every walk of life and every political persuasion, but on the right bullying holds a special, exalted position. It is no accident that two of the movement's greatest heroes—Tom DeLay

---

*Sticking with the sixties analogy, this would have been the right-wing equivalent of the moment in 1969 when Students for a Democratic Society took their famous lurch to the left. Only instead of splitting into factions and disappearing in a blast of farcical rhetoric as SDS did, the College Republicans became stronger and more influential as the years passed, watched their absurd rhetoric become mainstream AM radio fare, and advanced upward and onward to the point where they are today a big-spending 527 organization, loaded with direct-mail money, their national chairmanship a highly coveted position that carries with it a $75,000 annual salary. And instead of passing the remainder of their lives in ignominy, as did the radicals of the sixties, the young reactionaries of the eighties went on to careers in the highest reaches of government. This form of extremism is one that pays off.

and Oliver North—had the same nickname: "the Hammer." This is a movement that adores bullies, that cheers their bullying slogans at its conventions, that longs for a bully mean enough to put the wimps back in their place forever, that has lionized bullies from Joe McCarthy to Westbrook Pegler to Bill O'Reilly to George Allen to Michelle Malkin, a pundit with the appearance of a Bratz doll but the soul of Chucky.

In the long history of the joyful pummeling of the weak by the strong, nobody tops the Young Americans for Freedom (YAF), the legendary shock troops of the 1964 Goldwater campaign. In their sixties heyday the YAFers were famous for their campus counterprotests and for an abusive imagination that sometimes bordered on the Auschwitzian. During the Vietnam era, for example, it amused the YAFers to sing:

> Back to back, belly to belly,
> Burn their bodies with Napalm jelly.

The song proceeded from general to specific, ending with a lyrical call for the immolation of folksinger Joan Baez, then a favorite hate-object of the right.[14]

A remnant YAF soldiered on into the eighties, even making headlines once when, dressed in jackets and ties, they raided an antinuclear vigil in a Washington park, tearing down the protesters' signs and replacing them with more patriotic placards.[15] But by and large, the YAF was a spent force by the time our story begins, reduced by schisms, coups, and purges to a fraction of its former membership.

The College Republicans simply filled the vacant market niche. Their chairman, Abramoff, fit the bill perfectly. He had reportedly been something of a bully in high school and had grown into a "hard charging" and "dynamic" leader, in the assessment of conservative magazines, an ass-kicking weight lifter who could quiet the commies with his fists if they got out of line.[16]

My own impression of this wish for a bully messiah was cemented forever at the 2006 Conservative Political Action Conference (CPAC), the annual gathering of the right-wing tribes. After numerous speakers had failed to rouse the audience, the throb of what sounded like Lambeg drums summoned the neat young attendees into the auditorium for the main event: Ann Coulter, then the most popular conservative orator in America. Well-dressed wingers filled the available seats and packed the staircases and aisles. A journalist friend of mine chatted excitedly with her neighbors, anticipating something like a rock concert. Then Coulter loped onto the stage, the crowd roared, and suddenly we discovered that what we had wandered into was closer to Orwell's Two Minute Hate.

Coulter's style is the comic monologue; in her trademark offended-patrician accent she blurts out a series of short anecdotes and one-liners connected only by the liberals and Muslims which they target. At CPAC, some of these fell flat; the meanest and most insulting jabs triggered standing-Os and paroxysms of delight. Coulter called for war on Syria. She urged us to punish the uppity "ragheads." She joked about the time she "had a shot at Clinton." The crowd whooped its approval. My journalist friend, I noticed, had stopped chatting. Her eyes were wide, and the blood had drained from her face.

"If you're going to be a conservative in America," Coulter announced to the crowd, "you can't be a pussy."

Jack Abramoff certainly wasn't, and the right loved him for his pugnacity. His gangster fetish is by now familiar to the whole world—his constant references to *The Godfather*, his black trenchcoat and fedora, his Meyer Lansky memorabilia, the murderer argot which will no doubt serve him and his friends well during their prison years.[17] But the attitude was there from the beginning. The young College Republican leader was a master of "confrontation politics," crowed the right-wing magazine *Human Events* in 1983. This was another term borrowed from the sixties, and what it meant in this case was that Abramoff's CRs liked to fight. They taunted campus leftists in a hundred inventive ways. They mocked the libs by setting up fake student groups, like "bestiality clubs"[18] that were supposed to make gay-rights organizations seem ridiculous.* They produced a series of insulting posters that "hit back—hard," as Jack put it: one mocked supporters of a nuclear freeze as Soviet dupes; another noted how both the federal budget and Tip O'Neill, the Democratic Speaker of the House, were "fat"; a third listed the crimes of the Soviet dictator Yuri Andropov, evidently on the assumption that the reader wouldn't otherwise know Andropov was a bad guy.

Seen from this perspective, politics is a showdown in which the soft and the weak get pounded by the hard and the strong. The symbolism is important in winger Washington, with its heroic "hammers" coming down implacably on the people it calls "squishes." Abramoff himself, for example, derided the moderates whom he ousted from control of the CRs as "wishy-washy country-clubbers" and insisted that he had transformed the organization into an "ideological, well-trained, aggressive, conservative" outfit.[19] Another son of Reagan gloried in the "bare-fisted journalism"—shorn of "limp-wristed euphemism" and unpalatable to "the sissies"—that was sweeping the college scene in those days.[20]

---

*In the heat of the right-wing revolt at Dartmouth College, for example, Dinesh D'Souza and his friends actually set up a Dartmouth Bestiality Society, demanded funding, and duly screamed "discrimination" when it was denied. See Dinesh D'Souza, "D'Souza Remembers the Early Days," *Dartmouth Review*, September 22, 2005.

Liberals, of course, were the softest of all. When *Conservative Digest* asked Abramoff whom he supported in the 1984 presidential contest, the young roughneck exploded: "Are you kidding? Wally Mondale is a boring wimp."[21] Others on the right taunted "Fritz" Mondale as a "quiche eater," after the squishy food for which "real men" were said to have no appetite, and a squad of CRs mocked the "wimp" to the catchy theme from *Ghostbusters,* dancing and singing, "It's Ronnie's time; Fritz is a slime." The group reportedly sold almost fifty thousand T-shirts emblazoned with their "Fritzbusters" logo and along the way gave me my own first taste of the tradition of gleeful malice that is observed so carefully in conservative circles.[22] Today the symbolism has spun off a full-blown political theory. According to the pundit Michael Barone, history itself is a confrontation between "Hard America" and the parasite "Soft America" (labor unions, civil servants, and nicey-nice schools), which "lives off the productivity, creativity, and competence" of the Hard.[23]

These themes would be repeated countless times as the conservative revival unfolded, and as it unfolds still: the country's leaders lacked both the mettle and the muscle of their ancestors; they had grown squishy and weak and could stand up to neither the Soviets nor the strikers, muggers, pornographers, and bureaucrats who were destroying America from within. But marching forward to steel the nation's will were the legions of youth. They had the toughness to crack down, to fight where the moderates only appeased.

War was the new generation's rallying cry. "Fighting the Left with a goal of victory" was now the official, stated purpose of the College Republicans, according to an essay Abramoff wrote for the group's 1983 *Annual Report*. The CRs were "fighting America's last stand," he blustered; they would "defund the enemy wherever possible," one of his lieutenants added.[24] According to the journalist Nina Easton, CR officers had their underlings memorize the gory opening monologue from the movie *Patton*, only with the word *Democrat* standing in for the word *Nazi*. Others went a step further. The editor of the *Sequent*, a right-wing newspaper published at George Washington University, actually took breaks from red-baiting professors in order to zip down to Central America and hang out with the Nicaraguan Contras and the death squad faction in El Salvador.[25]

What all this represented was not just a coup against the moderates in the GOP but a grander historical shift. The liberal consensus was over. War was the order of the day, from President Reagan's fight with the air traffic controllers right down to the college campus, where Abramoff became famous for his fiery declaration: "It's not our job to seek peaceful co-existence with the Left. Our job is to remove them from power permanently." Rollback was the strategy now, not détente.[26]

The right's favorite term for its war was *revolution*. The College Republicans were, Abramoff liked to say, "the sword and shield of the Reagan Revolution." The group's slogan, as printed on its campaign buttons, went from "The Best Party in Town" to "Join the Revolution"—from beer-soaked to bloodstained, as it were. "Fighting for the Revolution" was the official theme of the group's 1983 national gathering. And in 1984 the CR's maximum leader used his moment at the rostrum of the GOP convention in Dallas to lecture the assembled small-business types on revolutionary theory.[27]

A morbid obsession with betrayal and conspiracy is a recurring pathology of the revolutionary mind-set. The leaders of the French Revolution, for example, sank so deep into their fantasies of plots, traps, and subterfuge that, before too many years passed, they had killed one another off for imaginary acts of treason. The conservative revolutionaries of our own day also see enemies lurking everywhere. All the setbacks that befall the capitalist system and the United States generally are said to be the work of a hidden hand—meaning, in the eighties, a network of traitors supposedly guided by the infinitely evil, infinitely clever men in the Kremlin.

Here, too, the sons of Reagan showed a special fervor. Almost every American detested the Soviet Union in those days, but the Reagan youth always had to detest it more than everyone else, as though only they were aware of the danger. The CRs, for example, were constantly organizing anti-Soviet demonstrations: They built and demolished a model of the Berlin Wall, they demanded that the Soviets allow more emigration, and one day they got up real early to protest the Soviets' destruction of a civilian airliner.

I remember being mystified by all of this as I watched the Abramoff-era College Republicans shout their anti-Soviet slogans. After all, I thought, who in the world *supported* the destruction of civilian airliners? There was obviously nothing daring or confrontational about being loudly against the Soviet Union here in the cities of its sworn enemy. In fact, I thought the whole thing reeked of official propaganda; it was the kind of bogus demonstrating that college students might do in a place like . . . the Soviet Union.

The reason I didn't get it is that I missed the next step, in which the war with the Soviets morphed into the war on liberalism here at home. By Abramoff's own accounting, there were bona-fide communists everywhere in early-eighties America. A "cadre of 12,000 Marxist professors" were poisoning the minds of youth, he insisted, and once he proudly described his plans to checkmate students worried about the war in El Salvador by calling attention to the crimes of "their beloved Soviet Union."[28] But this was kid stuff compared to what the big leaguers were pitching in those days. Consider a 1981 essay by Reed Irvine, a dogged hunter of the liberal media, in which he asked why bad things had happened to America over the preceding few decades and pointed the finger at "those who staff and control the mass communications media."

> It was they, after all, who determined to set America awash on a sea of guilt over the killing by American troops of some 100 civilians at My Lai while virtually ignoring the communist massacre of 5,000 civilians at Hue in February 1968. It was they who decided that we lost the battles known as the Tet Offensive. . . .
>
> Such anomalies are perplexing and seemingly irrational if we make the standard assumption that all Americans share a common interest in preserving and expanding freedom and defeating the efforts of the communists to extend their totalitarian dominion.
>
> They make sense only if they are viewed as part of the effort of the enemies of freedom to confuse its defenders and undermine their morale.[29]

Treason was all around: this was the worldview that saturated the books favored by the Reagan youth. The best example was *The Spike,* a best-selling 1980 spy novel by *Newsweek* editor Arnaud de Borchgrave that was promoted as "the secret history of our times!" Its characters had to go from Vietnam to Washington to Europe and back until it dawned on them that reality is a constant showdown between soft Westerners and hard, ruthless Soviets, who control the consciousness of their enemies with a secret army of liberal journalists and other puppets. To the burning question *Why do liberals do the awful things that they do?* the book supplied the classic answer: because lots of those liberals are traitors, roped into the communist conspiracy by a satanic liberal think tank in Washington. Once this was understood, all the frustrating mysteries of history could easily be answered: Where did the debilitating "Vietnam Syndrome" come from? Why, it was designed by the KGB and spread by these infernal libs. The SALT treaties? Devastating for the United States and harmless to the USSR because that's how the liberals wanted them. The liberals' congressional hearings on covert activity? Merely the Soviets' war with the CIA carried out by other means.

The Spike deserves our attention not merely because it was a popular book but because a number of prominent American conservatives regarded it as essentially true, a shaft of harsh light cast on the dark truths of the media/think tank conspiracy.[30] Even spookier are the echoes of the book that we shall encounter in the pages to come—by which I mean not that we'll uncover lots of liberal treason, but that we'll see the Reagan youth mimic the imagined behavior of their spy-novel enemy.

Stranger still was a 1980 book called *What Will Happen to You When the Soviets Take Over,* an effort to translate the strategic pessimism of the seventies into detailed descriptions of the Soviet threat to *each of us as individuals.* The author quickly dispensed with that little matter of the arms race; of course the Soviets were winning it, and as a result "the United States of America and its government could fall as early as 1982 or 1984."* After a short pause to make the familiar accusation of (liberal) treason in high places—"errors of judgment as vast as these can hardly be viewed as anything less than a gross betrayal of the American

---

*One of the recurring obsessions of the conspiracy-spotting genre is the exact date on which the communists, with all their scientific cunning, have scheduled their triumph over us. Daniel Bell first took notice of this theme in 1962 (the wingers of those days believed the communists had set the date for our downfall in 1970), but we find the same morbid fascination with the particulars of our coming disaster in *The Spike,* where we get to eavesdrop on the thoughts of a KGB agent:

> The Plan, Barisov had gleaned . . . was a blueprint for achieving Soviet domination of the West by a certain date. The deadline had been revised once or twice already. The current deadline, Barisov had been told, was 1985.

people"—the author gets down to business, instructing Americans from all walks of life on just how bad it's going to be when the commies run things. Will the Soviets be hard on, say, automobile mechanics? Why, yes, the Soviets will make life difficult indeed for auto mechanics, who will look back at their prosperous days under the red, white, and blue as "almost unbelievable in retrospect." Well, what about bankers? They have "dismal fates in store."[31] Bar owners and bartenders? Barbers? Bondsmen? Bureaucrats? Businessmen? Awful, awful, awful, awful death.*

The College Republicans' national office, I am told, sent a copy of this preposterous, panic-peddling work to every campus chapter in the nation. And they kept pushing the idea long after the threat had disappeared. In a televised 2003 address to the national College Republicans convention, Abramoff could be heard warning the young activists to be vigilant in their defense of liberty, else "the bad guys, the Bolsheviks, the Democrats, in ascending order of bad," would return.

The organization also made original contributions to the genre. The CRs' "deputy projects director" in 1983 was one J. Michael Waller, a writer and editor who would go on to spend years spinning amazing webs of liberal-commie interconnectedness in book after book—and in articles for the conservative press, and in congressional hearings, and in his campus newspapers, the *Sequent* and *Freedom Fighter in Central America*.[32]

In theory, Waller was a rising expert on Latin American affairs, specifically on the left-wing movements that had sprung up in Nicaragua and El Salvador. But like so many red-baiters be-

---

*The "editor" of *What Will Happen to You* was a man named Ingo Swann. He is not widely known as an expert on communism or on the Soviet Union or even on issues of strategic power. According to his Web site, however, he is one of the nation's greatest practitioners of "remote viewing" and other "superpowers of the human biomind." See http://www.biomindsuperpowers.com.

fore him, the bulk of his work targeted liberals and leftists here at home: peace activists, Democrats in Congress, earnest college students who liked to think they were down with the *campesinos*. Waller took special umbrage at a group called the Committee in Solidarity with the People of El Salvador (CISPES), writing and rewriting an attack pamphlet that denounced this annoying but harmless left-wing outfit as a "terrorist propaganda network."

The problem with these liberal American groups, Waller argued, wasn't merely that the policies they advocated were mistaken; it was that, witting or not, these people were servants of communism, doing the evil empire's work. This Waller sought to prove in the time-honored style: by drawing the connections between one person and another, tracing "radical ties" from dot to dot until he arrived at a bona-fide subversive who would then light up the whole grid with his amperage of evil, instantly discrediting everything that the connected people had ever said and magically exposing everyone's secret malign intentions. The methodology was weak, but the conclusions Waller drew from it were robust indeed. Under the Carter administration, "the pro-Castro lobby was the government itself," he wrote. Liberal Democrats were "Congress's Red Army," he insisted; "they aren't taking their lead from the Soviets, but they wouldn't vote much differently if they did." One reason the CIA and Congress classify documents, he reported, is "to keep the public from knowing the extent of cooperation between liberal politicians and Soviet front groups."[33]

Before we brush off all this ignorance and panic, consider how much conservative Washington owed to this hyperpessimistic, conspiracy-minded form of anticommunism. This was the source of the fifty-megaton notion that liberals are by nature treasonous, forever betraying their country and selling out our allies. As Oliver North put it in his famous testimony before the Iran-Contra

Committee, "We didn't lose the war in Vietnam. We lost the war right in this city." The idea remained potent even after the Soviets were gone. John Kerry's presidential campaign, for example, was torpedoed with innuendo of this kind in 2004. Both Ann Coulter (*Treason*) and Michael Savage (*The Enemy Within*) filled best-selling books with the stuff in 2003; Dinesh D'Souza, an old hand at this sort of thing,[34] tossed yet another (*The Enemy at Home*) onto the pile in 2007. All that changed was the foe—it was Muslim terrorists, rather than Russian communists—that liberals pined to appease.

Let us not lose sight of the central fantasy, however outlandish it might seem. The conservatives we are considering imagine themselves "revolutionaries"—"outsiders," "radicals," "rebels-in-chief"—and in those early days of the Reagan administration they looked abroad and discovered a perfect embodiment of their insurgent fancy. This idol, this incarnation of winger-boy daydream, was the "freedom fighter," a ragged warrior who had, according to myth, spontaneously taken up arms against communism in third world countries around the globe. American conservatives came to love these freedom fighters intensely, and for a simple reason. These tough anticommunists in faraway lands validated the conservatives' most cherished fantasies of the sixties turned right side up. *Their revolution was for real.*

Needless to say, conservatives had not traditionally cheered for rebellions or guerrilla movements. When the right cast its eyes overseas, it instinctively identified with the forces of law and (the old) order: the British Empire, the shah of Iran, whites-only regimes when in Africa, local oligarchies when in Latin America, generalissimos when in a pinch. It neither loved nor saw itself in any of these brutes. They were ugly regimes, doing ugly but necessary work. There was nothing particularly exalted about anticommunist insurgencies, either. For decades the CIA had been assembling guerrilla armies wherever a left-wing government needed to be toppled, but these units were generally regarded as bands of sadists, blackguards, and hirelings . . . another necessary evil.

But in the transforming fire of the Reagan Revolution, all the cutthroats were now "freedom fighters"; all the mercenaries were now patriots. And all the cultural templates of the Vietnam period were inverted. It was our guys who were the heroic underdogs now, disrespected and ill-supplied, going up against the high-tech, organization-men monsters of the Soviet Union—and its liberal proxies here in the United States.

The great guru of the freedom-fighter cult was a sort of right-wing Jonny Quest named Jack Wheeler who had, in his youth, climbed the Matterhorn, swam the Hellespont, and done just about everything else on the checklist of Victorian boyhood fantasies. In the early eighties Wheeler took it upon himself to visit the various anticommunist guerrilla armies of the world, trying to knit them into a movement that, once he popularized it back in the United States, would carry as much cultural voltage as had left-wing guerrillas twenty years previously. Remembering "all the Che posters on all the college dorm walls in the 1960s," he told the *Washington Post,* "Now it's our turn. . . . Now there are anti-Marxist guerrilla heroes . . . the whole anti-imperialist liberation struggle is just all shifted around, 180 degrees."[35]

Wheeler's vision of a unified, global anticommunist insurgency may have started as the peculiar notion of a peculiar individual, but by the mid-eighties it had become a great shimmering idée fixe of the American right. The ultraconservative Free Congress Foundation proposed that the United States get behind some kind of interguerrilla alliance, with "coordinating meetings" where "international solidarity" could be nurtured. Another right-wing group issued a freedom-fighter fanzine, with news about the latest shoot-outs in all the different theaters of insurgency plus pics and bios of the bravest anticommunist warriors from around the world. The zine seemed to show the love in direct proportion to a guerrilla unit's viciousness, with the most murderous thugs drawing fits of trembling ecstasy from the wingers back in Washington. Its authors worked hard to glamorize the RENAMO rebels in Mozambique, for example, an army that was then engaged in what a State Department official called "one of the most brutal holocausts against ordinary human beings since World War II." The zine even published a fawning profile of the Afghan rebel Gulbadin Hakmatyar—a "liberator" heading an outfit "notable for its . . . freedom from corruption and strongly Islamic orientation"[36]—who is currently a terrorist ringleader sought by the U.S. Army.*

The peerless darling of the freedom-fighter fan club was Jonas Savimbi, a charismatic Angolan guerrilla leader whose every utterance seemed to strike eighties conservatives as a timeless profundity. Angola had been one of the very last countries in Africa to be freed from colonial domination, but unlike so many other "national liberators" over the preceding decades, Savimbi was not a Communist. In Angola, the Communists were the ones who grabbed power in the capital as soon as the Europeans left; Savimbi, who fought them with the backing of the apartheid government in South Africa, believed in free enterprise and balanced budgets.[37]

---

*All of this probably strikes you as a curious monstrosity, no more. But in fact it wasn't even the only freedom-fighter fanzine out there. J. Michael Waller had one too, aimed at college students and titled *Freedom Fighter in Central America*. Staying true to the Reagan youth ideal of the-sixties-in-reverse, its masthead featured a fierce-looking guerrilla, cartridge belts crossed over his chest and machine gun at the ready. One can only imagine the excitement that must have swept across the campuses of America when a new issue would appear and everyone got a chance to read up on the adventures of their favorite band of Contras and then dig into "The Fifth Column," a regular feature in which Waller would expose some liberal organization as a nest of reds. In the January 1985 issue, there was even a chance to purchase a brass cartridge that had actually been fired at a Nicaraguan commie!

Conservatives were smitten with this self-made general who struggled for free markets in his remote land. They fell for Savimbi as romantically, and as guilelessly, as sixties radicals once did for Che, Ho, and Huey. Savimbi was "one of the few authentic heroes of our time," roared Jeane Kirkpatrick, queen of the neocons, when she introduced him at the 1986 CPAC.* Grover Norquist followed the great man around his camp in Angola, preparing magazine articles for Savimbi's signature. Jack Abramoff made a movie about him, depicting Savimbi as a tougher, African version of Gandhi.[38] Even Savimbi's capital—the remote camp called "Jamba"—was described in conservative literature with elevated language: "liberated Jamba" or "Savimbi's Kingdom."

The conservative organizer Howard Phillips fell the hardest. For him, virtually no American politician was worth a winger's damn. But deep in the Angolan bush Phillips found his hero. And contemplating the great Savimbi brought him instantly from the crankiest sort of pessimism to an exuberant credulity. "Jonas Savimbi," he sang, was "the Real Leader of the Free World." In his newsletters Phillips reprinted long excerpts from Savimbi's bombastic lectures and added to them his own burbling praise.

> Savimbi is an extraordinary man. Charismatic, articulate, and well schooled, the Angolan patriot, fluent in several languages, could enjoy a sumptuous life in virtually any Western country. Instead, he has cast his lot with his people, choosing to live hip-deep in the dust of southern Angola, with few of civilization's amenities. . . . Whatever material progress his people have made is largely attributable to his sacrificial leadership.[39]

---

*In one of my favorite images of Washington in the eighties, the assembled CPAC crowd of clean-cut young careerists was actually moved to chant the name of Savimbi's guerrilla faction, UNITA, while Kirkpatrick rhapsodized from the podium about the weapons Savimbi deserved to have.

This is embarrassing stuff on the face of it, but the last sentence also inverts reality so monumentally that I cannot simply let it pass. Contemporary observers of southern Africa almost universally agree that the "material progress" of Angola is precisely what Savimbi destroyed, and not as a "sacrifice," either, but because of his grotesque personal ambition. The civil war that Savimbi kept going for nearly thirty years made Angola one of the worst places on earth—its population impoverished, its railroads wrecked along with its highways and dams, its countryside strewn with land mines by the million, even its elephant herds wiped out, their tusks hacked off to raise funds for Savimbi's army.[40]

This was the man whom the rebel right chose for the starring role in one of the strangest spectacles in American political history, a media event designed to cement conservatism's identification with revolution. The organizer was Jack Abramoff; the place was Jamba; the model, I am told, was Woodstock—only with guerrillas instead of rock bands.[41] The "rumble in the jungle," as skeptics called it, came to pass in June of 1985. Of course, bringing it off required considerable assistance from Savimbi's South African patrons, as anyone could have predicted. Hell, nobody else even knew how to *find* Jamba.[42]

Every kind of freedom fighter was there, joining hands in territory liberated by arms from a Soviet client regime. There was a Nicaraguan Contra, some Afghan mujahideen, an American tycoon—and they all got together at Savimbi's hideout. Since these freedom fighters had no actual issues to discuss—no trade agreements or mutual-defense plans or anything—they signed the Jamba Declaration, a bit of high-flown folderol written by Grover Norquist that aimed for solemnity but sounded more like the work of a fifth-grader who has been forced to memorize the Gettysburg Address and the Declaration of Independence and has got them all jumbled up somehow. Or else something dashed off by a hungover adult on the plane ride up from Johannesburg.[43]

The journalists who covered the freedom-fighter summit mainly treated the event as a curiosity, remarkable primarily for the extremely primitive conditions under which it was held. Conservatives, on the other hand, announced themselves awed by the majesty of it all.[44] The *Washington Times* editorialized about the "jolt of Jamba," gleefully speculating about the pain it must have caused "a '60s assistant professor" to see his Marxist world turned upside down.[45]

Two decades later, it is difficult to find meaning in something so banal. One is tempted to forget about Jamba the way we have forgotten other empty media spectacles of the eighties like "Hands Across America" or the hundreds of Elvis impersonators who performed at the Statue of Liberty on Independence Day in 1986. Jamba was like a parody of a great moment in history, a gathering at once so portentous and so farcical that it doesn't so much resist interpretation as send interpretation reeling in disgust.

But interpret we must. And the first impression that is forced upon us is the threadbare shoddiness of even the grandest ideas of the Washington right. Jamba was meant as a celebration of *freedom,* a word revered by Americans generally and a term of enormous significance to conservatives in particular. As freedom's embodiment, though, Abramoff and Co. chose a terrorist: Jonas Savimbi, the leader of an armed cult. To fill the main supporting role in this great freedom-fest, meanwhile, the organizers turned to apartheid South Africa, a place where only a small, correctly complexioned percentage of the population possessed the most basic democratic rights.

But there was also a certain cynical brilliance to it. Jamba was officially sponsored by a long-forgotten Washington group called Citizens for America whose leading members were typical conservative plutocrats: oil barons, Wall Street kings, and agribusiness lords. The group's founder, Jack Hume, was one of the California millionaires who had funded Ronald Reagan's political career from the beginning. ("He made a substantial investment and has backed Reagan ever since" is one apt description.)[46] To represent its conservatism to the world, though, this 24-karat group did not choose a contented white yachtsman snoozing in an easy chair, but a black African fond of camouflage and handguns; a ferocious warrior who single-handedly kept a real rebellion burning against the government of his country year after year. Aflame with the gorgeous idea of their own radicalism, the wingers of the eighties admired Savimbi in almost precisely the way that fashionable, upscale leftists of the late sixties looked to the Black Panthers.

This brings us back to the idea with which this chapter began: conservatism's understanding of itself as a movement of outsiders, an assembly of root-and-branch antigovernment radicals. Even when they rule in Washington, they do so, remember, as an "occupying army of insurgents." As tenacious as it is ludicrous, this myth has many functions, but its primary purpose is evasion. Never again will conservatives shoulder the blame for catastrophes like the Great Depression or even the many blunders of the Bush years; no matter how much of it they control, the government is never theirs, and they cannot be held responsible for its actions.

The myth unfolds into a vast array of self-exculpating pettifoggeries. To those who complain that years of conservative rule have not changed the size of government, they reply that it will take a long time to unbuild all that the libs have contrived. In fact, this was how Jack Abramoff himself brushed off the matter when speaking to a crowd of College Republicans in 2003: "I guess the problem is really this, the liberals and the Democrats set an ocean liner on a voyage and they had forty great years of running it, and turning it around is very tough."[47]

Refute this, and the wingers fall back on another favorite bit of buncombe: that their leaders weakened and failed because once they got to Washington they had "gone native"; they had gotten "cozy with Beltway mores."[48] The city's ability to hypnotize even the staunchest conservatives—to repel assaults from the right with an invisible force field—is a folk belief of long standing in winger circles. Grover Norquist, for example, blames "the siren sounds of Georgetown society" for his colleagues' alleged deviations from the true faith.[49]

When we challenge these views—when we note that liberals really don't have special hypnotic powers, that conservatives have been in charge of at least one of the federal branches for most of the last thirty years, and that you can't call yourself a "dissident" when you have claimed, as did George W. Bush, that it is your right to unleash the world's most powerful army on any country you choose—conservatives will often retreat one step more, to what they believe is an impregnable defensive position: the Republicans who have held those high positions in Washington *haven't been conservatives at all.* Nixon talked a good backlash game, they will admit, but he didn't follow through.[50] Ronald Reagan may have been the very soul of the conservative movement, but he shrank government not at all.[51] George Bush Senior was no good from day one. Newt Gingrich caved when the crisis came.[52] George Bush Junior inflated the deficit, expanded Medicare, and claimed to believe in government, making him an *Impostor,* to use the title of a popular 2006 book.[53] The result: *Conservatives Betrayed,* as another recent title puts it.[54] The conservative state? Who knows? *It's never been tried.*

There are bits of all this that are undoubtedly true. Rank-and-file conservatives *have* been betrayed by their leaders, and repeatedly, on those matters commonly referred to as the culture wars. Conservative leaders *are* impostors in many ways, as we will see in the pages that follow. They have never managed to cut big government down as much as they promised. But even the most embittered winger has to concede that conservatism, by which I mean the free-market faith, enjoyed sweeping and unambiguous triumphs all over the world in the years after 1980.

That's why it's difficult to see all this pishposh about rebels, hypnosis, and hard-to-turn ships as anything but the baldest kind of opportunism, with conservatives ardently embracing Nixon/Reagan/Gingrich/Bush when those men were riding high and then claiming to have been tricked once their blunders were publicized. (And then embracing them anew when their image improves, as Reagan's eventually did.) But whether it's Bush as rebel or Bush as impostor, the larger message is the same: when government fails, conservatism can't be held responsible for it.

CHAPTER 4

Marketers of Discontent

Conservatism's triumph was the result of two innovations that were first rolled out on a massive scale in the seventies. The first of these was the adversarial fantasy, discussed earlier, which allowed the movement to survive blunder after blunder. The second, which was discovered accidentally in the course of movement-building, was that enormous profits could be made from conservative activism. The right began to understand in those years that there was fantastic potential for synergy between business and politics.

By this I do not mean merely to point out that conservative politicians tend to serve business interests, which they have always done, or that businesspeople tend to be conservatives, but that *conservatism itself became a business,* a source of profit for the people Jack Abramoff once referred to as "political entrepreneurs."[1]

In its embryonic form, conservatism-as-industry consisted of peddling right-wing grievances to the like-minded. There were dealers in precious metals who used a towering contempt for liberalism as a sales pitch for gold coins. There were outfits raising money to help beleaguered conservatives who were in fact not beleaguered and had not asked for the help. There were anti-union charities and even fake anti-union charities, all of them capitalizing on the keen hatred for labor shared by so many businessmen. "There was so much money ready for conservative organizations in the United States," said Spitz Channell, a freelance conservative fund-raiser later involved in the Iran-Contra scandal, that the problem was finding "ways to spend that money."[2]

The visionary up-builders of industry conservatism were a group of entrepreneurs who called themselves the "New Right" and who appeared on the Washington scene in the seventies. Most of them had been Young Americans for Freedom together, and now as adults they discovered that the YAF's trademark air of confrontational pessimism was not only politically attractive but an excellent marketing strategy as well. Working out of the suburbs of northern Virginia,* meeting together every week, the New Right leaders became the unlikely political superstars of the time, spreading their nightmares across the land, forging a mass movement, and making a tidy profit in the process.

The New Right's story began at the retail level. The operation is familiar by now to just about everyone who owns a mailbox: letters, mailed by the millions, written in tones of the highest outrage, soliciting donations for conservative causes. The advertising term for this technique is *direct mail,* and in the early days the New Right used it to spread a dark vision of treason in high places, of Panama Canal giveaways, of crazy lawsuits filed by the thousands, of imminent takeover by homosexuals or bureaucrats

*Conservatives have always favored the Virginia suburbs over those located in Maryland, I believe, because of their residual southernness and their reassuring proximity to the Pentagon.

or the United Nations—with the only hope for a happy ending residing in your personal checkbook.

Richard Viguerie was the prodigy of the form, the direct-mail guru who held the fledgling movement together with his amazing mailing lists and his uncanny knack for persuading middle America to part with its dollars. Viguerie is, when you meet him, a hearty and congenial fellow who just happens to hold fairly pronounced right-wing views. He traces these back to the days of his youth, before Goldwater, before the YAF, back to the early fifties when he would skip classes to watch the Army-McCarthy hearings on TV. Roy Cohn, Senator McCarthy's boyish attorney, was a particular object of the young man's admiration. "Gosh, he's doing all these neat things!" Viguerie remembers thinking. "I wish I could do that!"

Viguerie eventually decided to make his contribution by bringing the wisdom of marketing to the conservative movement, and he set out methodically to educate himself on the subject. The meeting room of his office today is lined with volumes like *Persuasion for Profit, Zig Ziglar's Secrets of Closing the Sale,* and a number of direct-mail guides from the sixties; on the wall hangs a framed photograph of the legendary twenties adman Claude Hopkins. Scattered among all this is Viguerie's collection of political books, including classics of the paranoid genre like *The Rhodesian Sellout, Target America,* and *Surrender in Panama*.

Viguerie's master stroke was to merge the two: modern marketing and the far right, two great tastes that taste like nitroglycerin together.

The offspring of this union were discussed in lively detail in their heyday. "The fund-raising letters of the New Right groups depict a world gone haywire, with liberal villains poised to destroy the American Way of Life," wrote the conservative author Alan Crawford in 1980. The emphasis was on shrillness, on prose that would " 'make [people] angry' and 'stir up hostilities.' "[3] Like all propaganda, direct mail was rank, contemptible stuff.

Still, awestruck observers came to regard it as a magic medium capable of persuading anybody of anything. Conservatives in particular could be heard celebrating it with the same frenzied hoopla they would expend on the Internet in the nineties. In both cases wingers believed they had found a way to get around the traditional mass media, which they despised as much then as they do now, and to reach out directly to like-minded people suffering liberalism in silent frustration across the land. "You can think of direct mail as *our* TV, radio, daily newspaper and weekly magazine," Viguerie wrote in a 1981 book called *The New Right: We're Ready to Lead*.

Curiously enough, given the world-shaking significance of direct mail, the thing itself—the actual letters that were sent out by the millions in the seventies and eighties—has largely disappeared today. No library that I know of made a comprehensive effort to keep up with the stuff.[4] This form of prose changed the country, and yet it is today as obscure and inaccessible as the lost plays of Menander.

Direct mail moved the country to the right, and, more importantly for our purposes, it made the direct mailers rich. Countless conservative entrepreneurs entered the field looking for a piece of the action. The reason, according to Alan Crawford, is that in case after case, most of the money raised in direct-mail appeals went to compensate the professional fund-raiser, with only a tiny remainder going to the actual cause that the donors had been told they were supporting. Viguerie responded, accurately enough, that direct mail is primarily a mode of advertising; that advertising is expensive; and that clients should be pleased that this form of advertising brings in anything at all.[5]

Direct mail could be *so* expensive, in fact, that political groups often found themselves in debt to their direct-mail fund-raisers.

One conservative activist I spoke to compared the relationship between political organizations and certain smaller direct-mail companies to sharecropping. It would begin, he says, when the fund-raisers approached the political outfit, offering it an advance on proceeds of a direct-mail campaign. Since some of these organizations were chronically starved for cash, they would accept, and the mail bearing their name would go out. But somehow the campaign would never break even, and the organization would find itself in debt to its fund-raiser. To make good, the fund-raiser would offer another advance for another direct-mail effort, and the cycle would repeat itself.

Viguerie, for his part, went far beyond direct mail. By the early eighties he had built a cross-promoting empire of discontent. He published *Conservative Digest,* the house journal of the New Right; he had a syndicated newspaper column and a radio commentary; a TV production company; and a "tax revolt" organization that promised both to fight for tax cuts and to offer advice on "your personal tax situation." He also became an author, publishing a history of the New Right and a manifesto of conservative populism—both of which were extensively advertised in his other ventures.[6]

Today Viguerie is an elder statesman of the right, telling and retelling the story of how he and his friends did it. He has branched out onto the Internet, naturally, where he continues to police the boundaries of the movement he built, inveighing against George W. Bush and other former heroes for "betraying" the conservative cause. Few are pure enough for this great salesman, but in today's climate Viguerie no longer sounds like an extremist; when pronounced by his resonant bass voice, all these verdicts sound so *reasonable* somehow.

Viguerie's genius was for marketing and sales. His New Right colleague Terry Dolan, the director of the National Conservative

Political Action Committee (NCPAC, pronounced "nick-pack"), developed political entrepreneurship into a more advanced business form, making a singular contribution to America's long descent into cynicism and corruption. His innovation was to sell political results—in particular, the destruction of liberal U.S. senators, and in general, the destruction of the campaign-finance rules that limited individual contributions to a specific campaign. Subverting these two simultaneously made for a profitable business model indeed.

NCPAC's trademark was to use terrifying national direct-mail solicitations to pay for local TV commercials that, in turn, set new standards for viciousness and mendacity. The model was a runaway success when Dolan rolled it out during the 1980 elections: NCPAC targeted six Democratic senators from the West and Midwest and knocked off four of them with TV spots accusing them of weakness in the face of the Soviet threat and letters describing all they had "done to ruin America. Each of their Senate votes is like another nail in our nation's coffin." The resulting victories made him an overnight sensation, and as his next target Dolan chose a Democrat from Maryland, so that residents of Washington, D.C., might tremble as they saw the nick-pack attack come roaring across their own TV sets.[7]

Dolan was a leader in that long parade of right-wing bullies whose open contempt for fair play exerts such a fascination over the media. He was cynical about voters, boasting that he could elect Mickey Mouse to the U.S. Senate if he chose. He was cynical about political ethics: Dolan once told a member of Congress to vote his way on a particular legislative measure or face the attack-ad consequences. And, of course, he was cynical about government: "The biggest threat to America—it isn't the commies, it isn't the oil companies," he once said. "The biggest problem is the United States government."[8]

Indeed, in Terry Dolan one finds enough of the signature

attitudes of Washington conservatism as to make him a virtual prototype of the species. He reveled openly in gaming the system, in carefully obeying the letter of the law while trampling exuberantly over its spirit. The law, in this case, had to do with campaign finance, and Dolan gloried in the ease with which he brought big money back into the game, raising and spending enormous sums to run political commercials that were nominally independent but that all attacked liberals. "Dolan is not only finding loopholes in the Federal Election Reform law, he is taunting the FEC, the lawmakers and everyone else," a shocked *Washington Post* reported in 1980. "It's a stupid law," Dolan himself said. "They're gonna take me kicking and screaming to jail before I stop my activities."[9]

NCPAC's commercials earned a reputation for error, but this too Dolan embraced, as just another wrench rammed into the works of reform. "Groups like ours are potentially very dangerous to the political process," he bragged to the *Post*. "Ten independent expenditure groups, for example, could amass this great amount of money" and undermine the whole notion of "accountability in politics. We could say whatever we want about an opponent of a Senator Smith and the senator wouldn't have to say anything. A group like ours could lie through its teeth and the candidate it helps stays clean."[10]

Like direct mail, NCPAC was a money machine, at least for some. Its contractors—pollsters, mailers, and media buyers who always seemed to be either NCPAC insiders or personal friends of Terry Dolan—did well enough. Other friends could count on Dolan to push their personal profit schemes with legislators. There was even a NCPAC effort to set up a conservative organization modeled after Amway, with early joiners poised to grow rich off the membership dues of late arrivals. "Jesus Christ built his church in the same way," said Dolan's designated organizer. "He got 12 people involved, and they got 12 others involved, and so on." Also like Jesus's church, the scheme was ruled illegal soon after its launch.[11]

The political innovations of Howard Phillips would prove most lethal of all. Phillips was—and remains—a serial launcher of organizations: the Conservative Caucus, a grassroots outfit; the Moral Majority, a religious-right outfit; and the Constitution Party, a political outfit on whose zany platform Phillips has thrice run for president. He lives to "organize discontent," as he once put it, personally recruiting the legions of the embittered.[12] Some of his organizations succeeded; others are best forgotten. What distinguished them all was the obsessive but admittedly brilliant imperative Phillips used them to promote: *defund the left*.

As political entrepreneurship goes, this was something new: a plan to systematically destroy or redirect the income of the other side. Phillips rarely gets credit for anything these days, thanks to the ever-widening gyre of his right-wing radicalism, but as we look back over conservatism's decades of dominance in Washington, "defund the left" appears more and more to be the seed from which sprang the whole vast boodling enterprise of conservative governance.

We have encountered Howard Phillips and his works a few times already—he was a founder of Young Americans for Freedom; he was an admirer of Jonas Savimbi—and he will come up again and again as our story progresses. In the early eighties, when the Reagan administration came to town, Phillips was the right's champion peddler of alienation and bitterness. "Our country is going down the drain," he would rage,[13] and in the succeeding thirty seconds he could tell you more about what ailed us than Jimmy Carter could in all his meandering conjecture about our national malaise. My God, it was obvious: Liberalism was soft in the face of a hard world. The liberals were burdening small business with an impossible regulatory load;

they were spending beyond our means; they were cracking down on friendly regimes while playing footsy with the Communists; they were kind to criminals while throwing the book at business owners; they rewarded sloth and punished hard work; and now they were actually starting to give away pieces of our national territory.

The definitive Howard Phillips issue was the 1978 treaty that arranged for the eventual return of the Canal Zone to Panama. The treaty had been a bipartisan, consensus undertaking, but Phillips and his New Right colleagues saw in it a political promise that the establishment Republicans completely missed—not so much a chance to stop the treaty, but to use the "surrender" of the canal to build up public fury: you've always suspected liberals were weak, bordering on treasonous, and here they are collaborating in the actual, physical dismantling of the country! Phillips rode the canal for all it was worth, buying advertising space, setting up phone banks, touring the country, appearing at rallies, giving speeches and press conferences, and eventually sending out more than 3 million pieces of mail on the subject. The cause was also one of the New Right's greatest financial successes, and winger fund-raisers took Panama to the bank again and again over the years, although never quite managing to reverse the treaty or any of the other traitorous "giveaways" that they claimed to have unearthed.[14]

Conservative Caucus literature from the mid-eighties implied that the group had 700,000 members, but Howard Phillips was so energetic one senses he didn't really require them. He was a movement of one, traveling constantly, plotting strategy, and endlessly generating books, articles, magazines, newsletters, broadsheets, speeches, TV shows, testimony to Congress, direct-mail missives—all of them pouring forth from his headquarters in suburban Virginia and bearing his trademark glowering photograph, the original angry man logo.

Eventually Phillips developed other logos as well. A heap of babies in a trash can symbolized "abortion." A big red zero, printed on Conservative Caucus stationery, on posters, and even on bumper stickers, meant "defund the left."

Phillips was a talented organizer, but he had little faith in the masses. "Politics is not a battle of the millions, nor of the majorities," he once wrote. "It is a battle of the militants," in which his "army" practiced what he called "guerrilla politics," striking damaging blows here and there. The key to disabling the liberal Leviathan, he thought, was not some single pitched battle, but a long campaign of sabotage and disruption that would cut off the supply lines to liberal organizations and eventually shut them down.[15]

In explaining his "defund the left" approach, Phillips was fond of quoting a famous Thomas Jefferson pronouncement—"To compel a man to furnish funds for the propagation of ideas he disbelieves and abhors is sinful and tyrannical"—the idea being that by spending tax dollars on programs conservatives disliked, the government was violating basic American rights.[16] The document from which Phillips drew this favorite Jefferson quote is the Virginia Statute for Religious Freedom, which was designed to prevent any alliance between government and religion. In Phillips's mind, Jefferson's dictum about church and state does not apply to something like a Ten Commandments monument in a courthouse,* say, but it makes a heck of a lot of sense when brought to bear on government spending programs that somehow benefit liberal goals, private liberal groups, or even liberal individuals.

Such spending constituted "faith-based advocacy," Phillips raged in 1981, and with a little creativity, virtually any federal

---

*Phillips believes that the nation needs a strong dose of "biblical law" and so admires former Alabama chief justice Roy Moore for his famous Ten Commandments provocation that he tried to get Moore appointed to the Supreme Court.

program at all could be indicted: the National Endowment for the Arts, which funds (liberal) artists; the Department of Energy, which has a (liberal) "Earth Day" program; even public health clinics, "with aspirin tablets, in a sense, becoming instruments of patronage," since they were handed out by liberal doctors. If we squint hard enough, we can almost see, as Phillips did, that "Harvard, Yale, and Berkeley are Establishments of Religion" (since "they advance a world view based on a rationalist faith") and that "Left-wing Professors Pick Our Pockets" through all the various federal grants, subsidies, and student loan programs that keep the universities afloat. Defund the "atheistic" scoundrels! After all, "by what moral principle do you have the right to require me, through your exercise of political power, to subsidize the education of your children?"[17]

Despite all the badges and bumper stickers it has adorned, I doubt that "defund the left" ever had much popular appeal. It is, in its essence, strictly an inside-the-Beltway slogan, concerned not with votes but with the way the federal agencies do their business. Political candidates seldom debate the duties of the Department of Education or the practices of the Department of Labor; not even the Washington media bother much with that subject. Nevertheless, as Howard Phillips saw, the Washington bureaucracy was the true battlefield. This is where the great victories were to be won.

Cut off federal funds to liberal programs, and not only would you kill organizations like the Legal Services Corporation—Phillips's bête noire, a federal program that furnishes lawyers to poor people—but you would close career opportunities for the sort of people drawn to the Legal Services Corporation, which is to say, liberals. Undermine the Department of Labor, and you simultaneously shut off funding to labor unions, pitch prolabor bureaucrats out into the street, and make it that much harder for unions to do their private-sector job. "Defund the left" was thus a plan for a negative patronage scheme, whose effects would reverberate through the political system, as liberal groups found their budgets squeezed and payrolls slashed.

Phillips wails today against the Bush administration for its big-spending ways, but perhaps what he really should be complaining about is its failure to share the credit for its accomplishments. After all, his "defund the left" doctrine eventually became a sort of keystone idea for conservative Washington, repeated by everyone and polished to deadly perfection by Grover Norquist and Tom DeLay. It was the explanation for Republican sabotage of everything from the EPA[18] to the Department of Agriculture, and its unspoken flip side—*fund, fund, fund, fund, fund the right!*—was the obvious inspiration for the Bush administration's program of channeling public money to "faith-based" organizations, to private contractors with the right politics, and to the clients of favored lobbyists. Howard Phillips, the eternal outsider, may rage on in his strip-mall office in northern Virginia, but there are millionaires swanning all across this city who owe their fortunes to his brilliance back in the day. For every federal dollar that we steered to some idealistic social worker in the sixties, we have now paid it back many times over, with millions upon millions flushed down the pipe to Blackwater, Halliburton, A.I.G., and whoever it was that Homeland Security's executives were "consulting" for last year. Surely the judgments of the Lord are true and righteous altogether.

No one absorbed the political teachings of Howard Phillips better than Jack Abramoff. In those heady days of the early eighties, Phillips was, as another College Republican leader remembered, "a father figure to Jack in politics." Close readers of Phillips's newsletters found countless stories of Phillips's encounters with his young protégé, of discussions he had with the brilliant young provocateur, of how he brought Abramoff on board one of his organizations.[19]

Abramoff, for his part, dutifully parroted the older man's views on nearly everything: The CRs' many wars on campus, for example, were youth-auxiliary versions of Phillips's obsessive campaign to "defund the left." In both the professional and the varsity versions, the politics were identical: Neither taxpayers nor tuition payers, the argument went, should be required to fund views they found disagreeable. To bolster their efforts, the CRs used the very same quotation from Jefferson that Phillips had latched onto; Abramoff's CRs even gave out a "Jefferson Award" to the most zealous defunder of the campus left.[20]

Abramoff and Co. also reconfigured the College Republicans for entrepreneurship. When the "campus radical" took over as chairman in 1981, the CRs' budget came directly from the Republican National Committee, then a bulwark of the moderate establishment. That had been sufficient for the old CRs, who liked to party and aimed to anger nobody. But Abramoff started to complain about the arrangement in his first year on the job. And he schemed to achieve autonomy.[21] He didn't want "to be the youth arm of the Republican National Committee," his onetime lieutenant David Miner remembers. He wanted

> a very strong, viable organization. And instead of once a year sitting down with the budget director and the political director of the RNC and making a twenty-minute case about why they should donate $100,000 a year to the College Republicans, Jack decided he was going to run the College Republicans just like the Republican National Committee was run, he was going to have his own direct mail list, he was going to have prominent members of Congress sign letters for him, and he was going to raise his own money. That's a pretty bold statement for someone to do at twenty-two years old.

It was so bold, in fact, that it infuriated the RNC officials charged with supervising their college auxiliary. In late 1983 they kicked the CRs out of their building.

No matter. Under Abramoff's leadership, enthusiasm was high, membership soared, and revenues far surpassed those of the previous period. The College Republicans' *Annual Report* for 1983 claimed that the group's income had quintupled since the last year before Abramoff took the reins; what's more, fully 70 percent of that income came from individual donors, dwarfing the contributions of the RNC. "Jack was a very creative, smart executive," continues Miner. He was "a hell of a CEO."*

Just like entrepreneurs are supposed to do, Abramoff and his MBA sidekick, Grover Norquist, opened their organization to the market, setting up incentives for growth and looking for investors outside the parent organization. And what did the College Republicans have to offer these investors, these donors?

Outrage. Activism. The right-wing position rammed home with force. One reason the CRs staged so many anti-Soviet protests, for example, was that they were popular "with people who wrote us the checks," remembers Mike Simpfenderfer, who served as the organization's secretary under Abramoff. "The older establishment was willing to pay the bill because they were like, *that's what we need.* Somebody to shake this place up." To see conservative kids in the street, chanting the slogans of the hard right—this was a spectacle for which aging wingers were willing to pay a good price. And Jack's CRs delivered. "The people that had the ability to . . . keep us in business looked at it and said, 'we agree,'" Simpfenderfer continues.

---

*Before Abramoff's name became so poisonous, College Republicans generally regarded the Abramoff era as their finest hour. In 2001, then-chairman Scott Stewart introduced the lobbyist to the CRs' convention as "probably the best national chairman that we have ever had."

" 'Not that we're going to go out there and protest with the youngsters, but considering that we had to watch what we didn't agree with in the sixties, we kind of like watching what we agree with in the eighties.' "

Another way of escaping the RNC's funding straitjacket was through direct mail. The single specimen from the CRs' Abramoff period that I have managed to unearth is typical of the genre circa 1983: by turns chummy, frightening, confiding, and apocalyptic. As was common in those days, the letter is signed by an elected official—in this case New York representative Jack Kemp, then the best-known conservative in Congress. It pleads with the reader to "dig down deep" for the College Republicans, led by "my good friend Jack Abramoff." And why should Mr. and Mrs. America give to Jack Abramoff's CRs, of all groups? Because, according to Kemp, they were "the most important Republican organization in America today," prepared to do all manner of grassroots electioneering in the upcoming 1984 contest. And why should the reader care about that? Because "our nation is in grave danger of sliding into another depression" should liberals be permitted to resume their tax-and-spending ways. "That's right," Kemp warned. "A depression worse than the so-called Great Depression." Thankfully, though, Jack Abramoff and his "dedicated group of young leaders . . . understand what must be done to return economic prosperity to America."

The larger mechanism that CEO Abramoff used to break free from the stodgy Republican elders was a tax-exempt and technically nonpartisan fund-raising group called the United Students of America Foundation (aka USA Foundation or sometimes just USAF). The nonprofit USAF had an office in the Heritage Foundation building; its officers were drawn from the cast of characters who accompanied Abramoff from group to group; and its purpose was to lay down supporting fire for whatever assault the

College Republicans were then making.* Like the Polish army in Iraq, the USAF allowed the CRs to describe whatever they were doing as the deed of a high-minded alliance, such as the Student Coalition for Truth, in which the CRs joined with the USAF to hold a panel discussion assailing the nuclear freeze, or the Committee for Democracy in Grenada, which took to the park in front of the White House in 1983 to show the enthusiasm of youth for the U.S. invasion of that country.[22]

Going freelance with a tax-exempt foundation, as Abramoff did with USAF, soon became a popular career move among the sons of Reagan. Ralph Reed launched a group called Students for America, a southern outfit designed to bring evangelicals into the conservative mix. Students for a *Better* America, which warred on liberal professors, was set up by Steve Baldwin, also a onetime Abramoff lieutenant. The Conservative Youth Federation of America was launched by Amy Moritz, still another Abramoff associate. Then there was the Conservative Action Foundation, the Conservative Student Support Foundation, and the mysterious Young Conservative Foundation, aka "America's premiere Human Rights organization."

What accounts for this organizational flowering on the right? The answer is clearest in the case of the USAF: Foundations like these allowed the Reagan youth to pursue hefty contributions from the real powers of Republicandom—corporations, which prefer to donate to tax-exempt organizations. It was through his not-for-profit that Abramoff seems to have discovered the profitable side of politics.

---

*The College Republicans were quite open about the direct relationship between the party organization and the "nonpartisan" foundation. Paul Erickson, an officer of the CRs as well as the USAF, explained to the *Chronicle of Higher Education* in 1984 how his colleagues "began to realize that the Republicans' 'educational' activities could be done by a tax-exempt foundation instead, so 'the educational program we conducted as College Republicans was brought over here.' "

The occasion for this discovery was the College Republicans' ongoing war with Ralph Nader's Public Interest Research Groups (PIRGs), student activist outfits that were funded at most colleges by "activity fees" all students were required to pay (unless they checked a box on a form).[23] This was the point on which the CRs challenged them, insisting on campus after campus that it was "sinful and tyrannical" to compel students to fund an obviously political organization.[24]

Like other Nader groups, the student PIRGs were something of a pain in the neck to business, always agitating for container deposit laws and other environmental causes, and at some point it apparently occurred to Abramoff or Norquist that defunding and thus killing PIRG chapters was a service for which the targeted businesses ought to be paying. Up to now, dedicated conservative students had fought to defeat liberalism—to defeat the force that regulated business, that raised taxes on business, that fined business for polluting, that sided with unions against business—and the kids had done it all for free.

This had to change. In a 1986 interview, one USAF spokesman described how his young charges were to attract investments from business interests. "Listen, [PIRGs are] involved in all these campaigns to increase regulation against business," the young conservative was to say. He or she was urged to mention Nader: "You say Ralph Nader's name and any educated businessman will take interest." Norquist himself was more specific, pointing to the PIRGs' bottle-bill campaign as an example. "We say: 'We're fighting PIRGs and you know that they go after you bottlers all the time, and try to get nickel-a-bottle [deposit] laws passed. And we're going to go after 20 PIRG fights this year . . . and you have an interest in this, or you ought to.' "[25]

Thus did the young entrepreneurs of the USAF get out there and sell themselves as political hit men. According to one 1986 study, the group managed to collect tribute from canning and bottling companies, two oil companies, an electric company (PIRGs were then working to set up utility watchdog groups), Amway, Coors, an assortment of San Francisco landlords worried about the possibility of rent control, and the Campbell's Soup Company, which reportedly paid USAF to attack a campus support group for a migrant farmworkers union.[26] It was pugnacity for pay.

Grover Norquist explained the strategy to an interviewer as a simple matter of cost-effectiveness. "PIRGs have cost the bottlers and the auto industry millions of dollars, hundreds of millions of dollars," he said. "And to the extent that we've been able to get people ginned up and kill PIRGs off, . . . we've cost the left a couple hundred thousand dollars a year in funding." For a mere $20,000, Norquist figured, the USAF could hire a campus disorganizer to mount perhaps ten campaigns against PIRGs per year; if he won half of those, that's "50,000 to 100,000 less money that the left has."[27] Funding the right to help it defund the left made for a most excellent return on political investment.

The USAF's motto was "Promoting a free market of ideas on the nation's campuses," and here we encounter yet another signature theme of the Washington right. Like many winger ideas—anticommunism, for example—it sounds good at first. A "free market of ideas" sounds like "free inquiry," or a "free exchange of ideas"; an environment in which hypotheses are tested and bad ones are weeded out while good ones go on to earn the respect of the community of scholars. But this is not what the phrase means at all. Markets do not determine the objective merit of things, only their price, which is to say, their merit in the eyes of capital or consumers. To cast intellectual life as a "market" is to set up a standard for measuring ideas quite different from the standard of truthfulness. Here ideas are bid up or down depending on how well they please those with the funds to underwrite inquiry—

which effectively means, how well they please large corporations and the very wealthy.

To make this market work, though, you had to get businesspeople to understand which ideas served their common interests, which ones didn't, and then to act together as a class—supporting the good ideas and crushing the liberal ones. Say "you kill ten PIRGs this year," Norquist speculated back in 1986. "Well, were those PIRGs going to do bottling this year or were they going to do airbags this year? Well, maybe fifty-fifty but you know in general that they're coming after you at some point."[28] Norquist would repeat a similar argument to me twenty years later. Businesses were still not spending enough on the political war. They had to be instructed on big-picture thinking, on the amazing returns to be realized through funding conservatism. In 2006, however, Grover Norquist was not some campus activist; he was the architect of the most effective defund-the-left program Washington has ever seen.

Less imaginative entrepreneurs continue to work the old USAF game to this day. Take David Rothbard, a USAF officer who traveled from campus to campus organizing the campaign against the PIRGs. In 1985 this budding political entrepreneur set up his own nonprofit, the Committee for a Constructive Tomorrow (CFACT), and continued the war against the left as a freelancer. CFACT specialized in alerting the energy industry to "consumer group activities that directly affect them," as a fund-raising letter put it, and reeled in contributions from the usual suspects: electric utilities, oil companies, right-wing foundations. Rothbard still fights the libs today, with columns in the *Washington Times* and proclamations by countless "experts" that pour forth from CFACT's Washington offices, pooh-poohing global warming, leading the cheers for nuclear power, and moaning about EPA "regulators gone wild."[29] It is a remarkable accomplishment, in a way; for two decades now, this fellow has enjoyed a corporate-subsidized career based on lib-bashing articles written for a newspaper subsidized by the Reverend Sun Myung Moon. The "free market of ideas" in action, I suppose.

It should come as no surprise that the biggest scandal of the eighties resulted from a combination of the two great conservative themes I have been describing: revolutionary "freedom fighters" and political entrepreneurship.

The outlines of the Iran-Contra story are well known. President Reagan's CIA was waging a "secret" war against the Sandinista government of Nicaragua; the Democratic Congress objected because we were technically at peace with that nation. So, in 1983, Congress cut off funds to the Contras, the Nicaraguan "freedom fighters" that the CIA had recruited and trained. Over at the National Security Council, however, Marine lieutenant-colonel Oliver North came up with a scheme to get money to the Contras using a network of private donors, weapons sales to Iran, and private supply operations. He also organized private efforts to lobby Congress to change its mind.

Quite early on in the annals of Iran-Contra our pioneering political entrepreneurs make their inevitable appearance. Jack Abramoff crops up in Oliver North's notebook for February 14, 1985, his name misspelled, but the beginnings of a great lobbying career soon becoming clear. On March 26, Abramoff and Howard Phillips show up on a list of people helping North to influence the upcoming Contra-aid vote in Congress; later that day, Abramoff phones North and tells him that a number of "votes" are available in exchange for some other legislative favor.[30]

We do not ordinarily remember Iran-Contra for the business opportunities it generated, but in the long, winding history of conservatism-as-industry it remains a particularly instructive chapter. The aforementioned Spitz Channell, for example, sensed the Contras' potential early on and used them to become the most successful fund-raiser in all of Washington, circa 1985. Channell's marks were conservative widows; his politics were far to the right, verging on Bircherite; he made his pitches in person, often using a scary slide show about the dangers of Nicaraguan communism put together by Oliver North.[31] Not only did his donors reap tax write-offs by giving to one of the many nonprofit groups Channell had set up, but they sometimes got to meet President Reagan too, a favor the fund-raiser arranged simply by throwing some change to one of the president's former aides.[32]

None of this put much money into the pockets of the Contras, though. On the right, as we have seen, the fund-raiser always prospers, but the cause itself sometimes languishes. And Channell was a professional; he later admitted that he only became interested in Nicaragua after he noticed how the subject ticked off rich folks and it dawned on him that these "freedom fighters" had fund-raising possibilities. He proceeded to take the customary profiteering to dizzy entrepreneurial heights. Of the $12 million raked in by Channell's empire of nonprofits in 1985 and 1986, the historian Theodore Draper calculates that only $2.7 million actually made it to the Contras. Huge sums were diverted to Channell's friends, his lover, and his friends' lovers. All the middlemen between here and Managua took a cut, too.[33]

The similarities between Channell's machinations in the eighties and the scandals of today's Washington are so remarkable that they form a persistent pattern of conservative misbehavior: the luxury meals, fancy condos, and web of nonprofits that in both cases masked the movements of the money, yielding tax deductions for the chosen, punishment for the uncooperative, and nice things for friendlies. Also, an unmistakable cynicism toward the chumps who are taken in. Just as the corrupt lobbyists of our time famously sneered at the Indian tribes they represented as "monkeys" and "troglodytes," Channell expressed his private contempt for his aged donors in colorful terms: "Hamhocks," "Dogface," "Mrs. Malleable."[34]

Exposing all this did not reduce the racket's profitability. Iran-Contra was the scandal with the Midas touch, and it continued to rain money on the faithful even after the whole rotten operation had been rolled up. One day in July 1987, as the Democrats in Congress screeched hysterically about the White House and its illegal foreign policy, Ollie North put on his uniform, stood before the cameras, raised his hand, and summoned up a backlash tsunami that crushed the liberals and brought a flood of prosperity to the political entrepreneurs of the right.

Richard Viguerie sent out 5 million Olliemania letters within three weeks after North's testimony ended. NCPAC's phone pledges were up 200 percent in the same period. Jack Abramoff started selling copies of an Ollie North videotape made up of a slide show that was almost certainly the one Spitz Channell had used to scare his dotards, advertising it with a photo of the stern-faced marine testifying before "the so-called Iran/Contra congressional committee."[35] Oliver North videotapes eventually became something of an industry unto themselves, but the one made by Abramoff, titled *Telling It Like It Is,* is surely the only bit of filmed entertainment ever to be dedicated "to the memory of William J. Casey," the CIA director famous for his towering contempt for Congress.[36]

The trade in Olliania boomed for years, as the persecuted patriot was indicted for his crimes and came to require a legal defense fund. (And also, apparently, a host of fake legal defense funds.) Jerry Falwell compared Ollie to Christ. Howard Phillips compared him to a brand, calling him "the most marketable political commodity that I know of in the whole United States." And so he was: there were Oliver North key chains and pocketknives and T-shirts and eventually even a TV show in which

Ollie told America the secrets of war. There was the usual round of plunder, as funds raised to help Ollie stayed with the fundraiser instead. And inevitably there was "Ollie, Inc.," as the former marine finally went into the nonprofit direct-mail business on his own behalf. By 1994, when he ran for a Senate seat in Virginia, Oliver North had become the most successful political fundraiser in the land, bringing in some $20 million in the course of the campaign. He lost anyway.[37]

Prodigious though they might seem, these acts of retail profiteering were minuscule beside the colossal entrepreneurial gambit that the Iran-Contra investigation revealed. The insiders called it "the Enterprise": Private money, raised through the sale of government favors and property, would go to fund private armies of "freedom fighters" operating overseas. The ultimate aim of the Enterprise, as envisioned by CIA director Casey, was privatization on the grandest scale imaginable: the construction of a foreign policy instrument that was free from the meddling of Congress, financed by sales of weapons and another precious commodity that government had in abundance but which it had hitherto been reluctant to market—access.[38]

As a foreign policy venture, Iran-Contra was a disaster, and the Enterprise eventually fell apart under congressional scrutiny. In the George W. Bush administration, however, this very bad idea was back in even more grandiose form, encompassing a vast selling-off of government favors to those willing to fund the conservative movement, a wholesale transfer of government responsibilities to private-sector contractors, and even private armies, unaccountable to Congress or anyone else.[39]

Underneath it all, then as now, was the bedrock cynicism of the right. According to his boss at the National Security Agency, Oliver North was "quite cynical about government," and this cynicism was critical to what North proceeded to do. He broke the liberals' law against funding the Contras because he disagreed with it; he kept secrets from the State Department and Congress because he had little respect for them. Contempt for government and contempt for the liberals who built that government thus led irresistibly to North's curious blend of self-righteousness and corruption, a combination we shall encounter again as our story progresses.[40]

Industry conservatism has come a long way since the days when liberals sputtered at NCPAC's brutality and gaped uncomprehendingly at the letters pouring out by the millions from Richard Viguerie's computers. At its height in the Bush years, the industry included specialists in dozens of fields. There were professionals and amateurs; those who did it because they were paid to do it and those who did it because their eyes had seen the glory of the coming of the entrepreneur. It had establishment firms and feisty start-ups—megacontractors taking billions to do work that the government used to do itself; young men with a nice smile and a single client who just wanted to do a little clear-cutting out West somewhere. In conservative circles you would encounter entrepreneurs both formally and casually, at carefully programmed events laying out the opportunities for profit opened up by Hurricane Katrina, or in conversation at a banquet celebrating some conservative anniversary or other. At one such event in 2004, waiting for the presentation of the "Charlton Heston Commemorative Firearm," I made the backslapping acquaintance of a freelance motivational speaker who, upon discovering that one of my tablemates was an officer of the Transportation Safety Administration, immediately sought his confirmation that "we're gonna privatize that, right?"

For some in winger Washington this was an idealistic business, but what gave it power and longevity was that it was a *profitable* business—a far more profitable business than the one employing the guy on the other side of the table, the EPA drudge who went home at night to a brick-colonial cube and a garage that would accommodate no vehicle wider than a Model A.

I mean this not as polemic but as a statement of fact. Washington swarms with conservative ideologues and operators not because conservatives particularly like it here, but because there is an entire industry in D.C. that has sprung up to support conservatism—an industry subsidized by the nation's largest corporations and its richest families, and, until recently, by the government, too. We are all familiar with the industry's flagship organizations—Cato, Heritage, AEI—but the industry extends far beyond these, encompassing numerous magazines, hundreds of lobbying firms, and a daily newspaper published strictly for the movement's benefit, a propaganda sheet whose distortions are so obvious and so alien that it puts one in mind of those official party organs you encounter when traveling in authoritarian countries.[41] There are think tanks that specialize in reaching highly specific parts of the conservative demographic—interns spending the summer in D.C., for example. There are political strategists, pollsters, campaign managers, trainers of youth, image consultants and makers of TV commercials, revolutionaries-for-hire, and, of course, direct-mail specialists who still launch their million-letter raids on the mailboxes of the heartland.

In a curious way, Washington truly became a winger wonderland. All the nation's prize tories gravitated here. Remember the guy who wrote those sputtering diatribes for your student newspaper at college? Chances are, he ended up in D.C., thinking big thoughts from an "endowed chair" or churning out more of the brilliant usual for one of the movement's many blogs or publications. The campus wingnut whose fulminations on the Red Menace so amused my friends and me at the University of Virginia, for example, resurfaced here as a full-blown columnist for the *Washington Times* before transitioning inevitably into consultancy. A friend of mine who went to Georgetown recalled for me the capers of *his* campus wingnut, which he had completely forgotten until the guy made headlines as the lead culprit in a minor 2004 scandal called "Memogate" (it involved the distribution of Democratic strategy memos to the press). A while ago I read in the newspaper that he was working for the U.S. embassy in Baghdad teaching democratic civics to Iraqi politicians.

There was so much money in conservatism then that Grover Norquist could boast, "We can now go to students at Harvard and say, 'There is now a secure retirement plan for Republican operatives.' "[42] The young people who came pouring into Washington in the thirties and forties could have had little expectation of getting rich there, but the youngsters who answered conservatism's call over the last three decades were making a canny career move in addition to obeying their conscience.

This was not what the well-meaning centrists of the nineties had in mind when they used to sing about how the "entrepreneurial spirit is transforming the public sector," but this was what the transformation looked like nonetheless. It was no well-meaning centrist affair. It was industry conservatism, constantly seething and effervescing; tens of thousands of individuals coming and going, each avidly piling up their own tiny pile; but collectively, and with the guidance of the market's invisible hand, engaged in the common project of reconfiguring the state.

CHAPTER 5

From Paranoia to Privatopia, by Way of Pretoria

Even with all the innovations I've described, industry conservatism was not yet the perfect entrepreneurial weapon it would one day become. Conservatism-for-profit was still missing an essential ingredient: its ideological rationale. Only with the end of the cold war would the final catalyst be brought into the mix.

The Ollie North episode was one of the final spectacular flare-ups of the right's long-burning love affair with anticommunism. Just a few years later, the collapse of the Soviet Union rendered the wingers' tenderly crafted treason dreams as obsolete as know-nothingism.

What came to take the place of anticommunism as the wingers' inspiration was the great god market. In truth, of course, this idol had been there all along, gathering dust on a shelf at the American Enterprise Institute. But as the more compelling causes of cold war and culture war began to recede, new and amazing properties of the free market were discovered. Free markets, it occurred to the conservative world, were the very essence of democracy itself. Free markets were the path for all to reach prosperity. What's more, free markets were advancing by an ineluctable dialectic of their own, leaving liberalism in the dust and forcing every government on earth to privatize and deregulate and do all the other things that business demanded.

The awakening wasn't limited to wingers, either. Before the end of the eighties, centrist Democrats were crowding the pews too, and as the NASDAQ worked its miracles even liberals abandoned the shrine of the state and raised their voices instead for the new god, the infallible setter of prices and the savior of the third world; hallelujah for mammon, all-seeing, all-enriching.

The public face of conservatism changed so radically in those years that it was difficult, sometimes, even to understand that it was still conservatism. The ecstatic economic optimism of books like *Dow 36,000* supplanted the deathly pessimism of *What Will Happen to You When the Soviets Take Over*. Suspicious hypernationalism of the *None Dare Call It Treason* variety gave way to the breathless globalism we find in the newspaper columns of Thomas Friedman. Even the culture wars seemed to recede, as the new capitalists made their pronouncements to an Iggy Pop beat and the offices of America went "business casual." The crew-cut factory owner in Akron was joined in his denunciations of big government by the hipsters at *Wired*—and, mirabile dictu, by a Democratic president.

All across the land wingers changed their plumage. Onetime red-baiter Dinesh D'Souza became an authority on Silicon Valley, the site of the deregulated New Economy's greatest achievements. Jack Wheeler, erstwhile leader of the cult of the freedom fighter, discovered that the Internet was the weapon that would destroy the liberal state here at home.[1] Leadership of the conservative movement passed from Pat Buchanan, warning darkly about the coming "New World Order," to Newt Gingrich, extolling the coming Information Age and referring reporters to the glorious free-market future as revealed in *The Third Wave*.

The most telling metamorphosis was that of the conservative writer George Gilder. Like so many others, Gilder started his career as a culture warrior, denouncing feminism as a mortal threat to civilization. In his 1981 best seller, *Wealth and Poverty,* he expanded the attack, describing poverty as a result of bad values and blaming society's breakdown on permissive liberalism. Then, in the late eighties, Gilder discovered that the microchip, the motor of American prosperity, contained in its very design a political commandment: *thou shalt embrace free-market economics*. This astonishing insight lifted Gilder to an entirely different plane of celebrity, made him a member of the "digerati," a clairvoyant of technology itself, and then, of all things, the greatest stock picker of the late nineties. (Subsequently, one of the worst stock pickers of the early oughts.)

These people all seemed to change, but their essential political views did not. For Gilder as well as D'Souza and Gingrich, liberalism was always evil while private enterprise carried within it the spark of the divine. Their superficial changeability reveals a truth about American conservatism generally: The interests of business are central and defining, while every other aspect or strategy of the movement is mutable and disposable. Indeed, even the cult of the free market, which appears to be such a solid, fixed element of the business mind, is malleable as well, with conservatism handing out the bailouts as soon as the going gets tough on Wall Street.

These mutations are particularly remarkable when considered as the statements of a movement that claims to ground itself in "tradition." One year, the working-class, values-voting "hardhats" are trumpeted as all-American heroes; on another occasion they are an uppity canaille requiring a whiff of grapeshot. Thinly veiled racism elects a host of Republican free marketeers; soon afterward, the system's big thinkers can be heard proclaiming racism to be the great enemy of free markets. Patriotism is a virtue under all circumstances—until the time comes to declare the nation-state a relic of the protectionist past. Combat veterans are to be venerated—until they run for office as liberal Democrats. Even communism itself becomes perfectly acceptable when, as in Red China, it mutates into a way of enforcing market discipline.

The needs of business stand like a rock; all else is convenience, opportunism, a bit of bushwah generated by some focus group and forgotten the instant it is no longer convincing. Fundamentally amoral, capitalism is loyal to no people, no region, no heroes, really, once they have exhausted their usefulness—not even to the nation whose flag the wingers pretend to worship.

Hence the eternal frustration of the conservative rank and file with their leaders. Unless you are solely interested in the welfare of business, Washington conservatives will all turn out to be "impostors" to you, always ready to compromise on family values or their adherence to the Founders' "original intent." Every ally is an ally of convenience for them, every ironclad principle subject to revocation without notice, every noble ideal advanced merely to shore up popular support. Although there is no central command barking out the talking points, the movement nevertheless seems almost naturally to behave like an agitprop bureau.

This is why, I think, one of the most telling illustrations of the right's malleability—its fundamental loyalty to business, its opportunism in all other matters, and its essential kinship to propaganda—can be found in the career of an obscure but well-connected Washington think tank, the International Freedom Foundation, or IFF, which campaigned vigorously on behalf of South Africa from 1986 to 1993. The IFF waved the conservative flag with admirable energy, but the costumes it donned to lead the parade changed dramatically as the years passed. Without even a blink the IFF would go from decrying the Panama Canal give-away to puffing the North American Free Trade Agreement. Like the other organizations we have examined, this one, too, was well outside the mainstream, but don't brush it off for that reason; many of the positions the IFF took became standard Beltway wisdom. They are ideas that you and I will contend with for the rest of our lives. Its story is not that of an ideological exotic but of the movement's very essence.

You don't have to dig very deep in the conservative literature of the eighties before you hit apartheid South Africa. Today their onetime association with that country makes conservatives uncomfortable, naturally, and few will own up to the passion with which they once worked to rationalize the apartheid regime or to vilify its foes. But in those days, South Africa's agonizing racial problems, its prosperous but beleaguered business community, and its stout defiance of all things communist made it a potent symbol for American conservatives. South Africa was essentially like us, conservatives seemed to believe, and yet with the airy moralism of the do-gooders—with their sanctions and their disinvestment strategies—the liberals were preparing to sell out this loyal friend, just as they had sold out so many others.

In fact, the apartheid government made an ideal love-match for the American far right. South Africa was the place where all the strands of eighties conservatism came together. It was a God-fearing land where American corporations did well, where Christianity was written into the constitution, and where the government wasn't squeamish about the death penalty. South Africans were unassuming people who ate American fast food and relished American movies. Howard Phillips even led tours of this "beautiful, peaceful, productive country," doing his part to teach "the truth that has *not* been allowed to appear in the national media."[2]

South Africa was one of the only Western nations that had successfully resisted the liberal currents of the preceding forty years. While America had moved toward equality and full civil rights, South Africa raced in the opposite direction. While American blacks gathered political strength and scored a series of victories, South Africa's white regime clubbed its black population down, stifling the barest peep of political expression with bannings, torture, prison terms, assassinations, massacres. Liberals managed to make "police brutality" an object of horror in America; in South Africa it became an everyday tool of governance, something you just got used to. As for the cultural upheavals of the sixties and seventies, they barely intruded in the highly moral Republic of South Africa, thanks largely to the censor's heavy hand and the complete absence of television until 1975.[3]

It was also one of the only spots on planet Earth where the crackpot social theory of the far right—in which communists are everywhere and liberals are their "useful idiots"—was the official ideology of the state. Indeed, white South Africa had staked its very existence on this lunacy. Claiming they faced a "total onslaught" from secretive and superpowerful communist foes, the government had made it a crime not merely to *be* a Communist, but to *agree* with the Communist Party about certain things. The government defined its main internal opposition as "communists" and then banned and imprisoned them; it propped up vicious neighboring regimes and, when those fell, vicious guerrilla groups in order to hold the line against "communism"; it built up an enormous security establishment and a notorious secret police force so that it might stand ever-vigilant against suspected "communists," both domestic and foreign.

South Africa's huge investment in the communist threat is easy enough to understand. To begin with, there really *was* a sizable

Communist Party in South Africa once, and there really *were* Soviet arms in the hands of apartheid's enemies. But faced with the implacable hostility of an overwhelming majority of the people it ruled, the apartheid regime chose to exaggerate these threats in the most inflammatory way. If the choice in southern Africa could be reduced to apartheid or communism, then Pretoria could appear, to some in the West at least, as the holders of the "lesser evil" title.

All this made the Afrikaners the most aggressive crisis peddlers of them all, more alarmed about the Soviet buildup than the Committee on the Present Danger, more contemptuous of liberal weakness than Oliver North, more paranoid than all the unmedicated Birchers of Orange County combined.

Meanwhile, back in America, and despite our country's broader shift to the right, public opinion was turning rapidly against the white South African regime. There were constant protests at the South African embassy in Washington, miniature shantytowns on college campuses, codes of conduct for companies that did business there, meetings between American officials and representatives of the African National Congress (ANC), and, crowning it all, the Comprehensive Anti-Apartheid Act of 1986, which slapped sanctions on South Africa and which Congress passed over President Reagan's veto.

To the white government in Pretoria, these were the harbingers of disaster. It desperately needed to fight the American left with a goal of victory. It needed a political hit man.[4]

Jack Abramoff was ready to sign up. As it happened, he had been pursuing opportunity in South Africa for years. He had visited the country in 1983 to meet with businessmen and South African student leaders, most notably one Russel Crystal, who headed an energetic right-wing outfit on that nation's campuses. Crystal was a sort of antipodean doppelgänger to Abramoff, echoing not only the American's tactical thinking but his truculent style as well. In the early eighties, Crystal's group declared "all-out war" on its campus adversaries, who, the South African said, were "undermining the will of the Western world"; on one occasion his followers reportedly attacked a peaceful left-wing demonstration with baseball bats. Just like the College Republicans, Crystal's student organization spent lavishly, and Crystal boasted about its financial "support from the business community." Its publications even borrowed language from those of the CRs. Naturally Crystal and Abramoff became allies, with the CRs organizing a tour by Crystal of American college campuses and Crystal, in turn, helping to set up the Jamba spectacle in 1985.[5]

Then, one month after Jamba, conservative college students from the world over got together in Johannesburg for a second right-wing Woodstock, this one hosted by Crystal's group. The event was called "Youth for Freedom," and a "Dear Delegate" letter given to each participant explained its purpose: Here it was 1985, the UN's "International Youth Year," and high-minded youth congresses were happening all over the world—most of them "under the leadership of . . . communist front organisations . . . to propagate their own marxist/leninist agenda." The duty of the righteous was "to gather the true defenders of liberty and freedom"; to ponder "the security and prosperity of the free world"; and to draft a statement to which "conservative students worldwide" might rally.

Norquist, Abramoff,* and a gaggle of CRs made up the American contingent. Howard Phillips regaled the youngsters with tales of "the revival of conservatism," and also on hand was the American diplomat Charles Lichenstein, then a hero of the right for having told the United Nations how tickled he would be to see that organization pack up and leave the Home of the Brave. A little color was added by a representative of the German

*Although Abramoff is listed as the very last speaker on the official "Youth for Freedom" program, none of the attendees I talked to remember seeing him there.

extreme right (bonus points: he had been a U-boat captain during World War II). The delegates listened to a denunciation of disinvestment. They received a full-color, expensively printed book about the martial and philosophical achievements of Jonas Savimbi. The South African author Leon Louw, whom we shall encounter again later, limned for them the glories of free enterprise. After the conference was over, the kids were given a treat: some of the "youth for freedom" got to go to a military base to see a riot-control demonstration.[6]

Coverage of the conclave in the South African press focused on the lavishness of the proceedings and the great expense involved in flying everyone first-class to Johannesburg. Youth for Freedom participants stayed in what was then the finest hotel in the city, and the conference featured a squad of interpreters and a video crew to document it all. Obviously Russel Crystal's tiny student group couldn't have paid for all this by itself, and Crystal himself was keeping mum about the financing. But other freedom youths confirmed that the gathering had been at least partly funded by South African corporate concerns, in the now-familiar political-entrepreneur pattern: "The business community in South Africa is very enthused about any face-lift possibility that they can gain," explained one of the organizers.[7]

Out of that 1985 conference came an organization called Liberty and Democracy International, which didn't last long, perhaps because of the neck-snapping contradiction between its dreamy title and South African reality. And out of *that,* in 1986, came the International Freedom Foundation—the IFF—the strangest scheme yet hatched by the sons of Reagan for bringing the power of money to bear on politics and the world of ideas.[8]

In the course of researching this book, I found many conservatives who were happy to share their memories with me. When my research reached the IFF, however, I encountered a solid wall of evasion and refusal. Not one of the many former IFFers that I contacted, either in the United States or in South Africa, would consent to an interview. Their reticence was prompted, I believe, not only by the Abramoff connection but also by the fact that the IFF was an advocacy group set up and funded by the apartheid government of South Africa. Since no one would talk, what I know about the group comes mainly from the blizzard of publications and documents that the IFF produced in its short life and the smaller flurry of news stories that attended the exposure of its connection to the Pretoria regime.

We do know the most fundamental facts. According to volume 2 of the official report of the South African Truth and Reconciliation Commission, the duties of the IFF included supporting Savimbi and fighting trade sanctions against South Africa. The IFF's head office was in Washington, where Jack Abramoff initially served as executive director. But the shots were actually called by the organization's South African branch, headed by Russel Crystal. There was an office in London and, eventually, one in West Germany.

We also know that the IFF was an expensive proposition and that the apartheid government spent millions of dollars propping it up. The group hosted speakers, conferences, and presentations; it published several magazines and a flock of newsletters; its principals constantly traveled the globe, talking up their toxic trinity of "Liberty, Prosperity, Security."

The Washington branch of the IFF, it seems, was particularly successful at courting politicians. The group's "advisory board" included Senator Jesse Helms; Representatives Phil Crane; "B-1 Bob" Dornan; James Inhofe, a stout family-values supporter; and "Buz" Lukens, an egregious family-values violator. Charles Lichenstein, who had been present at the creation, was the board's chairman and, according to one writer I talked to, the guiding hand behind the foundation's American magazine.

The group also apparently tried its hand at influence-buying. In 1987, the IFF's Washington office requested $400,000 from South Africa in order to buy a jet plane for the presidential campaign of Jack Kemp, then the darling of the conservative movement. According to internal IFF documents, this bauble would be an investment sufficient to make Abramoff's gang "the 'kitchen cabinet' types of the Kemp administration." The South Africans turned the proposal down, realizing even then what a long shot Kemp was.[9]

The IFF approached its mission in a roundabout manner. Its backers well understood that apartheid could not be sold in the West for the simple reason that racism as a philosophy of government was flatly irredeemable here.[10] Instead the organization was to tarnish apartheid's enemies, "to paint the ANC as a project of the international department of the Soviet Communist Party."[11] This it did, energetically red-baiting the ANC. In this respect, the IFF was merely a large-scale replay of the political entrepreneurship we saw at the USAF, with Jack and the gang yet again hiring themselves out to a wealthy client to perform a hit on a troublesome left-wing group.[12] High points in this campaign included hearings by the House Republican Study Committee in 1987 to blame "the plight of the children of South Africa" on the commie-terrorist ANC; reports playing up the ANC's commie-derived taste for atrocities against kids; newspaper ads designed to throw cold water on Nelson Mandela during his triumphant visit to America in 1990; and an endless war on Ted Kennedy, a leading proponent of the 1986 sanctions.[13]

All of this specifically South African stuff was mixed in with a large quantity of standard-issue winger-talk. The IFF manifesto was a 1987 statement bearing the ultimate conservative seal of approval: a photo of Jack Abramoff proudly shaking hands with Ronald Reagan. Its contents were a draft of highly rectified ideological piffle: pointless, labored meditation upon a cliché—in this case, the word *freedom*—with an occasional dash of hot indignation directed at those who don't share the author's noble feelings about said cliché. *Freedom* means being free, being free is what freedom is all about, we support people who support freedom, we oppose people who oppose freedom, and so on. According to this document, the IFF was "dedicated to the promotion of individual freedom throughout the world"—surely something everyone could support. The problem, though, was that there were "distorted interpretations of the concept of freedom" out there, and so the foundation committed itself to "exposing the cynical use of the concept of freedom" by governments that say they are free *but really aren't.* That the IFF was itself from the very beginning a cynical effort to use "the concept of freedom" to shore up a racist prison state is merely another whopping duplicity that we must wearily add to conservatism's rapidly growing account.

Amid this mush of freedom-talk could be found three more solid points: freedom equals "the free market system"; the foundation supports "freedom fighters in their struggle for liberty and democracy," meaning Savimbi (but not the ANC); and the foundation will create "forums for dialogue" where people can freely contemplate the majesty of freedom, as opposed to those bogus forums where "uniformity and sloganizing is [*sic*] mistaken for freedom of expression and free thought." Then one final freedom-fib in closing: the IFF "accepts no government funds and maintains its total independence from governmental entities."[14]

After dizzy nonsense like this, the IFF's official designation as a *think* tank must be marked down as one of the lesser ironies of winger history. A handful of genuine thinkers did actually publish pieces in *International Freedom Review,* the group's respectable-looking American magazine, but for the most part it was a showplace for pontifications by Congress's rightmost members, gripes about betrayal from embittered South Africans, and gussied-up undergraduate term papers.

It was also a showplace for the right's unrelenting suspicion toward the world. Nothing was as it seemed; everything was an act of cold-war trickery or deception. *International Freedom Review* featured articles with titles like "Getting Beyond the [Nelson] Mandela Smokescreen" and "Afghanistan: Has Reagan Sold Out the Mujahideen?" In issue number one, a red-baiting book coauthored by Dinesh D'Souza is lauded as a well-observed description of how the sly Soviets are "manipulating public opinion" in the United States. In issue number two, the IFF lavishes its highest praise on *Requiem in the Tropics*—a feverish tract the foundation also happened to be selling via mail order—describing it as "the book they don't want you to read."

> Who are *they*?
>
> *They* are the career State Department officers who have, naively or otherwise, argued that the Sandinistas pose no threat to the Americas and who have recently redoubled their efforts to appease the Leninists in Managua with various "peace plans."
>
> *They* are the media . . . whose lies about Nicaragua are exposed in *Requiem*.
>
> *They* are the world's masters of mis- and disinformation, the Soviet KGB and their Kremlin masters, who have much to gain from America remaining ignorant.

As late as 1990, with the Warsaw Pact itself having rebelled successfully against the Soviets, the magazine was still insisting that Mikhail Gorbachev's reforms were merely "strategic deception," a clever trick staged to cause headaches for the Western "pro-defense consensus."[15]

Ridiculous though this stuff seems today, the IFF had good reason to believe in a world in which grand conspiracies gulled the masses and public opinion was manipulated by the hidden hand of a foreign power. After all, that's what they themselves were doing. As it turns out, the IFF itself was steered and subsidized not just by the government of another country, South Africa, but by its military intelligence.

This peculiar entrepreneurial form was not completely without precedent. Back in 1967, the National Student Association, a consortium of liberal American student leaders, had been exposed as a front for the CIA, which liked to send these young idealists to international student conclaves so they could make friends, influence people, and wave the banner of the noncommunist left, the big idea at the time for responding to Soviet advances in the third world. The news of covert CIA funding for the group snowballed into an enormous scandal, and the *New York Times* vituperated against the agency for destroying the National Student Association's credibility in the eyes of the foreigners it was supposed to woo. "It should have been clear long ago to the C.I.A.'s overseers in the White House," the paper fumed, "that the end effect of clandestine subsidies to groups representative of the detachment and diversity of a free society must inevitably taint the genuineness of their detachment." It was an old, familiar, and even obvious lesson: Ideas had to stand on their own merit, and government subsidies had to be granted in the light of day.[16]

But conservatives in 1967 did not share the liberals' squeamishness toward covert ops. They had no objection to clandestine funding of political groups; all they wanted to know was why *they* hadn't *also* received a helping of the CIA's sugar.[17]

The Reagan youth, for their part, believed that the "enemy," meaning the American left, was routinely funded and steered by the KGB and other supersneaky Communist organizations. They also suspected that one of the main conduits through which the libs got their marching orders were covert operations masquerading as think tanks. The master villain in *The Spike,* after all, had been a KGB-controlled think tank that pulled the strings on its many puppets in journalism and government.

So why couldn't conservatives do the same thing? All that was required was a sharp political entrepreneur who could hook up with some funder comparable to the KGB, with deep pockets and an even deeper need. And so the young man who had dreamed of being the "sword and shield of the Reagan revolution"—a variation, after all, on the official motto of the KGB—finally found a foreign power willing to take him on in a similar capacity.

Code-named "Pacman" by military intelligence, the IFF was connected to the highest levels of spookdom. Neither Abramoff nor Russel Crystal had dreamed up the IFF by themselves. The real, confessed eminence grise behind the organization was in fact South Africa's infamous "superspy" Craig Williamson, a man whose bloody escapades deserve an entire chapter in the annals of cold-war espionage—that is, if South Africa's war on its own people can in fact be glorified as a part of the cold war. Williamson infiltrated South Africa's main leftist student group in the seventies and rose to its leadership; he used the connections thus made to assist in the imprisonment and the murder of the movement's other leaders.[18] A respected South African historian, asked for his opinion of the man, said simply, "Craig Williamson was the scum of the twentieth century. He murdered friends of mine. I spit on the ground he walks on."

When the IFF's true identity was ultimately exposed in 1995, each of the Americans whom the media questioned denied any knowledge of its ugly provenance.[19] And in most cases this was plausible enough; after all, the basic principle of a clandestine operation is secrecy. Back when the National Student Association was a CIA front group, for example, only its top officers were aware of the connection.

Within the IFF, though, total ignorance seems unlikely for a number of reasons. To begin with, the "Youth for Freedom" conference at which the group was launched was swarming with spies, former spies, and people who believed that covert activity was just the way politics worked. The German right-winger who attended, for example, had been the head of West German military intelligence in the sixties.* Charles Lichenstein had once edited the CIA's classified, in-house magazine and continued to write on intelligence issues all through the eighties.[20] And here they all were, traveling to a police state in order to attend a lavish but mysteriously funded right-wing youth conference whose explicit purpose was to counter *other* youth conferences that

---

*This was Günter Poser, a leader of the far-right German Republikaner Party who caused a momentary outrage twelve years after the conference by declaring that the Nuremberg trials had been nothing but "legalized lynching" and "political show trials." (Berlin *Tageszeitung*, December 8, 1997.)

Poser's participation in "Youth for Freedom" gives us a hint of the shadowy world of extremism which the IFF brushed up against. For example, in 1987 the group sent a delegation to the annual meeting of the World Anti-Communist League (WACL), a body comprising three main groups: representatives of Asian dictatorships, death-squad organizers from Latin America, and surviving remnants of the Nazi empire in eastern Europe. (Scott Anderson and Jon Lee Anderson, *Inside the League: The Shocking Exposé of How Terrorists, Nazis, and Latin American Death Squads Have Infiltrated the World Anti-Communist League* [New York: Dodd, Mead & Company, 1986].)

Another example: Dr. Myron Kuropas, a Ukrainian nationalist who sat on the advisory board of *International Freedom Review*, and who later turned out to be something of an anti-Semite. This only came to public attention when Kuropas was sent to the Ukraine by the Bush administration in 2005 as part of an official delegation, bringing his writing under wider scrutiny. (See "Controversial professor donated $1,550 to Speaker of the House," *The Hill*, February 3, 2005.)

Another: Abramoff's great friend and fellow student leader Russel Crystal, who was quoted in a 1981 Associated Press story about the troubles in South Africa as saying, "Hitler had a democratic right to do what he did." Whether Crystal meant this as a vindication of Hitler (and hence of South Africa's treatment of blacks) or as a comment on the worthlessness of democracy, it should have been a strong disqualification for someone wishing to run a "freedom foundation" of any kind.

were thought to be "communist front organisations." The only way their suspicions would *not* have been aroused, I think, is if their various intelligence services had in some way condoned the whole rotten thing.

The odor of spookery clung to the IFF throughout its life. Its magazines ran articles by former CIA officials and contemplated the role of intelligence agencies in the post-cold-war world. In 1992 the IFF's principals apparently met with the top brass of the FBI.* A short while later the group sponsored a conference on intelligence at the same palace in Potsdam where Truman, Churchill, and Stalin had met in 1945. The featured speakers at this second-time-as-farce Potsdam Conference were a former CIA director and a former KGB counterintelligence chief, men extremely unlikely to be tricked by a South African front group.[21]

Jack Abramoff almost certainly knew who was footing the bill.[22] Still, he denied it—"categorically," he exclaimed—when the truth came out. Plus, he had a typically conspiratorial explanation for the story: "It's pay-back time in South Africa," he fumed. All this exposure—this truth and this reconciliation—was just another trick, just the ANC using a novel weapon to get back at its old foes.[23]

It was in the difficult period after the Soviet Union's collapse that Pretoria's bought-and-paid-for propaganda organization really distinguished itself. With communism in tatters, the panic-spreading style of winger Washington became an instant museum

*During the eighties the FBI spent enormous time and resources monitoring the leftist group CISPES on the mistaken suspicion that it was a front for a foreign power. Given that, I wondered if the FBI had put a similar effort into spying on the IFF, which actually *was* a front for a foreign power. What I found, in response to a Freedom of Information Act request, was not only that the FBI did *not* monitor the IFF, but that the bureau's director, William Sessions, apparently met with the IFF's officers in 1992 and even set up a tour of the FBI academy for them when they hosted the U.S. visit of some former KGB chieftains.

piece. Sovietologists became historians. The world no longer cared about the "total onslaught" faced by brave South Africa. In these circumstances, the International Freedom Foundation had to come up with a new strategy to get its client off the hook, and in a remarkable episode of conservative reinvention, what it chose was libertarianism. The IFF became an early exponent of the idea—soon to be echoed by the assembled tycoons of the world from the heights of Davos—that unregulated markets not only brought perfect freedom but also could solve virtually any economic or social problem.

Its publications quickly evolved into organs of the purest libertarian globaloney. In 1991 the IFF's American magazine was renamed *terra nova: A Quarterly Journal of Free-Market Economic and Political Thought*. Its European journal became *laissez-faire,* a showplace for "radical free market articles." The foundation dumped its old advisory board of cold-war hawks in favor of a more Information Age set, including both the chairman of the libertarian Cato Institute and the president of the Mont Pelerin Society, the free-market club founded by the economist Friedrich Hayek. As communism receded, Hayek's sacred name came to loom ever larger in conservative circles, and the IFF deftly made itself the leader of the cult: A 1992 issue of *terra nova* was dedicated to Hayek's memory, and on one of his many trips to South Africa, the IFF's chairman presented a lucky politician with an autographed copy of a Hayek book. On a trip to Prague he presented the "IFF Freedom Award" to Hayek's disciple Vaclav Klaus, who soon became prime minister of the Czech Republic. The prize was supposed to go, the IFF newsletter explained, to a person who demonstrated "how the free market is the best mechanism for mobilizing people's freedom. Such individual freedoms are necessary for self-reliance through entrepreneurship." You read those ringing words right: freedom is good because we need it to succeed in business.[24]

And libertarianism is good because it helps conservatives pass off a patently pro-business political agenda as a noble bid for human freedom. Whatever we may think of libertarianism as a set of ideas, practically speaking, it is a doctrine that owes its visibility to the obvious charms it holds for the wealthy and the powerful. The reason we have so many well-funded libertarians in America these days is not because libertarianism has acquired an enormous grass-roots following, but because it appeals to those who are able to fund ideas. Like social Darwinism and Christian Science before it, libertarianism flatters the successful and rationalizes their core beliefs about the world. They warm to the libertarian idea that taxation is theft because they themselves don't like to pay taxes. They fancy the libertarian notion that regulation is communist because they themselves find regulation intrusive and annoying. Libertarianism is a politics born to be subsidized.* In the "free market of ideas," it is a sure winner.

Were we to invent a way to compare the number of foundation employees now toiling in the capital to the number of people abroad in the land who hold those foundations' views, we would probably find that, in per capita terms, libertarianism is the most overrepresented philosophy in all of Washington. Everywhere you go in the city you meet its disciples. Libertarians in black leather. Libertarians drinking beer. Libertarians puffing the stocks they've bought. Libertarians shooting deer.[25] It's hard to remember, but there was a time when libertarians were regarded as the most exotic of all the right-wing tribes. One memorable 1973

---

*The purer the libertarians, the more serious they tend to be about marketizing politics. In 1980 the Libertarian Party made the oil billionaire David Koch its vice presidential nominee. The reason, according to a well-placed observer: "Koch bought the nomination; it cost him a half-million dollars. There is no law against selling a slot on the national ticket to the highest bidder, and in the Libertarians' case, it made a good deal of financial sense." (Mark Paul, "Seducing the Left: The Third Party That Wants *You*," *Mother Jones*, May 1980.)

newspaper column described them as "far, far, far righties who are so much around the other side of the political sphere that they're backing into the far, far, far lefty anarchists."[26] In the nineties, however, libertarianism's dogmatic faith in markets seemed to capture the spirit of the moment.

And what, precisely, could libertarianism do to solve South Africa's social and economic problems? For one thing, it made for a potent argument against trade sanctions, and Pretoria's pet intellectuals in Washington became the most ardent free-traders of them all, pounding home the notion that restrictions on trade are the result of self-serving political pressure exerted by brutish, xenophobic labor types.

Libertarianism also served to neutralize the "corporate conscience" movement, whose leaders had spent the eighties demanding that American companies run their South African operations according to certain moral guidelines. For a true free marketeer, of course, such demands are so much balderdash; a company exists to make a profit for its shareholders, period. Interfering with that directive is the truly immoral act, since it reveals the interloper's presumption to know better than the market almighty.

The doctrine's real attraction, however, was in the vision it offered for South Africa's future. By the late eighties it was obvious that apartheid was done for. Out in the streets a burgeoning black labor movement was demanding social democracy. What would come after the white-minority regime was anyone's guess, and a mania for "scenario planning" swept over the South African business community as its leaders tried to set the stage for a favorable outcome.[27] The government privatized and downsized itself, even dismantling its collection of atomic bombs, working frantically to close off the possibility that some future South African government might nationalize basic industries (as Nelson Mandela confirmed in 1990 that the ANC still planned to do) or take some other costly step toward social democracy.[28]

The ideal scenario espoused by the IFF addressed just these fears: a country where everyone could vote but where those votes had no bearing on private property. Foundation publications constantly offered advice for the framers of a future South African constitution, recommending, for example, that it include "clauses establishing and protecting free enterprise."[29] White supremacy was not going to survive for long, but with a covering barrage of free-market propaganda, the country's ruling class might yet come through the revolution unscathed.

The first step for the South African business community was to put some distance between itself and the collapsing old regime. So a top priority at the IFF—an apartheid front group, remember—became *depicting apartheid as an enemy of capitalism.*[30] And here we see conservative malleability at its most cynical. For many years, of course, apartheid had been capitalism's friend, its staunchest supporter in the global battle against communism. The regime's onerous racial policies were capitalist in origin too, having evolved out of the needs of particular South African industries for cheap, voiceless, unskilled labor. But now, the argument went, the country had developed, and apartheid had become a liability for business. It made skilled labor expensive. It required a massive security establishment, paid for through taxes. And it provoked ostracism and trade embargoes from the rest of the world.[31]

Capitalism needed to be shed of its old pal apartheid, and quickly. Libertarianism was the way to do it. In politics, taught the International Freedom Foundation, there are really only two possibilities. Either you have *freedom,* or you have *government.* There is no middle ground worth wasting your time on; it's either a 1 or a 0; either government interferes in the economy, or it doesn't. And simply by studying the debacle of communism—a good example of the *government* option—we can see that "government necessarily screws up anything it touches; individuals do not."[32]

So by 1991, with apartheid tottering over the grave, the IFF was ready to denounce it as another system of government interference in the economy . . . *just like socialism!* After all, both apartheid and social democracy involved a "top-down system of control of the economy," one of the foundation's magazines proclaimed, and therefore the two were essentially identical, with the only *real* alternative being a plunge into the healing waters of unregulated capitalism. All the old oppositions were instantly transformed into kinships by this logic: instead of being the most zealously anticommunist government on earth, the South African regime was now rather pink itself—"apartheid is South Africa's war against capitalism," was how one IFF staffer put it. The social-democratic plans of the ANC, on the other hand, could now be seen to bear "a remarkable resemblance . . . with the abominable economic means of the system of apartheid." More deep thinking from the IFF's tank: "If black South Africans really want to see a fairer distribution of wealth, they must insist not that property be taken over by the state, but that state-owned enterprises be turned over to the people," by which our innocent young winger meant, of course, privatized.[33] The most fantastic formulation of the IFF's point came in a 1991 article about "energy markets": "The former Soviet Union has abandoned Stalinism. Perhaps so should South Africa with respect to electricity generation."[34]

With a little free-market sorcery, the traditional concerns of the South African business class were thus transformed into another, purer wing of the antiapartheid movement. The black majority wanted the government to stop torturing and murdering people, and business wanted the government to stop running the electric utility. In both cases, the theory went, the malefactor was the same: big government. A minimized state would make everyone happy.

The most concise explication of the theory came from the South African libertarian Leon Louw, who remains today that country's high priest of the free market. Testifying in Washington at a 1987 hearing, Louw insisted that the real problem in his country was "unlimited power" in the hands of the state. The country's economy was "centralized," he complained, and state power also suppressed the majority of the population. This left South Africans debating the devilish question: "who should have that power?"

> It is like a tank out of control, and people are saying, "Who should be in the tank? Should it be whites, or blacks, or a mixture, or power sharing over there?" That cannot produce a solution. . . .
>
> What one can do, however . . . is to just remove the power, to reduce the power.[35]

And shut down the tank altogether.

As libertarianism became respectable, so did the International Freedom Foundation. Abramoff turned over the wheel to Duncan Sellars, another Howard Phillips protégé whose politics were even more extreme[36] but whose PR instincts seem to have been considerably more adroit. The IFF's leadership soon grasped that prestigious Washington institutes don't put their message across with bullhorns in the street; they get their way in quiet lunchtime conversations. They give out awards. They testify before congressional committees. They send observers to monitor elections. They sponsor visits by foreign dignitaries. They commission studies and place op-eds in newspapers. Thus did the IFF become mainstream.

It also became something of a prophet. When we flip through its later publications, we notice something remarkable: here we find, in larval state, many of the standard arguments of winger Washington, the bad ideas that chewed through the nation's brain. In 1991 and '92, Pretoria's pundits repeatedly sang the coming glory of NAFTA, with an occasional improvised verse deploring American labor unions and the absurd notion of "fair trade."[37] They chortled at environmentalism and laughed merrily at the very idea of global warming.[38] They put out an entire issue of *terra nova* dedicated to the magic of privatization. (High point: a plan for "Privatizing the Oceans.")[39]

And then they disappeared. The crumbling South African regime cut off the IFF's subsidies in 1992, and, like most libertarian groups, the organization was unable to get by on its own. Before it passed, though, it served up one final course of irony. In what turned out to be its last issue, *terra nova* ran an article suggesting a bold new strategy to hammer down armed rebellions. What was recommended was "privatizing counterinsurgency," developing a system in which guerrilla-plagued nations could hire companies that specialized in exterminating such infestations. During previous outbreaks of insurgency, *terra nova* pointed out, the West had foolishly relied on government (that is, armies) to solve the problem, and with the usual disastrous results. Now that we know about the science of markets, however, we understand that we must use "free-market techniques to secure a world of free markets."[40]

Quick on the heels of this call for "privatizing counterinsurgency" came the debut of the first major private counterinsurgency company. The firm in question was called Executive Outcomes; it was made up of former members of the same South African military that had subsidized the IFF and defended Jonas Savimbi; its first big client was the Communist government of Angola; and its assignment was to give apartheid's old friend Savimbi a thrashing. Which it did, with dispatch, in 1993.[41]

In this ugly coda, I submit, we find another perfect little parable of the market. Here was Savimbi, beloved by the wingers of America for a free-market piety that mirrored their own, merrily torching and land-mining his way through life on Pretoria's dime. Then one day the cold war ends, apartheid weakens, and his subsidies are cut off. Next thing you know, his ideological comrades, heeding the entrepreneurial call, have changed sides—it seems the commies have shown them the money—and are now hounding his ragtag band of "freedom fighters" all the way back to Jamba.

The lesson Savimbi learned was the same one that everyone in this story gets schooled in, sooner or later: that the market is a faithless sovereign, disloyal and deceitful. That there is no tradition or patriotism or ethics that it holds sacred. That it will even devour its own if the payoff is right. One day it defends the apartheid government against all comers; the next it undergoes an amazing metamorphosis and declares that apartheid's crimes are indeed hideous—but that the guilt for them tarnishes social democracy as well.

More amazing still is that the South African free marketeers essentially got what they wanted, albeit more because of the IMF than the IFF. The country's new constitution was indeed written to protect private property. The apartheid government began the privatizing, and the ANC, once it controlled the state, embarked on one of the most ambitious deregulatory schemes in the world. It sold off state-run operations from airports to waterworks. The results have been precisely what you'd expect: spectacular prosperity for some, little improvement for everyone else. In fact, and although it's difficult to believe, income inequality in South Africa has actually widened since apartheid was dismantled. South Africa is again a one-party state, with rampant corruption and Afrikaner-style cronyism. But money—thank God—is free at last.

The International Freedom Foundation is gone, along with the government that propped it up, but its spirit triumphed.

Freedom-talk in the service of business became a vast, booming industry in Washington. All across the city free-market techniques were used to secure a world of free markets. Political entrepreneurs even breached the liberal state itself. What they proceeded to do there is enough to make any tough old Boer proud.

PART II

Saboteurs

CHAPTER 6

"The Best Public Servant Is the Worst One"

Until now we have mainly been concerned with conservatism as a private-sector operation, as a constellation of cynical theorists, amateur red-baiters, and libertarian ideologues-for-hire. More significant by far, however, was its public-sector correlative, the conservative state. This was where the rubber hit the road—or, rather, where the buzz saw met the flesh. This was where all the cynicism, the revolution-talk, the market-worship, and the conspiracy-spotting came together to make up the leviathan of waste and misgovernment that, for many years, was the glory of conservative Washington.

Conservatism made its first and most essential departure from the traditional liberal model for the state on the key question of personnel. Among conservatives the idea of excellence in government has long been a favorite joke. "The best minds are not in government," Ronald Reagan famously said of the federal apparatus he led. "If any were, business would steal them away." Even so, conservatives took staffing decisions very seriously. One of the movement's favorite adages is "personnel is policy," and the importance of who gets hired is a subject on which its leaders have expended vast reservoirs of ink.[1]

In 1981, for example, we find Morton Blackwell, then a special assistant to President Reagan, describing the difficulties of building a conservative government: you could either fill positions with people who were "competent to do the work" but politically unsound, he noted, or fill them with movement types who knew little about the actual job to be done. There were precious few who had both expertise and a "demonstrable commitment" to conservatism. Blackwell's candor is unusual; more typical were the remarks made three years later by the young Grover Norquist in which competence doesn't figure at all. What concerned Norquist were the tactics of seizing and holding power, which he adapted straight from the playbook of Joseph Stalin. Or, as he put it:

> First, we want to remove liberal personnel from the political process. Then we want to capture those positions of power and influence for conservatives. Stalin taught the importance of this principle. He was running the personnel department, while Trotsky was fighting the White Army. When push came to shove for control of the Soviet Union, Stalin won. His people were in place and Trotsky's were not. . . . With this principle in mind, conservatives must do all they can to make sure that they get jobs in Washington.[2]

Norquist was describing, not merely exhorting. The Reagan administration had, in fact, placed one of its most reliable soldiers in charge of federal personnel, a former YAFer named Donald Devine, and he had duly launched an all-out effort to beat the bureaucracy into submission. Conservatives fought bitter battles to wrest seemingly insignificant positions away from members of the hated moderate faction. At the same time, the adminstration was seeding Washington with carefully selected young wingers, building a "farm system" in which senior conservatives across the country sent their most loyal charges to the capital to become "credentialed" members of the city's class of rulers. The player of note in all this was the Heritage Foundation, which boasted that it could pluck from its résumé files a conservative who would fit any special need the administration might have.[3] This most powerful of think tanks reprised this role during George W. Bush's administration, when the streets of Baghdad's Green Zone swarmed with eager young appointees who were found to have one peculiar thing in common: They had sent their résumés to the gatekeepers at Heritage.[4]

Sometimes the ruthlessness with which conservatives pressed their war on the bureaucracy does indeed put one in mind of Uncle Joe. During the Justice Department scandal of 2007, the world learned that one Monica Goodling, a graduate of Pat Robertson's Regent University Law School and a novice lawyer, had helped fire nine far more experienced U.S. attorneys for reasons of basest partisanship. She habitually vetoed other supposedly nonpartisan federal hires on suspicion of liberalness and, to help her with her purges, kept a tote board tracking who was and was not a member of the right-wing Federalist Society. She was just one "goodling" among many, we learned; there were supposedly 150 Regent grads toiling for the administration, plus several others hailing from Patrick Henry College, a fanatic factory that had been set up in Loudoun County specifically to supply the movement with functionaries.[5]

Conservatism's push to fill the bureaucracy with cronies, hacks, partisans, and creationists is properly seen as a part of its wider war with intellectuals. The right has always regarded liberalism as a bid for political dominance by a supposed "class" (the highly educated) over the common people (which is to say, businesspeople), and thus it arrogates to itself all the gaudy symbolism of a populist rising, in this case against Harvard* and the rest of the "East Coast schools."[6] This perception is at least partially attributable to the historical circumstances of the New Deal, which, remember, replaced rule by wealth with its "brain trust," its "bright young men," and Felix Frankfurter's "hot dogs," down from Harvard to do their bit. But it also reflects a deeper, more philosophical conflict: American conservatism defines government as meddling in the market, which is, in turn, conceived as a force of godlike omniscience; Rooseveltian liberalism, on the other hand, understands that markets are unstable and must be controlled by the organized intelligence of mankind.[7]

In the liberal era, and in other lands where the idea still persists, talent is central to public service. This is not to suggest that liberal bureaucracy is always an effective or lovable institution, but that when it is properly run it is capable of performing the difficult jobs for which it was designed. Conservatism, on the other hand, seems actively to want an inferior product. Believing effective government to be somewhere between impossible and undesirable, conservatism takes steps to ensure its impotence. The result is predictable enough: another sour truckload of the mother's milk of conservatism, cynicism toward government.

"A Plea for Inefficiency in Government" was the title of this

---

*In his book *Rock the House,* Grover Norquist, a Harvard graduate himself, proudly told the story of the competing introductory seminars for brand-new members of the House of Representatives offered by Harvard and the Heritage Foundation. In the dismal years before the Gingrich revolution, almost every freshman chose the Harvard seminar; now, in the glorious year of 1994, "as the tumbrels pass through town," they all chose to go to Heritage, and humiliated Harvard was forced to cancel its offering. "Indeed," Norquist gloated, "why would Members of Congress who were elected to tear down the present Establishment wish to sit at the feet of those who built, defended and still believe in it?"

doctrine's most concise expression; it appeared in 1928 in the pages of *Nation's Business,* the magazine of the U.S. Chamber of Commerce, and it took the form of an interview with Homer Ferguson, a former president of that august organization. "The best public servant is the worst one," Ferguson declared.

> A thoroughly first-rate man in public service is corrosive. He eats holes in our liberties. The better he is and the longer he stays the greater the danger. If he is an enthusiast—a bright-eyed madman who is frantic to make this the finest government in the world—the black plague is a housepet by comparison.

Ferguson was a defense contractor by trade, a builder of warships for the navy, and if our government came to be filled with talented people (his interlocutor explained), it might be able to build its own warships and then poor Homer would be out of work. That, plus a few obligatory remarks about quality-in-government being the first step to communism, and the argument was complete: business needed lousy government so that no one would ever consider handing over more responsibility to it.[8]

It was the most cynical of arguments, bluntly made, handed down from the highest councils of industrial wisdom, and absolutely impossible to misinterpret. "If public officials are and remain inefficient, the public will sicken of incompetence and rely exclusively upon corporate enterprise," wrote one astonished reader. "That means less competition and more profits."[9] Especially for defense contractors, whose interests in a dumbed-down government were as obvious then as they are today.

For decades after the 1929 crash the nation ignored the Chamber's plea for lousy government, bent instead on using government to build a more equitable society. Through depression and war and postwar boom the civil service continued to grow and grow, hitting its postwar peak in 1968.[10] Conservative Washington, however, is Homer Ferguson's kind of place, a point made quite explicitly in 1987 by the conservative pundit Doug Bandow, once a special assistant to President Reagan, who announced that for conservatives, "excellence in government" was not an acceptable goal. "We shouldn't want a proficient public sector," he wrote. "Given that government absorbs and redistributes wealth rather than creates it, we desperately need to keep the very best people out in the private sector where they can do the most good." "The definition of public service," this former public servant went on, "should be doing what is right, not doing anything well."[11]

No politician wants to appear to turn the reins over to imbeciles, however, and ultimately conservatives got out of this problem by defining it away. "We have told members of the Cabinet we expect them to help us place people who are competent," Lyn Nofziger, Reagan's political affairs director, told a reporter in 1981. "As far as I'm concerned, anyone who supported Reagan is competent."[12]

In the mythology of the American right, federal rank-and-file workers are villains whose wickedness is surpassed only by that of the Soviet Communists themselves. They have just four concerns in life, sneered the journalist Don Feder in 1985: "pay, pension, sick leave and throwing their not inconsiderable weight around. No one has to teach us to detest public workers. It comes naturally, by a process of observation and experience."[13]

Their tendency to join unions makes these public workers even more detestable. Once organized, civil servants support liberals, with both votes and campaign contributions—and these liberals, once in office, return the favor by making generous concessions to their unionized employees. Or so it seemed, anyway, back in the seventies when everyone from teachers to trashmen was going on strike—and winning, too. In that unhappy decade, the conservative mind began to dimly perceive a diabolical scenario unfolding, a disastrous endgame in which its two greatest enemies came together as one: government remade as a tool of its unionized employees, who would use its tax power to plunder the hardworking businessman.[14]

The famous "Prop 13" tax revolt that swept California in 1978 was inspired at least partially by this doomsday vision, with the rebellion's leader thundering, "We're not going to permit public employee unions to run this country." The issue also spawned an obligatory bout of direct-mail profiteering, with an outfit called Americans Against Union Control of Government sending out appeals for funds to help them fend off the "very real possibility of a relative handful of union bosses seizing control of America's government."[15]

The vivid colors of this particular catastrophe-dream have long since faded in the public mind, but Washington conservatives never forgot. Their policy toward career government personnel has always been to club them down, and by putting it into effect they have delivered massive rewards both to their political faction and to their primary constituents in the business community.

The Reagan administration rode to power on a wave of vituperation against the federal system. Its principals regarded the "permanent government" of nonpolitical or career civil service as irretrievably liberal and implacably hostile; their own position among them was like that of the French army at Dien Bien Phu, surrounded by Communists.[16] Military metaphors apparently came up often when the Reaganites expressed their feelings toward the career civil service: the director of the Office of Personnel Management, the aforementioned Donald Devine, once declared it was time to "bring the tanks up to the border" to deal with the bureaucracy; looking back on his days of public service he wrote that "the only way bureaucracies got reformed was when barbarians took them apart brick by brick and head by head."[17]

Proposals for improving the system bubbled up from all sides, but the ones that were eventually implemented "reformed" the bureaucracy in the same way that a twelve-thousand-pound bomb "reforms" a railroad bridge.[18] The assault began in earnest in the first days of the Reagan administration, with the New Right demanding jobs for wingers and shrieking every time a moderate Republican received an important position.[19] The resulting politicization of government operations was unprecedented, with loyalists in and career civil servants out. By the summer of 1981, according to one report, 59 percent of the "subcabinet appointees" confirmed by the Senate had no experience in government, as did 78 percent of Reagan's hires at the independent agencies and a full 100 percent at the independent regulatory agencies. The politicization was especially conspicuous at the all-important Office of Management and Budget, formerly "an institution of high integrity" that began producing laughably optimistic budget projections, insisting surpluses were just around the corner instead of the world-record deficits that everyone knew Reaganism was racking up.[20]

So much for the new hires. Everyone else got to face the tank. Reagan fired striking air-traffic controllers in that first summer and set in motion the systematic pummeling of organized labor that continues to this day. Senior civil servants were evaluated and retained if they were found ideologically pliable. On the other hand, if they were "program loyalists," one bureaucracy scholar wrote, "the offices they supervised were stripped of functions, or they were sent on assignment to a U.S. trust territory or given an office in an empty suite with nothing to do."[21] "Reductions in force" (RIFs) brought down the numbers of federal workers at the programs not in favor with conservatism. By 1984, morale was gratifyingly low in the "permanent government": a full 72 percent of senior public servants said, in response to a poll, that they would not encourage their children to take a career in public service.[22]

The killer statistic, though, was the one that bureaucrats call the "pay gap." If the government wants to attract talented workers to the civil service, its pay must obviously be made competitive with the private sector's offerings. If the government believes its employees are ideological villains, on the other hand, it will do the opposite.

It did the opposite, of course. Convinced that civil servants were the left, it defunded them. In 1975, federal workers earned around 10 percent less than people doing comparable work in the private sector, which was not worrisome given federal employees' benefits and job security. By 1987, though, the pay gap had widened to around 30 percent. By 1990, when the government's method of calculating the difference was changed, federal executives at the top grade were making almost 40 percent less than people with the same skills who had chosen to work for private industry.[23]

For a moment in 1989 the nation's media paid attention. There were rumors of a "brain drain" from important agencies and, in the *Los Angeles Times,* a story about a grocery store checkout clerk who turned down a job at the Drug Enforcement Administration because the pay cut would have been too great. Alarm bells clanged. With all the best people leaving, wouldn't that mean disaster for NASA? And the National Institutes of Health? What would happen to the CIA and the air force? Or the Federal Reserve, which held the whole economy in its hands?[24] Then up stepped the *Wall Street Journal* to reveal the "hidden agenda" of this imaginary "federal pay scare." It was all, of course, political—a coordinated attempt by members of the sinister "permanent government" to keep their jobs and thus "perpetuate existing federal policies in the face of political change." What's more, government had no business hiring the nation's most talented people. Doing so necessarily meant taking them from the private sector and helping "to deprive the U.S. economy of its driving force: the skill and knowledge that result in the production of wealth."[25] Pay is policy, too, and good pay is the devil liberalism.

I suppose it would have been expecting too much of Bill Clinton to ask him to take a stand against these attacks on the civil service. That just wasn't the sort of thing "New Democrats" did. Instead he joined in, posing with huge, sinister volumes of federal rules and declaring his own war on bureaucracy and red tape. He continued the policy of blowing off the pay gap, even though there was now a law, passed by a Democratic Congress, that required federal wages to be brought up to par with the private sector. But Clinton found a loophole, offered only the tiniest raises to federal workers, and set about revising, again, the methods by which the pay gap was calculated, hoping to conjure the problem away in a puff of theoretical smoke.[26]

The Clinton team spoke of "entrepreneurial government" as reverently as any Republicans, and they huddled with the nation's leading management theorists to figure out how to deliver it. The answers were what you would expect: downsizing and outsourcing, concealed in a fog of fake existentialism. *Reinventing Government,* the instruction manual of the Clinton administration, exhorted us to think of firing bureaucrats as a way of freeing them, allowing them to be born again in the zestful private sector.

> Many employees in bureaucratic governments feel trapped. Tied down by rules and regulations, numbed by monotonous tasks, assigned jobs they know could be accomplished in half the time if they were only allowed to

> use their minds, they live lives of quiet desperation. When they have the opportunity to work for an organization with a clear mission and minimal red tape . . . they are often reborn. When they are moved into the private sector, they often experience the same sense of liberation.[27]

This is an improvement on "bring the tanks up," I suppose, but in practical terms it meant roughly the same thing.

George W. Bush, the "MBA president," then arrived with his own variation on the theme: He promised to bring the "managerial revolution" to Washington. The all-powerful Heritage Foundation, the conduit through which so many job seekers passed, drew up a plan to guide the president's attack on the civil service—again identified as a sinister "permanent government" that would thwart his aims unless he dealt with it quickly and severely.[28]

This he did. The result was the old Reagan-style politicization times ten, with wingers advancing powerfully on all the old battlefronts. We have described how political considerations came to warp the Department of Justice, and how hacks and cronies found their way into virtually every job Bush was permitted to fill, regardless of competence, right down to the most minuscule federal agencies. Career employees began to run up against politics in all sorts of unexpected places, with expert testimony by government officials altered by political staff, proposed regulations dismissed, and senior scientists overruled by college dropouts who happened to be loyal conservatives.[29] Those who resisted these initiatives, says Hugh Kaufman of the EPA, were sent to the "hall of zombies," in which "you're at a desk, and you don't do anything of substance. Most of the career bureaucrats in Washington in [the Bush] administration are in the hall of zombies."

For the civil servants who remained at their posts Bush promised "the discipline of competition." The system of advancement by seniority, always derided for its antiquity in administration documents, was to be replaced with "merit pay," which sounds like a good idea until you realize that it was the political zealots in the White House who would decide what constituted "merit." The outrage surrounding the pay gap gradually faded until modest wages became another one of the things you simply accepted when you took a government job. By 2008, starting salaries at top Washington law firms for kids straight from law school were higher than the highest *ending* salaries for most career civil servants.[30]

Each of these components was harmful enough on its own, but added together they gave us something truly awful. "All the people with institutional knowledge, who know how to do stuff, have taken early retirement. Very few of the old pros are left in," the EPA's Kaufman told me in 2008. "The whole domestic government will have to be rebuilt, because it's been hollowed out."

There are many ways of measuring the disaster, but one that has stayed with me comes from a 1986 article on the civil service that I happened to read in the course of my research. Although the federal bureaucracy had been much vilified, the author wrote back then, it remained excellent in a number of ways; federal employees, for example, had won seven Nobel prizes in medicine since 1968.[31] How many have they won in the intervening years, I wondered, since conservatives really went to work on them? The answer: one.[32]

Almost every career civil servant I met during the Bush 43 years told me the same general story: they were dispirited; they were depressed; they were afraid of speaking up; they were thinking about leaving. "Federal employees feel under siege," said John Threlkeld, the assistant legislative director for AFGE, a federal employees' union.

> Every now and then I'll hear someone say if their job's not going to get contracted out or if they're not going to get stripped of their collective bargaining rights, then they're going to lose their civil service protections against politics and favoritism. I think there's very low morale, a feeling that their services are not valued and that their careers are disposable. You know, there's an increasing emphasis on federal employees having very short-term careers and then going back out to the private sector. . . . I think to some extent it's designed to reduce the independence and autonomy of the civil service.

The professional civil service is an organizational form that every advanced society adopted a hundred years ago for the same reason: to ensure the state would not be the tool of money. That its wrecking has coincided with the greatest wave of political corruption in living memory is no mere coincidence.

The "market-based" system that conservatives installed in place of the autonomous civil service was *government-by-contractor*, also known as "outsourcing." Clintonites used to gurgle about how "entrepreneurial" and "Information Age" this strategy was, but in fact Uncle Sam has always turned to private companies to build his gunboats, fighter planes, tanks, and so on. Uncle Sam getting ripped off by contractors was not new, either. Many of the great "robber barons" got their start as crooked contractors during the Civil War.[33]

What was new was the *ideological* commitment to outsourcing. Contracting out government work was one of the basic recommendations of the 1984 Grace Commission, which found that this would both save money and help to break up the supposed mutual-aid network between government workers and liberal politicians.[34] The commission made this suggestion in the driest of prose styles; in personal appearances, however, J. Peter Grace would rage hotly against federal employees, who, he claimed, were just "looking for a cushy deal," resided in "the posh suburban communities of Washington, D.C.," lived for years on undeserved disability payments, and often traveled in first class.[35]

Of all the "disciplines of competition" that the Bush administration brought to Washington, the most consequential was outsourcing. Fully half of federal positions, the president's 2001 management manifesto asserted, could be opened to bids from the private sector. Agencies were even to be graded according to the number of federal jobs they privatized.[36] Say what you like about Bush as a conservative "impostor": With outsourcing he emphatically delivered on his promises. "Contractors have become a virtual fourth branch of government," wrote two *New York Times* reporters in 2007. "Contractors still build ships and satellites, but they also collect income taxes and work up agency budgets, fly pilotless spy aircraft and take the minutes at policy meetings on the war. They sit next to federal employees at nearly every agency; far more people work under contracts than are directly employed by the government."[37] As the general counsel of a group called the Project on Government Oversight told me in 2005, "It's very difficult to determine where the government stops and the contractors start."

It is a basic principle of conservatism—an axiom, a cornerstone, an immutable law of human nature, world history, and all the planets and stars—that turning over government operations to private businesses is the most efficient way to get things done. In reality, the conservatives' outsourcing system has been a ripoff of such massive proportions that it deserves a Grace Commission all its own. In each of the Bush administration's great initiatives—antiterrorism, the recovery from Hurricane Katrina, and Iraq reconstruction—privatized government played a starring role and proved itself a gold-plated botch. Again and again, and despite a veritable river of dollars, it failed to deliver what it promised. The Departments of Defense and Homeland Security routinely accepted contracts so ill-crafted they seemed designed more as a way to sluice billions into the contractors' pockets than as a device for getting something done.[38] And, being private, the contractors were largely shielded from oversight and accountability. Indeed, a favorite conservative tactic was to shut down offices that supervised the outsourced operations—in 2006, the General Services Administration actually tried to contract out the job of supervising contractors—allowing the market to perform its miracles without any scrutiny from government at all.[39]

But I digress. The subject that concerns us here is the conservative effort to bring the federal workforce to heel, and in this respect contracting-out was a notable success. Although the Bush administration presided over one of the greatest expansions of federal spending in history, the number of federal employees actually *decreased* during Dubya's term of office. Bush administration documents even boasted about the government having "achieved its lowest level of civilians on payroll since 1950."[40]

The chief consequence of the conservatives' unrelenting faith in the badness of government is . . . bad government. The one follows from the other not by casual happenstance but as a rule; not because of George W. Bush's personal weakness for cronyism but because a hostility to talent is how his movement approaches the job. It is a classic self-fulfilling prophecy, and today we behold its fulfillment all around us, in the prodigious money-burning bungling enacted by an antigovernment president working (until 2007) with an antigovernment Congress.

"You cannot run on a platform that government is the problem and expect the best people in the country to want to be part of the problem," says Carl Auerbach, a lawyer who worked in the Labor Department during the thirties. The blunders of the Bush administration were not "an accident," he asserts. The incompetence reflected "a philosophy toward the role of government and the people who are in it."

As public policy, destroying the quality and morale of the federal workforce was so obviously stupid it requires no elaboration here. From Baghdad to New Orleans and right down to the toxic spinach and peanut butter that fill your neighborhood grocery store its folly was plain. What does require constant reiteration as we survey all this wreckage is that from the perspective of the right this was not a disaster; *this was a triumph*. Screwing up the civil service was a *good* thing; it rewarded conservatives in all sorts of larger, structural ways.

Most obviously, weakening public-sector unions advanced the larger campaign to defund the Democratic Party, which has always been the recipient of most of such unions' political spending. Slightly less obvious were the effects that all this undoubtedly had on the private-sector workforce. One of the results of government being a "good" employer was to put competitive pressure on the private sector to be "good" also; by changing all that, by minimizing what government offered its workers, conservatives reduced that pressure. Like Reagan's termination of the air-traffic controllers, these strategic degradations of federal labor signaled to employers nationwide that the days of job security and benefits are over.

It was also deregulation by other means. When the Chamber of Commerce called for "inefficiency in government" and when Doug Bandow wrote that we ought to "keep the very best people out," they did so because they objected to the meddlesome things government did; keeping government shorthanded and ineffective was explicitly seen as a way to keep government from doing those objectionable things.[41] To you it may have seemed like a bad idea for the USDA to cut way back on food inspectors—especially in this age of mad cow and rampant E. coli—but it was a wonderful idea when seen from the perspective of the food processors, who could run their assembly lines as if the nineteenth century had started all over again.[42]

One of the marked peculiarities of American conservatism is the way it persistently mimics its enemies: the John Birch Society organized itself after its archrival, the Communist Party; the Goldwater campaign, according to the boasts of one of its directors, used Maoist methods to capture the Republican nomination in 1964; and Grover Norquist takes lessons from Stalin and Brezhnev.[43] Sometimes this is done deliberately and is proudly announced to the world; on other occasions it seems like an unconscious reflex—but always what the conservatives choose to mimic is not so much the actual behavior of the bad guys but their own *perceptions* of what the diabolical Other is up to.

We shall see many examples of this mimicry as we proceed, and what conservatives have done to the federal workforce is one of them. Having hallucinated for years that the civil service was ripping off taxpayers in satanic cahoots with liberal politicians, conservatives built a mirror image of their nightmare in thousand-times magnification, a system in which certain federal contractors—whom conservatives hired to do work formerly done by civil servants—actually *did* rip off taxpayers and actually *were* in league with prominent conservative politicians.

It took me a long time to understand the way this worked. Like everybody else, I had heard all the talk about Dick Cheney's "ties" to Halliburton, about Condi Rice and Chevron, and I had brushed it off as so much liberal hysteria. Sure, these people came out of the oil industry, I thought, but no way will they actually do *favors* for their old friends while they're in office. It would just be too obvious, too sinister—like something out of a silent movie melodrama.

It was just after Hurricane Katrina had destroyed New Orleans that I started to get it. Everyone who was able to turn on a TV knew the disaster was coming, and yet of its six thousand employees the Federal Emergency Management Agency (FEMA) managed only to station a single person in the city before the storm hit. As I read about the thirty thousand desperate people in the Superdome, my mind turned to the billions and billions and billions that we had spent on "preparedness" since 9/11—the great levee of public money that was supposedly necessary to keep us safe—and it slowly dawned on me that it had all been a waste. These inconceivable expenditures—this greatest security effort ever, mounted by the mightiest nation in history—and it was all for nothing. We might as well have piled the banknotes up in a pasture somewhere and set them afire.

From first to last the New Orleans disaster was a test of Bush's "market-based" government. To start with, we have FEMA as it was in 2000, a well-run, freestanding federal agency whose employees reported high morale and job satisfaction; candidate George W. Bush even praised the agency in one of his debates with Al Gore. *President* George W. Bush then put FEMA under the charge of Joe Allbaugh, a Texas winger with no disaster experience but a long history at Bush's side; Allbaugh proceeded to fill the place with political appointees and incompetent pals like the soon-to-be-notorious Michael Brown. Two years later Allbaugh left "Brownie" in charge and opened a lobby shop, representing companies that specialized in disaster relief and big reconstruction projects, much needed in Iraq in those days.

FEMA, meanwhile, had become part of the Department of Homeland Security, where outsourcing was the normal practice, bungling was the normal result, and where, by 2006, fully two-thirds of top officials had departed for a job with the contractors (or their lobbyists) to whom the department outsourced its work.[44] At FEMA, the brain drain was more like a hemorrhage. Between the dispiriting leadership of Allbaugh and Brown and the market-based opportunities dangled by the rising homeland security contractors, the old hands had rich incentive to get out. Morale among the career types at FEMA sank so low that the president of the union local wrote a letter to Senator Hillary Clinton in 2004 begging her to do something to save the agency.[45] "This administration really distrusts government workers. Just right across the board," Leo Bosner, a FEMA career man, told me in 2005. But outside consultants? "We can trust those guys [the administration thought], and they're the private sector, and they'll do it right."

So the hurricane hit, FEMA failed completely—and then came the really big money. Bosner told me that standard disaster procedure had previously been to hire recovery workers locally, because doing so helped the people most affected. This time, though, the idea was apparently to help the people most connected. The no-bid reconstruction contracts poured out like gravy, and clients of Bush's buddy Joe Allbaugh just happened to be among those who won them. An emergency housing contract went to the engineering conglomerate CH2M Hill, a client of a different lobby shop that also featured a detachment of former top Homeland Security officers. Still other contracts went to the Fluor Corporation, whose patriarch had been one of the original trustees of the Heritage Foundation, and to Bechtel, a longtime donor to right-wing organizations and employer of retired right-wing politicians.[46]

A month after the disaster, the contractors got together to chortle over their good fortune at a "Katrina Reconstruction Summit" held in a Senate office building. The air tingled with talk of the billions that were to be handed out, and a former Reagan administration official named Ed Badolato was particularly ebullient. His employer, the Shaw Group—an enormous construction company and a client of Allbaugh's—had already bagged a $100 million contract. In the past, he related, people "around town" would say, "Shaw Group, we never heard of y'all." But today Shaw men were walking tall in the corridors of power. "Right now, I'm sure that with the large contracts that we have been receiving," Badolato boasted, "everybody [every subcontractor, that is] who had my name in a Rolodex . . . has been calling me and everyone else they knew at Shaw to get a piece of that." He gave a shout-out to "our consultants, people who really delivered the bacon to us . . . when we needed it"; reminded the crowd that Shaw had done "a lot of lobbying and consulting efforts, both in Louisiana and in Washington"; and allowed that this "really pays off when it's time to get some contracts."

By 2008 over $100 billion had been spent, but parts of New Orleans remained empty. Repairing public housing seems to have been a low priority; rebuilding casinos an urgent one. All this might seem like social engineering in a cruelly nineteenth-century mode, but in fact it was the unavoidable result of a recovery plan composed of tax cuts for entrepreneurs, fat handouts to chosen contractors, and toxic trailers for those who can't afford large donations to the GOP.

Once we recognize the pattern, we start to see how the model once extended all across the winger wonderland. Outsource the job, commands the free-market ideology, and a contractor was duly chosen. But not just any contractor, and not even the low bidder, necessarily; it had to be a contractor whose conservative bona fides were well known, who was ready to donate a part of the take to the movement that gave the job to him.

Alphonso Jackson, Housing and Urban Development secretary during the Dubya administration, has told the world quite bluntly how it works: you use contracts to reward your friends and punish your enemies, with friendship determined by campaign contributions. Speaking to a real estate conference in 2006, Jackson bragged about firing a HUD contractor who criticized President Bush. "Why should I reward someone who doesn't like the president, so they can use funds to try to campaign against the president? Logic says they don't get the contract."[47]

The law, unfortunately, says something else, and soon Jackson found himself under investigation. Although nothing is settled as of this writing, it appears that Jackson obeyed the logic of the market, as he had defined it, in a number of instances. One Jackson buddy got lavish no-bid contracts to run public housing in the Virgin Islands, even though he had no public-housing experience and even though his predecessor in the job had been paid one quarter of the amount that the newbie received. Another pal got a sweet job overseeing work in New Orleans. For a third friend anxious to develop some publicly owned properties, Jackson allegedly leaned on a reluctant city housing authority.[48]

Possibly the most baroque contract hustle in the capital is the one involving "Alaska Native Corporations," legal entities engineered specifically to reel in federal contracts. Their designer, the former Alaska senator Ted Stevens, got the laws passed and the rules adjusted so that these particular corporations, unlike all other corporations in America, were allowed to receive no-bid federal contracts *without restrictions,* should some government department decide to toss one their way. And, lo and behold, someone did. Under a president anxious to outsource government's duties as fast as he could, this little loophole became extremely valuable, causing Alaska Native Corporations to spring up all across contractor-land.

There are three main pieces to the Alaska Native con. First is the use of indigenous authenticity and exceptionalism to camouflage the outsourcing of jobs government used to do itself, a maneuver we shall see our wingers use again and again. While some of the Alaska Native companies have grown immense through their special loophole, the impoverished and remote Alaska Natives who technically own them have little to do with their operations and even less to do with their profits. The companies' executives do not have to be—and apparently rarely are—Alaska Natives, and many of their headquarters are in subtropical northern Virginia, where the federal contracts hang from the trees like ripe fruit. What the members of the various Alaska tribes receive from their corporations are charity and dividends, averaging about three hundred dollars per shareholder per year.[49]

Not much capitalism for the owners, in other words, but the companies themselves are ingeniously entrepreneurial. This is the second piece of the puzzle: these Alaska Native Corporations seem to be forever winning contracts for technical work they cannot do, like maintaining radiation screening devices for the country's ports (to use a recent example).[50] So they may subcontract the job, usually to a conventional federal contractor such as SAIC or American Science & Engineering. Since the companies are privately held we can't be sure about any of this, but the implications seem clear: many of these corporations appear to exist to grease the skids between the government and its usual private-sector favorites,[51] allowing our MBA leaders to toss a quick $20 million to, say, Bechtel or SSA Marine whenever the mood strikes them, without having to go through the usual time-consuming bidding process.[52]

Giving back is the final, predictable piece of the picture. Certain employees of the Alaska Native Corporations I looked into donated generously to Ted Stevens and the other members of the

Alaska delegation. Each of the bigger corporations is also a client of one of three prominent Washington lobby shops: at the first, a former Stevens aide and a current Stevens brother-in-law are principals;[53] the second is a nest of enthusiastic Republican partisans and is headed up by former Homeland Security brass;[54] and the third seems to specialize in employing former aides of Alaska politicians.[55] One of the Alaska Native companies even rents office space at a building former senator Stevens partially owns in Anchorage.

Of the multitude of contractor scams to come floating along in the Bush years, though, it is the story of Brent Wilkes that makes plainest the squalid possibilities of the industry. Wilkes, of course, is the defense contractor who gained international fame for the cloudburst of bribes he showered upon Representative Duke Cunningham, a conservative of distinctly neanderthal tendency,[56] in exchange for Cunningham's help in obtaining contracts from the Defense Department. Wilkes's company, ADCS, specialized in converting paper documents into digital files, another operation that the government would probably have done itself in an earlier time. Today, however, we know better than letting the bureaucrats run things. We have the market do it.

In theory, market forces are supposed to save the government money by having contractors compete to get the job, but with supervision switched off and with the "very best people out," as per the conservative dictum, things got messy. Some contractors competed through bribery, with the most competitive offers being those of Brent Wilkes. He proceeded to build a lucrative business out of government jobs that he obtained via influence; as he told the *New York Times*, "campaign contributions were a prerequisite" for winning contracts. Over the years Wilkes handed out impressive donations not only to Cunningham but to high-ranking conservative congressmen Jerry Lewis, John Doolittle,

Roy Blunt, Duncan Hunter, and Tom DeLay, that champion of clean living. Wilkes was even a Bush "Pioneer" in 2004.[57]

So far, Cunningham is the only one of this bunch whose winnings can be tallied comprehensively. We know about the yacht, the Rolls, the Sea-Doo, the Glock, the second Sea-Doo; the tickets to see Jimmy Buffett, the tickets to see the Super Bowl, the "fully automatic machine gun shooting session," the vacation in Palm Springs, the vacation in Key Largo, the vacation in West Virginia, the vacation at the princely Prince Hotel on the island of Hawaii; the corporate jets and limos required to ferry his personage about the land; the fine wines that chuckled into his waiting glass; the steaks and lobsters and rare fishes that lined up to pass through his digestive tract; and the hired love of market-based women.[58]

And here is one sample, chosen from numerous others, of the goods that Duke Cunningham delivered in exchange for these fine gifts, as related in the grand jury's indictment of Wilkes for bribery.

> In or about April 2001, coconspirator Cunningham summoned a Deputy Assistant Secretary of Defense (Resources) to Cunningham's office and sternly lectured her about the need to allocate more money to ADCS [Wilkes's company] as she was not executing his vision. Subsequently, Cunningham attempted to get the same Deputy Assistant Secretary of Defense fired for not awarding to ADCS all the funds appropriated to the N[ational] G[round] I[ntelligence] C[enter] FIRES program.[59]

Take a good leisurely read back over the preceding two paragraphs. Go online and savor the original court documents on which they are based. Look up the riches scored by the congressmen and lobbyists who spent the last few decades deciding which contractors got our taxpayer money. Read until you've got a bellyful. And remember: none of it was accidental. These were the fruits of the free-market theory of government. This was political entrepreneurship in action. Ideas have consequences, and this revolting state of affairs was the direct consequence of the idea that "government is not the solution to our problem; government is the problem."

CHAPTER 7

Putting the Train in Reverse

After the war on the workers was won—after the tanks were brought up, the contractors put in place, and the bureaucrats baptized in the spirit of entrepreneurship—there still remained the logistical problems of compelling government to do the bidding of business. Much progress was made, though, before conservatives lost their hold on government, and several mechanisms were perfected to ensure that the state conformed to the wishes of its masters.

The first of these, for reasons of sheer ubiquity, was the famous "revolving door" by which government employees moved into the private sector and vice versa. Instances ranged from the entirely unremarkable—after all, people should be able to change careers if they choose—to the blatantly corrupt, with the revolving door ensuring that those who serve private enterprise most loyally during their public career were rewarded after their service was complete. Although with a little diligence one can find examples of the phenomenon dating back to the beginnings of the Republic, the revolving door as we know it only really picked up speed once the Reagan revolution swept through Washington in 1981. A study of the Defense Department done in the mid-eighties found that from 1975 to 1985, the number of former Defense personnel taking jobs with private contractors had increased by 491 percent. This was thought to be shocking then because the implied corruption was so obvious: "If a colonel or general stands up and makes a fuss about high cost and poor quality," sniped an air force memo from the time, "no nice man will come to see him when he retires."[1]

It shocked far less by the end of the Bush years. For one thing, prominent journalistic watchdogs decided that the revolving door wasn't really a problem after all: By making government procurement a deal between friends, it helpfully accelerated the whole business of buying jet planes or disaster equipment.[2] For another, it became almost impossible to study the revolving door systematically. An early, little-noticed act of the Republican Congress that took power in 1995 was to discontinue record keeping on the subject; today no one really knows for sure how many military people—or any other kind of federal employees, for that matter—have left to work for the private defense contractors whose office towers crowd the northern Virginia hills like a besieging Confederate army.[3]

Anecdotally, though, the phenomenon became so well known—and so uncontroversial—that any resident of the capital during the Republican period could come up with a dozen examples just from memory. The Defense Department procurement exec who tossed Boeing a $20 billion "gift" just before taking a job there in 2003 was a notorious example, but others spring to mind just as easily.[4] Think of the briefly infamous Steven Griles, for example, who did great favors for the oil and coal industries while a public official in the Reagan and Bush years, and who passed his time between tours of duty on the payroll of oil and coal lobbying groups. Or the main author of the Bush administration's Medicare prescription drug benefit plan, whom the Bush people plucked from the for-profit medical industry and who returned there as soon as he had finished his work—work that was shoddy from a public perspective but immensely profitable from that of his once and future employers. Or the *fifteen other* public officials involved in crafting that drug law, including one powerful House committee chairman, all of whom departed for Big Pharma's green pastures once the job was done.[5]

The Department of Homeland Security, built from scratch by the Bush administration in 2003 according to its principles of "market-based" government, was naturally the worst. While the department's career employees were initially stripped of bargaining rights, its top political officers, responsible for doling out gargantuan contracts, were apparently free to wheel and deal with all the entrepreneurial zest they could summon. According to the *New York Times*, by 2006 fully two-thirds of them had already departed for private-sector jobs in the ultralucrative homeland security industry, which subsists almost entirely on government contracts. One example suffices to explain it all: a deputy administrator of one of the department's agencies earned $155,000 while in the government's employ, the *Times* reported in 2006; one month after going to the private sector, she was making six times that from a contractor with offices out in McLean. With all the merry moneymaking that surrounded it in those days, one suspected that the entire department was, as columnist Frank Rich put it, no more than "a networking boot camp for future private contractors dreaming of big paydays."[6]

As with other fields of entrepreneurial endeavor, a constant innovative ferment kept the revolving door spinning faster all the time. Huge special payments and stock options, for example, were sometimes delivered to former public servants upon their hiring by a private employer, in return for we know not what.

Ever the leader in these matters, Jack Abramoff, in his lobbyist years, devised a secret "credit" system whereby one trusted confederate would use his position as aide to a powerful congressman to serve Abramoff's clients and then, later on, when he had joined Abramoff's lobbying firm, collect a reward commensurate with what he had delivered.[7]

As I have pointed out, conservatives deliberately tried to make public service an unattractive career option, opening up a "pay gap" between the public and private sectors and muttering about a "wage freeze" when federal workers complained about it. What this meant in practical terms was that the pay of government workers stagnated at the same time that Washington rose to the wealthiest tier of cities, making the carrots of private-sector success that dangled in every inhabitant's face seem that much juicier. It wasn't planned that way, of course, but by bidding the price of home and (private) college so high, plutocratization had the effect of making bureaucrats more and more anxious about their declining status, and ever more desperate to please those who might someday offer them a berth in the class that was going up instead of down. It was a self-reinforcing cycle.

In fact, the chasm between public and private employees was so vast by the end of the conservative era that even members of Congress routinely hit the revolving door, anxious to get started lobbying their former colleagues. Fully 43 percent of the senators and representatives who left Congress from 1998 to 2008 became lobbyists, one good-government group determined; that's up from about 9 percent in the seventies.[8] Again it was the financial math that overwhelmed all other considerations, moral or civic. U.S. representatives earned $165,200 a year in 2008—good money in most places, but certainly not enough to win them a Grand Monet in McLean or even a Grand Norman Rockwell. Congressmen who became lobbyists, however, often took in that much from a *single client*, frequently a public university or utility whose interests they were supposed to be representing in their term as an elected official.[9]

Former congressman Bob Ney, who was imprisoned for accepting bribes, furnishes the most poignant example. A U.S. representative from a working-class part of Ohio, Ney spent the sunny days of the conservative revolution selling his votes for little bites of raw fish, a luxurious golf trip in Europe, and other nibbles of the good life. Then, when the floor fell in, the incentives worked just as well in the other direction. With Ney's reputation shredded by exposure, the Republican leadership pressured him to withdraw from the 2006 election by pointing out that Ney had two kids of college age and that, if he embarrassed the party by losing, he "could not expect a lucrative career" as a lobbyist.[10] The influence peddlers would not forgive such a breach of party discipline; they would latch their thousand-dollar briefcases and walk away, leaving the Neys to sink back into the Appalachian soil from whence they sprang.

Ney, of course, did as he was told.

Putting federal operations under the direction of people who are hostile to those operations' existence is the second main tactic of conservative governance. When some aspect of the state is of no conceivable use to the conservative movement—when all the business community wants it to do is die—the standard method of dealing with it is to put the department in question under the control of someone who is either spectacularly ill-suited for the job or vocally opposed to that department's mission. Since the parts of government that conservatism most despises are often supported by the public, this strategy avoids the tactlessness of repealing or abolishing agencies while achieving the same results.

Many were astonished to see the veteran UN denouncer John Bolton nominated in 2005 to be our ambassador to the UN, but seasoned winger watchers knew that this was merely the creature doing what comes naturally. Nor were they startled to see Andrew Biggs, who has spent years campaigning for Social Security privatization, be made the number two at . . . the Social Security Administration. They may actually have yawned to read about the crusaders against birth control whom President Bush appointed to run the federal office overseeing . . . birth control assistance to the poor. But even the most hardened are surprised to learn that William Bennett, the secretary of education in the Reagan years, once expressed a desire to withhold resources from public schools, according to a high-ranking public official: according to this official, Bennett "wanted them, he said, to fail so that they could be replaced with vouchers, charter schools, religious schools, and other forms of private education."[11]

Like the clouds of poison gas that rolled across the Ypres battlefield in 1915, this tactic shocked the world when conservatives first used it on a large scale in 1981. *Why, they're flouting the law!* the goo-goos expostulated. Indignant editorials were published.[12] Hearings were held. But it seems there is very little you can do to make the president appoint people of a type he doesn't feel like appointing. Time passed, and so did the libs, and eventually conservatives came to use the weapon so brazenly and so casually that the capital just learned to live with it. Today everyone simply knows that when the wingers are in, one of the things you will get is deliberate mismanagement.

Not everywhere, of course. Traditionally, the damage is worst at those agencies that most inconvenience business: the Labor Department, the Environmental Protection Agency, and virtually anything else having to do with pollution, strip mining or oil drilling, product safety, or workers' rights.

For modern purposes, the model for this style of governing was established by the remarkable Howard Phillips, who served as director of the Office of Economic Opportunity (OEO) for five crazy months in 1973. As we have seen, this man Phillips is renowned for the purity of his right-wing views. The OEO, on the other hand, was set up to administer Lyndon Johnson's very liberal "War on Poverty"; it included a legal aid program that made lawyers available to people who could not afford them and which had thus led to thousands of lawsuits against landlords, banks, employers, and so on. Johnson had appointed Sargent Shriver to run the OEO. Nixon chose Howard Phillips.

What happened next is the stuff of right-wing legend. Then only thirty-two years old, Phillips immediately commenced wrecking the agency he headed. He purged the OEO of moderate Republicans and brought in his colleagues from the YAF, who reportedly got one hundred dollars a day to serve as assistant hatchet men. Budgeted funds were withheld; OEO employees around the country started to get termination notices; and soon newspapers were reporting the closing of legal aid offices in far-flung places. Congress had approved OEO's operations well into 1974, but according to a leaked memo, Phillips believed that if he acted quickly enough he could smash the agency and scatter its pieces before the libs had a chance to stop him. The young, idealistic winger became an overnight sensation—"the man of the week in Washington," the columnist David Broder called him—handing out lists of his "general principles" to the curious and denouncing the agency he ran as a product of a "Marxist notion."[13]

The editorial pages screamed. Phillips's unilateral obliteration of the OEO, said the *Washington Post,* was "a brazen usurpation of the powers of Congress and as crass an assault on its prerogatives as we can imagine." And, sure enough, a judge stepped in with a stop-work order only two and a half months into the demolition. "If the power sought here were found valid," the judge reasoned, "no barrier would remain to the executive ignoring any and all Congressional authorizations if he deemed them to be contrary to the needs of the nation." Tighten up the judge's prose a little, and you would have a concise motto for all the conservative high jinks to come over the next thirty-five years, from Iran-Contra to 2008's last gift from the USDA to the beef industry. But Nixon himself had no stomach for the OEO battle and replaced Phillips a short while later, allowing the conservative idealist to growl forever after about the first great lesson in the perfidy of politicians he learned during his stint at the OEO.[14]

But that episode was just the prototype, a forgotten secret weapon from Richard Nixon's war with the world. When Ronald Reagan took over, it was dusted off and put into mass production.

The true beginning of the age of political vandalism came with the appointment of James Watt, Reagan's first secretary of the interior. Before taking over the reins at that bureaucracy, Watt had directed a legal foundation dedicated to fighting that very department's conservation policies; naturally he did so with donations from wealthy ranchers, oil companies, and timber interests. Once in charge of the department itself, he promptly opened vast amounts of federal acreage to exploitation by same. Watt was also a walking caricature of a right-wing crackpot. He spoke in tongues. He accused environmentalists of trying to "weaken America." He thought the Beach Boys were disreputable. He looked like a space alien. And ultimately he had to resign because of an off-color joke.

Watt's spectacular oafishness made him easy to laugh off. But he was only the most conspicuous member of the crew. In fact the jovial actor-president had chosen similarly minded people to administer each of the federal government's pollution and conservation operations: a rancher to run the Bureau of Land Management, a former coal executive to run the strip-mining office, and a lumber industry lawyer to run the Forest Service.[15] Each had been picked to demonstrate the administration's hostility or indifference to the agency in question.[16]

The Reagan team was also worried that if it named competent people to run objectionable agencies, its actions might "be interpreted as sanctioning the regulatory enterprise," in the words of an academic study.[17] Therefore, to direct the Environmental Protection Agency, Reagan chose one Anne Gorsuch, a Colorado state legislator with virtually no experience in environmental issues. And here we see the cynical science of administrative sabotage come to maturity, incorporating each of the tactics that would define conservative governance.

In the seventies, the EPA had been "noted for its efficiency and esprit."[18] It was the government's largest regulatory agency, and its mission was broadly popular, as people generally dislike being poisoned.

Gorsuch wrecked it in two short years. First, she antagonized the agency's career employees by stripping them of authority and concentrating power in a handful of cronies drawn largely from the ranks of industry lobbies.[19] Then she made plans to whittle down the agency's workforce—even though its responsibilities were increasing. One civil servant, a high-ranking expert who talked to the press, was considered particularly heretical by Reagan's EPA team, and so they actually had investigators spy on the man, apparently in hopes of finding some cause to fire him.[20]

All these things were explained in the modish language of management theory. "I come from business and my initial impression when I got here was that this agency is fat. It has more money and people than it needs," said one of Gorsuch's assistants. "It offends my sense of efficiency as a businessman." Maybe he came from the school of management-by-mustard-gas; as a previous EPA administrator observed in 1982, "Any manager knows that firing, causing to quit, and demoting or transferring downward 80 to 90 percent of an organization's workers in a little more than a year means the end of that organization."[21] Thus we have the first general rule of conservative administration: cronies in, experts out.

Rule two: Congress can regulate all it wants, but without enforcement it is meaningless. Immediately upon taking office, Gorsuch actually did away with the EPA's Office of Enforcement. She then came up with a series of schemes that seemed designed to make the agency's work impossible: turning over enforcement power to the states; making toxic waste reports that had been mandatory into questionnaires that would go to only a handful of polluters; and developing a "peer review" plan that would run every new proposal by scientists—scientists whom she was busy firing. She even directly promised one worried company that she wouldn't enforce certain troublesome EPA rules. But for the true believing wingers it was never enough. In a memo leaked in 1983, a particularly zealous member of Gorsuch's inner circle assailed a slightly less zealous colleague for being too strict on pollution enforcement and thus "systematically alienating the primary constituents of this Administration, the business community."[22] It is a memo every American should have gotten.

Both Nixon and Reagan had confronted a Democratic Congress and a media establishment with real clout, countervailing forces that had either disappeared or withered by the time George W. Bush took the presidential chair. Consequently, his administration was less constrained in its approach to the federal agencies and was able to demolish the regulatory state far more completely.

Which is to say, we saw the train wrecks repeated over and over, in full speed and in slow-mo, on the nightly news and the front page, one after another until the sight of the exploding locomotives no longer astonished and the twisting of the cars barely rated a comment. Wasn't that just what trains did? When I heard, in the second month of the Bush administration, that the vice president appeared to be crafting the nation's energy policy with the help of oil, coal, and electricity companies, I was infuriated. When I read, in 2007, about the various means by which the vice president had contrived to undermine the Clean Air Act, I couldn't even be bothered to finish the story.[23]

At the EPA and the Interior Department, Dubya's cover band played a note-for-note version of the old Reagan air. Indeed, Gale Norton, the new secretary of the interior, was plucked from the very same winger legal foundation that had produced James Watt. She was a far more genial figure than the truculent Mr. Watt, of course, but the administration resumed his early-eighties course with such decisiveness that Watt himself was moved to pay this ringing tribute: "Everything Cheney's saying, everything the president's saying—they're saying exactly what we were saying 20 years ago, precisely," Watt told the *Denver Post*. "Twenty years later, it sounds like they've just dusted off the old work."[24]

And what could the new and improved Interior Department do for you—excuse me, for your trade association? Well, for irrigation-dependent farmers in California's Central Valley, whose lawyer the department hired to oversee irrigation in California's Central Valley, the department could furnish water abundantly and cheaply. For oil drillers, the department could ignore overdue royalty payments owed the U.S. government. It could open up new land for drilling, for mining, for logging—why, it could even open up national parks to achieve these wonders. Then, the inevitable quo for this juicy quid: what could your trade association do for the Bush appointees who had faithfully piloted the ship straight into the iceberg? A million-dollar job at your D.C. office—plus a plywood pile in McLean—would be just the thing, thanks!

At the Environmental Protection Agency, just as in the Gorsuch days, the chosen course was not so much taking robust action on behalf of industry as taking a few pills and lying down for a nice long nap. As per the script, the first thing to go was the enforcement department, which was quickly ratcheted down to its lowest staffing level ever. Then, with a series of deft moves, the administration stopped EPA action against air polluters and reversed the actions that agency had taken against them in preceding years; it even tried to undo a rule reducing arsenic in drinking water.[25] "Peer review" made its return as a delaying device, but industry review seemed to be the operative method, with the administration simply dismissing expertise it found inconvenient.[26] Indeed, cooperation with industry reached such a state of refinement that at one point the EPA proposed a new pollution rule that had largely been written by lobbyists.[27]

The rot was visible nearly wherever we chose to lift the rug and take a peek. The Mine Safety and Health Administration, we read, decided to reduce the fines it charges mine owners for safety violations, and sometimes it didn't bother to collect the fines at all.[28] Over at the Consumer Product Safety Commission, a much-downsized agency that paid no mind while lead paint oozed back into the toy market, the chairperson bitterly opposed measures that would have given her more power to weed out the dangerous toys—but readily accepted free trips paid for by toy industry lobbyists.[29] In 2003 the baby-formula industry, aided by a team of conservative lobbyists, induced the Department of Health and Human Services to dilute a planned ad campaign promoting breast-feeding.[30]

And on and on, to the regulatory horizon. The Minerals Management Service, a division of the Interior Department charged with extracting royalties from oil companies that operated on public land, was discovered in 2008 to have grown so close to the industry it was supposed to be overseeing that several of its employees were having affairs with oil company personnel. The Food and Drug Administration embraced market-based government so enthusiastically that it essentially became an arm of the pharmaceutical industry. The FDA's top officers were, in the Bush years, largely drawn from Big Pharma, its drug evaluation operation was funded in part by the drug companies themselves, and on numerous occasions the agency tried to silence critics of drugs that made it through its approval process.

The most revealing exchange at the agency came during the uproar over Vioxx in 2004, after a career FDA scientist had discovered that one of this already-approved drug's side effects was heart attack; his politically appointed superiors were distinctly displeased with his findings. "A former manager of mine from the Office of Drug Safety told me that industry was our client," the whistle-blower recounted on the TV program *Now*. "And when I said to him, 'No, the public is my client,' he said I was wrong and it was industry."[31]

We have heard some version of this phrase twice now from conservative appointees in the EPA and the FDA—business as the "primary constituent"; industry as "our client"*—but the third place we will encounter it is the strangest: the Department of Labor, which exists specifically to advance the interests of workers, but where one assistant secretary was by 2002 exhorting her colleagues to "*focus* on business as the primary customer."[32]

Should we really be surprised? The Labor Department is, after all, the branch of the federal government most hated by organized money. The series of moves with which the Bush adminis-

---

*Another example cropped up in congressional hearings held in the spring of 2008: The Federal Aviation Administration, which began referring to airlines as its "customers" in 2003, had eased up on aircraft inspections, allowing dangerous passenger planes to remain flying. Read about the FAA's "Customer Service Initiative" on its Web page, http://www.faa.gov/about/office_org/headquarters_offices/avs/cust_service/.

tration wrecked it was a masterpiece of misgovernance that incorporated injury, insult, and every spiteful little thing in between.

Start with sarcastic staffing. It had long been the custom with Republican administrations to treat Labor strictly as spoils, making its top jobs into sinecures for loyalists. But the Bush people took this a big step further, stuffing the department with cranks and zanies of the deepest hue, giving special, snickering priority to antilabor activists. The man who oversees the Employment Standards Administration, for example, was the author of a 1995 report titled "How to Close Down the Department of Labor." The man in charge of the Occupational Safety and Health Administration came to the job from a union-busting law firm. The president's choice as the Labor Department's chief lawyer had spent the nineties fighting doggedly against the one major new regulation OSHA had approved during the Clinton years. (It had to do with ergonomics; Congress repealed it in Bush's second month as president.)

For secretary the president first proposed Linda Chavez, whose principal qualification for the top position at Labor was her smoldering hatred of the labor movement.[33] When that didn't work, Bush replaced her with Elaine Chao, who believes it is a crushing indictment of her department's regulations to point out that they contain more words than the Bible and whose main—possibly only—credential for the job was her marriage to the powerful Republican senator Mitch McConnell. The department's chief economist was not only a ferocious enemy of unions but an advocate of allowing entrepreneurial prison wardens to bring back convict labor. (He departed early on in the Bush years to start a new career as a 9/11 conspiracy theorist.)[34] The department's chief information officer was formerly a right-hand man to Jack Abramoff. There was even a senior adviser to the secretary who appeared regularly on Fox News to talk about Intelligent Design.

And this gang didn't just idly collect paychecks; they worked hard to get the locomotive speeding in reverse. Policing labor unions became an important priority of what they proudly called the "new Department of Labor." They even set an example for American business by cracking down on their own unionized workers: in 2003, DoL management decreed that members of the government workers' union would not get the one-hundred-dollar monthly transportation subsidy that every other federal worker in the city receives; they had to *bargain* for it, giving up some other item in order to obtain a benefit that everyone else got automatically.[35]

With regard to its traditional job of policing the workplace, the Department of Labor announced that it was ready to forgive and forget. Business was the "primary customer" now, after all, and the secretary herself apologized for the "regulatory jungle" in which misguided liberals once entangled the country's employers. "Voluntary compliance" was the obvious solution; after all, everyone in that enlightened age knew that the free market exerted "much stronger financial incentives than OSHA penalties" on employers who let their workers get hurt.[36] (As indeed it might, were conservatives not constantly capping lawsuit damages and slashing workers comp.)

The market was on the job, so who needed regulators? In 2007, the Department's Wage and Hour Division fielded only half as many inspectors as it had in 1941 when it was first set up, although it was now supposed to be looking after eight times as many workers. Going forward, the "new Department of Labor" agreed to give Wal-Mart a fifteen-day notice before investigating it for any possible child labor violations. The bosses at OSHA, meanwhile, got busy smothering their staff's proposed regulations. The division's leader even gave a humorous speech blaming workplace injuries on stupid mistakes by workers themselves.[37]

The rightful protector of the worker, according to the conservative view, is enlightened management—not contracts, or rules made by Washington bureaucrats, or even a voice for labor in how the business is run. And the Labor Department itself eagerly led the way into this white-collar utopia, becoming what the management gurus might call a Department of Excellence. It has an "MBA outreach program"; its chief information officer holds Washington spellbound with his lectures on the need to "recognize project champions" and to let "programs create and own their goals."[38] And the management community returns the love. The DoL is "like a star pupil that keeps asking the teacher for more assignments," raved *Government Executive* magazine in 2004; from the very worst among federal departments it "fought [its] way to the Number 1 position," marveled Maurice McTigue, a theorist of government much in vogue in conservative Washington.[39]

Judged by the goal it was founded to meet—to improve the lot of American workers—the Bush Labor Department was a colossal failure. Although the economy grew at a decent pace from 2001 until the collapse of 2008, blue-collar workers as a group did not participate in the good times. Median family income actually fell, rather than rose, in those years. The lower on the wage scale a worker stood, the more his or her wages shrank.

But so what? The "primary customer" was different then. So was our understanding of how organizations worked. In 2005 the aforementioned McTigue could be heard urging an assortment of Labor Department bureaucrats to open their hearts to the almighty CEO, to remember that this godlike figure must always have "full control over the number of staff, their remuneration and terms and conditions of employment."[40] In management-land this kind of talk is unremarkable: there, the Lord Boss omnipotent reigneth. What made McTigue's talk a moment to remember was that the people being inducted into the cult of the CEO were the official protectors of the American worker.

None of these things is the object of conventional political debate, but at least they still made the headlines now and then. The antiagencies that were another staple of conservative governance didn't even do that. They were designed to dismantle the liberal state under cover of bureaucratic mystification; only academics and impoverished good-government groups seemed to know that such organizations even existed.

This strategy, too, had its beginnings in the Reagan administration, which rode to power on a wave of antiregulatory fervor. And Reagan delivered, too: in his first weeks in office he suspended hundreds of regulations that federal agencies had developed during the Carter years but that had not yet gone into effect. In so doing, Reagan created a precedent that conservatives have observed ever since, tossing out the regulatory work of their more liberal predecessors immediately upon taking charge.[41]

Reagan then gave the task of blasting regs a permanent institutional incarnation: the little-known Office of Information and Regulatory Affairs (OIRA), originally an unassuming paperwork-monitoring outfit buried deep in the Office of Management and Budget. On these humble foundations conservatives built OIRA into a mighty fortress dominating the strategic chokepoints of big government and passing judgment on all proposed federal regulations. Its administrator, the nation's "regulatory czar," is traditionally drawn from the ranks of dernier cri conservative economists. In its early days, OIRA apparently answered to industry pretty much directly. Jim Tozzi, a regulation fighter who ranked high in the office during Reagan's first term, is said to have solicited the advice of business leaders about which rules he should strangle and to have taken care to make no records of his conversations with them; "I don't want to leave fingerprints" is how he summarized his management style.[42]

What was in those days a battle over regulation eventually became a rout, a one-sided contest in which a bombardment of criticism from winger think tanks and institutes muffled the occasional musket shots of the other side. John D. Graham, who began running OIRA in 2001, advanced Tozzi's legacy. He had come from Harvard's Center for Risk Analysis, where he solicited and received donations from a large array of companies, all of which stood to benefit from an ingenious critique of the regulatory process that Graham had invented.[43] Once seated behind the big guns at OIRA, Graham proceeded to put his theories into effect, soliciting the opinions of industry on proposed regulations and acting, in case after case, as they urged him: weakening, delaying, or overturning rules altogether.[44]

But Graham was not the worst of it, as I discovered when I visited the Mercatus Center in Arlington, Virginia, one of Washington's foremost free-market institutions. The think tank is housed in an enormous glass turret that reminds one both of Silicon Valley office buildings and of a gigantic revolving door. These two hints give us a good idea of what Mercatus actually does: its walls are lined with plaques listing the many corporate sponsors who have come together to construct this free-market fortress (Enron is there, among others),[45] and its offices are filled with exuberant scholars ready to testify about the foolishness of regulation, offer advice on making government more like a business, or take jobs in friendly administrations.

I myself was there to look about the legendary library,* which, I had heard, boasted a collection of right-wing literature

---

*Although housed in the same building as the Mercatus Center, the library turned out to belong to a different libertarian outfit called the Institute for Humane Studies.

spanning everything from the gold standard to Christian reconstructionism. It also had plenty of room left over, I found, for the *pensées* of the British crank Enoch Powell, long-forgotten studies of media bias, two competing Ayn Rand magazines, and copies of *Reason* going all the way back to 1969.

On my way out I found, literally on the floor, a pamphlet called *A Day in the Life of a Regulated American Family,* signed by one Susan Dudley of the Mercatus Regulatory Studies Program, and apparently published by this PhD-flaunting institution with the goal of frightening small children. It is the perfect inversion of that story from 1945 about the happy dime, whose wanderings showed generations of schoolkids the many ways government improves our lives. Using the same kid-friendly technique, Dudley gives us a parable of deepest paranoia: Nearly everything in life, the pamphlet tells us darkly, is tainted by the hand of government. It regulates the radio stations, inspects our food, fiddles with our cars, restricts what we can do with our employees, and it might just declare our backyard a wetland if we don't look out. Each of these examples is meant to terrify, and when the totalitarian threat isn't immediately obvious—I, for one, wish the government would do more food inspecting, not less—Dudley sticks in an extra sentence establishing its awfulness ("John . . . is not made safer by the airbags"). The pamphlet is illustrated with clip art of the kind found for free on the Internet and used to enliven elementary school newsletters.

The trash was where this thing belonged, and I hastened to deliver it to its rightful resting place. But for some reason I hesitated, brought it home, looked up its author—and behold: a few years after excreting this thing, Susan Dudley succeeded John Graham as chief of OIRA; in the final years of the Bush II administration she was our government's chief regulatory officer. The effect is like a hammer to the head, like learning that they've put a ten-year-old Quaker lad in charge of the Strategic Air Command.

Although he is seldom included on the roster of great conservatives, George Bush I came up with an even more brilliant antiregulatory innovation: the Council on Competitiveness, a secretive executive branch office empowered to review, alter, or overturn any regulation it chose. The brilliance resided in the direct way the council achieved the conservative goal of applying market forces to government—or, I should say, apparently achieved, since nearly everything it did was secret, and council staffers refused congressional requests to appear in public and explain their decisions. (The council's director did meet with the Chamber of Commerce, however.) "No fingerprints" was again the rule.[46]

According to those who studied it, there was nothing mysterious about the council's duties. It was a venue in which business could inform the administration which upcoming regulations would hinder its profitability—its "competitiveness," in the management slang of the day—and get those regulations nixed. In its short lifetime (it was abolished on day one of the Clinton administration), the council overruled the EPA on air pollution; slowed down an FAA effort to deal with noisy airplanes; speeded up the FDA's drug-approval process; and, with the help of a lawyer named Ken Starr, churned out a plan for suppressing the sort of lawsuits that consumers file against industry. Naturally, the council instantly became an object of passionate lobbyist lust; and just as naturally, the love songs of business leaders who contributed to the Republican Party seemed to be the ones that charmed the council most.[47]

In the meantime the race went on for the bureaucratic neutron bomb—a device that would kill regulation but leave the regulatory agencies themselves intact and, apparently, on the job. In

2001 a figure from OIRA's glory days built that device: the Data Quality Act, drafted by none other than Jim Tozzi and passed into law with a little help from a friendly Republican representative but with no hearings and no public notice. As implemented by George Bush II, it allowed outside parties—usually corporations or their lobbyists—to challenge the studies on which regulatory agencies based their decisions. OIRA and the Council on Competitiveness worked by shooting down regulations at the terminus of the process, after agencies had labored over their proposed rules for years; the Data Quality Act exposed the regulatory process to interception and attack at every point.

And, yes, *attack* is the correct word. Although technically the law merely provides for the familiar give-and-take of the scientific method, it has in fact been used almost exclusively to slow things down and screw things up; studies of global warming, action on dangerous herbicides, and warnings against eating too much sugar have all been crushed in the regulatory logjam. According to one reporter, Tozzi, the author of the law, has been "gumming up the regulatory works," dreaming of finding a way "to induce regulatory sclerosis." And with the Data Quality Act he found it.[48]

We have here another uncanny illustration of conservative mimicry. Back in the seventies, the regulators themselves stood accused of inducing sclerosis, of gumming up the nation's economic works. But in the aughts conservatives paid this imaginary debt back, compounded and with plenty of interest.

And they did it with lots of help from good old American entrepreneurship. After having figured out how to expose the regulatory process to the kicks and blows of private industry, Jim Tozzi turned around and hired himself out as an assassin of annoying regulation. He filed Data Quality petitions on behalf of different trade associations; he set up the humorously named Center for Regulatory Effectiveness, which monitors the regulatory agencies in pseudo-objective style, and, under the more straightforward name Multinational Business Services, he is simply for hire.

This supremely inventive anti-bureaucrat seemed quite at ease amid all the controversy. Tozzi's office, when I visited him in 2008, featured a humorous caricature of himself as a Godfather type with the motto "We don't leave no fingerprints"; on his walls were framed copies of a critical newspaper story and a review of a book that dealt with him harshly. The man himself struck me as a genial fellow with an extraordinary knowledge of both federal-agency procedure and—of all things—Dixieland jazz. Also as quite a prosperous fellow: He received me wearing an expensive tie and a shirt with his initials monogrammed on the cuff; in years gone by, he admitted, he traveled the city in his own chauffeured limousine.

This all made good economic sense, of course. It seemed natural that the market should reward those, like Tozzi,[49] who accept its eternal truths and spend their lives carrying its holy war deeper and deeper into the heart of its enemy, the state. It seemed equally natural that the market should withhold its blessings from those who don't embrace the laissez-faire way.

Visit the offices of the good-government groups, and you will see what I mean. In the period I am describing, the Project on Government Oversight, which has probably saved taxpayers billions by illuminating the deepest recesses of the federal contracting system, did its work from offices where posters were thumbtacked onto plain white walls, and where battered old desks served as conference tables in rooms piled high with office supplies. In the lobby was a plastic houseplant; next door was an abandoned building.

I got my own, comic lesson in this simple principle of D.C. life years ago, during an earlier period of Republican government. I was a graduate student then, in town to visit a friend of mine who worked for a U.S. senator. We went to a house party crowded with members of our generation, all of them fresh out of college and just starting their careers at law firms or committee staffs. Then, as now, the bit of information everybody wanted to know upon introduction was where I worked. But telling them the truth—that I was studying history—proved to be so distasteful that people would actually turn away and walk off before I could finish the sentence. My friend, a Republican, suggested a better strategy: *Tell them you work for the Council on Competitiveness,* he advised, a federal agency I had never heard of before. For reasons I did not understand until I came to write this book, the line made me an instant social success.

Tom Geoghegan, a labor lawyer in Chicago, has spent his career watching the New Deal system get taken apart by measures like those I have described here. Thanks to the Bush administration's "partnership" with the Union Pacific Railroad, he wrote in 2007, one fine day the Federal Railroad Administration simply decided to stop enforcing many of its rail safety rules. The Labor Department no longer fielded enough inspectors to enforce its wage and hour regulations on Wal-Mart, let alone the country's multitude of smaller enterprises. In one of Geoghegan's cases, as he told the story, the employer he was suing offered this defense for letting his workers go without any advance warning: how was he to know the government would decide to enforce its pure food regulations and shut down his filthy chicken-processing plant? It never does that anymore. And the judge agreed. "In other words," Geoghegan wrote, "the application of the rule of law is the equivalent of an act of God. Completely arbitrary. Like a hurricane."[50]

Through the smoke and the wreckage of the old regulatory state we could, in those days, make out a new and unfamiliar America rising in its place. This colossus was not the product of some awesome and irresistible force like "globalization," but rather of decades of hard right-wing work, of careful bureaucratic sabotage and an occasional shot of lobbyist money. The accomplishments of the new conservative state were unmistakable: productivity galloped along, but with workers' organizations out of the picture, only the people at the very top benefited from the advance. For the rest of us there were sudden outbreaks of deadly food poisoning. Toxic securities. Deadly mine accidents. Tap water that was unfit to drink. Mysterious workplace plagues that, upon investigation, could have been easily avoided at only a slight expense to management. But all of it made possible—unavoidable, even—by a philosophy of government that regards business as its only important constituent.

CHAPTER 8

City of Bought Men

Although the lobbyist's reputation is only slightly better than the purse snatcher's, there is nothing really sinister about the lobbying industry when it is considered in terms of its formal components. Just as businesses hire specialists to hymn their brand, put their books in order, and smooth their production process, so they engage lobbyists to explain their needs to the government.* The essential operation of the trade is also fairly benign, if you consider it abstractly enough: lobbyists meet with legislators and regulators to plead their client's case, and the side with the best argument prevails.

Except that's not how it works. Persuasion may be the least of the methods through which lobbyists get their way. Above all else is money, applied strategically to the right politician, sometimes

*There are also thousands of "advocacy" lobbyists in the capital who toil for non-profits, labor unions, consumer organizations, and civil rights groups. Here, however, I will be examining only the more mercenary lobbying that is done on behalf of industry.

as a campaign contribution, sometimes literally as the price of admission to a party known as a "fund-raiser," which you, too, can attend for a few thousand dollars on any given weekday on Capitol Hill. Sometimes the lobbyists even host the fund-raisers, an innovation that relieves the senator in question of the burden of collecting his own campaign contributions. There are meals: steaks and sushi and caviar and wine. There are gifts and vacations, which for reasons of maximized face time generally focus on the game of golf.* There is—or there was, anyway—an ever-more complete integration of lobbying with the day-to-day work of Congress, with lobbyists writing bills, helping see proposals through the legislative process, and running politicians' reelection campaigns.[1]

There are the CIA-style operations about which we know little, since lobbyists don't have to disclose them: the gifts and donations to pundits and journalists, the subsidies arranged for useful think tanks, the establishment and support of fake grassroots groups. And there are the ex post facto services, about which we know even less, in which well-upholstered chairs are held open at lobby firms for cooperative regulators, judges, and elected officials when those personages are ready to make their move into the private sector.

Amid all the squalid splendor in which he deals, the lobbyist is also a specialist in human friendship. He is, by the requirements of his profession, an amiable fellow: a bon vivant, a gourmand, a raconteur. If you're a man of power, he's always got your back, and the reason you can count on him is that friendship is a valuable commodity in Washington. Former committee staff members deal in access to existing committee staff members. Onetime aides to senators trade on their special relationship to

---

*Perhaps this is also because golf allows the lobbyists and elected officials to take one another's moral measurements. After all, as Tom DeLay intones, "golf is a game of character, and you can tell who a man really is by how he plays." DeLay with Mansfield, *No Retreat, No Surrender*, p. 110.

their old boss . . . and their old boss comes to them looking for a job when it's time to cash in. Before the fall of Tom DeLay put many of them out of business—in late 2005 he resigned as House Majority Leader after being indicted for campaign finance violations—a constellation of his former aides made up an entire branch of the lobbying industry, reeling in the clients and the campaign contributions, receiving countless favors back, and one of them even hiring DeLay's wife to do some subclerical work at vastly inflated wages.

The industry itself is difficult to categorize. Is it a cousin of the advertising industry, for example; a branch of marketing where coolness is *verboten,* where offices have desks instead of beanbags, and the casual-wear revolution never happened? Are lobbyists minor-league politicians, possessing that profession's conviviality but lacking its appetite for public affection? Or is lobbying a form of legal practice in which laws are made, not merely interpreted? Lobbyists have sometimes been con men, ripping off their clients; they have historically been drawn to gambling and casinos; the most exalted members of the profession seem always to own restaurants; and it often occurs to journalists to describe them in the language of pimps and prostitutes.

However we classify lobbying, nearly everyone agrees that, by putting a tollgate between the people and their government, the industry has been in some way responsible for Washington's prosperity. Lobbying was "Washington's biggest business," proclaimed the *Washington Post* in 2007, supplying residents of the capital with "a new Washington aristocracy" of which they could be proud.[2]

It was also the signature activity of conservative governance, the mechanism that, in its heyday, translated market forces into political action. Lobbying is how money casts its vote.

The lobbying industry is frequently referred to by the term *K Street*, after the main drag of downtown Washington, but just as ad agencies are often located far from Madison Avenue and stockbrokers work from places besides Wall Street, lobbyists can actually be found all over the city. In the sunny noontime of conservatism, the command center of corporate lobbying was the spectacular white office building at 101 Constitution Avenue, across the street from the Capitol itself.

You knew you were getting close to the place when you would start seeing lobbyists buzzing around like bees near a hive. With a little practice, the pressure boys were easy to distinguish from lesser drones: they were the ones who looked like caricatures of prosperous men, dressed in a way that was no doubt meant to suggest "affluent businessman" but in which no proper businessman in Chicago or Kansas City would ever, in fact, dress himself. In most of the United States, male office-wear tends toward the drab; the lobbyist, by contrast, fancied himself Beau Brummell. He appeared to choose each element of his ensemble for its conspicuous priciness, and you could spot him in the field by his perfectly fitted thousand-dollar suits, usually blue; his strangely dainty shoes; his shirts, which often came in pink or blue with white collars and cuffs, the latter of which displayed cuff links of the large and shiny variety; his vivid, shimmering ties, preferably in orange or lavender; his perfect haircut; his perfect tan; the tiny flag attesting to his perfect patriotism on his perfect lapel.

One of the most arresting sights in conservative Washington was one of these fussily dressed and pleasant-smelling creatures out of their element—say, dragging a piece of Tumi down a broken sidewalk near the bus station in the one-hundred-degree heat. But, here at 101 Con, they felt right at home. They would come striding into the Charlie Palmer Steak restaurant, and the air-conditioning would be blasting and their teeth would be exactly right and their ties would jut gamely from their collars. The gang was all here, a bunch of real straight shooters, and they would extend their hands to the congressional committee chairman, and all the handsome fellows would share a laugh as they took their seats among the huge vases of cut flowers and scurrying waiters.

You could offshore nearly any kind of job in those days—ship your factory to Mexico and send your back office to India—but your lobbyists had to stay in Washington. The rest of the hard, old, face-to-face world may yet dissolve, but lobbying always remains stubbornly rooted in the necessities of physical proximity to power and, of course, to tasty eats. At 101 Constitution, both of these could be found in fantastic abundance, and this made the building a landmark for the time. 101 Con was K Street in a box, a private-sector Pentagon where ten stories of lobbyists plotted their next thrust on behalf of the life-insurance industry, the mining industry, or the retail hardware industry.

Form follows function, as they say, and 101 Con is admirably suited to the task of paid persuasion. To begin with, 101 Con is the closest commercial property to the Capitol building, literally just across a traffic island from the Capitol grounds. This means "members," as they are called, can scoot over and back in a matter of minutes. The building's upper stories provide an astonishing view of the Capitol dome, a quality exploited by the prominent turret that juts toward Constitution Avenue. This protuberance is topped by a rooftop terrace, where fund-raising events were often held against the striking panorama (rent started at $10,000 a night, I was told in 2006); smaller balconies on the lower floors permit regular tenants to hold their own parties with the same backdrop. The tangible value of this view—namely, that it impressed clients—was often mentioned in news stories. The intangible value, I imagine, is that it also allowed the lobbyists, like captains of industry in old advertisements, to look out grandly over the assembly line where their product was manufactured.

The building's ground floor houses the aforementioned Charlie Palmer Steak restaurant, very large and very luxurious and world famous for its "artisan meats" and fine wines. This latter being one of the baseline currencies of the influence trade, the bottles are stored in an ostentatious glass "wine cube" perched on a platform over an indoor pond, like a Richard Neutra building in captivity. In theory, I suppose, having the wine room elevated and transparent in this way means that a dedicated, score-keeping fan of lobbying, if such a thing even existed, could actually have determined which particular vintage was being uncorked to advance which particular political cause.

The building's architects did their job well. 101 Con is a "trophy-class" building where even the elevators have a role to play. "Since many of these tenants make regular trips to lobby their powerful neighbors across the street," their manufacturer's Web site boasted, "we're proud to think of the 15 custom elevators that we fabricated for the building as the first stage in the journey toward the creation of new laws."[3] All that was missing, really, was a bullet train to the golf course.

Visitors to Washington who want to see democracy in action traditionally waste their time at the viewing galleries of the Capitol building, where—if they are lucky—they might see one or two legislators mumbling mechanically for the C-Span cameras. It is, as everyone knows, a big letdown—a disillusionment that is cited whenever smart young people relate how they got to be so wise to the world.

However, had those visitors merely walked across the street to Charlie Palmer Steak, they would have seen the machinery of conservative governance in action. *This* was the place for political spectatorship, where you could see the questions before the nation actually being resolved—and you could do it over a meal, too, saving yourself a trip to Applebee's later.

You could start with the miniature lobster corndogs, a nod to the deep-fried treats of your red-state youth (but made with lobster, get it?), and then you could slyly bribe yourself with a plateful of the domestic Kobe sirloin, sixty-eight dollars. If you were smart, you would wash the whole thing down with a half dozen Manhattans—you'd need them. If you looked around while you ate, you would have noticed that this was not the dim, windowless steakhouse of your weekend debauches in Topeka. It was light; it was open; its polished limestone walls were accented with delicate Wedgwood blue; a curtain of glass showcased the prosperous diners to the sweating world outside. And did you notice that pond burbling in the middle of the restaurant? And the heavy steel ingot that propped up your menu?

It's because of classy touches like those that your congressman never did move back to your home state, regardless of what he used to say about "sharing your values." Speaking of that congressman of yours: If you were lucky, you'd see him here. Indeed, for the price of that steak you could watch him and his fellow members make decisions on matters that would affect you for the rest of your life. And you might have noticed that he was making those decisions in close consultation with nonmembers—people just like you, in fact, only with better hair, better clothes, better teeth, better manners, and a better job working for far richer and more important people than you.

There is nothing new about persuasion-for-hire in Washington. What was new in the conservative years was the size of the lobbying industry and the blithe acceptance of its enormous role in matters of public significance. Years ago, Americans understood very clearly what a development like this would mean for democracy, and their indignation was expressed best by the Supreme Court as it tossed out an 1874 case in which a lobbyist sued a client for nonpayment after he, the lobbyist, had duly secured the passage of an agreed-upon measure. "If any of the great corporations of the country were to hire adventurers who make market of themselves in this way, to procure passage of a general law with a view to promotion of their private interests," the Court thundered, "the moral sense of every right minded man would instinctively denounce the employer and the employed as steeped in corruption and the employment as infamous."

Corruption and infamy are just about the only contexts in which the public takes notice of lobbying. Indeed, the milestones of the business are identical to a list of the great American scandals: the Ulysses S. Grant administration, Crédit Mobilier, Teapot Dome, Bobby Baker, Watergate, Koreagate, Deavergate, Bill Clinton's White House coffees, and the Abramoff affair. But the industry chugs merrily along nevertheless.

No one can agree on a uniform standard for measuring the lobbying business, but for a long time its fortunes only seemed to go up and up. During a fleeting burst of anti–K Street outrage in 1986, the population of lobbyists was reported to have doubled in the preceding ten years—"the biggest growth industry around," expanding so fast that Washington was said to be close to lobbyist saturation. But the monster continued to grow. By 1992 K Street's numbers were said to have doubled again. In 1993 a political scientist came up with a total head count, including all the staffs of the city's advocacy organizations, registered or not: ninety-one thousand was the amazing figure he settled on. The current system for registering lobbyists gives us a smaller number—only about thirty-five thousand—but whenever that number was cited in the Bush years, it was said to represent a shocking increase in size.[4]

While the number of lobbyists has doubled and doubled again, so have the dollar amounts associated with the business. According to Jeffrey Birnbaum, the *Washington Post*'s man on the lobby beat, lobby shops charged their clients twice as much in 2005 as they did in 2000. By then lobbyists themselves earned more than ever before: The standard beginning salary for a staffer fresh from Capitol Hill was $300,000, up by more than a hundred grand from the start of the Bush days.[5]

Perhaps these fees seem unremarkable to you, something you should expect from an industry in such a state of zooming expansion. But in fact they represent something of a puzzle. With more firms competing in the field and more lobbyists than ever for the provincial businessman to choose from, the price of lobbying should have been going *down,* not *up*. Unraveling this mystery requires a close look at K Street's role in the great changes of the last few decades.

Lobbying's contribution to the prosperity of the capital encourages what we might call the institutional or centrist school of lobbying commentary. Lobbyists come from both parties, the centrists point out; lobbyists make campaign donations to members of both parties; lobbying is therefore politically neutral and is best evaluated not moralistically but as a normal modern business. A prime example of this school of interpretation is the twenty-seven-part series written in 2006 by *Washington Post* editor Robert Kaiser that told the story of lobbying's fantastic growth by narrating the rise of Gerald Cassidy, the proprietor of a prominent lobby shop.[6]

The story is an epic of crassness. Virtually the only aspects of Cassidy's life to come persistently through are his "restless ambition for the really big bucks" and his creative application of Wall Street financial maneuvers to the political-influence biz. Readers learned how he used an employee stock-sharing scheme "to extract wealth" from his lobbying firm, how he tried and failed to go public, how he launched a merchant banking firm, how he acquired other influence operations, how he sold out to an ad agency holding company, and so on, to the point where Cassidy was able to dress in fine clothes and own a big house on the Chesapeake.[7]

"Cassidy got rich," Kaiser writes, "by sticking to his knitting," a phrase so thick with small-town wholesomeness that the reader wants to stand up and cheer for the young entrepreneur with the can-do attitude. What Cassidy's "knitting" turns out to be, though, is the marketing of earmarked appropriations, those specific spending items inserted by an elected official into some larger piece of legislation. Wasteful earmarks like Alaska's $200 million "Bridge to Nowhere" were the target of a storm of public anger in 2005 and 2006; Gerald Cassidy is said to have *invented* the form back in the seventies and then used a platoon of salesmen, working on commission, to travel the country selling the idea of earmarks to potential clients. Any takers turned up by the salesmen would then pay Cassidy a retainer; Cassidy would do his lobbying magic; the clients would eventually get their millions in taxpayer money; and the legislators responsible for inserting the earmark got a nice campaign contribution. Says Kaiser: "All the parties profited handsomely from this enterprise." Sure, good-government types complained that Congress had no business spending money without some kind of formal review by experts, but they and their experts were simply "blown away," as Kaiser puts it, by the win-win brilliance of the transaction. One Cassidy client, the former president of Boston University, actually produces a calculator during his conversation with the journalist Kaiser and figures out the return his institution got on its political investment.[8]

Each new chapter in the Cassidy saga made me want to curl up with a bottle of scotch, set the Sex Pistols record on infinite repeat, and forget this city of bought men. But for the *Post* editor Kaiser, the story was one of triumph: the rise of an industry, the financial ingenuity of its leading figures, and the corresponding transformation of Washington into "one of the wealthiest regions in America."[9] Any possible objection to lobbying, the author apparently believed, is canceled out by the bipartisanship of the thing; Cassidy started life as a liberal D, working for George McGovern himself, but he went on to party just as comfortably with hard-core Rs like Tom DeLay and Roy Blunt, the former House minority whip.

You hear this view pretty frequently in Washington. Members

of both parties are tainted by lobbyist money, and if we invented a third party it would accept lobbyist money, too. Besides, people say, lobbying is just business competition on another playing field, with the lobbyists for one trade association fighting with the lobbyists for a different trade association. Surely all those dollars just cancel each other out.

Despite all this competition and all this bipartisanship, though, lobbying brings a constant pressure in a single direction. There have always been many diverse lobbies fighting with one another, acknowledges a classic history of the industry, but "all of them, working in coalition, were struggling to capture the government itself" on behalf of those with the means to pay their fees.[10] Lobbying is how business pulls the levers of the state.

The all-time classic example was exposed in 1906, when the New York state legislature appointed a committee to investigate the insurance biz, and discovered, among other things, that industry's highly successful efforts "to control a large part of the legislation of the state." The various companies in that highly profitable field, while technically in competition with one another, had come together to fund a "House of Mirth" in Albany, a combination headquarters and trysting spot for their brigade of lobbyists, who would receive instructions on which legislative measures to suppress and what news items to plant in the papers. What shocked the nation back in 1906 was the systematic, businesslike way that the lobbyists had subverted the democratic process. But when confronted about its tactics, the insurance industry was unrepentant: its interests were "continually menaced" by the state government, it responded, and thus it had to "resort to secret means to defeat [it]."[11]

Then there were the exploits of the National Association of Manufacturers (NAM), the megaphone of American capitalism. During a 1913 investigation, Congress discovered that the NAM was home to a sort of superlobbyist *avant la lettre,* one Martin

Mulhall, who had at least one but probably many U.S. representatives in his pocket, enjoyed powerful influence with the House minority leader, and even had his own office in the Capitol building, from which he tried to control the committee assignments of members of Congress. This particular influence peddler was unusually versatile; he also lent his shoulder to the NAM's great push against labor unions, traveling to places where strikes were in progress and doing his part to carry the day for management.[12]

This seems perverse to the modern reader—lobbyists are supposed to love fine clothes and good food, not the company of skull-cracking goons—but there is a larger consonance that makes the match both natural and predictable. Both union-busting and lobbying, as it was practiced in those days, involved the subversion of democracy through bribery, propaganda, and the well-placed news story. Both were—and are—legal services demanded by the same entities, namely corporations. And to this day there persists an eerie alliance between the two. Akin Gump, an international law firm that runs one of the largest lobby shops in Washington, also advertises its ability to help employers defeat labor union initiatives. Burson-Marsteller, the PR giant, offers clients a similar array of "integrated solutions": lobbying in Washington by the well-connected firm BKSH; advice to "companies facing strikes" when that's what's called for.[13] (On the other hand, I know of no corporate lobby firms that sell themselves to workers as a "solution" for getting management to the table.)

These stories of the NAM and the House of Mirth come to us from an era when American businessmen knew where their class interests lay and acted accordingly, a conservative might sigh. But in the years after World War II, he would continue, corporations started to get soft; they started to get comfortable with big government.

There was more than a little truth to this complaint. The

classic study of the American corporation in the sixties, John Kenneth Galbraith's *The New Industrial State,* described an organization in which shareholders had virtually no role at all and managers answered instead to government and to one another. For average citizens this arrangement made for the greatest period of mass prosperity in the nation's history. For conservatives, though, it was an intolerable state of affairs, and the upper stratum of society watched as its cut of the nation's wealth fell to its lowest level ever in the mid-seventies.[14] The point of the business enterprise is to maximize shareholder value, they started to scream, nothing else.

Schemes to return the corporation to the free-market paths of righteousness and profitability have danced through the conservative imagination ever since. The list of innovations designed to discipline the corporation—to force managers to concern themselves solely with profit—is long and getting longer every day: leveraged buyouts, stock options for senior management, shareholder revolts, stock buybacks, mergers, spinoffs, downsizing, outsourcing, and offshoring, to name a few.[15]

Lobbying could be a valuable weapon in the war for profit, but conservatives had apparently lost sight of its potential. Although it seems inconceivable today, conservatives in the seventies and eighties routinely attacked lobbying on the grounds that, by pleading for bailouts and special favors, K Street had both softened capitalism's competitive edge and encouraged government to grow big. Even Ronald Reagan railed against lobbyists as part of the Washington "buddy system," with everyone in the city doing favors for everyone else and leaving taxpayers to get the bill.[16] This, of course, didn't stop corporate lobbyists from gaining unprecedented influence in his pro-business administration.[17]

The cycle was repeated in 1994, when a second Republican revolution swept the land, howling once more against the malign influence of lobbyists and other Washington insiders. The leading figures this time were Newt Gingrich and the famous "Freshman Class" of 1994, a cohort of angry Republicans often depicted as idealistic everymen rising in fury against corrupt Washington power.[18] Although his triumph would mark the beginning of the most corrupt and lobbyist-friendly Congress in a hundred years, Gingrich actually climbed the ladder by denouncing what he called "money politics."

> Congress is a broken system. It is increasingly a system of corruption in which money politics is defeating and driving out citizen politics. Congress is a sicker and sicker institution in an imperial capital that wallows in the American people's tax money. . . . Corruption, special favors, dishonesty and deception corrode the very process of freedom and alienate citizens from their country.[19]

Newt's Freshmen confronted "a town controlled by an establishment trying to fight off outsiders," in the words of one *Washington Times* columnist; "a town run by a system comprising career representatives and senators, expensive lobbyists and establishment journalists."[20]

And how Newt's boys cleaned up, once they got their hands on the broom! They passed a ban on certain kinds of lobbyist gifts, they required lobbyists to register themselves, and in an outpouring of idealism David McIntosh, an *enragé* Freshman from Indiana who took the lead in the attack on lobbying, even tried to pass a complete ban on lobbying by certain groups.[21]

This was a form of idealism in the way that poison ivy is a tasty and nutritious salad green. McIntosh's antilobbyist bill, as it turned out, would have applied solely to organizations that received federal funding and would thus have damaged only advocacy lobbyists like environmentalists and good-government types; in Republican circles his proposal was commonly referred to as a "defund the left" bill.[22] Instead of staving off government-by-money, McIntosh's measure would only have eliminated the competition for corporate lobbyists.

McIntosh was, in fact, as perfect an advocate for business government as my generation has produced. He didn't rise to Congress from behind a plow somewhere; he came from the Bush I administration's antiregulatory Council on Competitiveness. Before that, he helped found the Federalist Society, the extremist lawyers' club from which the Bush II administration has drawn so many of its federal judges.

This fiery poseur against lobbying became a lobbyist himself the same year he left Congress. Today the idealistic McIntosh wages his war for good government on behalf of Big Pharma and the U.S. Chamber of Commerce.

The real visionary of '94 was Grover Norquist, who had left Savimbi behind and attached himself to Newt Gingrich instead, helping to draft the famous "Contract with America." Norquist, I think, understood the simple fact that has eluded so many others: that lobbying has the potential to become the greatest "defund the left" scheme of them all. If business interests were united in the age-old political fight—if business leaders could remember how their forefathers used to operate, if they could set up a modern "House of Mirth" or take a page from the old NAM, if they could learn to *act as a class*—they could easily overmaster every other institution in society. They could win the final victory over liberalism.[23]

When it comes to defunding the left, Grover Norquist is the city's true genius. Over the years he has outlined countless schemes for wrecking the Democratic Party by starving its constituent movements or shutting down the avenues by which its leaders receive contributions. His master stroke was the K Street Project,* which aimed to force businesses to behave as conservative loyalists, in line with their correct interests: that is, to hire only conservatives as their lobbyists and to donate strictly to the campaigns of conservative politicians. It was a win-win proposition. Businesses would reap the rich rewards of their political investments; the political entrepreneurs of the right would prosper; and the left would simply starve. Put differently, the object was to make the dim-witted corporate world—with its vast reservoir of dollars—understand who its genuine political friends were.

"The business community's soul," Norquist wrote, is as much an object of contention as a battlefield. In the seventies and eighties, conservative ideologues encouraged the formation of business PACs in the belief that they would be a sort of silver bullet for the laissez-faire agenda. They were then bitterly disappointed to see those PACs give roughly half of their funds to Democrats.[24] From a pragmatic standpoint, of course, this made a great deal of sense. The Democrats were the majority party in those days, and under the leadership of the so-called New Democrats the party was moving steadily to the right. Bill Clinton turned out to be the most pro-business Democratic president since Grover Cleveland, and his triumph over more liberal Democrats was a development corporate types wanted to encourage. They were happy to support a Democrat who took their side on

---

*The "K Street Project" is the specific name for the efforts to influence the lobbying industry mounted by Americans for Tax Reform, Norquist's group, as opposed to the similar enterprise of Tom DeLay and other members of the late Republican Congress. Norquist was so annoyed by the media's failure to distinguish between these not-so-different operations that in 2006 he tried to trademark the phrase "K Street Project." According to Norquist's filing with the U.S. Patent Office, "The K **Street Project** promotes the hire of lobbyists at corporations and trade associations who understand free-market economics, who support their principled positions for free trade, against tort law abuse, and for lower and more transparent taxation." The trademark application was marked "abandoned" in 2007.

NAFTA, welfare, and banking deregulation; who eliminated the federal deficit; who retained Alan Greenspan at the Federal Reserve; and who made the chairman of Goldman Sachs his treasury secretary.

For deeply dyed conservatives like Norquist, though, it was a standing outrage that the true believers in the free-market way did not receive 100 percent of the funds and the K Street employment opportunities that corporate America had to offer. Take away the Democrats' majority in Congress, as the GOP did in 1994, and this sort of even-handedness became sheer perversity in the wingers' eyes, an offense against nature, the free market, and stockholders themselves. "If people want to change Washington to make it a better place for the free-market system to operate, they have to hire Republicans," one aide to Majority Whip Tom DeLay fulminated back in 1998. Hiring Democrats was "not a shrewd business decision," agreed Michael Scanlon, another DeLay aide.[25]

An additional problem, as Norquist explained it to me in 2006, was that business seemed unable to control its lobbyists, to train them to discern between the company's interests and their own personal feelings. Norquist recounted with some disgust the story of a long-ago battle over enhanced fuel-efficiency standards, which would essentially have mandated smaller cars. Norquist worked to oppose the new standards by putting together a coalition of auto manufacturers and cultural conservatives who, he says, like big cars because they have big families. But the auto industry's representative would have none of it.

> A woman in the room said, *I would rather lose the issue than work with "those people."* Somebody being paid by one of the three major car companies explaining, *I'm not for what's good for General Motors or Ford*—I forget

> which one she worked for—*but my prejudices and my hatred and my bigotry override the needs of the company that pays me.*[26]

Prejudices were just the beginning. Norquist also attributed business's obstinate refusal to act in its own best interests to Stockholm syndrome, in which hostages grow sympathetic to the terrorists who have imprisoned them. Business interests, he told me, "were completely mau-mau'd. They were threatened. I was at the Chamber of Commerce, 1983–84, and I would hear the horror stories of [former House Speaker] Jim Wright threatening the Chamber of Commerce. *We will get you!*" In other words, business funded Democrats in those days because it was forced to.

For Norquist, the biggest, baddest mau-mau of them all was California representative Tony Coelho, a leading Democratic fundraiser in the eighties, who appears to live in Norquist's imagination as both a horror and an inspiration. His obsession with Coelho seems to derive from a 1988 book by the reporter Brooks Jackson called *Honest Graft,** which, in Norquist's interpretation, shows the Ds practicing their own sinister version of the K Street Project, telling business, "*If you wish to lobby us, you will hire our staff and give us money.*" Coelho's operations amounted to political extortion, according to Norquist, with Democrats shaking down the feeble giant of corporate America by threatening to use their power to destroy its profits. Here is how he described it to *The American Enterprise* during an interview in 1996.

---

*Norquist's fascination with this book is shared by other former leaders of the Reagan youth. Ralph Reed, for example, writes that *Honest Graft* revealed to him how "politicians shook down special interests" and thus caused him to lose his "lofty ideals." Ralph Reed, *Politically Incorrect: The Emerging Faith Factor in American Politics* (Dallas: Word Publishing, 1994), pp. 25–26.

> A "juice spill" [*sic,* he means "juice bill"], a term from the California state legislature, is where politicians say to businessmen, "I have a bill here that crushes your industry." Everybody in that industry hands in $1,000, and the politician says, "O.K., we won't crush your industry this month, we'll crush some other industry." And you threaten industry after industry and everybody antes up, and the guy who refuses to ante up sufficiently gets hit. The Democratic Party under Tony Coelho perfected this.[27]

Ten years later, writing in *USA Today,* Norquist was still roaring about how "Democrat enforcer Tony Coehlo [*sic*] operated to get free-market businesses to act against the interest of their shareholders": "Businesses were told to hire Democrats and contribute to Democrats (or else!) even though most opposed the goals of American business. Many businesses hired and contributed as they were told. They 'paid to play.' "[28]

When Norquist explains his work as a response in kind to "Coelhoism," it may be the most glaring case of Freudian projection that we will encounter in our tour of the Washington right. *Honest Graft,* the book on which Norquist has based this dark worldview, contains dozens of examples of self-aggrandizement by Democratic legislators, some of them quite revolting, but no stories of lobbyists being forced to hire Democratic staffers, and all of three instances in which Democrats made threats, only one of which they followed up on (and that was directed not at a corporation but at an idealistic liberal who wanted to get PAC money out of politics).* Across the board, the message taken

*Turning to the larger realities of the time, the conclusion is even more wildly off. Perhaps the most famous abuse of official power in that period was that of the "Keating Five," a bipartisan group of U.S. senators who did the bidding of the savings-and-loan fraudster Charles Keating. What made the Keating Five notorious was not squeezing money out of an honest businessman by threatening to regulate him; they

from *Honest Graft* by reviewers for major publications and business magazines was that big money in politics was drowning out the voices of average, nonrich people—not that big money was vulnerable to marauding liberals. As for Coelho, his stated goal was to reposition the Democratic Party itself as a "businesslike" outfit in order to please corporate types, a program in which his model was . . . the more advanced Republican organization. Big business was the winner in this process, not the loser.[29]

And, in truth, Norquist seems to have read *Honest Graft* less as a cautionary tale and more as a blueprint for the bruising partisanship that his Republican friends proceeded to inflict on the lobbying industry. As the record clearly shows, it was Norquist himself who urged retaliation against those who refuse to play ball with his K Street Project. Here is how he reacted in 2004 to the news that a prominent biotech concern had hired a Democrat to lobby for it, according to the lobbying columnist for the *Washington Post*: " 'That's not very wise on their part,' he said. Speaking of key Republican leaders, Norquist added ominously, 'People are aware that this has happened. It's going to be treated seriously.' "[30]

And that is as patty-cake compared to the reaction of Newt Gingrich, Tom DeLay, and the rest of the House leadership when they discovered in 1998 that the Electronic Industries Alliance, a Silicon Valley industry association, intended to hire former Democratic congressman Dave McCurdy as a lobbyist. Here is the *Post*'s account of that ugly episode.

> House GOP leaders became so enraged when the EIA announced McCurdy's selection last week that Gingrich

---

became famous because they took campaign contributions from a crooked businessman and then used their official power to protect him from government regulators. In other words, the biggest scandal of the day showed politicians behaving in precisely the opposite of the way Norquist's theory would have had them behave.

> declared in a closed-door meeting that he would not discuss legislation with the former lawmaker, according to Republicans who attended. Gingrich and most other top Republicans also instructed their staffs not to meet with any EIA officials. Republican leaders, who had hoped the group would select retiring Rep. Bill Paxon (R-N.Y.), also delayed passage of noncontroversial legislation concerning international copyrights, a bill the EIA supports, for four days in an effort to send a message to the group.[31]

It fell to the young Michael Scanlon to wrap it all up with a cynical insult to the world. After Jerrold Nadler, a Democrat from New York, suggested that the episode merited an ethics investigation, Scanlon puffed himself up and said, "We don't appreciate his heavy-handed tactics."[32]

The larger message sent by all this message sending was this: corporations must be forced to act in their owners' interests; without strict guidance from the political right, they will fall for one smooth-talking Democrat after another. Norquist, for his part, was emphatic about this. When it comes to politics, he growled, corporations were "morons, idiots." When I told him how strange it was to hear a politico like him instruct business on market principles, he replied, "I'm telling corporate America when you hire a goddamned Democratic staffer . . . and he sits here and tells you to absorb tax increases, and protectionism, and trial lawyers, because that's the best deal you can have, you're being lied to and misused."

Fortunately for stockholders, the Republican revolutionaries who ran Congress after the 1994 election were willing to use the muscle required to turn the business community right side up. Soon the party of the free market was dragging the corporation, kicking and screaming, to its own coronation. Ponder the images from those days: the big book that sat on the coffee table in Tom DeLay's office, where every visitor could see it and notice how carefully DeLay was following the campaign contributions he or she had made. DeLay's refusal even to speak to lobbyists who weren't Republicans. ("We don't like to deal with people who are trying to kill the revolution," he said in 1995. "We know who they are.") Senator Rick Santorum's Tuesday morning get-togethers at which job openings in the lobbying industry were assigned to deserving Republicans. The big meeting at which the chairman of the Republican National Committee informed the CEOs of the nation's biggest corporations that they needed to replace their Democratic lobbyists with Republicans.[33] The idealistic freshman who boasted how he bullied a trade association that had given to his opponent, saying, "They made a bad political choice, and they chose to do it in my face, and then they got rolled."[34]

Throughout my research for this book I was often impressed by the absurdity of my subjects' views. But I'll be damned if Grover's contrivance didn't work. Like the other efforts to discipline the corporation that I described earlier—leveraged buyouts, stock options for CEOs, and so on—the K Street Project had an immediate effect on business behavior. Corporate contributions began listing to starboard. Prominent K Street Democrats became rare enough that, by 2004, the appointment of a Democrat to the head of a trade association was considered a newsworthy event.

What the famously idealistic Gingrich Congress achieved—by purging liberal operatives and heaping rewards on the conservatives—was oneness with the market or, at least, with its political arm, the lobbying industry. It took a few quarrels to get there, but the groping lovers eventually found each other; K Street and the Capitol, joined in a torrid embrace. In their very first term in office, according to two *Washington Post* reporters, Newt's principled Freshmen turned out to be such zealous fund-raisers that most of them "hired professional consultants to run their events and solicit contributions," and for good measure they also "formed steering committees of lobbyists to advise them." And happily ever after did they live: almost half of the 1994 Freshmen to leave Congress have become lobbyists, up from about 9 percent of the congressmen to quit during the seventies.[35]*

Among the multitudes who came to Washington with the revolutionaries of '94 was Jack Abramoff. The onetime leader of the Reagan youth had left the capital in 1988 to churn out low-budget movies, but now he returned, got a lobbying job on the strength of his connections to the newly ascendant conservatives, and immediately became the perfect embodiment of his friend Grover's new vision for K Street.[36]

He was, the media discovered, an idealist. He would not take just any client, Abramoff told the *New York Times* at the height of his power; "he represents only those who stand for conservative principles."[37] Abramoff would fight exclusively for what he believed in; I guess it's just one of history's happy coincidences that what he believed in was the market. He would use the free-market techniques of K Street to secure a world of free markets.

The idealist Abramoff seemed to specialize in supporting the idealist Freshmen. The new Congress had only been in session for a few months before he declared, to the *New York Times*,

---

*The same is true, incidentally, of other outbursts of conservative idealism. The prototype for the '94 Freshmen was Newt Gingrich's Conservative Opportunity Society, a caucus formed in the early eighties to press the agenda of the New Right. Of the eleven members of the group to depart Congress, seven became lobbyists; the three who remained in public service in 2008—Duncan Hunter, Jerry Lewis, and Larry Craig—were each mired in scandal. Of the ones who became lobbyists, one was indicted in 2008 for terrorist-related money laundering.

The original roster of the Conservative Opportunity Society appears in *Conservative Digest* for August 1984; among others, it included Robert S. Walker (today the chairman of the Wexler & Walker lobby shop) and Vin Weber (today the CEO of lobby powerhouse Clark & Weinstock).

that "assistance for the freshmen" was the number one priority of the revolution, "the most important goal from the political contribution point of view."[38] During the 1996–97 period, Abramoff's famous lobbying team made contact with the offices of at least thirty-four of these idealistic firebrands, nearly half of their entire number. In 1997 Abramoff even managed to recruit his very own '94 Freshman as a team member: David Funderburk, a one-term congressman from North Carolina and a conspiracy-minded extremist of the sort we have by now begun to expect whenever a new character appears in the Abramoff story.* Over the succeeding years, the single largest recipient of Abramoff's contributions would be J. D. Hayworth of Arizona, a particularly bombastic member of the '94 class who fancied himself a crusader against corruption.[39] Bob Ney, a '94 Freshman from Ohio, was the first congressman to hit the cellblocks as a result of his dealings with the superlobbyist.

Abramoff was doing a "new kind of lobbying," he once told Amy Moritz Ridenour, a friend from his College Republican days; she rejoiced to discover that it really "was not lobbying at all, but educational work."[40] A better word might have been *propaganda*. All that was new about it was the profits involved.

---

*Funderburk first surfaces in the Abramoff files in 1989, when he published an unfortunate essay in the IFF's magazine arguing that glasnost was a trick, that the "brilliant elitists at State" were "appeasing" the Communists, and that the Soviets would never permit the Eastern bloc countries to break away. The Berlin Wall had the bad manners to fall while the issue was still on the newsstands. But Funderburk would not be deterred. He extended his streak two years later with a book called *Betrayal of America: Bush's Appeasement of Communist Dictators Betrays American Principles* (Dunn, N.C.: Larry McDonald Foundation), in which he elaborated on his theory that glasnost was a ploy by "the old Bolsheviks [who] finally found the ideal front man to win over the West while they continue to carry out their objectives" (p. 50). This time the Soviet Union itself collapsed, and only months after the book's appearance.

What to do with a man who gets it wrong so consistently? Elect him to Congress, of course!

Abramoff himself directed the campaign on behalf of his clients. He no longer needed to make posters, run a nonprofit, sponsor panel discussions, or publish a magazine to get his views across; all of these could be done through one of the thousand points of dim light that make up winger Washington—such as Ridenour's own curiously named outfit, the National Center for Public Policy Research, which did Abramoff's bidding so loyally that, according to one official finding, it "functioned as an appendage of Mr. Abramoff's lobbying operation."[41]

But then, a skeptic might say, that's how the entire conservative movement functioned. Abramoff's basic lobbying strategy was simple: it was to sell his clients to the assembled soldiers of the right at one of its regular gatherings. Indian casinos, which became the mainstay of his practice, were cast as an amazing libertarian success story, an object lesson in how the weak could triumph if government just left them alone. Channel One, a controversial educational venture that included commercials in the free programming it offered public schools, was promoted as a money-saving (and hence tax-reducing) scheme suffering persecution by hysterical, antibusiness leftists. There were dozens of others that signed up as the superlobbyist's reputation grew: Internet gambling concerns, mysterious European shell companies, enterprises at the murky edges of American sovereignty.

On top of his staggering fees, Abramoff had his clients tithe to the galaxy of nonprofits that make up a big part of winger Washington, cementing the relationship between them and the movement. Essays supporting his clients' causes were easily ginned up and placed in conservative newspapers and magazines, sometimes apparently written by a member of the lobbyist's team for a prominent winger's signature.

For liberals who made trouble there would come a devastating cascade of invective from those same publications. For good, conservative legislators there were campaign contributions and free trips, usually sponsored by some cooperative think tank. And for his clients, there were tax hikes suspended, labor laws that went unenforced, and rival businesses that were closed down. As his practice grew, Abramoff tried to realize some economies of scale, maintaining various skyboxes around the city and opening his own ultrapricey restaurant for the express purpose of dishing out luxury meals to important men.

In certain ways Abramoff's lobbying career was the consummation of the political-entrepreneurial dream with which the Reagan youth began. Abramoff was a field marshal of the movement now, and from the heights of a prestigious Washington law firm, he and his team of power rangers managed the ideological battle: blocking legislation and terminating bureaucrats' careers; ordering a journalistic bayonet charge here or a banquet of comped meals there. What's more, all this power was in private hands, and all of it was for sale.

At astronomical prices, of course. Which returns us to the basic mystery of lobbying I raised earlier. How is it that the explosive growth of lobbyists and lobby firms did not cause prices to fall? By the rules of supply and demand, the entry of hundreds of new lobby firms into the field should have driven the price of lobbying down, not up.

Were we to pose the question to our conservative friends, they might attribute the avalanche of money to the political enlightenment of the Fortune 500, a wising-up that required a few lessons from Professors Norquist, DeLay, and Gingrich, but that was no less real for that fact. Were we to ask our colleagues on the left, they might identify the K Street Project as having been a kind of influence cartel, driving prices up by restricting entry to the field.

The most credible explanation, though, is that clients grew more and more confident that their lobbyists could deliver something of value in exchange for their fees. This confidence, in turn, was the result of a basic change in the larger world of government, with first Congress and then the executive branch turned over to that wing of the Republican Party that regards business as something holy but that understands the regulatory state as a criminal enterprise. When empowering business and neutralizing that regulatory state suddenly became the very object of government—oh, how the money rolled in.

The reason companies started buying, in other words, was that *Congress began selling*. The boom began with the arrival of the conservative idealists in Washington in 1995. In that first, noble term of the Gingrich Congress, according to two *Washington Post* reporters who covered the '94 revolution, the entry price to a congressman's fund-raiser rocketed from $250 to $1,000.[42] This was not because fund-raisers had become four times as rare or because the new Republican majority was preparing a long list of "juice bills" threatening private industry, but the very opposite: because of a dramatic improvement in the quality of the goods for sale.

Consider a few of the better-known examples of the goods that the free-market believers made available. There was the 1995 legislation weakening OSHA, an agency despised by the business community, which was substantially written by a group of industry lobbyists.[43] There was the two-day get-together between House Republicans and media company CEOs, after which the various broadcasters and publishers were asked to replace their Democratic lobbyists with Republicans; the Telecommunications Act of 1996, almost certainly written by industry lobbyists, followed soon afterward, deregulating the airwaves and trailing clouds of glorious profits for the media companies.[44]

There was Tom DeLay's "Project Relief," a bill that shot down numerous workplace and environmental regulations and that was actually drafted by a team of lobbyists representing some 350 different industries; as the bill went to the floor the lobbyists set up a field command in a room off the House chamber, where they responded to challenges and reassured the wavering. It was "an unambiguous collaboration of political and commercial interests," wrote the *Post* journalists who witnessed the episode, and when the bill had passed by a veto-proof margin, DeLay and a chain-store lobbyist jointly presided over a celebration in one of the House office buildings at which they cut symbolic red tape off of a miniature Statue of Liberty.[45]

All these were rational political investments, as Grover Norquist would no doubt say. And the Republican Congress continued to reward investors. In 2004, a group of the country's largest companies reportedly paid some unnamed K Street firm $1.6 million to secure a tiny modification of the tax code; once the law was rewritten in accordance with their wishes—and with almost no public notice—they saved $100 billion in taxes, an amount which you and I will eventually have to replace in the public treasury. If you do the math on this, you will find that the rate of return these companies made on their lobbying investment was some 6 *million percent*.[46] These are the wages of conservatism.

Let's say you are a civic-minded sort and you went to Washington in those days to see the wheels of your market-based government turning. Let us return, then, to the building at 101 Constitution Avenue, and the golden conservative year of 2006. Had you taken an elevator to one of the building's upper stories and strolled around, you would have noticed that the offices were often decorated with those handshake pictures that are so popular in Washingon—photographic proof of a given lobbyist's intimacy with a politician and a much more useful tool in establishing one's professional bona fides than any framed degree. You would also have seen model airplanes, model motorcycles, and other carefully arranged bric-a-brac that in ordinary offices would serve as reminders of leisure-time fun in the outside world. Here, though, they were strictly business: emblems of the industry for which legislative favors were sought. And, always, looming magnificently in the background, was That View: the bleached dome of the U.S. Capitol.

Think of the elevator ride upward as Dante's descent into Hades, but in reverse and with ten stops instead of nine. At the midway point, the fifth floor, we might have visited the National Mining Association (NMA), an industry group that was mainly concerned with promoting coal and that furthered its agenda with large campaign contributions, mainly to Republicans. In 2004, this outfit sponsored a grassroots effort called "Mine the Vote," in which mine owners introduced mine workers to their favored candidates. Very plutocratic of them, but also very effective: the program is said to have helped George W. Bush prevail in the once reliably Democratic state of West Virginia.[47]

Until 2005, the head of the NMA's in-house lobbying operations was one John Shelk, an expert on energy issues who got his start, like many lobbyists, working for the congressional body charged with overseeing those issues—in this case the House Energy and Commerce Committee. He later proceeded to lobby his old colleagues on behalf of none other than Enron, which was then spending tens of millions "spreading the gospel of deregulation," as a Shelk profile in a trade magazine put it. When pushing coal for the National Mining Association, of course, Shelk claimed to have only the consumer in mind, but the religion was essentially unchanged from the Enron days: "The point is for people who believe in markets to stick together," he said.[48]

Now it's on to floor six, where you could visit the offices of Van Scoyoc Associates. The first time I heard about Van Scoyoc was when a lobbyist friend insisted to me, in hushed tones, that the people at this prestigious and respected D.C. firm were specialists in earmarks. I didn't believe him at first. After all, earmarks were in those days the very symbol of misgovernment and corruption. They were the "Bridge to Nowhere"; the menu of bribes that Representative Duke Cunningham drew up for the convenience of his regular customers. I knew in the abstract that lobbyists were involved in the process, of course. But, I wondered, could it really be so open, so unconcealed? A firm that *specializes in earmarks*? That's like putting a sign on your door that says "Shameless Dealers in Graft and Boodle."

So naive was I. According to a 2006 story in the *New York Times,* the buying and selling of earmarks was by then so routine that even municipalities were getting into the act, hiring lobbyists to induce their own elected representatives in Washington to do their jobs. According to a story from that same year in *CQ Weekly,* the number of clients looking for earmarks (that is, "budget and appropriations") had tripled since 1998; procuring earmarks was, by then, the single largest category for lobbying activity. The top firm in the field: Van Scoyoc Associates, of 101 Constitution Avenue.[49]

The firm employed a staff of ninety then and claimed to have a client list of over three hundred, including (according to the firm's publicity materials) fifty universities and twenty of the nation's largest corporations. Van Scoyoc seemed particularly proud of its success in the rapidly growing field of academic earmarks, whereby some research project or institute is funded directly by Congress instead of through the usual process—you know, where scholars or experts look the proposal over and decide whether it's a good idea or not. One example of how this works, according to data provided by Public Citizen: from 1998 to 2006, the University of Alabama paid Van Scoyoc $1.5 million; over that same period, the various officers of the firm contributed at least $123,500 to Alabama senator Richard Shelby (two of the firm's vice presidents are, in fact, former staffers of

Shelby's); and, during those years, Shelby earmarked some $150 million for the University of Alabama.

Every element of this chain was, of course, formally unconnected to every other—innocent and wholesome as a newborn babe. But imagine, for a moment, that this was exactly the racket it appeared to be. That is to say, the company's officers were charging clients $1.5 million for making contributions of $123,500 (a twelvefold increase), and the University of Alabama turned that $1.5 million in lobbying fees into $150 million in research earmarks (a hundredfold increase), and Shelby himself pocketed $123,500 in campaign donations just for voting the right way when the phone call came from 101 Con.

We all know the liturgy of conservatism: government doesn't work, the private sector is so much more efficient, and so on. Still, I can't help but marvel at how much everyone would have saved had we just cut out the middleman and had Shelby do his job.

Up another floor, we would have found the offices of the Federal Policy Group. Though the tenants of 101 Con wielded great power over the public welfare, they were generally not public figures. An exception to this rule, however, was the boss man of Federal Policy Group, Ken Kies. Unlike most other lobbyists of that period, Kies did interviews, wrote articles, and even appeared on television. This was because Kies was no mere chortling backslapper in a turquoise tie but, rather, a bona fide expert on a difficult subject. Indeed, he was said to be one of the greatest living authorities on the U.S. tax code; over the preceding twenty years, Republicans came to him whenever they wanted to rewrite tax law.

It turns out, however, that letting a lobbyist have a say in writing the tax code is a risky proposition. The lobbying expert Jeffrey Birnbaum tells the story of a 1989 incident in which Kies, who had left the staff of the House Ways and Means Committee a short time before, came back to his old friends at the committee seeking a tax exemption for his *new* friends—at an iron-ore outfit that had hired him as a lobbyist. Not only were Kies's pals on the Hill happy to oblige; they actually let Kies come up with a tax increase on somebody else (in this case, cell phone users) to replace the revenue lost in the tax cut they granted Kies's client.[50]

With the Republican Revolution of 1994, Kies returned to the public payroll, now as chief of staff for the Joint Committee on Taxation, a position of such authority and prestige that articles from the time reported him to be more popular on the corporate lecture circuit than his nominal bosses on the committee. In 1998, Kies went back through the revolving door for good, once again dreaming up justifications for the very particular changes to the tax code that his new and very wealthy clients wanted. "I've never seen a guy who's got an influence over the tax chairman like he has," a tax official told the *New Republic* in 2000.[51] His lobby shop's Web site used to list the results: regulations reversed, laws averted, rulings withdrawn, corporate tax deductions retroactively allowed—more lawmaking activity than Congress itself, almost. And all of it could be yours, if the price was right.

On floor nine, you would have noticed the conference rooms where public policy was made by the private sector, the leather upholstery and star-spangled light fixtures, and domed ceilings made of polished wood. Just beyond lay a large, empty triangular room with the balcony beyond and the by-now-tiresome view. This may well have been the site of one of the most storied events in lobbying history: Tom DeLay's Thanksgiving fund-raiser of November 17, 2005. Those were dark days for "the Hammer": he had been indicted in Texas and had resigned his position as majority leader; several of his former associates had been implicated in the growing Abramoff scandal, and guilty pleas were just around the corner.

But Tom DeLay would not be intimidated. He stared the world down with those unblinking exterminator's eyes and conspicuously scheduled one last, great blowout—the biggest fund-raiser of the year. And it was a success, too. A lobbyist friend explained the rationale to me: *DeLay just might survive this episode,* the participants thought, *and if he does, I want to be his friend.*

So the call went forth, and the private sector arose as one, a mighty host shoveling the money in a colossal show of "moral support," as one of them described it to the *Washington Post.* The good old NAM sent an emissary, as did the Refiners and the Truckers. The roll call of industry went on—Oil! Coal! Gas! Finance! Electricity! Petrochemical!—late into the night, on that delirious ninth floor of 101 Con, as they did homage to their friend and paid their dues for the years of good government he had given them.[52]

On the tenth floor you would have found the building's magnificent rooftop terrace, the site of countless political fund-raisers and memorable winger celebrations. You would also have found, near this most desirable space of all, the offices of the United Brotherhood of Carpenters (UBC). Which supplied the final twist in the story of 101 Constitution: this showplace of corporate power was owned by a labor union, the UBC. In earlier days, the 101 Con site was occupied by a standard-issue union headquarters, a "marble mausoleum," as one Carpenters official described it to me. The considerable revenue that their new building generated was dedicated by the union to their organizing efforts.[53]

Though there were few overt signs of the union presence, if you had looked closely there were clues indicating the building's provenance. From the parquet marble floor in the lobby to the finely polished elevator doors to the exotic wood paneling, you were always aware of the building's slightly excessive craftsmanship. If you happened to forget who was responsible for all this quality, you were reminded by an enormous mural in the lobby depicting a hard-hatted carpenter, naked from the waist up, taking a break from his construction job to gaze at the Capitol dome. As presumably the sole bit of monumental social realism executed in the nation's capital during the Bush years, by the way, this mural ought to have put the building on the tourist's map all by itself.

If you're a liberal optimist, you might have seen 101 Con as an ingenious détournement of Washington's hypercapitalist culture, its rent helping to strengthen the ranks of the labor movement, the very thing the hypercapitalist culture dreads most. Buy that senator another slab of artisanal meat, Mr. Lobbyist! Sip your fizzy Italian water and poke at your BlackBerry with both thumbs! Surely the joke was on you.

Only it wasn't, really. While I myself find it gratifying to see corporate types obliged to pay rent to a labor union, the UBC wasn't exactly the adversarial organization that one might have hoped. For one thing, its president, Douglas McCarron, was virtually the only labor leader to win the friendship of George W. Bush, the most antilabor president since . . . maybe since Karl Rove's hero, William McKinley. McCarron hosted Bush at the union's Labor Day picnics; Bush hosted McCarron on Air Force One; McCarron was the only labor leader to speak at Bush's economic summit in 2002; that same year, Bush spoke at the UBC's political conference, where he congratulated the union for—of course—opening its new building at 101 Constitution. The payoff for Bush: in the 2004 election, which many unionists perceived as the most important in their lifetimes, the Carpenters proudly and with great fanfare endorsed nobody.[54]

In Bush's salute to 101 Con, he claimed to find inspiration in the attendance of both Senator Teddy Kennedy and Labor Secretary Elaine Chao at the building's dedication. The implied bipartisanship, the president said, was "a good sign as to how . . . Washington ought to deal with problems."[55] Democrats and Republicans, labor and big business—all of them coming together under one roof.

Should you ever happen to find yourself on that roof, turn

your back on the view and walk over to the other side. What you will see there is the brutal concrete shoebox of the Frances Perkins Building, in whose bowels toil the employees of what was, in the conservative days, the most disrespected federal department of them all, the Department of Labor. It was here that the adminstration's philosophy of *slam that sucker into reverse* achieved the amazing results I noted above: the elevation of hilariously unqualified people to positions of great authority; the shift of emphasis from protecting workers to policing them.

The two buildings are not just neighbors on Constitution Avenue; they are opposites, physical representations of two different visions of government. As one worldview sank, the other rose, clad in glowing white limestone and ringing with the happy hubbub of commercialized politics.

One summer day in 2006, while wandering the neighborhood, I paused to rest outside the Labor building for a moment and noticed that there were actual workers present—a crew of bricklayers silently replacing the pavers in the terrace outside the building's main entrance. What kind of workers, I wondered, did George W. Bush's Department of Labor hire when it needed work done on its own building? The first worker I approached couldn't say; he didn't speak much English. The foreman, though, was happy to answer the question: nonunion.

Maybe they could use a lobbyist.

CHAPTER 9

The Bantustan That Roared

Let us now put all these pieces together. We have examined conservative ideas toward government, conservative use of government power, and the acts of political entrepreneurship, great and small, that made conservatism a profitable industry. What did we get when all these elements were allowed to converge and flourish, unencumbered by the annoying strictures of liberalism?

What we got was Saipan, the largest island in the American territory known as the Commonwealth of the Northern Mariana Islands, or CNMI. Located on the far side of the Pacific Ocean, the CNMI is the most distant part of the United States. It is much closer to Japan (1,300 miles) than to San Francisco (5,600 miles). To travel to Saipan by airplane from Washington is a daunting journey that eats up at least twenty-four hours. To telephone people in Saipan during business hours, a resident of the capital must place his call at seven or eight the night before. Naturally the island boasts great physical beauty, tropical sunsets, glorious beaches, and so on. Every prospect pleases.

But the system that men devised for the place is what concerns us here. Variously hailed as "a perfect petri dish of capitalism" (Tom DeLay), a "laboratory of liberty" (*Washington Times*), a demonstration that "pro-business policies are pro-people policies" (Amy Ridenour), or as a place to seek "answers for the rest of the American family," in Congressman Brian Bilbray's immortal words,[1] the CNMI economy was, during the conservative era, the product of a unique economic deal the islands struck with the world; a deal in which wages could be kept extremely low, workers had no citizenship rights, and virtually the entire power of the state stood behind employers as they extracted profits from the toil of others.

For most of the workers who came to the islands over the last few decades, this arrangement meant indentured servitude; for a few, it was tantamount to slavery. For Tom DeLay, the situation was so gratifying that he promised personally to block all efforts to divert Saipan from its chosen course. "Stand firm," he once told a gathering of the island's overlords. "Resist evil. Remember that all truth and blessings emanate from our Creator."

I almost retched the first time I read that. Most liberals I know reacted the same way. Their mouths hung open; they could not believe what they were hearing; they seethed with rage. They shook their heads at that scoundrel DeLay and wondered how these people ever got to be such liars.

But in some fundamental way Tom DeLay was right about Saipan. So were all those newspaper columnists and feature writers who described the place as "America's Hong Kong" or "a free-market model" or "a vibrantly successful experiment in the unregulated free market."[2] Let us give them their due here: what happened on Saipan really *was* an experiment in the free market, in about as unregulated a state as it gets. It really *was* a model from which all the world could learn what happens when the laissez-faire believers get their way.

Even better: it was a proving ground of the conservative political philosophy. From the power of industry to the hounding of liberal critics to the deliberate sabotaging of good government, the CNMI episode was as fine a demonstration of the way conservative government works as we are likely to find anywhere.

If we include in this experiment not only the labor abuses that took place on Saipan proper but also all the political machinations that made those labor abuses possible—if we throw Tom DeLay into the petri dish along with Jack Abramoff, the CNMI's lobbyist, and if we add to the mix the various magazines and newspapers made to dance by the islands' money, and if we consider the $10,000-a-player golf outings and the "think tanks" for hire, and if we also toss in the ways in which conscientious civil servants were impugned, incompetence was rewarded, and the Department of the Interior itself was suborned, all so that a handful of manufacturers could enjoy slightly juicier margins—then we have *my* perfect petri dish of conservative governance.

So let us look closely at Saipan, this laboratory of misgovernment and exploitation. It was here that conservatism confronted—and vanquished—its original, fundamental enemy: labor. The war mobilized the entire right wing—from Christian soldiers, to national securitarians, to populists and libertarians. Saipan was where the fight against the left distilled itself down to its one essential and irreplaceable component: the war on the worker.

The story of American involvement in the Northern Mariana Islands began with World War II. The United States invaded Saipan in the summer of 1944, closing in on the Japanese home islands. The land battle was short but bloody: thousands of Japanese civilians who had settled on the island killed themselves rather than be captured. The naval battle was even more lopsided, with virtually all of Japan's remaining carrier-based air force shot down in two days. The Americans quickly built the neighboring island of Tinian into a vast airfield, servicing the B-29s that proceeded to reduce the cities of Japan to ashes.

Although it may not have been obvious at the time, World War II would eventually kill colonialism just as surely as it killed the fascist empires. While European administrations would limp along for a few years more in Africa and Asia, the racist doctrines that legitimated them were now as discredited and forgotten as the invincible European armies that had once propped them up. Decolonization became the irresistible wave of the next thirty years, spawning uprisings from Vietnam to Angola and setting the two superpowers in a desperate race to identify themselves with the black and brown people who were now, apparently, on history's winning side.

The remote Pacific islands that remained in American hands after the defeat of Japan were many thousands of miles from the main fronts of the war against colonialism, but the winds of history blew there nonetheless. Over the centuries the islands had been the property, successively, of Spain, Germany, and Japan, but by the 1960s and '70s the era of the colonial masters had passed. The novelist P. F. Kluge, who was a Peace Corps volunteer in Micronesia in the late sixties, had a front-row seat at the revolution. He watched the islanders refuse to be treated like just another Indian tribe, and he developed a romantic admiration for their leaders. "These were nation builders," he wrote, "San Martíns and Bolívars, Paines and Washingtons, and my pleasure, as I got to know them, was to wonder who was who."[3]

The Marianas played it differently. Here there was no question about whether or not to bind themselves to the United States: "The Northern Marianas leapt right into America's bait box," Kluge writes, "Charley the Tuna finally conning his way into a Chicken of the Sea can."[4] The only question was the deal's particulars, and the United States was ready to make concessions: the Saipanese had suffered much in the war, they lived in a remote place, and they had no industry to speak of. For these reasons, the 1978 covenant that made the islands an American commonwealth allocated a number of state powers to the CNMI itself. In order to jump-start their economy, the islanders were exempted from American quotas, tariffs, and minimum-wage laws. They also received control over immigration because they feared, in the words of the American diplomat who negotiated the covenant, "that U.S. immigration laws would permit an influx of aliens that would dilute the indigenous population."[5]

Within twenty years the Saipanese had imported so many outsiders to work in factories and construction that they, the "indigenous population," were a minority in their own country. From 1980 to 1997, when the Clinton administration issued a report on labor conditions on the islands, the population of the CNMI had increased by 250 percent, with aliens filling fully 90 percent of the private-sector jobs.[6]

It would be nice if we could point to a single individual or industry—Tom DeLay or the Chinese garment business, say—and blame them for the cinder-block Hades of toil and whoring that came together on Saipan. But the real culprit is something far more powerful than these limited, earthly actors. Consider the legal situation into which the CNMI had maneuvered itself by the mid-eighties.

- Immigration was, in effect, unlimited.[7]
- Immigrants were to be "guest workers," bound by contract to a particular employer; they could not become citizens or vote or even change jobs without the say-so of island labor authorities.[8]
- Guest-worker contracts ran for one year and were renewable

at the discretion of the employer; guest workers could also be deported instantly by their employer for the slightest offense.[9]

- The minimum wage, which most of these guest workers received, was much lower than in America; with a little ingenuity wages could be driven far lower still.[10]
- Enforcement of basic labor laws was extremely lax, and workers could even be confined to their "barracks" if their employer so desired.[11]
- On the other hand, there were "virtually no restrictions on investment and capital flow."[12]
- Taxes on capital were much lower than elsewhere in the United States.[13]
- Business owners were free to open and close, build and raze as they saw fit.[14]
- Anything manufactured on the islands could be tagged "Made in U.S.A." and exported to the American domestic market—the richest in the world—without quotas or tariffs.[15]
- Manufacturers and their property were protected by the laws and the armed forces of the United States.

Put such a list before the world, as Saipan did,[16] and any qualified MBA would instantly recognize it for what it was: a plan for a labor gulag; an island maquiladora. Tom DeLay was right to describe this as the free-market state in perfect miniature. This is what the management gurus worship under the name "flexibility": business would have every possible protection; labor would have virtually none.[17]

It doesn't require some evil genius to see the opportunity in this plan, although Saipan has been blessed with many of these. The personalities are in fact completely interchangeable, as are the locations. What happened in Saipan could have happened anywhere, had the locale in question been able to furnish the above political conditions. Had Nantucket Island or Yellowstone National Park been able to make such a proposal to the bankers of the world, the results would have been precisely the same. Colombians might have been the guest workers. Congolese might have been the investors. The winners might have built their castles in an English Baronial style rather than going with feng shui; they might have driven Harleys to the office instead of Rolls-Royces, they might have gotten tattoos and spent their vacations doing extreme geyser-boarding, but none of it would really have made much difference. Nor would the physical beauty of the locale in question, nor the intricate culture of the locals, nor the ancient traditions revered by the society's elders. Those would all be vaporized like Nagasaki. All that matters is that the offer was made—that the political conditions existed which allowed the offer to be made.

The market would do the rest.

The international garment industry was the first to buy what Saipan was selling. John Bowe, a journalist who has observed the islands' system firsthand, recounts how CNMI representatives in the eighties laid their wares before global "loophole shoppers" and quickly struck deals with manufacturers in Hong Kong and Korea. Within a few years there were thirty-six garment factories in operation on Saipan, running on the labor of workers imported from Korea, the Philippines, Thailand, and, above all, Communist China.[18]

What happened next on Saipan is a well-known media story. The garment manufacturers recruited their guest workers—most of whom forked over a hefty fee, usually borrowed, in exchange for the opportunity to work in "America"—and transported them to Saipan, where they lived in barracks specially built for the purpose. They worked unusually long shifts in unpleasant conditions, sometimes up to twelve hours a day, with extra pay for overtime an iffy proposition. And that was the whole of the workers' experience, by and large: factory and barracks, little more. In many cases they were prohibited from leaving the company compound, and some of them were required to sign contracts agreeing not to join unions, talk to American officials, or even to go on dates before they were permitted to work in the "laboratory of liberty."

Before long the guest worker system became a way of life on Saipan. There was a bottomless ocean of Asians out there to be hired, and human resources departments in every conceivable industry simply had to turn on the spigot: farmers, housekeepers, security guards, checkout clerks, gas station attendants, bookkeepers, hotel maids, casino workers, and even professionals (nurses, newspaper reporters, and engineers) were brought in. Although their contracts typically ran for only one year, they could be renewed by their employers, and guest workers in many occupations were essentially permanent residents of Saipan.

In the late eighties a typhoon of Japanese tourism swept over the CNMI and the construction and hospitality industries became major employers of imported labor. Casinos and luxury hotels made their inevitable appearance, along with the golf courses that would later make such a romantic backdrop for the visits of Saipan's conservative admirers. The indigenous islanders had also won from the United States the exclusive right to own land on the island, and many of them made millions leasing their property to resort developers. "The late eighties and early nineties were not just good years," writes John Bowe, "—they were amazing ones. The sleepy little island that hadn't even had traffic lights ten years earlier had suddenly become the Western Pacific's miracle of economic development."[19]

It was a great way to run a country, provided you were one of the group born with the right to vote and the right to own land—and not one of the poor fish who had signed away your freedoms in order to spend twelve hours a day sewing khakis for the frolicking youth of California.

Other than those who owned factories or stores, native-born islanders learned to stay away from the private sector, with its sub-lousy wages and abusive conditions. They tended either to work for the local government, where the wage scales were closer to American standards, or not to work at all. Even the locals who chose the latter quickly discovered the nifty advantages to which the island's magic wage-suppressing system entitled them. The hourly pay for domestic servants was driven so low—sixty-four cents an hour in the mid-nineties—that even people on relief could afford maids. We know this because in 1995 the local government actually had to forbid food-stamp recipients from employing housekeepers.[20] I guess it looked too unseemly.

But there was no disguising it. The class divide between indigenous islanders and the guest workers who supported them was so vast and so distasteful that virtually every independent account of Saipan to appear in the last ten years commented on it. Accounts of guest worker abuse—beatings, rapes, murders—grew so numerous it takes only a lazy Google search to unearth them.[21] Guest workers were routinely hit by cars according to John Bowe; in one incident he described, the police simply forgot about the case once they discovered it was a local who did the hitting-and-running.[22] An assistant U.S. attorney in that part of the world recalled for me how he once saw CNMI immigration police chase, beat, and then haul off a man who was almost certainly a garment worker who had displeased his employer in some way. "Perhaps later he was escorted back to his sewing machine, bloodied, ruffled, the defiance gone, and all the other workers got the message," this official wrote me. "Or maybe they cleared out his room that night and someone whispered that he was seen being taken to the airport, sent home penniless and in shame."

The sex industry was another central element of the CNMI setup. It arose, predictably enough, from the other two mainstays of Saipan's economy: the garment mills and the tourist trade. One part of the island was swarming with young, desperate, and sometimes even hungry female garment workers; the other part was filled with rich men on a spree. The most elementary economic forces dictated what came next, as a lush jungle of brothels and massage parlors and karaoke joints came to flourish on Saipan.[23]

All this brought about the unsavory sexual dynamic that always seemed to astonish visitors to Saipan. The place was an open sexual buffet for otherwise undesirable American men, a geriatric surf city with two girls for every geezer. One anthropologist who has studied the place described for me in 2007 how the men

> park outside the garment factories at shift changes waiting for girlfriends, they meet girls in clubs; men 50 and up walk around with women in their early 20s, old men marry teenagers—all these things exist everywhere in the world, but here they are common. Men sleep with a series of women who would not give them a second glance in any other society; men and women marry who have no language in common. . . . Marriages end very easily, when the wife ages and the husband finds a younger contract-worker wife.

The political effect of all this was to take the edge off the society's ugliness. Being swarmed nightly by easily accessible females apparently brightened even the gloomiest male dispositions. John Bowe saw the transformation many times. "Suddenly, it was okay that three quarters of the population lived as second class citizens and were frequently abused, even though this was supposedly the United States," he writes. "Three or four blow jobs into Saipan, most white men's reaction to Saipan seemed to evolve from 'Gee, this is wrong,' to 'Well, it's complicated.' "[24]

There were plenty of indigenous islanders who were disgusted by what has happened to their home, of course.[25] But the reaction that sticks in my mind is the utter complacency radiating from the following conversation, reported by the *San Francisco Chronicle* in 1999. "We've got a good thing here," one fellow said, standing on a Saipan beach, beer in hand. "If someone wants to come work for me for pennies, why shouldn't they be able to? I mean, why stop them?"[26]

Oh, there's been indignation. In the mid-nineties, the island system came under ferocious assault from the mainland media. Newspapers across the country ran exposés of the working conditions in the CNMI. Even *Reader's Digest* went after the place, calling it a "Shame on American Soil." The government of the Philippines, which furnished a good part of Saipan's labor, became so enraged that in 1995 it forbade its citizens to take jobs there until conditions improved.[27] In 1996, the legislature of Hawaii passed two resolutions denouncing the CNMI system.[28] The big-brand clothing companies came under pressure to drop their CNMI suppliers.

But this is a clinical examination of conservative governance, not a catalog of horrors, and once we have recovered from our initial shock, what intrigues us about this story is how, with no evident expertise in nineteenth-century history, the leaders of the Saipan garment industry proceeded to reconstruct the "satanic mills" of a century before in astonishing detail: the indebted workers, the company stores, the tricks used to extract unpaid hours, the exits that one researcher found to be nailed shut. A nice touch, that last. Very Triangle Shirtwaist. Very realistic.

This wasn't the work of some robber-baron reenactment club, however. It was simply the market doing what the market will always do, should it somehow get loose from the political cage. The animal is predictable. It will bid wages down and push profits up by any means it is permitted to use. Freed from the restraints built up over the years by unions and government, for example, every factory manager on earth will quickly discover that he can save a few pennies by, say, never having the toilets cleaned.

Another thing that outsiders always tended to notice about the CNMI was epic political corruption. As in the heroic period of American public venality, corruption on the islands generally took two basic forms. The first was petty nepotism, the appointing of friends and relatives to government jobs regardless of their qualifications. This practice was the subject of scrutiny ranging from the anthropological to the bureaucratic,[29] and it is of little concern in our analysis of conservatism, except for its indirect—but no doubt pleasing—effect of turning certain branches of government over to incompetents and thus helping to wreck them.

More significant, for our purposes, is the second, grander species of corruption: the conquest of government by private industry. As Interior Secretary Bruce Babbitt told Congress in 1998, the CNMI's government was "deeply in league with factory owners"; it was a place where American labor law effectively did not apply because "the [local] government has abdicated that responsibility in totality."*

What went on in the CNMI could not have happened without the active involvement of the state. Yes, this was a free-market paradise, as the libertarians assured the world on dozens of occasions, but a free-market system never simply means *do what thou wilt.*

---

*With a few exceptions, federal labor law did apply formally, of course. But thanks to the defunding of the Labor Department over the years, there was virtually no enforcement presence in the CNMI in those days.

Babbitt's remarks can be found on pages 18 and 44 of the March 31, 1998, hearing before the Senate Committee on Energy and Natural Resources.

To begin with, the state was required, at the most basic level, to maintain order in an unpleasant system where the impulse to down tools and say *take this job and shove it* must have run strong indeed. Contracts—sacred contracts—had to be enforced. Someone had to run down and beat the garment workers who needed beating. Even more important, the state had to ensure that workers were imported as industry saw fit. Were the immigration process regulated according to any other criterion, the CNMI's manufacturers might quickly have found themselves in some kind of bidding war for labor that would have caused wages to rise all on their own, minimum wage laws notwithstanding.

The state also had to maintain the pseudodemocracy that made all of this possible, with some inhabitants possessing only minimal civil rights while others voted, received benefits, sat on juries, and served in the legislature. Last, the state was required, in this imperfect, bureaucrat-ridden world of ours, to mollify the external powers-that-be—the fretful investors; the liberal fact-finders; the anxious home governments of the guest workers; our own federal government, sporadically wondering what the hell was going on—and to convince them that everything was being taken care of.

The Saipan experiment showed, once again, that a large and powerful government does not necessarily contradict the conservative credo. What makes a place a free-market paradise is not the absence of government; it is the capture of government by business interests.

Consider the islands' labor agency. As we have noted, the formal mission of the U.S. Department of Labor is to ensure that workers have a voice in government and that they are protected in the workplace. The reason the department exists and is so charged is that workers fought to make it this way. In the CNMI, however, workers had little voice and even less power. The islands' voters, by and large, benefited from cheap labor; the islands' leaders, by and large, sympathized with employers—hell, they *were* the employers, in some cases. In 1996, for example, the chairman of the CNMI's Wage and Salary Review Board also happened to be the personnel director of the island's largest garment manufacturer.[30] And the public servant who wrote the CNMI's guest worker law, Ben Fitial, went on to become a high-ranking officer of a related garment company and then an even higher ranking officer of the commonwealth itself.[31]

The main labor issue on Saipan was not protecting workers but disciplining them, a job that fell to an entity known until 1994 as the Department of Commerce and Labor and charged by legislation "to do any and all things necessary to stimulate economic growth in the private sector."[32] This, would have been an obvious contradiction anywhere else,[33] and, indeed, the department's name was eventually changed to Labor and Immigration (DOLI). But its mission apparently stayed the same. If you dig deep enough, for example, you will find a 1996 letter from the commonwealth's governor to the director of the local Chamber of Commerce advocating a "partnership between the Department [of Labor and Immigration] and the private sector," and it is easy enough to see what such a partnership entailed. DOLI worked hard to keep the cheap labor coming but could never seem to get off its ass when it came to stopping the rampant sweatshop-style abuses in Saipan's workplaces—abuses so well known, remember, that even *Reader's Digest* covered them. "The alien workers were not seen as American workers are seen. They were seen more as the property of the employers," a former attorney general of the CNMI explained to me. The local Department of Labor did little to keep them from "being locked up in barracks with fences around them, . . . and didn't even think there was any reason to investigate it."[34]

In 1994 and '95, the islands' raw material—the imported guest workers themselves—started refusing to play their assigned role. A wave of union organizing swept across Saipan, and the government was put to the ultimate test. Workers at grocery stores, restaurants, and several of Saipan's hotels decided to take matters into their own hands, with the assistance of an organizer sent by a hotel workers' union in Hawaii, one Elwood Mott.

But this kind of liberty—well, let's just say it might have blown up the laboratory altogether. CNMI officialdom reacted to the organizing drive with horror. It began with the first big push, at a Saipan hotel in 1994. The islands' legislative leaders insisted that the National Labor Relations Act, which establishes the right of Americans to join unions, did not apply to guest workers on the Marianas; besides, local representative Stanley Torres warned, if guest workers were permitted to organize, the resulting competition would make life harder for indigenous people "moving up the corporate ladder."[35] The hotel itself asked that its workers' right to unionize be suspended because, in the event of a strike, it might have trouble replacing them.[36]

The two sides fought their way through the courts for months, and—lo and behold—when the dust had settled, the guest workers had won. Panic convulsed the islands' employers as a nightmare scenario began unfolding before their eyes: the movement was going to spread from hotels to the garment industry and on across the islands' economy. " 'Stop the Unions,' " screamed a banner headline in the *Marianas Variety* in that summer of '95, quoting local business leaders. The labor movement "is like a disease growing at an epidemic proportion," one desperate corporate VP warned his colleagues; "we have to do something to control it." There were hurried meetings with legislators and fiery denunciations from the islands' elected officials.[37]

Representative Torres, a white-haired gent whom the newspapers sometimes pictured in an elegant panama hat, again took the lead. The fact that union members pay dues—that unions are not charitable organizations—struck him as a particularly poignant injustice, and he raged against the "profits" that the mother union back in Hawaii would make on the backs of the poor guest workers in Saipan, imagining how their dues would fill the bank accounts of "bigwigs in the States who drive around in limousines and smoke big cigars." He and his fellow legislators passed a right to work law in September 1995, and in December, with Torres leading the way, the CNMI's legislature unanimously declared Elwood Mott, the organizer from Hawaii, persona non grata. Ordinarily, this label is applied by a sovereign state to a foreign diplomat who has gotten out of hand; for an American territory to wield it against a citizen from another part of the country is like something out of the civil rights era, when southern tirades against "outside agitators" were an ugly commonplace.[38]

It was just the first of many such blows. Three months later Torres announced that he would introduce legislation limiting the stay of guest workers to only two years should they dare to join a union, and, in a statement released the same day, tacitly threatened them with blacklisting.

> Every worker should not forget that becoming a Union member will be a lifetime employment record and may haunted [*sic*] you everywhere you go when looking for a new job. And that is the truth. Think about your future, don't let Union [*sic*] destroy your BIO-DATA for future jobs.[39]

Meanwhile, Pete P. Reyes, the majority leader of the CNMI legislature, proposed another ingenious bit of legislation, this one requiring fired guest workers to be deported immediately rather than wait for any complaints that they might file to be resolved. Exasperated with uppity guest workers, Reyes told the local newspaper about a demonstration he had seen in which someone carried a sign that called Saipan "the island of abusers." "That placard is unnecessary, uncalled for and was done in poor taste," he steamed. "They have done injustice to their hosts."[40]

Against such opposition, and without resorting to massive civil disobedience, the guest-worker movement had little chance of gaining ground. But Saipan's rulers, whether frightened or furious, seemed to make the situation worse every time they opened their mouths.[41] Clearly they needed a practiced advocate, someone who could fight the left with the goal of victory. In the roar of the battle, they and Jack Abramoff found each other.

Abramoff's work for the CNMI was hugely successful: he beat back no fewer than twenty-nine efforts to bring the islands into line with American wage and immigration laws—one of them a bill introduced by a Republican and passed unanimously by the U.S. Senate[42] ("we stopped it cold in the House," Abramoff boasted to the CNMI's governor). More importantly, Abramoff managed to transform his client's petty and ugly political need into an ideological crusade. He was the ideal visionary for the job; throughout his career he had seen *freedom* where others saw ruin and exploitation, and now, on this distant Pacific island, Abramoff was going to drive his trademark hallucination home. Under his tutelage, and without changing a thing, Saipan was recast from a pariah state to a "laboratory of liberty,"* a shining beacon for the world.

---

*The phrase "laboratory of liberty" might well have been the official slogan for the CNMI lobbying campaign that Jack Abramoff ran. It showed up in the very first pro-CNMI article to appear after Abramoff was hired, "Tinkering with the Success of Liberty" by Peter Ferrara, which ran in the *Washington Times* on October 10, 1995, and which Abramoff faxed proudly to his clients on Saipan the next day, assuring them that "the Ferrara article hit yesterday with great fanfare."

In a July 24, 1996, letter to the governor of the CNMI, Froilan Tenorio, Abramoff boasts that the slogan is catching on. "Word is spreading fast among the free market conservatives that the CNMI is a 'laboratory of liberty,' " he writes, enclosing a manuscript copy of another essay, this time an effort by F. Andy Messing and Milton Copulos, two colleagues from his Conservative Caucus days.

The phrase was repeated again in a study authored by Doug Bandow and published by the Competitive Enterprise Institute in November 1996.

The very particular problems that the CNMI hired Jack Abramoff to solve in 1995 were similar in some ways to those of South Africa when *it* hired Jack Abramoff in 1986. Saipan, like South Africa, was a minority-run state in which most workers—or "labor units," as Pretoria sometimes called them—could neither vote nor own land, regardless of how long they had been there. And on Saipan, just as in the posh suburbs of Johannesburg, members of the ruling race protested the harsh way the outside world treated them just because they happened to live among multitudes of ethnic Others—people who had, after all, taken jobs of their own free will.

More to the point, Saipan considered itself, as had apartheid South Africa, a victim of bad press that scared off business and brought boycotts from other countries. South Africa's prosperity was threatened by corporate disinvestment, which came in response to widespread antiapartheid agitation; much of Saipan's troubles, meanwhile, came from clothing companies that didn't appreciate being linked to sweatshops. In both cases these skittish corporate types had to be reassured.

The "trips" program, Abramoff's great scheme for fighting back, was explicitly modeled on the tours South African business leaders once offered to influential outsiders.[43] The very particular way Abramoff ran his trips program—flying influential people to Saipan, maintaining a database of travelers, and constantly asking these travelers both to help with political efforts and to suggest new travelers—might well have been drawn from an article about South African PR efforts that appeared in one of the IFF's magazines in 1988.[44] A good number of those who eventually took trips to Saipan were also retreads from the IFF, either officers or contributors to one of the foundation's magazines.[45]

We get another glimpse of the strategies Abramoff would use from a memo dated January 31, 1998. Here the superlobbyist can be found describing how he and his colleagues would get ready for upcoming congressional hearings on the CNMI, "preparing questions and factual backup for the friendly Senators and Congressmen," and finding "friendly workers (one Chinese, one Filipino, one Bangladeshi)" to attest to the garment industry's wholesomeness. He boasts about the "positive pieces" he has been able to generate in the media; he lays plans to "develop Democrat friends" in Congress; he urges an expansion of the trips program. He also outlines a plan to "impeach" the character of Allen Stayman, an Interior Department official who oversaw the CNMI, and then to reduce the funds available to Stayman's office to an incapacitating minimum. (Defunding the office was better than abolishing it, Abramoff reasons, since it would not draw the attention of the media and also because it would prevent the Clinton administration from simply transferring the terminated office's duties elsewhere.) All this will require money, however, and Abramoff asks for more of it.[46]

The men he asks are the garment manufacturer Willie Tan and his then-employee Eloy Inos. Abramoff officially worked for the CNMI government, but it was simply understood that these men were the ones in charge.[47] Indeed, it is impossible to read an account of Saipan politics without sooner or later coming across Tan's name. He was one of the first to spot the opportunities Saipan presented, and to open a garment factory on the island. At the zenith of his power, he controlled garment factories, an airline, hotels, shipping, a fishing fleet; at one point he was the largest employer on the island, the largest taxpayer, and even the recipient of the largest fine ever levied by the U.S. Department of Labor, an accomplishment viewed with admiration in some circles. In classic robber-baron style, Tan also owned one of the two local newspapers, the *Saipan Tribune,* where a staff of crusading journalists deplored "the dirty infestation of labor unions into our economy and society," penned masterpieces such as the 1997 editorial "Thank You, Willie Tan!," and wished upon "those who flaunt the rights of employees" what a columnist tastefully called

> punishment Mexican Style: Sent [*sic*] the bastards to jail and while looking to see you off, flush the keys into their own toilet bowls. That ought to do the job loud and cleeeaaaa![48]

The job of politicians, Willie Tan has said, is to work "with those that have invested a great deal here," and if he is not by this definition the outright political boss of Saipan, his role is, at the very least, quasi-governmental.[49] When Abramoff's contracts with the CNMI government came up for renewal, Willie Tan's newspaper provided support for "Our Freedom Fighter in DC"; when relations between the government and the superlobbyist soured, Tan organizations took up the slack, paying Abramoff's fees and keeping him working on the same targets.[50]

On one such occasion even stronger measures were called for. The CNMI had declined to renew Abramoff's contract, and in a kind of extreme case of his K Street strategy, Tom DeLay dispatched two emissaries to Saipan to make sure his man was rehired. As it happened, the former Tan executive Ben Fitial was standing for the speakership of the CNMI House of Delegates. But his victory looked unlikely. Using promises of federal largesse, DeLay's envoys persuaded two members of that body to change their votes in Fitial's favor. Order was restored: Fitial won; the delegates got their federal project; the Marianas House, now led by Fitial, pressed for Abramoff's rehiring; Abramoff was duly reappointed the CNMI's white knight. And the whole crooked operation was paid for by Willie Tan, with a check routed through Amy Ridenour's National Center for Public Policy Research.[51]

That was in 1999. Before long the conquest was complete. Tan's man Eloy Inos eventually took a job in the government proper, the secretary of finance for the CNMI. At the top of the roster, as governor of the commonwealth, was smiling Ben Fitial, hailed by Tan's newspaper as a "man of vision."[52]

Fitial was quite direct about the whole thing: it was a business government. Here is *Pacific* magazine's account of his January 2006 inauguration.

> Fitial also had a warning for all government officials at departments and agencies that deal with the economy: "All must adopt a pro-business mindset, ready to welcome and facilitate lasting investments into our islands. If you have a different agenda, then be prepared for a permanent reassignment elsewhere." That phrase drew the loudest cheers from the 1,500 people who attended the ceremony at the Marianas High School gymnasium.[53]

Forget trying to reform Saipan, said Tom DeLay in 1998. An entire commonwealth organized as a corporate labor camp, with wages free to fall as low as the market sees fit, an electorate drawn only from the winners, a wildly pro-business government, and savagely pro-business newspapers—why, this was an arrangement that we should be studying and learning from. We should emulate Saipan, he told the *Houston Chronicle*; we should set up a program just like theirs, "where particular companies can bring Mexican workers in" and pay them "whatever wage the market will bear."[54]

There is something about the combination of isolated places and free-market ideology that conservatives find irresistible, and over the years their fancy has turned to a series of low-tax Shangri-las, each one even more fabulous than the one preceding: Switzerland, Hong Kong, Singapore, Bahrain, the Isle of Man, air-conditioned Dubai, and beautiful Andorra, where, a promotional Web site promises, "there is no hint of a 'socialist mentality' among the natives." The wingers' dreams shimmer with visions of enterprise zones and bank accounts in the Caymans; of maquiladoras and SEZs; of liberated spaces where, by some accident of history, the leaden workings of leftism have been suspended. And when they can't offshore it all, they can join the movement to transform New Hampshire, through a massive *voortrek* of wingers, into a true "free state."[55]

Then there are the "lessons" that conservatives ask us to learn from these remote free-market paradises. The experience of Chile, for example, was long thought sufficient to compel, all by itself, the privatization of America's Social Security system. Singapore offers entire volumes of lessons, instructing us in everything from market-based traffic solutions to the magic of "depoliticization."

No one looks for a role model in apartheid South Africa anymore. But perhaps they should. This was the place where first world met third, the Afrikaners used to say; the land where a civilization of Mercedes-driving suburbanites came face-to-face with people who lived in huts made of sticks and plastic bags.[56] Today, this idea of "first world meets third" is no longer such an exotic concept. In some ways that's us. That's Europe, too. That's Ireland and France and Brazil and India and Malaysia and Mexico. It is now such a common feature of the "New Economy" that business gurus frankly insist on this mix: you can't have a properly profitable system *unless* you have plenty of surplus third worlders around to work their magic—that is, to work for pennies.

Apartheid was a costly and murderous way of managing this situation. But South Africa pioneered other models as well, half-remembered schemes in which low-tax zones and union-free labor forces were delivered and disciplined not by brutal white cops but by indigenous leaders bubbling over with ethnic pride.

One of these was the Republic of Ciskei, a black "homeland" set up by the apartheid regime as part of its scheme for gerrymandering South Africa into a permanent white majority. As a supposedly independent country, Ciskei and the other Bantustans allowed Pretoria to transform the country's labor force into foreigners.[57] The white government could declare black people who met certain criteria to be citizens of Ciskei—and possibly move them there by force—even if they had never been there before. The ministate was ruled over by a "president for life" who installed his brother as military chieftain, built monumental statues of himself, and even provided a haven for an alleged mafia kingpin so this figure could set up a bank in his savage little republic.[58] For the labor movement, however, he had a special malevolence, regularly beating and imprisoning its partisans. Poets and playwrights, too, were warned to watch their step.[59] And all of it was done in the name of ethnic pride, monumentalized with a Ciskeian national shrine and aristocratic pedigrees that were trumped up for the Bantustan's leaders.[60]

English-speaking conservatives loved Ciskei, the self-proclaimed "Hong Kong of Africa." Promotional materials trumpeted its corporate tax rate of zero, its flat income tax, its "unparalleled labor peace," and its "generous concessions—acknowledged as of [*sic*] the best in the world—to industrialists." The president for life not only busted union heads but also abandoned virtually all economic regulations.[61] Besides, the Bantustan's number two talked precisely like an American wingnut. Sitting through a session of this grandee's ferocious anticommunist oratory, the *New York Times* reporter Joseph Lelyveld was astonished to hear the man quote from a book popular with the John Birch Society and marveled that "there is an international traffic in cast-off conspiracy theories as well as cast-off machinery and garments."[62]

For the kind of conservatives we have been considering, however, these ideas were anything but castoffs. Howard Phillips's heart went pitter-pat for the union-free Bantustan with the big libertarian ideas. "The investment opportunities and the low-tax, regulation-free, pro-free enterprise attitude there will surprise you!" he wrote.[63]

The South African libertarian Leon Louw, although an opponent of apartheid, was one of Ciskei's great boosters. In a best-selling book, Louw speculated about the Bantustan's glorious future as a "libertarian mecca" should it be permitted to proceed in its chosen path: "Radical deregulations" would free up its economy and its libido alike, making it a fantastic success. Oh, there would be pornography, prostitutes, and all the dope you could smoke; there would be a seaside resort with casinos, yachting, and "oriental pleasure palaces"; and there would be . . . *golf*. A cartoon is included to make the idea memorable: a lumpy white guy, golf clubs bouncing on his shoulder, runs excitedly into the welcoming arms of ecstatic nude showgirls; on a distant hill, two scolding figures wag their fingers in disapproval. One is in a top hat and tie, representing the moralistic right; the other is in a Mao suit, representing the moralistic left.[64]

The Ciskeian fantasy ended in 1994, when the Bantustans were reincorporated into South Africa. The distant Pacific island of Saipan, however, lived out the Bantustan-capitalist dream with uncanny success, right down to the clucking disapproval of the moralistic liberals, who could never seem to lighten up about the sweatshop thing. Saipan never had a problem with moralistic conservatives, though. Indeed, if the prayerful Tom DeLay is any indication, moralistic conservatives were among the most enthusiastic Saipan supporters of them all, their precious values forgotten as soon as they caught a glimpse of the money on the table.

The summit of the liberal campaign to federalize the CNMI's wage and immigration laws was reached during a 1998 Senate committee hearing on conditions there, at which the secretary of the interior himself described the islands as "a plantation economy." Abramoff had prepared carefully, and as part of his program the committee heard from a representative of the Saipan Chamber of Commerce. "To quote Dr. Martin Luther King, Jr." she ended her testimony, " 'We must not allow . . . any force to make us feel like we don't count. Maintain a sense of dignity and respect.' A federal takeover of immigration and federalization of minimum wage laws strips the CNMI of its pride, dignity and respect."[65]

This was the final tactic of Abramoff's grand lobbying strategy. Virtually whenever he was called upon to defend the economic policies of Saipan, he or his colleagues pulled ethnic victimhood. The good people of the CNMI, they would plead, were merely a downtrodden people—an *indigenous* people—desperately trying to lift themselves up from decades of dependency. They were the victims of racism. They were the victims of colonialism. And to question their economic arrangements was an act of racism against the people of Saipan. Abramoff never claimed that importing bonded labor was a sacred Micronesian tradition the world needed to respect, and he never talked the commonwealth's governor into building a national shrine featuring heroic-sized statues of himself. But otherwise, his CNMI campaign seemed to come straight out of old Ciskei.

Thus did a hired gun for apartheid South Africa remake himself as a hair-trigger antiracist, fighting colonialism and deploring bigotry in places where most people saw only disputes over treaties and concerns about low-wage workers. Every defense of the CNMI followed the same script. First, to enforce U.S. labor and immigration laws on this U.S. commonwealth, as liberals wanted to do, was an act of colonialism, if not racism or genocidal fascism. Second, low taxes, low wages, and an unrestricted guest-worker program were the true components of "freedom" and also, between them, the policies that brought independence from colonial powers.

Abramoff's comments to the press about the CNMI's cause were a fine example of the strategy. Leaving aside the denials that are a routine part of a lobbyist's business—*nope, no sweatshops here*—he repeatedly flashed the anticolonialism card. "You know what all this fuss is really about?" he asked the *Seattle Times*.

> It's that the people of this beautiful island finally have broken out of U.S. dependency. They live on a warm, tropical island with beaches and they've always been dependent, but now they want to make their own economy and not be on welfare.
>
> I think what's going on here is the radical left simply is not happy about that.

He told the *Washington Post* that forcing the CNMI to comply with American law was, in the newspaper's paraphrase, like "the Nuremberg Laws restricting Jews' activities under the Nazis."

> "These are immoral laws designed to destroy the economic lives of a people," Abramoff said. Conservatives

> "see in this battle a microcosm of an overall battle. . . . What these guys in the CNMI are trying to do is build a life without being wards of the state."[66]

It was freedom-fighting all over again, with independence defined as a matter not so much of self-government for the islanders but of the islanders' right to reap the human harvest that the vagaries of the global economy had sent their way.

The paroxysm of sympathy for the CNMI's struggle against colonialism that seized America's conservative press beginning in 1996—and which we now know to have been organized by Abramoff—followed this line slavishly. "Keeping Uncle Sam out of Saipan," chided a typical 1997 op-ed in the *Washington Times*, a paper that ordinarily defends Uncle Sam's right to be wherever he chooses. The Democratic push to enforce U.S. law in the CNMI, its author insisted, was nothing but a reversion to the high-handed ways of the islands' Spanish conquerors many centuries ago.

One point that proved tricky was deciding just who the American liberals were being racist against. Some writers thought it was the very guest workers the libs meant to help. After all, since those Chinese and Filipinos had *chosen* to come to Saipan, according to free-market theory they had thus endorsed the peculiar institutions of the CNMI in every particular; to assume that bureaucrats in Washington knew better than them was ipso facto the vilest sort of ethnocentrism. "There is a hint of racism," thundered an editorial in the *Journal of Commerce*, a shipping industry trade magazine, "when U.S. officials imply that these thousands of workers ignored their best interests to go to Saipan."[67]

On the islands themselves, the answer was always the reverse: Efforts to relieve the plight of the guest workers were the unmistakable mark of racism toward the indigenous islanders.[68] The columnists for Willie Tan's newspaper played this particular chord loud and often. The liberals, they would insist, were engaged in a demonic attempt "to curtail freedom, eradicate local self-government, and impose their imperialistic will." They had a "racist agenda of economic annihilation—equivalence [*sic*] of the Nuremburg [*sic*] case." They were trampling "the rights of the indigenous people to self-government and the freedom to build upon wealth and jobs creation." All of which, by extension, made Jack Abramoff "a kind of hero to the indigenous people of the CNMI"; "an ardent champion of the little guy—of the much maligned Northern Marianas as well as the Choctaw Indian tribe of Mississippi." [69]

Abramoff apparently thought this picture of indigenous people resisting liberal imperialism was so compelling that it could pull onto the Marianas bandwagon the leaders of the African-American community, who had traditionally been strong critics of imperialism. According to a 1998 memo, members of the Congressional Black Caucus were to be particular targets of Abramoff's campaign to "develop" Democrats for the CNMI; two of them actually took trips to the islands (since their trips were sponsored by yet another friendly nonprofit, these representatives were unaware of Abramoff's involvement). Another tactic in this quixotic campaign was school vouchers, the issue which always seems to come up when conservatives are moved to consider the black electorate. Proclaiming in 1997 that the CNMI—as part of its well-known devotion to free-market principle—was about to approve a vouchers program, Abramoff's team brought various CNMI officials to the mainland and hooked them up with leading conservative voucher advocates and inner-city education activists in Cleveland, Milwaukee, and Washington, D.C.

What the superlobbyist seems to have understood was that any consideration of labor abuses in Saipan could be stopped cold by a fusillade of righteous ethnic authenticity. Abramoff was not the first to figure this out, of course. Applying the "racist" label to critics of outsourcing, offshoring, and even business generally is a familiar reflex of the "New Economy" mind. Surely you know the litany by now: the new, exuberant capitalism is leveling the barriers between peoples, flattening the world, and bringing us all closer together; to resist or even to criticize this new capitalism is to align yourself somehow with the forces of racist "protectionism." Entire books have been written to push this rattlebrained notion. It is the stuff from which D.C. think-tank careers are made. Even South Africa got into this act, as we have seen, transferring the guilt for its system of apartheid, once it was no longer defensible, to the regime's great enemy, socialism.

With Abramoff, the maneuver seemed to become instinctive. When the *Washington Post* ran the 2004 story on his Indian casino lobbying that shattered Abramoff's career, the superlobbyist's immediate reaction was to accuse the reporter of racism—against Indians, in this case. The article's main point had been that Abramoff's tribal clients spent more on lobbying than the largest companies in America. And that was enough to trigger the predictable accusation: "The reporter was a real racist and bigot," Abramoff wrote in a February 23, 2004, e-mail, "but that seems pretty obvious with the implication that Native peoples don't have the same rights that companies do to defend themselves."

By the following day, Abramoff's team had prepared an antiracist counterattack against the *Post*. They had drawn up three accusatory letters to the paper that were to be signed by Abramoff's Indian clients, each one following the same deploring line: the *Post*'s writer harbored "racial prejudices against Native Americans"; she made "highly racist remarks" and showed a "racially prejudiced disapproval of [the] dollar amounts" that the tribes had paid Abramoff. What made her article so racist was its denigration, by the faintest suggestion, of "the decision-making capabilities of the members of my Tribe in choosing our own representation in the nation's capital." To say that the tribes were ripped off by their lobbyist, in other words, was to imply that they were too dumb to manage their own affairs and hence to "undermin[e] tribal self-determination."[70]

A Senate committee began investigating Abramoff's lobbying activities the following year, and by then this particular canard no longer swam. It had come out that, when he wasn't busy championing the rights of indigenous peoples, Abramoff had a habit of referring to Indians as "troglodytes," "monkeys," "idiots," and "morons." His career as a "freedom fighter" for the colonized was over—but the fatuous idea of free markets as benevolent protectors of the downtrodden continues on as strong as ever.

Saipan, eventually, reached its boiling point. With its champion lobbyist behind bars and the Democrats he antagonized in charge of Congress, the "federalization" dreaded so long by the islands—namely, the same minimum wage and immigration system as everywhere else in America—is finally coming to pass. Confronted with the terrifying possibility that the people they exploited for two decades might one day become citizens and vote, the CNMI legislature in 2007 enacted a measure obviously designed to make it even easier for business owners to cheat guest workers and deport them at will.[71] In response to this provocation, the workers on Saipan began organizing again, and in response to *that,* the rhetoric of indigenous pride reached new octaves of offended righteousness.[72] Thus do we take our leave of this angry paradise, this laboratory of loathing, as it makes itself ready for the reward that history assigns the market's truest believers.

CHAPTER 10

Win-Win Corruption

In the preceding pages, we have watched our Washington wingers be drawn by some weird ideological magnet to virtually every morally indefensible cause of the last thirty years. They cheered for South Africa, swooned for Jonas Savimbi, admired the Contras and the Central American death squads, and when Saipan needed help defending its monstrous labor system virtually the entire movement pitched in.

What's more, in certain cases we have noticed that conservative support for these causes ebbed or flowed depending on their profit potential. We have even seen, in a few spectacular instances, how conservative anticorruption outfits got involved in promoting these obviously corrupt causes.[1]

What makes all this particularly strange is that conservatives once understood themselves as warriors against venality. Until the offenses of the Bush administration and the DeLay Congress made such an image inoperable, clean politics was a subject the right thought it owned. Corruption was something that only conservatives really understood.

What should be clear after this by no means exhaustive accounting is that Washington conservatives merely understood corruption differently than the rest of us. Take the matter of intellectual integrity. What does it entail? Well, to professional scholars and, presumably, to the rest of us, it means a nonpartisan atmosphere in which research could be conducted free from economic or other types of coercion.

On the right, however, where professional scholarship is often regarded with suspicion, the situation was so different that even the most extreme bias was really no cause for shame. "We're not here to be some kind of Ph.D. committee giving equal time," an officer of the Heritage Foundation told a reporter in 1986. "Our role is to provide conservative public-policy makers with arguments to bolster our side. We're not troubled over this."[2]

Some of the intellectuals dirtied most by the scandals of the last few years struck similar chords. There was nothing really wrong with what they did, they insisted, and so they remained defiant. The libertarian pundit Peter Ferrara, who confessed to taking money in exchange for stories puffing up Jack Abramoff's various clients, said, "I do that all the time. . . . I've done that in the past, and I'll do it in the future."

After admitting to the same thing, the libertarian pundit Doug Bandow tried to cleanse himself by plunging the rest of the world in self-interest. In a fire-breathing *vostra culpa* published in 2006, Bandow insisted that everyone is compromised somehow, that every think tank and foundation has an agenda. "The number of folks underwriting the pursuit of pure knowledge can be counted on one hand, if not one finger," he scoffed. So where was his sin?[3]

Besides, Bandow was something of an expert on corruption. In 1990, he published an entire book on the subject, *The Politics of Plunder,* in which he attacked "legalized larceny" (farm programs), "mass transit robbery" (public transportation), and "consumer fraud" (the FTC and FDA).[4]

This, too, was typical of winger Washington. Corruption was a subject conservatives thought they understood well; it suffused their every statement about politics; they simply located it somewhere else—in the liberal state, whose very existence they knew to be a rigged game in which powerful insiders advanced their own interests. Conservatives thought they could spot bullshit a mile away; they saw lies and theft and even extortion in every bit of liberal legislation; and they were champion accusers, charging their enemies with corruption almost as a matter of course.

Bribery? Well, the wingers would demand, what do you call all the subsidies and welfare and food stamps and affirmative action and Social Security benefits that flow from Uncle Sam to the "special interests" who keep returning these damned liberals to Congress? *Self-aggrandizement?* How about the vast army of bureaucrats and Washington "experts" whose only concern is to grab more power for themselves, to exert control over every little aspect of the economy? *Theft?* Isn't that just a synonym for *income tax?* And isn't *waste* a synonym for all the idiotic pork-barrel projects on which they blow our money? *Political machine?* Why, isn't that what you call such an arrangement in its entirety?

The welfare state isn't a "safety net" or an improved, scientific form of civilization, according to this view; it's a systematically organized ripoff in which all the liberal elements—from the media to the trial lawyers—have a designated role to play. The liberal state has no more claim to legitimacy than the thief who robs you at gunpoint. *The system is corruption itself.*

In its heyday, conservative Washington was saturated with these ideas: The Federal Reserve as a "legal counterfeiter" because it is empowered to adjust the nation's money supply. The Community Reinvestment Act, which outlaws redlining, as "a blackmail tool." Social Security as a "Ponzi scheme." The EPA as "the

Gestapo of government." The operations of city governments as "looting." As for taxation, wrote Grover Norquist, "your average street mugger is an improvement. He knows it's your wallet. He knows you earned the money. He just wants it for himself and he is straightforward enough to say, 'Give me your money, I have a knife.' Muggers understand this transaction."[5]

The most improbable corruption theorist on the conservative scene was Michael Scanlon, the aforementioned aide to Tom DeLay. Scanlon went on to work briefly on Jack Abramoff's lobbying team and then started what appeared to be a freelance PR consultancy. In congressional hearings it emerged that the superlobbyist would push his tribal casino clients to hire Scanlon's PR firms, who would then do unremarkable propaganda work for them at exorbitant rates, and secretly kick back half of the take to Abramoff. Like a bumbling gangster in a mafia movie, Scanlon eventually blew the whole operation by flaunting his winnings, buzzing back and forth by helicopter from his apartment in one of the city's Ritz-Carltons to the seaside town where he had bought a mansion from the Du Ponts.

Once all this was exposed and Scanlon had pleaded guilty, he had plenty of spare time on his hands. So he went and got his expertise in corruption certified officially, writing a master's thesis in 2006 on the history of ethics enforcement in the U.S. House of Representatives.

Scanlon's conclusion: *ethics enforcement is futile.* The ethics process is hopelessly partisan, just a different way for the majority party to police and punish their opponents. What's more, Scanlon wrote, it has "always" been this way; it has changed "only slightly" since the earliest days of the Republic.[6] Even the House Ethics Committee was itself just another product of partisan warfare.* "Mem-

*Tom DeLay's thoughts on the matter: precisely the same! "Unfortunately," he wrote in his memoirs, "ethics charges in the House of Representatives have become so politicized that you can't trust what you hear about them anymore." (DeLay with Mansfield, *No Retreat, No Surrender,* p. 144.)

bers of Congress took bribes in 1870, just as Duke Cunningham did in 2006," Scanlon reasons; ergo, bribe taking is a historical constant, unaffected by silly contrivances like ethics committees.[7]

In reality, corruption changes and develops all the time, just like other types of entrepreneurship; it even evolved considerably during the years in which Scanlon himself plied the trade. Compare, for example, the congressional outrage that propelled the reformers DeLay and Gingrich to power in 1994—the House Banking Scandal, in which congressmen wrote lots of bad personal checks—with the revelations of 2006: the selling of earmarks, the wholesale sabotage of government agencies, the pissing away of billions in no-bid contracts to whoever threw the most lavish party. In those twelve years the art of the graft advanced at a gallop.

For Scanlon, though, corruption is eternal and therefore unremarkable—a bit of schoolboy cynicism we should probably expect from a man who at thirty-three years of age had already bribed a member of Congress, cheated his clients out of millions, tinkered with the legislature of an American commonwealth, and cheered on Tom DeLay's campaign to impeach the president of the United States.[8]

But Scanlon's theories of corruption were more than mere rationalization. His way of understanding corruption is an essential enabling ingredient of corruption itself. It is the ideology of thieves.

This view of government as a criminal gang is not limited to the wingnuts and chiselers who have been our subjects thus far; it also has an academic component. The field is a subset of economics, of course; it exists only in America, of course; and its leading scholar is one Fred McChesney, a professor of law at Northwestern whose ideas are well known in libertarian circles and whose essays appear frequently in *Regulation,* a magazine published by the Cato Institute.

McChesney's feats of interpretation all arise from his realization that *government*—sometimes he puts the word in quotes—is merely a collection of self-interested individuals. Being in government gives these special people "a property right, not just to legislate rents [winger-speak for *dish out special favors*] but to impose costs." This epiphany allows McChesney to turn the usual interpretation of money-in-politics on its head: where most observers see politicians doing the bidding of their paymasters, McChesney claims that what's really going on is "rent extraction," otherwise known as extortion, in which politicians demand a cut of a business's profits by "threatening to impose costs—a form of political blackmail."[9]

One way politicians impose these costs is through regulation, which is often tantamount to theft. By certifying that any product in a given field won't kill you, federal quality standards—pure food and so on—nullify the reputations for quality and goodness that individual companies in the field have built up at great expense over the years.[10] Regulatory agencies, meanwhile, are the bookkeepers for the gang: Figuring out the amounts to be gouged from industries is so complicated that the blackmail operation known as government requires specialized "knowledge of elasticities."[11]

As an example, McChesney gives the story of the Federal Trade Commission, which was ordered by Congress in the 1970s to regulate certain industries; the FTC duly came up with the requested rules, but Congress nixed them in 1982 amid a steady rain of PAC money from the affected businesses. What this reversal demonstrated, to most observers, was how big money gets its way despite the general interest.[12] But in McChesney's account, the only significant fact is that Congress and the FTC are both arms of the beast "government," which means that the FTC was deliberately sicced on those particular industries in order to precipitate the PAC-money cloudburst of 1982. McChesney offers no evidence to prove that this was anyone's intent or even that the congressmen who proposed the regulations received the payoff; the fact that the events happened in the order they did is supposed to be convincing enough to convict the system.[13]

The conspiracy theory of regulation is something you can hear at any Rotary Club in America, without the footnotes and economic equations: business is a legitimate institution, the theory insists; government is a bipartisan criminal conspiracy that marauds and steals and provides nothing. Even in the heyday of the free market, business was still supposed to be society's great victim, honest and hardworking; government was still the corrupt tyrant that exploited everyone else with its misbegotten power to tax and regulate.

Theories like these are the reason why, in conservative Washington, you could be an ideologue and a corruptionist at the same time; a true believer and a wrecker both. They are also the reason catastrophe and failure were the inevitable consequences of the movement's rule.

Let us take as an example, one last time, the various misdeeds of Jack Abramoff: soaking his clients, taking kickbacks from Scanlon, bribing government officials, and so on. Were they really violations of free-market principle?

Consider the original accusation of wringing unseemly amounts from clients. The 2004 *Washington Post* story that first broke the scandal, "A Jackpot from Indian Gaming Tribes," did not accuse Abramoff of bribing anyone; it merely pointed out that he received "10 or 20 times" what the tribes' previous lobbyists made—much more when you factored in the kickbacks he received via Scanlon—and that at this rate the tribes were spending almost as much on lobbying as General Electric, the world's second largest corporation.[14] Many of the details to emerge in the months that followed merely added color to this picture: Scanlon descending on one desperate tribe to grab "all their

MONEY!!!" Abramoff boasting how he told another tribe "to come up with the dough or prepare for another trail of tears!!!" And so on.

But who was to say what constituted overcharging or overspending? In conservative land, where the market was the only rightful setter of prices, if someone was willing to pay a price, that price was correct. To complain about "price gouging," as liberals often did, was to remind the *Wall Street Journal* of "the old Soviet politburo," to "defy even junior-high-school economics."[15] To legislate against price gouging was to criminalize the basic workings of supply and demand; to apply, by extension, such logic to lobbying would have been to criminalize a basic element of democracy itself, the right to petition Congress for redress of grievances.

Or take kickbacks, like the under-the-table payments Abramoff received from Scanlon after recommending him to his tribal clients. Sure, this was fraud, as well as a violation of Abramoff's fiduciary duty to his client, but "fiduciary duty" is an artificial construct that science can pierce at a glance. In fact, as economics believes it has proven, kickbacks can often be beneficial, since they give professionals an incentive to refer a client to a specialist instead of doing the work themselves.[16]

Other stigmatized financial activities can be vindicated just as easily. The anti-corruption crusader Doug Bandow not only had no problem with price gouging but during the eighties he was a prominent defender of insider trading. (Since "we are all better off the faster share prices reach their correct levels," as he put it.)[17] That friend of the freedom fighter Jack Wheeler has praised the Internet for making "money laundering available to anyone, not just to huge multinationals and international drug cartels."[18] *National Review* put up a spirited defense of Michael Milken's corporate takeover strategies throughout his troubles with the law.[19] And then there is price fixing, the defense of which was the subject of the first *Wall Street Journal* op-ed I ever read. It gave me such a shock that I remember the argument to this day: It wasn't that ADM (the agribusiness giant that was then much in the news) was innocent of conspiring to set prices with one of its competitors, but that government had no business criminalizing such things in the first place.[20]

Always would the argument thus return to the libertarian basics: the tyranny of the regulatory state and the oppression under which it ground the entrepreneur and the hardworking stockholder. The truly corrupt party was Uncle Sam himself, and virtually any tactic is justified to relieve those poor souls who suffered under his iron heel: the owners of casinos, the brave garment manufacturers of the Mariana Islands, the businessman subjected to political "rent extraction."

The bribing of politicians, however, is an operation so stigmatized that even *National Review* won't try to rescue it. But some dare. When government activity is a form of extortion, wrote Fred McChesney in 2006, " 'corruption' "—he puts the word in quotation marks—"actually can be a good thing, if paying a small bit of baksheesh avoids political depredations that would wreak even greater economic havoc." If government is the enemy of free markets, bribery is just the market acting in self-defense. After reminding us that a little corruption would have been a good thing in Nazi Germany, McChesney made this reference to our own federal government: "In the real world of rent extraction, the only thing worse than a corrupt government official is an honest one."[21] And the best public servant, as we know too well, is the worst one.*

---

*The godfather of this argument is surely political scientist Samuel Huntington. "In terms of economic growth, the only thing worse than a society with a rigid, overcentralized, dishonest bureaucracy is a society with a rigid, overcentralized, honest bureaucracy," Huntington wrote in his 1968 book, *Political Order in Changing Societies*. "A society which is relatively uncorrupt—a traditional society for instance where traditional norms are still powerful—may find a certain amount of corruption a welcome lubricant easing the path to modernization."

* * *

And when this bunch had finished their work, what did they tell us then?

They said, with a laugh, that the only way to keep them from doing it again was for us to give up. To have a government that tries to redistribute wealth inevitably attracts the gnawing and the blighting of creatures like them. "The problem is that the federal government hands out billions of dollars, and people will lie, cheat, steal, or bribe to get it," Grover Norquist once told a libertarian magazine.

> If you have a big cake, and you put it under the sink and then you wonder why the cockroaches are in your kitchen, I don't think any sprays or blocking the holes in the walls are going to get rid of the cockroaches. You've got to throw the cake in the trash so that the cockroaches don't have something to come for.[22]

It's a funny thing, though: I've been eating cake all my life, and I've never had problems with cockroaches. And just as there are millions of other people whose cake-eating experiences are largely cockroach-free, so there are also millions who live under governments run by capable professionals, not hacks bent on wrecking the operation; entire countries where American-style scandals are as rare as sweatshops. But conservatives blocked out this possibility as though it were some kind of schoolboy utopia, some French absinthe dream. For these hardheaded pragmatists it was always one or zero, remember, government or no government. If you didn't like what Norquist's buddies were doing in Washington, your only alternative was to give up on economic justice altogether, to throw the whole thing in the trash.

Although Norquist made this analogy back in 1997, it was

the conservative movement's standard, all-purpose reaction to the scandals of 2005 and 2006. If you don't like corruption, you had to do away with government.[23] Abramoff himself even made the point in a 2006 interview with *Vanity Fair*: "The only thing that a clever lobbyist cannot manipulate," he said, "is the absence of something to lobby for or fight against."[24]

This is a theory of political venality that is deeply entangled with venality itself. When a free-market theorist says that the answer to corruption is *no government* and is then seconded by the leading corruptionist of the time, a "free-marketeer"[25] who says that *no government* is the only way you will stop people like him, we have come very close to a union of theory and practice. Free-market theory, that is, and practices that should have turned the stomach of every believer in democracy. Seen this way, corruption is just another way to attack the liberal state, a sort of street theater in which the right-wing provocateur makes his point about government by demonstration. Give him what he wants, or he'll do it again.

The truly prodigious feature of corruption is that it is often self-reinforcing. Not only does it enrich the corruptionist in an immediate way, but when it is done grandly enough, corruption can actually destroy public faith in the very possibility of noncorruption. This is the unintentional lesson of *Making Democracy Work,* a book about good government that the sociologist Robert Putnam wrote comparing those parts of Italy where government functions well to those places where it is so hobbled by corruption that it scarcely functions at all. The main difference between these places, Putnam found, was the presence or absence of civic trust, which causes people to "deal fairly with one another and expect fair dealing in return." Where trust was absent and people behaved like the self-interested monads that classical economics holds them to be, on the other hand, government mainly existed to deal in favors, bribery, and patronage. Citizens in these regions were cynical and resigned.[26]

When Putnam published *Making Democracy Work* in 1993, he took it for granted that a functioning, democratic government was something everyone wanted, but one could just as easily view the book as a guide for how to make democracy *stop* working. As we have seen, plenty of conservatives regard a government that doesn't work as a positive thing, and we have heard from them at length in these pages. Reading Putnam makes it easy to figure out the steps you would take to achieve this upside-down utopia: instead of reinforcing the fragile institutions of civic trust you smash them, you encourage cynicism toward government, and if you get a chance you put the whole thing—conspicuously—on a for-hire basis.

This all reverberates in my head whenever I think about something Grover Norquist once told me, in his oddly cheerful way: instead of complaining "about all these obviously corrupt earmarks," as some conservatives were doing, "they should welcome those earmarks."

> Corrupt earmarks are like the National Endowment for the Arts funding "Piss Christ." They remind people of how abusive the government is. When the government was funding symphonies people didn't get angry. When the government uses your tax dollars to fund "Piss Christ," they get mad. When taxpayers thought the government was, quote unquote, building roads, they were happy. When they realized they were building bridges to nowhere and rail-lines to nowhere, then they get pissed off.

And people being pissed off at government was the very core of right-wing discontent. Corrupt earmarks, inserted by conservatives, ought to lead to conservative victory.

But, you protest, nobody really fell for this. Everyone understood that the guy who got the "Bridge to Nowhere" earmark was a conservative Republican. Everyone recognized that conservative deregulatory doctrines enabled the financial crash of 2008. People knew where the blame belonged, and they punished the malefactors.

True. But remember the long-term effects of Watergate. While the immediate consequences of Nixon's outrageous behavior were jail sentences for several prominent Republicans and the election of a bumper crop of liberals to Congress in 1974, Watergate permanently poisoned public attitudes toward government and stirred up the wave that swept Ronald Reagan into office six years later. Watergate made antigovernment cynicism the default American political sentiment.

Government's failures can be made into conservatism's fuel, even when it's conservative bungling that has brought them about. The ultimate expression of this doctrine came during the 2008 debate between vice presidential candidates Governor Sarah Palin and Senator Joe Biden. Palin, the conservative Republican, was heaping doubt on the Democrats' health-care plan; it would involve a "government-run program," she noted, and we all had learned the folly of government-run programs—from the disasters of the conservative Republican Bush administration! Her words, exactly: "Unless you're pleased with the way the federal government has been running anything lately, I don't think that it's going to be real pleasing for Americans to consider health care being taken over by the feds."

Or consider the massive and concerted effort to describe FEMA's spectacular incompetence in New Orleans not as an inevitable product of the "market-based" state but as typical government behavior, the sort of thing we should always expect from Washington, regardless of who's in charge.[27]

The wail arose from all quarters of the winger wonderland in that summer of 2005. "The lesson here is the failure of government," wrote one regular feeder at D.C.'s subsidized libertarian troughs. "Government Broke Down," proclaimed a huge headline on the cover of *Fortune* magazine. "Business Stepped Up." Daniel Henninger, a columnist for the *Wall Street Journal,* surveyed the wreckage of FEMA—brought about by market-friendly devices like outsourcing and the revolving door, remember—and declared that the answer was "outsourcing some of these functions, for profit, to the private sector." John Tierney, a columnist for the *New York Times,* saw that and raised it: The whole agency, he suggested, might well be turned over to Wal-Mart, which would no doubt be happy to deliver the market's answer to the unlucky and the indigent when they came looking for their place in the lifeboat.[28]

There is nothing new about corruption per se. A century ago just about every electoral contest, from the presidency down to municipal city councils, was the object of brazen, ingenious fraud. During that golden age of political plunder, the journalist Lincoln Steffens, who called himself a "graft philosopher," went around the country asking the corruptionists themselves what accounted for this state of affairs. The answer he always got was "business."

In every city he examined, the rot involved the most prominent members of society's upper crust. And in every case the corruption was merely an extension of market principles into the public realm. It happened "because politics is business. That's what's the matter with it. That's what's the matter with everything,—art, literature, religion, journalism, law, medicine—they're all business, and all—as you see them." Gradually Steffens came to understand that corruption was not merely a series of discrete crimes, each one separate from the other, but a "natural process by which a democracy is made gradually over into a plutocracy," a government by the wealthy.[29]

Steffens liked to tell how his "process" theory would disturb the various big-city bosses to whom he related it, how they would protest that plutocracy was not their aim, that they only wanted to make some money, that they had never thought about it that way before. They were merely opportunists, Steffens concluded, charming rascals whose company he enjoyed even as he deplored the system they were establishing.

Merely opportunists—it would be hard to say this of the principal actors I have described in this book. For one thing, the liberal state that they commenced demolishing in the eighties was a thing unknown in Steffens's day; wrecking it required a vast mobilization of resources. For another, it was impossible for our corruptionists to claim ignorance like Steffens's rogues. Our wingers knew what they were doing. Like Marxists trying to speed history on its way to utopia, they advanced Steffens's plutocracy process deliberately, with results that were visible everywhere from McLean to Iraq.

Indeed, it was in Baghdad, the other capital of George W. Bush's market-based government, where this process and its consequences could be seen most clearly. In Iraq the conservatives got their chance to remake an entire country into a free-market utopia, with minimal interference from media types, regulators, and liberals. Back home the goo-goos screamed about all the dirty deals, the no-bid contracts; but conservatives didn't see the problem. This was just the world turned right side up. "Iraq is open for business," declared Paul Bremer, the American viceroy.[30]

And Bremer got busy. Personnel is policy, remember, and so they flew in fresh-faced movement youngsters by the planeload and put them in charge of the stock exchange, the Halliburton complaints office, the budget for the entire country. There were winger kids from Capitol Hill, home-schooled kids, kids from the Florida recount, kids whose parents had been Iran-Contra players, kids who confidently expected jobs on the Bush reelection campaign once their Iraq gig was done. Expertise, though, was out, since it rarely coincided with the more important qualifications for service in Iraq—like opposing *Roe v. Wade*—and so the talented and the experienced stayed home. Sometimes the screw-ups were even intentional. Douglas J. Feith, the undersecretary of defense who pushed the falsehood that Saddam Hussein was in some way responsible for 9/11, deliberately withheld U.S. plans for postwar Iraq from the man charged with running the place in hopes that the resulting smash-up would induce this poor fish to bring in Feith's buddy Ahmad Chalabi.[31]

This was to be "a capitalist dream," the *Economist* magazine declared, and so the work of reconstruction had to go, of course, to the private sector, to corporations bidding for contracts from the American authorities. "Whatever could be outsourced was," wrote Rajiv Chandrasekaran, a *Washington Post* reporter who watched it all go down. We contracted out the work of reconstruction, and the contractors subcontracted it, and—who knows?—maybe the subcontractors sub-subcontracted it in turn, with a fat slice for each entrepreneur on down the great chain of profit and, at the very bottom, a few crumbs for the Pakistanis and Indians who were imported to do the sweated labor. Meanwhile, back in America, the lobbyists and consultants swung into action. "Getting the rights to distribute Procter & Gamble products would be a gold mine," one specialist in Iraq contracting crowed. "One well-stocked 7-Eleven could knock out 30 Iraqi stores; a Wal-Mart could take over the country."[32]

"The job of setting up town and city councils was performed by a North Carolina firm for $236 million," Chandrasekaran continued. "The job of guarding the viceroy was assigned to private [Blackwater] guards, each of whom made more than $1,000 a day. For running the palace—cooking the food, changing the lightbulbs, doing the laundry, watering the plants—Halliburton had been handed hundreds of millions of dollars." Bechtel got a chunk. So did GE. Even the job of training the Iraqi army was outsourced, with the predictable result of that army having very poor morale.[33]

And oh, how they privatized. Technically, the assets of the Iraqi state didn't belong to the United States, even though we defeated that nation's army in the field. But "USAID and Treasury knew what Iraq needed," Chandrasekaran observed, and it was to have its public property sold off. The job of planning the privatization was contracted out to a management consultancy from McLean, and what it recommended doing for this land with a wrecked infrastructure and staggering unemployment was the precise opposite of what (liberal) history suggested. Back in the thirties, Americans launched massive public-works and relief programs. We encouraged labor unions and coaxed companies to recognize them. But in the conservative era we knew better: we needed to sell Iraq's government-owned industries, pass a flat tax, let the inefficient local businesses die off, import cheap foreign labor, take a hard line toward Iraqi unions, and pass laws so business-friendly that outside capital would come falling over itself to buy a piece of sunny Iraq.[34]

In some cases, the free-market geniuses running Iraq even proclaimed looting to be healthful, a sort of privatization-by-the-deed. "I thought the privatization that occurs sort of naturally when somebody took over their state vehicle, or began to drive a truck that the state used to own, was just fine," one of them once said.[35] These geniuses have since returned to their cushy think-tank jobs and their estate homes in neighborhoods where you don't have to bribe the fire department and where the water gurgles gratifyingly forth every time you turn on the tap. So history does not record their views on the extreme privatization that soon overtook Iraq, pulverizing society itself, reducing the country to a jungle of pure individualism, with private armies ensuring the safety of those who could afford it, gangs of armed entrepreneurs controlling the electricity, and garden hoses snaking from window to window across Baghdad, the desperate water supply of a society brought finally to the libertarian utopia of every man for himself.[36]

CONCLUSION

Reaching for the Pillars

Back in its blooming Maytime, conservative Washington's fondest daydream was that liberalism could somehow be defeated, finally and irreversibly, in the way that armies are beaten and pests are exterminated. Electoral victories by Republicans were just a part of the fantasy. The larger vision was of a future in which liberalism was physically barred from the control room—of an "end of history" in which taxes and onerous regulation would never again be allowed to threaten the fortunes that private individuals made for themselves.

This was the longing behind Karl Rove's talk of a "permanent majority," Tom DeLay's airy hopes of a "permanent realignment," and, twenty years previously, Jack Abramoff's declaration to the Republican convention that "it's the job of all revolutions to make permanent their gains," a line that would not have been out of place at a Jacobin club debate over whether to send Louis XVI to the guillotine. Outlining the same idea, Grover Norquist claimed to take his inspiration from Leonid Brezhnev.[1]

When I was first moved to contemplate this peculiar utopian caprice, I was struck by its obvious futility. You can wear those "No Libs" T-shirts from now until the Rapture, I thought, but you can't just stamp out an idea. In fact, you won't even begin to *confront* the idea with leaders like Rush Limbaugh and Ann Coulter, who are to genuine political theory what a set of particularly insolent HotWheels are to the cars in the Monaco Grand Prix.

What I did not understand was that beating liberal ideas wasn't the goal. This wasn't about ideas at all. The Washington conservatives aimed to make liberalism irrelevant not by debating but by erasing it. Building a majority coalition was always a part of this program, and conservatives enjoyed remarkable success at it over the years. But winning elections was not a bid for permanence by itself. It was only a means.

The end was capturing the state and using it to destroy liberalism as a practical alternative. The pattern was set by Margaret Thatcher, who used state power of the heaviest-handed sort to permanently implant the antistate ideology. "Economics are the method, the object is to change the soul," she famously said, echoing Stalin. Her plan for privatizing public housing—renters were offered generous subsidies to buy their units—was designed not only to enthrone the market but to encourage an ownership mentality and "change the soul" of an entire class of voters. When she sold off nationally owned industries, she took steps to ensure that workers received shares at below-market rates, leading hopefully to the same soul transformation. Her brutal, unprecedented suppression of the mineworkers strike in 1985 showed what awaited those who resisted the new order. As a *Business Week* reporter summarized it in 1987, "she sees her mission as nothing less than eradicating Labor Party socialism as a political alternative."[2]

In their own pursuit of the free-market utopia, American

wingers did not have as far to travel as their British cousins, and they never needed to use state power so ruthlessly. But the pattern remained the same: scatter the constituencies of the left, hack open the liberal state, and reward friendly businesses with the loot.

Grover Norquist was bluntest about using the power of the state "to crush the structures of the Left," as he put it. He outlined the plan countless times in countless venues: The liberal movement was supported by a number of "pillars," each of which could be toppled by conservatives when in power. Trial lawyers give millions to their liberal confederates in the Democratic Party; Norquist suggested that conservatives undermine them with "tort reform," a lawsuit-quashing measure that "will potentially cost trial lawyers billions of dollars of lost income." Labor unions were number two; Norquist proposed that conservatives "crush labor unions as a political entity" with some sort of "paycheck protection" measure and weaken them more generally with strategic expansions of NAFTA, like forcing Teamsters "to compete with Mexican truck drivers." Third were school vouchers, which would put paid to what he called the "2.1 million Democratic precinct workers belonging to the National Education Association." Fourth, a few "modest reforms" at HUD and the Department of Education that would cut off funds to "big city machines." And then—the coup de grâce—the Democratic Party would become "a dead man walking" when Team R privatized Social Security, permitting everyone in the country to own stock and thus share in those pleasures heretofore known only to the elite: "watching their investments grow—rather than shrink in the face of trial-lawyer parasites, labor-union work rules, and government-worker-driven taxes."[3]

And much of this program was accomplished during the conservative era, if not on the precise terms Norquist suggested. The war on labor, for example, yielded dramatic successes for conservatism. Labor used to be the financial bulwark of the entire liberal establishment in Washington; beating it down effectively knocked the props out from under numerous other liberal efforts, from affordable housing to civil rights.[4]

The shimmering dream of privatizing Social Security, though, remained the great unreachable winger prize, and the right persisted in the campaign regardless of the measure's unpopularity or the number of political careers it cost. President Bush, for example, announced privatization to be his top priority on the day after his reelection in 2004, although he had not emphasized the issue during the campaign and although, in statistical terms, almost nobody had voted for him for this reason.[5] He proceeded to chase the issue deep into the land of political unpopularity, a region from which he never returned.

He did this because the rewards of privatizing Social Security justified any political cost. At one stroke it would have both defunded the operations of government and utterly reconfigured the way Americans interacted with the state. It would have been irreversible, too; the "transition costs" in any scheme to convert Social Security were so vast that no country could consider incurring them twice. Then, once the deal had been done and the trillions of dollars that passed through Social Security were diverted from the U.S. Treasury to stocks in private companies, the following effects would have been locked in for good. First, there would have been an immediate flood of money into Wall Street, boosting the net worth of the wealthy and lifting the boats of the various brokerages and mutual fund companies who handled the millions of new private accounts. Second, there would have been an equivalent flow of money out of government accounts, immediately propelling the federal deficit up into the stratosphere and defunding a huge part of federal activity.

The overall effect would have been to marketize the nation's politics, elevating forever the cold rationale of the financial markets over such vague liberalisms as *the common good* and *the public interest*. The practical results of such a titanic redirection of our politics would also have been easy to predict, given the persistent political demands of Wall Street: low wage growth, even weaker labor organizations, a free hand for management in downsizing, polluting, and so on. To hand Social Security over to Wall Street would have been to enshrine these demands as the foremost objects of economic policy. After all, who would legislate for higher minimum wages or safer food or cleaner air when such legislation could be construed as an attack on the portfolios of the nation's beloved seniors? Not only would privatization have changed the soul; it would have permanently reversed the political valence of the famous "third rail of American politics," transforming Social Security overnight from the bane of the business community into its most powerful weapon. Touch Wall Street and you're dead.

The longing for permanent victory over liberalism is not unique to the Anglo-Saxon world. In country after country, business elites have come up with ingenious ways to limit the public's political choices. One of the most effective of these has been massive public debt.

Naomi Klein, a journalist who has traveled the world documenting the great shift to the right, finds that in case after case, the burden of enormous debts—often piled up by dictatorships or other noxious regimes—forced democratic countries to accept a laissez-faire system that they otherwise found deeply distasteful. Regardless of who borrowed the money and the appalling ways in which it was spent, these debts had to be repaid—and repaying them, in turn, meant that a nation had to agree to restructure its economy the way the bankers preferred: by deregulating, privatizing, and cutting spending.[6]

The American version of the debt trick is the vast federal deficit that magically reappears whenever conservatives take the driver's seat. Its effects have been far less traumatic than in the third world, but they nevertheless push the country in the same direction: deregulation, privatization, social spending cuts.

The irony of it all has been noted so many times that it is unnecessary to describe it in detail here. Republicans have ridden to power again and again promising balanced budgets and howling against deficits—government debt was "mortgaging our future," Ronald Reagan admonished in his inaugural address—but once in office they proceed, with a combination of tax cuts and spending increases, to balloon the federal deficit to levels far beyond those reached by their supposedly openhanded liberal rivals. So mechanically and so predictably do they embark on this course that it has basically become part of their identity, their brand. Vote Republican and watch the deficit grow.

The formal justification for this is always the famous "supply-side" theory, one of the all-time great hoaxes of social science. By cutting taxes, it was once said, you would unleash such vasty waves of economic growth that federal revenues would actually *increase* as a result, so all the additional government spending would be paid for.

Even the theory's proponents didn't really believe it. David Stockman, the libertarian budget director of the first Reagan administration, did the math in 1980 and watched as the whole idea "slid into the grave of fiscal mythology forty days after the supply-side banner had been hoisted up at the GOP convention."[7] Supply side would not rescue the government, he realized; it would wreck the government. This is the point where most people would stop, put the cup of poison down, and walk away. Instead Stockman decided it had medicinal value.[8]

Poison is a weapon, after all, and this particular kind of poison could be used strategically to force the libs to accept the conservative model for the state. With their beloved government brought to the brink of fiscal collapse by repeated doses of supply side, the liberals would either have to acquiesce in the reconfiguration of the state or else see the country destroyed. Stockman was remarkably candid about this: Once the tax cuts had been enacted, the conservatives would have the "craven politicians pinned to the wall. They would have to dismantle [the government's] bloated, wasteful, and unjust spending enterprises—or risk national ruin." The Reagan tax cuts, all by themselves, would thus be a "frontal attack on the welfare state."[9]

Let us understand Stockman's confession for what it is: a plan for government-by-sabotage. Other high-profile conservatives celebrated the gigantic Reagan deficits—for example, Milton Friedman, the dean of free-market economists[10]—but in Stockman's thinking we see the political logic of deficits most clearly. Deficits were a way to smash a liberal state that voters could not be persuaded to part with otherwise.

And besides, it was liberals with their fancy Keynesian ideas who invented deficit spending, as Reagan loved to remind the world.[11] Conservatives would merely heighten the contradiction of the liberal system: the fact that deficit spending, while ordinarily healthy, could be ruinous if used in the wrong situation. So they would use it in the wrong situation. The logic is analogous to Norquist's defense of corrupt earmarks and even to the College Republicans' old scheme for proposing bestiality clubs on campus; in each case our friendly wingers were merely demonstrating what the liberal system allows should someone decide to push it all the way.

This may sound too sinister to be believed, and yet the Reagan deficits did precisely this. They brought on the crisis. Glimpsing the vast heap of debt rising up in Washington over the course of the eighties, the political class screamed louder and louder for spending cuts, pay freezes for federal workers, and swift action on "entitlements." A mania for privatization swept the capital, with wingers demanding a national garage sale in which Uncle Sam would raise money by selling off the highways, the broadcast spectrum, and Amtrak.[12] But the greatest effect—and the main reason conservative administrations immediately run up as large a deficit as possible—is that deficits defund the left.

When President Reagan took over in 1981, he inherited an annual deficit of $59 billion and a national debt of $914 billion; by the time he and his successor George Bush I had finished their work, they had quintupled the deficit and pumped the debt up to $4 trillion.[13]

Act 2: Enter Bill Clinton, who had built his reputation as something of a populist, promising in 1992 to "put people first" and to ensure that economic growth was shared equally by rich and poor alike. As President Clinton, however, he quickly became a very different creature. This, too, is a familiar story, with the Arkansas man of the people morphing magically into Alan Greenspan's favorite president of them all.

What is remembered less vividly is the role the enormous Reagan deficit played in Clinton's transformation. Bill and Hillary called it "Stockman's Revenge," and from the first few gatherings of the new administration's economic team, it dominated all other topics. The deficit-rattled bond market had to be appeased, Clinton's aides told him; Wall Street had to be convinced that the Democrats were trustworthy. Greenspan himself spoke of "financial catastrophe" unless steps were taken immediately to control Reagan's deficit. Bob Woodward's description of the 1992 meeting at which Clinton realized he was trapped has become justly famous. The president-elect's "face turned red with anger and disbelief. 'You mean to tell me that the success of the program and my reelection hinges on the Federal Reserve and a bunch of fucking bond traders?' " Before long, though, Clinton himself was a convert, and he readily sacrificed his populism on the altar of deficit reduction.[14] He contracted out; he got tough with the federal workforce; he even considered privatizing Social Security in his own centrist way. In his second term he ran the government on a balanced budget for four straight years.

And then, act 3: George W. Bush proceeded immediately to plunge the budget into deficit again. Indeed, after seeing how the Reagan deficit had forced Clinton's hand, it would have been foolish for a conservative *not* to spend his way back into the hole as rapidly as possible.

Besides, think of the possibilities that opened to our conservative friends as they realized they were now free to taxcut-and-spend their way deep into the red. Oh, the earmarks they could hand out to people working on privatizing outer space or building experimental jet airplanes.[15] All the different ways they could reward the right lobbyists, the right consultants, the right contractors. And after they'd burned through the bank account and brought on the crisis, think of the points they could win by screaming about too-generous "entitlements," the insolence of publicly funded art, and all the fat and lazy bureaucrats who needed a pay cut.

If, along the way, all this idiotic spending happened to bump up public cynicism toward deficit spending a notch or two—why, that was just gravy. "It's perfectly fine for *them* to waste money," says former labor secretary Robert Reich, summarizing the conservative viewpoint. "If the public thinks government is wasteful, that's fine. That reduces public faith in government, which is precisely what the Republicans want." It's not just sabotage; it's win-win sabotage, a charming addition to win-win incompetence and win-win corruption.

Conservatives have often discussed the vulnerability of their enemy to such acts of sabotage. The most famous example can be found in a 1964 book by the conservative political theorist James Burnham, which diagnosed liberalism as "the ideology of Western suicide." What Burnham meant by this was that liberalism's so-called virtues—its openness and its insistence on equal rights for everyone—were in fact fatal weaknesses.

> Either liberalism must extend the freedoms to those who are not themselves liberals and even to those whose deliberate purpose is to destroy the liberal society—in effect, that is, must grant a free hand to its assassins; or liberalism must deny its own principles, restrict the freedoms, and practice discrimination. It is as if the rules of football provided no penalties against those who violated the rules; so that the referee would either have to permit a player (whose real purpose was to break up the game) to slug, kick, gouge and whatever else he felt like doing, or else would have to disregard the rules and throw the unfair player out.[16]

For its very survival, in other words, liberalism depends on fair play by its sworn enemies, making it vulnerable, as Burnham observes, to assassination, hijacking, or sabotage by any party that refuses to play by the rules.

The "suicide" that all of this was meant to describe was liberalism's destruction at the hands of communism, a movement in whose ranks Burnham had once marched himself. But after many flagrant decades of unsportsmanlike conduct by conservatives, his theory seems more accurately to describe the strategems of its fans on the American right.

Liberalism has indeed proven vulnerable to the tactics of its swaggering, bullying foes, but to call this suicide is like saying that your window got in the way of my brick, or that your nose smacked my fist. The correct term for the disasters that have disabled the liberal state is *vandalism,* conducted by a movement that refuses to play by liberalism's rules. It loots the Treasury, dynamites the dam, takes a crowbar to the monument, and throws a wrench into the gears. It slams the locomotive into reverse, tosses something heavy on the throttle, and jumps for it.

Mainstream American political commentary, with its own touching faith in fair play, customarily assumes that the two great political parties do whatever they do as precise mirror images of each other; that if one is guilty of some misstep, the other is also automatically and equally culpable.[17] The idea has a geometric elegance to it, and to journalists this doctrine of symmetry is especially appealing: It is a shortcut to fairness, an easy way to brush off the accusations of bias that plague them. But when applied to the political war that I have described in these pages, it serves to advance our understanding barely at all.

There is no symmetry. Liberalism, as we know it, arose out of a long-ago compromise between left-wing social movements and business interests. It depends utterly on the efficient functioning of certain organs of the state, and it does not call for some kind of all-out war on private industry. Conservatism, on the other hand, speaks not of compromise but of removing its adversaries from the field altogether. While no one dreams of sawing off those branches of the state that protect conservatism's constituents—the military, the police, the legal privileges granted to corporations—conservatives, in their heyday, freely and openly fantasized about doing away with those bits of "big government" that served liberal ends. And while defunding the left remains the north star of the Washington right, no comparable campaign to "defund the right" exists; indeed, it would be difficult to imagine one. Even in the darkest economic times, liberals are hardly likely to crack down on the Fortune 500 with the same resourceful malevolence that business leaders, to choose one example, have used in their war on labor unions.

In its classic form, conservatism is supposed to spring from a desire to preserve the connections between the present and the past. But in America conservatism is different; it is a destroyer of tradition, not a preserver. Left unconstrained by other forces, the free-market system is one of the most restless, destructive arrangements ever contrived—tearing down and building up, obsoleting last year's fashions and praising this year's, driving up prices and bidding down wages, and moving populations willy-nilly about the map. None of which is a secret or even a particularly left-wing accusation. On the contrary, these are staples of management lit, ideas to which every motivational guru worth his PowerPoint has contributed. Consider just the titles of management books from the last few decades: *Disruption, Thriving on Chaos, Surfing the Edge of Chaos, Leading the Revolution, Rules for Revolutionaries, The Age of Unreason, Change Is the Rule, The Heart of Change, The Dance of Change,* and the table of contents of virtually any issue of *Fast Company* magazine.

Here is Tom Peters, guru of gurus, explaining in his 2000 book, *The Circle of Innovation,* the attitude that businesses must take in order to be successful.

> **DESTRUCTION IS COOL!**

Here he is again, a little bit later in the same book.

> DESTRUCTION IS JOB NO. 1.

And again.

> It's easier to kill an organization than to change it. Big idea: DEATH![18]

As I relate these dreams of death and destruction, I am reminded of the emotional eulogy given in 1983 by Jerry Falwell for Congressman Larry McDonald, the chairman of the John Birch Society, who had died on a Korean airliner that was shot down by the Soviets. McDonald, Falwell declared, was like Samson in the Bible story, killing countless Philistines (in addition to himself) by pushing the pillars out from under their house. In fact, Falwell continued, this was a metaphor for what the entire conservative movement was doing.

> Like Samson, some of us are reaching for the pillars. We may not clearly see the way . . . we may be lacking in wisdom . . . but we have the will and the confidence in a God who is sovereign, and cannot fail. . . . Larry McDonald was [*like Samson*] a victim, a prisoner of a society moving to the left. But he never moved with it. He still was looking for the pillars. And at a certain hour on August 31, 1983 [when McDonald died], he found the pillars, one with his right hand and one with his left.[19]

Let us pass over Falwell's confused suggestion that McDonald's murder was what changed America. What glares out at us here is the preacher's desire to wreck "a society moving to the left"—to knock out its props and pancake the whole arrogant thing, even if it costs conservatives their lives.

In 1983, they were "reaching for the pillars"; twenty-five years later, we are all living with the consequences.

The middle-class America that Falwell and Co. wrecked with such gusto is not going to be easy to rebuild. For one thing, the balance of social power has been so decisively altered since those days that the political landscape itself has been radically transformed. Dramatic economic inequality of the kind conservatism has engineered has inevitably brought political inequality with it. The rich vote at higher rates than others, they contribute greater amounts to candidates, and, should they choose, they are able to afford today's expensive campaigns for public office. They can also subsidize authors, newspaper columnists, academics, magazines, and TV shows; they can fund the careers of friendly politicians and buy off dubious ones; and they can reward right-thinking regulators and bureaucrats when these worthies' stints in government are done. They can launch cable TV networks, buy newspapers, and bankroll think-tank operations charged with making their idiosyncratic personal ideas into the common sense of the millions.

"Over the past thirty years, American politics has become more money-centered at exactly the same time that American society has grown more unequal," wrote the political scientists Jacob Hacker and Paul Pierson in 2005. "The resources and organizational heft of the well off and hyperconservative have exploded. But the organizational resources of middle-income Americans—from labor unions to mass-membership groups—have atrophied. The resulting inequality of resources and organization has not been neutral in its effects. It has greatly benefited the Republican Party while drawing it closer to its most affluent and extreme supporters."[20]

In this sense, conservative Washington was a botch that will keep on working even after its formal demise. It defunded the constituencies of the liberal state while constructing a plutocracy that will stand regardless of who wins the next few elections and that will weight our politics rightward for years.

On the other hand, the marketizing of politics also left conservatism vulnerable in a few spectacular ways. Just as markets generally tend to get carried away, to overbuild and then to panic when the slightest adversity is encountered, so did the lobbyist-fueled conservative boom of the last ten years give way to a distinct conservative bust. In 2007 and 2008, conservative senators and representatives could be seen heading for the revolving door in record numbers. Having lost the majority in 2006, they were desperate to secure some fraction of the lobbying fortune they thought was safely in the bank—to sell out before conservatism's share price fell all the way to zero.

While there is considerable amusement to be had at the sight of yesterday's Republican bravo—so tough he even impeached a president!—pounding for dear life on the door of some lobby firm, the decline of one party and the rise of the other does not, by itself, signal a change in the city's underlying political logic. For numerous entrepreneurial Democratic leaders, the party's revival has merely been an opportunity to accelerate their own courtship of K Street, to hold their own parties on the tenth story of 101 Con.[21] Some have begun earmarking with such zeal and promiscuity that entire cities now thrive on the pork sent their way.[22] Other Democrats have easily proven themselves the Republicans' equals in clever circumvention of campaign finance laws.[23] And certain of them have also shown that they can spin that ol' revolving door with every bit of their rivals' cash-lust—can even set up lobbying supergroups so profitable they must "hire Brinks to bring in the money every day," as an admirer described one such firm.[24]

Throwing the rascals out is no longer enough. A century ago, in the classic period of business government, an epidemic of public theft persisted despite a long string of reformers in the White

House, Republicans and Democrats, each one promising to clean the place up. Nothing worked, and for this simple reason: democracy cannot work when wealth is distributed as lopsidedly as theirs was—and as ours is. The inevitable consequence of plutocracy, then and now, is bought government. As Justice Louis Brandeis said at the time, "We can have democracy in this country, or we can have great wealth concentrated in the hands of a few, but we can't have both." It is a bitter lesson that we are relearning all over again.

While writing all this, I have been looking up at two books that are shelved next to each other in my office: Richard Hofstadter's *The Paranoid Style in American Politics* and an example of that very paranoid style, James Tyson's *Target America,* one of the books that Jack Abramoff's College Republicans used to distribute to its campus chapters. Every morning when I come downstairs I half expect to find them reduced to ashes, having combusted spontaneously overnight. They are, in a way, diametric opposites: thought and antithought; health and illness; reason and conspiracy theory. Between them, in a way, they also sketch the arc of history itself.

The Paranoid Style was published in 1965, the year of my birth. It was one of the last monuments of what was known as the "consensus" school of history, the house pedagogy of American liberalism in its golden age. Hofstadter had a refined taste for irony, and he gracefully incorporated the insights of sociology and psychology into his work. In the consensus school came together all the social sciences, then at the peak of their respectability and self-assurance, looking out at a world whose problems were understood, were capable of solution.

And the solution was liberalism: it had rescued the nation from the mindless boom-and-bust cycle of laissez-faire; it had defeated fascism; and it was then, in 1965, delivering one of the greatest periods of prosperity in history. In that year, American GNP grew by 6.5 percent—in these glory days of the billionaire it barely gets over 2 percent—in line with the official, stated goal of American economic policy: "a growing abundance, widely shared." Taxes were high, and the richest man in the world was the oil baron J. Paul Getty, worth between two and four billion dollars and fond of grousing about how tough it was to be rich in an era when even the middle-class man had access to what had once been the exclusive privileges of great wealth.[25]

In 1965 Americans had just elected a liberal president in one of the most sweeping landslides of them all. Liberalism's rightness was supposedly apparent to all but the confused, and Richard Hofstadter declared that the right-wing movement on the losing end of that landslide was afflicted with a kind of political paranoia, a delusional understanding of history-as-conspiracy. They had "lost touch with reality," he announced; they were striking "a vital blow at the American political order" itself.[26]

The other book I mentioned, *Target America: The Influence of Communist Propaganda on U.S. Media,* was published fifteen years later to the thrill of the far right. Here is how its author went about evaluating American political writing: articles that "appear to follow the current Communist line" earned the journalist in question a "debit"; articles that were "harmful to the Communist line" won him a plus mark. We do the math, and the "balance sheet" told the rest: all across academia and journalism people were mouthing Soviet propaganda. History *did* work through conspiracy, and readers were told, with childlike astonishment, about the existence of the KGB, about the millions spent by the Soviets on propaganda, about the fact that *Pravda* told lies.

And yet, in the great political contest of our times, it was the latter book that prevailed. The ones who read *Target America* and rode the paranoid wave were, for the last few decades, the ones who assembled in riotous celebration here in Washington, enjoying the good times in the capital city of the most powerful nation in history.

The rest of us were left to mourn for Hofstadter's nation—that warm middle-class world that I was born into: a place where blue-collar workers owned boats and suburban homes, where government seemed at least interested in fairness, and where art and learning were respected as much as accumulation. The wreckage of that America lies all around us today.

It would be nice if electing Democrats was all that was required to resuscitate the America that conservatism flattened, but I suspect it will take far more than that. A wholesale renovation of the federal apparatus, for one thing, must come before there can be any return to the middle-class state. More basic still—and infinitely more difficult—is a revival of the social movements of the left that brought liberalism into being in the first place.

At least we know where to begin. We must understand conservatism's cynicism for what it is, and hold it accountable for what it did to our world. Until now, wingers have swaggered across the national stage wrecking and smashing with impunity, secure in the knowledge that a little bit of scoffing toward big government would always get them off the hook, save them to wreck again some other day. We can now say of that philosophy which regards good government as a laughable impossibility, which elevates bullies and gangsters and CEOs above other humans, which tells us to get wise and stop expecting anything good from Washington—we can now say with finality that it has had its chance. Whenever there was a choice to be made between free markets and free people—between money and the common good—the conservatives chose money. Their day is done now. It is time to turn the page.

AFTERWORD

Götterdämmerung

What the wrecking crew ultimately wrecked was the economy itself. In 2008 the wealth of the world collapsed in a cloud of bad debt—debt that had been issued by unregulated institutions, sold on exchanges that lobbyists had made sure were unsupervised, and held by banks overseen by an agency that was so hapless and so industry-friendly that it dozed through every alarm.

Now, it is probably unfair to lay the blame for the financial disaster at the feet of any single federal policy or even one of the two national parties.

It is entirely fitting, however, to describe it as a sort of judgment day for the conservative philosophy, shared as it was by leaders in both political parties and by players all across the economy.

Before the fall of 2008, the most acute consequences of rule by a clique dedicated to "inefficiency in government" had mainly befallen distinct and limited groups of people: citizens of New Orleans, union members, Iraqis, people who happened to eat tainted food. What's more, the conservative state's screwups could each be clouded with an inky squirt of culture-war populism or dismissed with more of the usual rhetoric—*See? Government can't do anything right.*

The economic collapse of 2008 was different. It was an effect of the same strategies of misgovernment that had wrecked the EPA and the Labor Department, yes, but the consequences now were so vast that virtually no one escaped. Nor could the ruination be brushed off, although countless conservatives tried. This time the public's fury would not be diverted: Americans pinned the blame squarely on the ideas that deserved it and on the individuals who had pushed those ideas along. And so the final casualty of conservatism's Samson-like effort to knock down the pillars of the state was the movement itself. By the end of 2008 its economic theories had been badly discredited and its political fortunes lay in ruins.

The policies that eventually flattened the nation's banks, insurance companies, and investment houses had originally been put in place, of course, at those very institutions' request. These industries got what they wanted from Washington, and what they wanted wound up killing them.

This outcome was an ironic one, but there was also a certain cosmic predictability to it. After all, the financial regulatory structure that the banks so hated had been pieced together in the 1930s to mitigate the extremes of the business cycle. Take that structure away for whatever reason—because you think the market can self-regulate, because you believe God has suspended the business cycle, or because you've convinced yourself that regulation is an insult to free men everywhere—and before long you've restored the nineteenth-century system from which our ancestors worked so hard to escape, complete with its extreme short-sightedness and its terrifying crashes.

As the world now knows, the specific cause of the disaster was a real estate bubble puffed up by a largely unregulated and unsupervised mortgage industry, which generated a prodigious quantity of bad loans, packaged them up, and sold them off to the savviest bankers and brokers in the land. Conservative economic theory holds that markets, especially financial ones, are perfectly capable of discovering and avoiding fraud without the assistance of government.[1] In this case, however, the opposite happened: Those who generated the toxins were rewarded with performance bonuses and their companies were the companies that grew; those who played by the rules saw their careers stagnate and their companies' fortunes wither.

As for the branches of government charged with overseeing the financial industry, the usual practices were in full effect. Regulatory agencies were not abolished outright, but instead they were systematically restrained, defunded, depopulated, and dumbed down. Their new, conservative leaders were often hostile to the regulatory mission and sometimes drawn from the ranks of the regulated. As in other reaches of the conservative state, they tended to regard business—not the public—as their customer.

The disaster was, in this sense, a perfect test of the conservative state, in which its trademark features were each tried and found to be as worthless as the mortgage-backed securities moldering in Citibank's basement.

The landmark deregulations that made the whole mess possible to begin with were tributes to lobbyist power and the allure of the revolving door. Securing the great financial deregulation act of 1999, which permitted the megabanks that would be judged "too big to fail" nine years later, had been the object of decades of bank industry lobbying. When the man who finally got the bill passed, Texas senator Phil Gramm, left Congress, he promptly got a job as an investment banker. Gramm also co-sponsored the great financial deregulation act of 2000, which closed off the possibility of regulating futures and derivatives—the instruments that brought down Enron shortly thereafter and just about everybody else later on—although according to one knowledgeable account it was largely written by a financial industry lobbyist.[2] Phil Gramm's wife, incidentally, had been an ardent foe of futures regulation in her own right when she worked in the Reagan administration; she went on to serve as an Enron board member and then as a professor at the Mercatus Center, the Northern Virginia think tank dedicated to assailing regulation by whatever weapon presents itself.

The innovations that set the stage for the crash of 2008 were the now-notorious subprime loans and "liar loans," issued in fantastic numbers by largely unregulated institutions. Making the whole business possible were those institutions' pay-for-performance incentives, an innovation that theoretically made managers profit-minded but that actually caused them to hand out iffy loans like candy at a parade because such loans meant revenue and, hence, bonuses for those same bankers in the here and now. The consequences would be borne down the line by the suckers who bought mortgage-backed securities—and, of course, by the shareholders.[3]

The capture of the state by conservatives, meanwhile, ensured that no one would interfere. The Federal Reserve, which regulates banks in addition to setting interest rates, declined to intervene despite an explicit warning about risky mortgage lending practices received in 2000 by its chairman, the famous libertarian Alan Greenspan. In 2003, the Office of the Comptroller of the Currency, a different federal bank regulator, actually overruled action against lenders by state-level agencies.[4]

Scan the rest of the federal agencies assigned to regulate banks and you can see the movement's entire arsenal of sabotage weapons deployed to devastating effect. You want revolving door? Look no further than the Office of Thrift Supervision (OTS), which oversaw Savings and Loans, and which was led during the Bush years by a big Republican campaign contributor from the banking industry. You want industry-friendly? Well, this worthy slashed his agency's staff and pulled back on enforcement. Such was his dedication to deregulation that he once posed for photographers with a group of banking industry lobbyists holding a chain saw to a pile of rule books and red tape.[5]

Like so many other Bush-era agencies, the OTS referred to the industry it oversaw as its "customers," and it treated them with the sort of leniency one associates with such an attitude. One example, from many: In mid-2008, OTS permitted IndyMac Bank, which would soon be dragged under by bad mortgage debt, to alter its records to avoid the appearance of crisis. Thanks to the diffuse nature of bank regulating—there are several overlapping federal agencies from which a financial institution was permitted to choose—decisions like this made OTS a hot item, a big winner in the resulting "competition in laxity," as banks rushed to sign up for OTS supervision. Maybe it's only a coincidence that some of the biggest banks ever to fail were under OTS's watch, but I doubt it.[6]

The Securities and Exchange Commission (SEC), the top cop on Wall Street, was no better. Its overworked staffers, whose pay was comparable to that of other federal employees, were expected to face down some of the most highly paid corporation lawyers in the world—a disparity that led, here as elsewhere, to the revolving door. By the time of the crash, the SEC was so utterly clueless that it completely missed the greatest Ponzi scheme of all time, the investment firm run by Bernard Madoff, despite having received numerous tips on the megafraud.

It took years for conservatives to transform the SEC into the laughingstock it became in 2008. Their vandalism began, as we have seen elsewhere, with personnel decisions: Before the 1980s, SEC commissioners were drawn from within the agency; from Reagan's presidency on, they came from Wall Street. This new breed of SEC officer picked fights with career staff and schemed always to take a less adversarial, more voluntary approach to supervision. The Reagan administration's first SEC chairman, for example, had been a mergers and acquisitions specialist at a big Wall Street firm; one of his lieutenants declared in 1984, "The best of all worlds is the termination of federal regulation."[7] Even so, the agency was still able to pull off a few spectacular insider-trading busts in this period.

It fell to George W. Bush to really wreck the place. In 2001 he appointed as its chairman one Harvey Pitt, a securities lawyer who had coauthored a report for the accounting industry explaining why it wasn't a problem for auditors to also act as consultants for their clients. (The Enron and WorldCom accounting scandals arose from exactly such unregulated conflicts of interest.) Pitt announced, predictably, that the SEC needed to "listen" to Wall Street more and fight with it less; he told an audience of accountants that he aimed to make the agency into a "kinder and gentler place." Amid the Enron/Arthur Andersen accounting scandal that broke later that year this attitude looked more than a little peculiar; Pitt finally had to resign after he tried to appoint, as head of a commission overseeing the accounting industry, a board member from a company under SEC investigation.[8]

As new dereg zealots replaced the old dereg zealots at the apex of the SEC, the agency set new records for groveling subservience to industry. For example, it thoughtfully set up a telephone hotline for "members of the regulated community," as an official put it in 2005, so they could lodge complaints without too much effort.[9] During an investigation into a hedge fund at about the same time, an SEC lawyer asked to question a great captain of Wall Street; for this unforgiveable impertinence he was fired.[10] Most notorious was a "voluntary supervision" program that the commission set up at the request of the international holding companies that owned investment banks. This toothless measure, much denounced in the wake of the 2008 crash, was only taken because the European Union had announced plans to regulate the holding companies, and thus they needed nominal supervision from the friendly SEC to forestall actual supervision by real regulators.[11]

The combination of overwork and undercutting had utterly predictable results: Over the course of the Bush years, prosecutions of SEC cases fell by 87 percent. In 2008, the year when all financial hell broke loose, the SEC brought the fewest prosecutions it had since 1991.[12]

The crash also tested conservatism's extraordinary capacity for blame evasion. Conservatives had long insisted that, as outsiders to Washington, they could not be held responsible for government's mistakes. They would remind voters that theirs was a movement of insurgents, of humble middle Americans rising against the self-righteous elites of the East Coast. In 2008, they got busy again, depicting themselves as the true victims of organized power. The ruse had worked for decades, but this time it met its Waterloo.

When the downturn pushed its way into the headlines, the presidential election was already well advanced. The Republicans had chosen as their candidate Arizona senator John McCain, the greatest outsider they could muster. McCain was virtually the only well-known figure from his party's ranks who had taken a stand against government-by-contractor. He had fought for limits on political campaign donations. He had even directed the first investigation of Jack Abramoff.

McCain successfully distanced himself from a Republican

Party that had become a target of public indignation for its manifest corruption and its friendliness with lobbyists. Were one to point out, however, that in reality his economic and regulatory views were the same as those his party had pushed for years, one would swiftly encounter that grand obfuscation known as the culture wars. Here McCain had made a particularly bold move, choosing the outspoken Sarah Palin for his running mate.

This traditional Republican strategy was rendered obsolete almost overnight following the September 15 bankruptcy of Lehman Brothers, the sale of Merrill Lynch, the bailout of the gigantic insurance firm AIG, and the failure of IndyMac and Washington Mutual, each act played out against a backdrop of plummeting stock prices. Suddenly the only issues that mattered were the big economic ones that insurgency and culture war were supposed to blur: Government's role in the economy. Deregulation. The political power of private industry. The country's distorted distribution of wealth. After all, when your mortgage is under water and your neighbors are being laid off, the need to take up the sword against arrogant stem-cell scientists becomes considerably less urgent.

It was not a good time to be a laissez-faire believer, as Senator McCain repeatedly said he was, and the Democratic candidate, Senator Barack Obama, insisted on putting economic fairness at the center of the discussion. The right did make several half-hearted efforts to blame the ongoing disaster on government or liberalism, however. TV commentators blamed "minorities" for the disaster, others zeroed in on the government-backed mortgage companies Fannie Mae and Freddie Mac, and country singer Hank Williams Jr., traveling with Mrs. Palin, wrote a campaign song that included this bizarre verse:

> The bankers didn't want to make all those bad loans
> But Bill Clinton said, "You got to."

That Hank Jr. bills himself as "the voice of the common man" only heightens the weirdness of the episode.

The main conservative response to the disaster was to double down on the righteous rhetoric of red-state grievance and spin the wheel one more time. This is why McCain's campaign became a flamboyant culture-war pantomime, grotesquely exaggerated in each of its parts, and, ultimately, separated from the lives of the everyday Americans it claimed so extravagantly to revere. It was "overripe," to borrow the term historian Johan Huizinga once used to describe late medieval culture.

What previous Republican campaigns had whispered, this one screamed. What had been contained to the movement's feverish fringes moved to center stage. Traditional Republican talk about the heartland became the place Sarah Palin referred to as "real America." An exaggerated authenticity became the touchstone of the GOP effort. "Liberals hate real Americans that work and accomplish and achieve and believe in God," proclaimed North Carolina congressman Robin Hayes. Speaking of Obama on the day before that, Minnesota representative Michelle Bachmann expressed deep concern "that he may have anti-American views."

Conventional Republican appeals to the working class mutated into "Joe the Plumber," that most authentic of men, who strode forward on the hard streets of suburban Toledo to challenge Obama's tax plan. He was "the average citizen" in the flesh, according to McCain; "a real person," according to Palin, who deftly ruined Obama's "staged photo op there."

The Plumber's role in the campaign was predictable from the day he made his celebrated appearance: It would never be enough to agree with Joe on tax matters; he would also have to become a victim in some way, persecuted by the high and the mighty as are all proletarians everywhere. So, when the media mob checked up on Joe's plumbing license and suchlike, the script was set;

martyrdom commenced. *Chicago Tribune* columnist John Kass described Joe's treatment as a decapitation, with the Plumber's severed head impaled on a "media pike." Stock proletarian #2, "Tito the Builder," won his own GOP spurs when he showed up at a rally in Virginia, confronted a crowd of reporters, and demanded,"Why the hell are you going after Joe the Plumber?"

Sarah Palin, who liked to use a censored version of Tito's line in her speeches, made the elite's persecution of middle America her own special cause. At a rally in Pennsylvania she hailed a "Bill the Mechanic" in the crowd and told him, "I need to warn you, the press knows who you are now. You better duck, Bill the Mechanic." At her speech to the Republican convention in St. Paul, she asserted that Democrats "look down" on small-town officials and observed that not being "a member in good standing of the Washington elite" exposes a person to unfair criticism from "some in the media."

Then, the second remove: By defending the victims of elitism, Palin's followers maintained, she herself became . . . a victim of elitism, a walking example of the very persecution of middle America she had made it her business to deplore. Dizzying! Naturally, Rush Limbaugh put it best. "You're being told by the media propagandists that Sarah Palin is not qualified to be vice president. You're being told she's dumb." Then came the populist turn: "These attacks on Governor Palin are attacks on you and attacks on me. They are attacking every single person outside the Beltway, outside the New York–Washington axis, outside their social circle of elitist friends that represents what's great about this country."

All these attacks on the good people of the trans-Beltway region, and yet no actual, physical attacks to speak of! The need for such a manifestation was ontological; it had to happen, and before long a College Republican field representative in Pennsylvania stepped forward to reveal to the world the stigmata of

Middle America's persecution. She had been robbed and beaten, she told Pittsburgh police, by a tall mysterious black man who, upon discovering her GOP affiliation, proceeded to carve a backward "B" onto her cheek—a "B" as in Barack, that tormenter of average Joes everywhere.

The next day, however, the victim recanted her tale and the whole thing fell apart.

It was more than just one clumsy, apparently self-inflicted beating that fell apart in 2008. Maybe, with that grotesque backward "B", we finally reached the freakish conclusion of the GOP's long-running persecution melodrama itself. Outside the theater, things on Main Street were turning ugly. Middle America was heading for the exits. And so the curtain came down on a movement that once dreamed of permanence, now punching itself forlornly in the face.

One of the last dispatches to arrive from privatopia emerged from a Georgia food factory that was found in early 2009 to have shipped salmonella-laced peanut butter around the country. It was just one of many toxic food outrages to crop up during the final years of the Bush administration and, like the others, it was the fruit of laissez-faire politics. The company in question operated without much oversight from government: The Food and Drug Administration did not inspect plants like the one in question; regulatory authority was held instead by underpaid and overworked state agencies. Under the industry's "self-policing" rules, the company could blow off salmonella alerts if it wanted and choose its own inspectors, despite the obvious conflicts of interest these situations entailed. Even when the toxic stuff was finally recalled, the operation was voluntary—and done on the company's schedule.

There is no evidence that the peanut company in question fielded lobbyists or bribed legislators, but its story is emblematic of the conservative era nonetheless. Deregulation, the economics and law professor William K. Black says, is often "criminogenic," and when I hear that word I think not so much of clean electronic credit-default swaps, but of all the mold and filth that inspectors found in that peanut plant in Georgia.

Our ancestors understood that capitalism requires supervision; when you take it away—or when you defund the supervisors, or make them answer to the supervised, or replace them with a "voluntary compliance" program—suddenly you've got diseased factories shipping salmonella-laced peanut butter throughout the country. You've got worthless mortgage-backed securities—rated triple-A, backed up by useless appraisals, issued by defunct banks—sickening financial institutions from San Diego to Budapest. You've got the world's greatest Ponzi scheme spreading its gift of bankruptcy throughout the land.

Thus did the conservative movement keep its appointment with destiny. Free-market techniques secured for it a world of free markets; criminal techniques gave it a land in which crime was triumphant. And with their eyes fixed firmly on their nineteenth-century utopia, its armies of privatizers, pressure boys, PAC men, political entrepreneurs, and professional victims made the world safe for predation. Putting civilization back together again is a job they left for the rest of us.

Notes

Interviews

Scott Amey, March 9, 2006
Carl Auerbach, March 14, 2006
Daniel Bell, February 6, 2006
Leo Bosner, October 18, 2005
Albert Braunfisch, January 16, 2007
Pam Brown, March 8, 2007
Jim Burton, July 27, 2007
Mark Cooper, October 3, 2007
Alan Crawford, October 15, 2007
John Daniel, January 15, 2007
Paul Erasmus, January 18, 2007
Jim Jontz, January 12, 2006
Hugh Kaufman, February 21, 2008
Dennis Kilcoyne, February 12, 2007
Moonyeen Lee, February 19, 2007
Peter Leon, January 31, 2007
David Miner, April 24, 2006, and January 28, 2007
Elwood Mott, March 28, 2007
Grover Norquist, March 21 and May 1, 2006
Dan O'Meara, February 7, 2007
Richard Pierce, May 14, 2007

Robert Reich, October 14, 2007
Dana Rohrabacher, December 13, 2006
Jacque Simon, March 14, 2006
Mike Simpfenderfer, January 3, 2007
Allen Stayman, March 21, 2006, and March 12, 2007
John Threlkeld, March 14, 2006
Jim Tozzi, March 21, 2008
Richard Viguerie, October 24, 2006

Introduction: Follow This Dime

1. In 2005, the Bureau of Economic Analysis ranked the Washington-Baltimore–northern Virginia "combined statistical area" third in per capita income, surpassed only by the New York metro area and the San Jose–San Francisco area. When the various cities' per capita personal incomes are compared to the national average, the difference between these three richest metro areas shrinks to almost nothing; they are bunched together at a level well above the rest of the nation.

   When we examine the BEA's statistics over time, the historical rise and fall of the nation's cities becomes strikingly clear. In 1969, when "big government" was at its biggest, Washington ranked ninth in per capita income among the metro areas, behind Chicago, Los Angeles, and Detroit. Its fortunes were indistinguishable from these other big cities. In 1982, though, Washington began moving sharply upward, while Detroit and Los Angeles were heading south. The capital's numbers cooled in 1988 and then boomed again beginning in 1998. The Bush II years were a period of uninterrupted prosperity for the region.

   For a wealth of anecdotal information about the capital's rise to the top tier of American cities, see *Washingtonian* magazine for November 2006, the cover of which carries this headline: "In the Money: How Washington Got Really Rich—and How It's Changing Us."
2. Mary Elting, in collaboration with Margaret Gossett, *We Are the Government* (Garden City, N.Y.: Doubleday, Doran, 1945).
3. Abramoff as greedy: This is the thesis of *Heist,* Peter H. Stone's 2006 account of the Abramoff affair. The quote comes from p. 9. Abramoff as having "gone native": This was a common theme in scandal interpretation. See the various conservatives quoted by Dick Polman, "Republicans Fearful of Abramoff Backlash," a story which ran in Knight-Ridder newspapers, January 22, 2006; or the remarks of George Will on an ABC News program on November 27, 2005: "This is an example of the Republicans having gone native with a certain unseemly exuberance. This is called K-Street conservatism." Abramoff as "sui generis": Holman Jenkins, "Indian Taker," *Wall Street Journal,* January 11, 2006.

4. Public interest: I am referring here to former FCC chairman Michael Powell (son of Colin), who related in a speech in 1998, "The night after I was sworn in, I waited for a visit from the angel of the public interest. I waited all night, but she did not come. And, in fact, five months into this job, I still have had no divine awakening and no one has issued me my public interest crystal ball." The entire speech can be read here: http://www.fcc.gov/Speeches/Powell/spmkp806.txt. For examples of the others, read the rest of this book.
5. Others have suggested this before. For example, see Robert Borosage's essay, "Why Conservatives Can't Govern," published on TomPaine.com on March 19, 2007.

Chapter 1: Golconda on the Potomac

1. These are, respectively, Howard and Montgomery counties in Maryland and Prince William County, Virginia, which borders Loudoun to the south. These are the richest counties of more than 250,000 people, as measured by median household income. Bruce H. Webster Jr. and Alemayehu Bishaw, U.S. Census Bureau, *Income, Earnings, and Poverty Data from the 2005 American Community Survey* (Washington, D.C.: U.S. Government Printing Office, 2006), table 2, p. 6.
2. Compare this to the similarly sized metro areas of Atlanta (five BMW dealers) and Cleveland (six BMW dealers, if we include Akron).
3. This includes the Ritz-Carlton "leadership center" in Chevy Chase, the Ritz-Carlton suburb in Loudoun County, and the metro area's four Ritz-Carlton hotels.
4. I know because I read an article about the Reagan appointee who made it a showplace of outsourcing. John Rees, interview with Danford Sawyer, *Review of the NEWS,* July 7, 1982, pp. 39–50.
5. Joel Garreau, *Edge City: Life on the New Frontier* (New York: Doubleday, 1991), p. 351. Washington seems to exert a magnetic attraction on celebrators of suburbia. David Brooks's rosy meditations on suburbia in his 2004 book, *On Paradise Drive,* instantly mark him as an inhabitant of the D.C. metro area. The latest priest of this faith is Richard Florida, a professor at a university located in the Virginia suburbs, who finds the city "a booming, far-flung region that's a key node in what [he] call[s] the Creative Economy." Florida, "A Creative Crossroads," *Washington Post,* May 7, 2006.
6. Oliver McKee Jr., "Washington as a Boom Town," *North American Review,* February 1935.
7. New Dealers' stories: See Katie Louchheim, *The Making of the New Deal: The Insiders Speak* (Cambridge, Mass.: Harvard University Press, 1983). The transformation of New Dealers into lobbyists is a persistent theme of Joseph C. Goulden's *The Superlawyers,* which focuses in

particular on Tommy Corcoran, who had been a close adviser to Roosevelt; the law firm of Arnold and Porter, named for the trust buster Thurman Arnold and Office of Price Administration chief Paul Porter; and Clark Clifford, a senior adviser to Harry Truman who later became the very personification of Washington insiderdom. Goulden, *The Superlawyers: The Small and Powerful World of the Great Washington Law Firms* (New York: Dell, 1973).

8. In this connection see the final chapter of Thurman Arnold, *The Symbols of Government* (1935; reprint, New York: Harcourt, Brace, 1962). Arnold headed the Antitrust Division of the Justice Department in the late thirties.
9. Felix Frankfurter, "The Young Men Go to Washington," a 1936 essay reprinted in Frankfurter, *Law and Politics: Occasional Papers of Felix Frankfurter, 1913–1938,* ed. Archibald MacLeish and E. F. Prichard Jr. (New York: Harcourt, Brace, 1939), p. 249.
10. The chairman of TVA was David Lilienthal; the head of OPA was Leon Henderson, who eventually resigned in the face of all the enmity brought on by his refusal to do favors for lobbyists and members of Congress. The stories of both men's travails are told in David Brinkley's account of Washington during World War II, *Washington Goes to War* (New York: Knopf, 1988), pp. 116, 129–33.

    Roosevelt's nominee to head the Federal Reserve was Marriner Eccles. This anecdote is related in Alan Brinkley, *The End of Reform: New Deal Liberalism in Recession and War* (New York: Vintage, 1995), p. 81.
11. I am thinking in particular of Evalyn Walsh McLean, famous for owning the Hope Diamond, and Cissy Patterson, the owner of the fanatically right-wing *Washington Times-Herald*. Their stories are told by David Brinkley, *Washington Goes to War,* chap. 6. The point about imported wealth is also made by W. M. Kiplinger in *Washington Is* Like *That* (New York: Harper & Brothers, 1942), p. 8. David Graham Phillips, *The Social Secretary* (Indianapolis: Bobbs Merrill, 1905), p. 12.
12. "Pity the Poor Hostess," *Saturday Evening Post,* September 5, 1936, pp. 30, 82, 84, 86. This final remark is attributed by the anonymous author to "one of the most resourceful women living in the capital."
13. See an original sales brochure for Arlington Forest houses online at http://www.capaccess.org/forest/broc1.html.
14. Michael Laris, "Landowners Cry Foul Over Zoning Proposal; Hearing on Consent Issue Heated," *Washington Post,* June 8, 2000; Graeme Zielinski, "Political Fireworks Fly on the Fourth; Groups Promote Views For, Against Growth," *Washington Post,* July 9, 2000.
15. One case is described here: http://www.loudoun.gov/controls/speerio/resources/RenderContent.aspx?data=f25ed5c1610246ac8d7fd113195d8f5b&optimize=100&tabid=312&fmpath=%2fPress+Releases%2fSupervisor+Burton%2f.

16. Michael Laris and David S. Fallis, "Influence of Developers, Allies Runs Deep," *Washington Post,* January 21, 2007.
17. Citizens for Property Rights, the main organization of the developers' faction, ran several advertisements accusing county supervisor Jim Burton, one of the leaders of the "smart growth" faction, of self-dealing. These appeared in the *Loudoun Easterner* on November 15, 2000, and April 11, 2001. Burton rebutted the allegations in a letter to the *Loudoun Easterner* on April 18, 2001.
18. Laris and Fallis, "Influence of Developers."
19. Head of Planning Commission: David S. Fallis and Michael Laris, "Official Backed Plans of Business Connections; Former Planning Chief Had Ties to Companies," *Washington Post,* January 22, 2007. De facto leader: David S. Fallis and Michael Laris, "Loudoun Official Tried to Capitalize on Contacts; Supervisor Tulloch Sees No Conflicts," *Washington Post,* June 1, 2007.
20. Michael Laris and Rosalind S. Helderman, "Five New Players May Chart New Course for Board," *Washington Post,* November 9, 2003.
21. Delgaudio on Vince Foster: Susan Schmidt, "Million-Dollar Tales of Death and Danger; Fund-Raising Letters High in Drama Bring Contributions for 'Clinton Investigative Commission,'" *Washington Post,* July 22, 1996. Delgaudio on the gay menace: Michael Laris, "Anti-Tax in Loudoun, Anti-Gay Everywhere; Local Supervisor Leads National Lobbying Effort," *Washington Post,* April 8, 2002. See also the remarkable Delgaudio fund-raising letter posted at http://www.equalityloudoun.org/?p=86.
22. http://www.publicadvocateusa.org/photogallery/.

Chapter 2: Their Enemy, the State

1. Marshall E. Dimock, "Do Business Men Want Good Government?" *National Municipal Review,* January 1931, p. 33.
2. Read Harding's inaugural address here: http://www.presidency.ucsb.edu/ws/index.php?pid=25833.
3. See John T. Flynn, "Business and the Government," *Harper's Magazine,* March 1928.
4. In describing the laissez-faire faith, the historian Clinton Rossiter writes, "The men of the Right thought they had stumbled on eternal truth, and they were neither modest nor tentative in proclaiming their solution to the riddle of the ages." The role of the church, as conservatives saw it in the nineteenth century, was "to make the unsuccessful happy with their lot; to assure the successful that, in Bishop Lawrence's words, 'Godliness is in league with riches.'" Rossiter, *Conservatism in America* (New York: Knopf, 1955), pp. 160, 149.
5. "Why has American conservatism been so rarely marked by stability or political responsibility?" asked the historian Arthur M. Schlesinger Jr.

in 1948. "In great part because conservative politics here has been peculiarly the property of the plutocracy." *The Vital Center: The Politics of Freedom* (1949; reprint, New York: Da Capo, 1988), p. 25. See also Rossiter, *Conservatism in America,* p. 100.

In *A Brief History of Neoliberalism* (New York: Oxford University Press, 2005), David Harvey asks whether conservatism's commitment to the business class is "utopian" or merely "political." In other words, does it aim to bring about some kind of pure libertarian state, or does it merely intend to restore the social power that the business class lost during the age of liberalism—roughly, the thirties to the seventies? Harvey's answer is the latter; utopian libertarianism nearly always gives way to the needs and desires of the business class. See p. 19.

6. Phillips's articles are generally regarded as the zenith of the muckraking movement, evoking a famous rebuke from President Theodore Roosevelt. They were assembled into book form many years later. David Graham Phillips, *The Treason of the Senate,* ed. George E. Mowry (Chicago: Quadrangle, 1964), p. 59.
7. Phillips, *Treason of the Senate,* pp. 83, 210.
8. David Stockman, *The Triumph of Politics: The Inside Story of the Reagan Revolution* (New York: Avon, 1987), p. 37.
9. For example, see Fred S. McChesney, *Money for Nothing: Politicians, Rent Extraction, and Political Extortion* (Cambridge, Mass.: Harvard University Press, 1997).
10. This is former FCC chairman Michael Powell again, with his famous "angels of the public interest" speech.
11. Quotations are from Wallop's "Final Address," delivered on December 1, 1994. This speech used to be posted proudly on the Frontiers of Freedom Web site; you accessed it through a link reading "Genesis of the Frontiers of Freedom Institute."
12. P. J. O'Rourke, *Parliament of Whores: A Lone Humorist Attempts to Explain the Entire U.S. Government* (New York: Atlantic Monthly Press, 1991), p. 14.
13. These are proposals of Frank Chodorov (*The Income Tax: Root of All Evil* [New York: Devin-Adair, 1954]), and the law professor Richard A. Epstein, who writes in his landmark book *Takings*: "It will be said that my position invalidates much of the twentieth-century legislation, and so it does. . . . If my arguments here are correct, then any New Deal economic and social legislation that suffers from the vices of the labor statutes in principle should be consigned to the same constitutional fate [i.e., overturned]. The New Deal *is* inconsistent with the principles of limited government and with the constitutional provisions designed to secure that end." Epstein, *Takings: Private Property and the Power of Eminent Domain* (Cambridge, Mass.: Harvard University Press, 1985), p. 281. Emphasis in original.

14. Right-wing Washington chattered gleefully about how the good folks "outside the Beltway" didn't really care about the shutdown, and Texas senator Phil Gramm took to the airwaves to scoff, "Have you missed the government?" The conservative thinker John Podhoretz later confessed that he had wanted to see the great train wreck happen because "it would make the case for conservatism better than anything else. People would realize that the federal government did little for them, and they would see Clinton as the defender of bureaucrats and fiefdoms." "A Reaganite Reconsiders," *Weekly Standard,* February 5, 1996. Before long, though, the polling pendulum swung dramatically against the Republicans, and all such language disappeared.

    DeLay: Quoted in Joel Bleifuss, "DeLay May Be Gone, But His Legacy Isn't," *In These Times,* June 27, 2006. Gramm: Quoted in Michael Gerson, "Open Arms Conservatism," *Washington Post,* October 31, 2007. For examples of winger speculation about how little the outside world cared about the shutdown, see James C. Miller III, "Government Shutdown? 'See If Anybody Notices,'" *Wall Street Journal,* October 13, 1995; Donald Lambro, "Drawing an Essential Lesson . . . ," *Washington Times,* November 20, 1995; Nancy Roman, "For Both Sides, It's Personal," *Washington Times,* November 16, 1995; Donald Lambro, "'Nonessential' Tag Backs GOP Call for Cuts in Cabinet," *Washington Times,* November 15, 1995; Nancy Roman, "Outside Beltway, Who Cares About Shutdown?" *Washington Times,* November 10, 1995; Pete Du Pont, "Shutdown Syndrome," *Washington Times*, September 7, 1995.

    There are countless other examples of conservative glee over the shutdown. Jack Wheeler, who claims to have inspired the "Reagan Doctrine," rejoiced in 1996 about the problems the shutdown had caused for the Equal Employment Opportunity Commission. "Now this winter's government shutdowns have collapsed the EEOC into gridlock and paralysis. So 'Hooters,' the restaurant chain . . . successfully defied and publicly made fun of the EEOC. . . . What is happening to the EEOC is beginning to happen to federal bureaucracies across the board. The Washington Colonial Empire is imploding, collapsing in upon itself." Wheeler, "The Technology of Freedom: Why Governments Are Becoming Obsolete," *Policy Counsel,* Fall 1996, p. 66.

15. "We have had a tumultuous national referendum on everything in our half-trillion-dollar welfare state budget," David Stockman wrote in 1986. "By virtue of experiencing the battle day after day in the legislative and bureaucratic trenches, I am as qualified as anyone to discern the verdict. Lavish Social Security benefits, wasteful dairy subsidies, futile UDAG [Urban Development Action Grant] grants, and all the remainder of the federal subventions do not persist solely due to weak-kneed politicians or the nefarious graspings of special-interest groups.

    "Despite their often fuzzy rhetoric and twisted rationalizations, congressmen and senators ultimately deliver what their constituencies demand. . . . What you see done in the halls of the politicians may not be wise, but it is the only real and viable definition of what the electorate wants." Stockman, *Triumph of Politics,* pp. 408–9.

Public opinion has remained remarkably solid on these matters, despite Congress's dramatic swing to the right in the period 1995–2006. On this see Jacob S. Hacker and Paul Pierson, *Off Center: The Republican Revolution and the Erosion of American Democracy* (New Haven, Conn.: Yale University Press, 2005), pp. 34, 38.

16. Sam Tanenhaus, "Is Bush Conservative Enough?" *Los Angeles Times,* July 22, 2003. See also Bruce Bartlett, *Impostor: How George W. Bush Bankrupted America and Betrayed the Reagan Legacy* (New York: Doubleday, 2006), pp. 10–11.
17. Albert Jay Nock, *Our Enemy, The State* (1935; reprint, New York: Arno Press, 1972), pp. 45, 12, 17.
18. Ibid., pp. 94, 57, 120, 95. Nock's account relies heavily on the work of Charles Beard, a then-fashionable and very liberal historian, whose famous *Economic Interpretation of the Constitution* had been published in 1913.
19. Nock, *Our Enemy, the State,* p. 58.
20. Olney as quoted in Matthew Josephson, *The Politicos: 1865–1896* (New York: Harcourt, Brace and Company, 1938), p. 526. Ellipses in Josephson.
21. George W. Norris, "Boring from Within," *Nation,* September 16, 1925, p. 298. On the general political solicitude for business during the twenties, see also John D. Hicks, *Republican Ascendancy, 1921–1933* (New York: Harper and Brothers, 1960), pp. 62–68.
22. George J. Stigler, "The Theory of Economic Regulation," *Bell Journal of Economics and Management Science,* Spring 1971, pp. 12, 17. Stigler's larger criticism was that regulation had effectively formed cartels across the economy. In certain industries this was true: by creating barriers to entry and regulating prices, regulatory agencies made cartels possible; the agencies' capture by industry sealed the deal.

    Although Stigler got the Nobel Prize for pointing this out, the idea had in fact been spelled out in far greater and more convincing detail by the historian Gabriel Kolko in his 1963 book, *The Triumph of Conservatism.* Kolko's thesis was that the original regulatory agencies of the Progressive Era were deliberately set up *in order to* cartelize the economy; that politics furnished a means of achieving the monopolies and oligopolies that business could not build on its own.
23. J. Peter Grace himself made this point in his summary of the commission's findings: "Government-run enterprises lack the driving forces of marketplace competition, which promote tight, efficient operations. This bears repetition, because it is such a profound and important truth." Grace, *Burning Money: The Waste of Your Tax Dollars* (New York: Macmillan, 1984), p. 141.

24. The Grace Commission's final report was published as *War on Waste: President's Private Sector Survey on Cost Control* (New York: Macmillan, n.d. [1984]). The "top executives" are mentioned on p. vi; a list of their names and employers is given in chap. 10.
25. David Osborne and Ted Gaebler, *Reinventing Government: How the Entrepreneurial Spirit Is Transforming the Public Sector* (New York: Plume, 1993), pp. xix, 1, 70. Al Gore, *Businesslike Government: Lessons Learned from America's* <u>*Best*</u> *Companies* (Washington, D.C.: National Performance Review, 1997).
26. This undated quotation can be found in Office of Management and Budget, *The President's Management Agenda* (2001), p. 17. Read it online at http://www.whitehouse.gov/omb/budget/fy2002/mgmt.pdf.
27. " 'Winger' from way back": Quoted in Robert Dreyfuss, "Grover Norquist: 'Field Marshal' of the Bush Plan," *Nation,* May 14, 2001.
28. Matt Miller, "Make 150,000% Today! Looking for a Great Return on Investment? Hire a Lobbyist," *Fortune,* January 27, 2006.

Chapter 3: The World as War and Conspiracy

1. Sidney Blumenthal.: *The Rise of the Counter-Establishment: From Conservative Ideology to Political Power* (New York: Perennial Library, 1988), p. 6. Bush as dissident: These are the president's own words. Peter Baker, "As Democracy Push Falters, Bush Feels Like a 'Dissident,' " *Washington Post,* August 20, 2007. Rebel-in-Chief: Fred Barnes, *Rebel-in-Chief: Inside the Bold and Controversial Presidency of George W. Bush* (New York: Crown Forum, 2006), p. 14.
2. The punk band intended its name as a play on "Hitler Youth," but others used the term with complete ingenuousness. In the College Republicans' newsletter for September 15, 1983 ("Jack Abramoff, Chairman"), we read about the CRs' plans for the "Reagan Youth Effort" and about a "Youth for Reagan caravan" being set up for the GOP convention the next year. "We are the sons of Reagan," the band sang, and this phrase, too, has echoes across wingerdom. Grover Norquist wrote an essay called "Reagan's Children" for the *American Spectator* in May 1999, arguing that demographics now tilted in the GOP's favor. The pundit Hans Zeiger used the same phrase in 2006 as a title for his book about youthful conservatism.
3. Then again, this phenomenon is an evergreen perennial among journalists, who, it seems, rediscover young conservatism every ten years or so. For a particularly egregious example of this, see M. Stanton Evans's 1961 book, *Revolt on the Campus,* which foresaw the sixties as a decade of the right.
4. The twenty-year-old was Marc Holtzman, who was profiled in "Revenge of the Nerd," a story by Norman Atkins that ran in *Rolling Stone,* October 9, 1986.

5. Specifically, this was how the Abramoff crony Ralph Reed explained his generation's dawning self-awareness to a crowd of fellow conservatives in 1987. In those days, a "first strike" referred specifically to a nuclear attack on the other superpower, that is, the Soviet Union. To apply the phrase to Iran is confusing since that country could obviously mount no retaliatory, or second, strike, making it unnecessary to distinguish a first strike from any other. I suspect the phrase appealed to Reed because of its similarity to the labor/leftist slogan "strike now," which (incidentally) has nothing to do with nuclear war. Reed's fond memories can be found in the 1987 book *The Third Generation: Young Conservative Leaders Look to the Future,* ed. Benjamin Hart (Washington, D.C.: Regnery Gateway), pp. 68–69.

   Reed's story is retold as a Generation X archetype in *13th Gen,* the most substantial of the pop sociology books about youth to appear in the early nineties. Neil Howe and Bill Strauss, *13th Gen: Abort, Retry, Ignore, Fail?* (New York: Vintage, 1993), p. 50.
6. I am referring to the crowd of budding journalists surrounding the *Dartmouth Review,* the flagship of right-wing campus journalism and supposedly a beacon of hope to the young generation in the eighties. (Ben Hart, editor of the *Third Generation* anthology referenced in the previous note, had been one of the founders of the publication in 1980.) The persecution myth is so deeply instilled in the *Review* that its twenty-fifth anniversary Festschrift was titled *The Dartmouth Review Pleads Innocent: Twenty-Five Years of Being Threatened, Impugned, Vandalized, Sued, Suspended, and Bitten at the Ivy League's Most Controversial Conservative Newspaper.*
7. This was the assessment of John Rees, writing in the John Birch Society's magazine *Review of the NEWS* for September 8, 1982.

   Abramoff's achievement in Massachusetts was also described by S. J. Masty in "College Republicans Are the New 'Campus Radicals,' " a profile of Abramoff that appeared in *Human Events* on June 18, 1983. "In the 1980 election, Reagan carried Massachusetts by only 3,000 votes," Masty wrote. "The College Republicans, who registered and turned out nearly 16,000 students and others for Reagan, won him the state."
8. Fought the power: " 'In the '60s, the liberal element were "on the outs" and the conservatives were the "ins," ' Abramoff said. 'We are now on the outs and want to be part of the establishment. They are the establishment and we are the ones who want change.' " "College GOP Launches Covert Attack on PIRGs," Joshua Peck, Pacific News Service, photocopied newspaper article in PIRG files, n.d. (1983).

   "Campus radicals": Masty, "College Republicans," p. 12.

   Instructing kids: When I interviewed Mike Simpfenderfer, who had been the CRs' secretary when Abramoff was chairman, I asked if imitating sixties radicals was a deliberate strategy of theirs. "Yes," he said. "That's what we talked about when we taught our seminars. Don't criticize them. . . . The left knew how to get the attention, how to get the media tactics, we realized, why would we want to argue with that? They figured out a methodology that worked. Let's use that same methodology [for] what President Reagan wants to get done. And people were so hungry for something to happen. That's what caused a lot of the organizations to grow. Jack understood that better than anybody."

9. The photographs appear in the College Republican National Committee's *1983 Annual Report,* p. 12. This slightly cultish document includes at least seven other photos of Abramoff (two show him in the company of President Reagan), an essay bearing his signature, an interview with him, and a letter from Reagan to the future corruptionist.

 Ralph Reed went on to replicate the Abramoff approach with his own student organization, Students for America, which was designed to ignite a "conservative student upheaval in the 1980's modeled after the student movement of the 1960's." This is according to an unnamed leader of the group quoted in Stacy E. Palmer, "Conservatives Cheer Falwell, Excoriate Fonda," *Chronicle of Higher Education,* January 30, 1985, p. 17.

10. Rick Henderson and Steven Hayward, "Happy Warrior," an interview with Grover Norquist, *Reason*, February 1997.
11. These moves are partially described in Nina Easton, *Gang of Five: Leaders at the Center of the Conservative Crusade* (New York: Simon and Schuster, 2000), pp. 140–41.
12. Each of these men was featured prominently at some point in Richard Viguerie's *Conservative Digest*. Phillips wrote a column for the magazine; Buchanan was its hero inside government. The first story about Jack Abramoff can be found in the issue for November 1982.
13. Weyrich's famous remark can be found in John S. Saloma III, *Ominous Politics: The New Conservative Labyrinth* (New York: Hill and Wang, 1984), p. 49.
14. Jolly YAF song from 1971, quoted by Alan Crawford (a onetime editor of the YAF magazine) in *Thunder on the Right: The "New Right" and the Politics of Resentment* (New York: Pantheon, 1980), p. 22.
15. S. J. Masty, "Capital Sketch: Poster War Rocks Lafayette Square," *Washington Times,* July 5, 1985. According to the YAF's Web site, the "war" with the protesters went on all that summer: "equipped with a newly appropriated white van the Lafayette Park Liberation Squad tore through Lafayette Park liberating the Park from any would-be dwellers" until the city government threw the protesters out. See http://www.yaf.com/history.
16. High school bully: "He was the sort of person who would walk across the street to be unpleasant to somebody," recalls Jonathan Gold, a restaurant reviewer for the *LA Weekly,* who attended high school with

Abramoff. Gold also describes being knocked down a staircase by Abramoff (then a champion weight lifter) on the radio show *This American Life,* episode 314, aired June 23, 2006. Abramoff's lawyer denied that the incident took place.

"Hard-charging": *Human Events,* July 23, 1983, p. 18.

"Dynamic": *Conservative Digest,* January, 1985, p. 3.

Fists: " 'Another time,' said Abramoff, 'some Communist students tried to break up a College Republican meeting. One guy was throwing chairs and physically assaulting our members. He came up about three inches from my face, yelled obscenities, and pushed me. Well, I was taught that you don't have to take it from those people.' Abramoff decked him with a one-two punch, and was reprimanded by college authorities while the instigator didn't even receive a warning." Masty, "College Republicans," p. 13.

17. *Godfather* references: These occur regularly in Abramoff's published e-mail correspondence. My favorite example comes in an exchange between Abramoff and his lobbyist colleague Dennis Stephens on March 1, 2001. Stephens refers to Abramoff's efforts to get Stephens appointed to the Interior Department as "the Johnny Fontane project," after a character in *The Godfather* whose career the various fictional cutthroats are determined to advance. Abramoff got the reference, of course; it was his favorite movie. He replied the same day, "I just hope I don't have to put a horse head in his [Karl Rove's] bed."

    Meyer Lansky: Abramoff had a signed Meyer Lansky item on display at his restaurant, Signatures. Albert Eisele, "Signatures: A Special Place to Dine With History," *The Hill,* May 8, 2002.

    Example of murderer argot: "It will be a great day when stayman is whacked," a member of Team Abramoff rejoiced in 2001, referring to Al Stayman, a State Department official who had opposed the low-wage agenda of Abramoff's client, the Northern Mariana Islands. Stayman was fired soon afterward. The "whacked" e-mail is described in the Staff Report of the House Government Reform Committee, September 29, 2006, pp. 64–65. See also Peter Wallsten, "Displease a Lobbyist, Get Fired," *Los Angeles Times,* October 15, 2006.

18. A College Republican "technology manual" from the early eighties suggested that an effective response to the appearance on campus of "gay rights groups and the homoseual [*sic*] social clubs" was to "try imitating the left."

    > Form a "Beastiality Club," [*sic*] or "Straight People's Alliance". Charter the club and apply for student activity money. If the gays are able to obtain funds, you should be able to. If the student government refuses to give you money, hold a press conference and attack them for being 'sexists' and discriminatory. Complain to the Dean's office. . . . Threaten a law suit.

College Republican Technology Manual, from PIRG files, n.d. The same "technology manual" is quoted at length by Nina Easton in *Gang of Five,* p. 151.

19. "Wishy-washy"/"ideological": *Human Events,* June 18, 1983, p. 13.
20. He also warned that "the lesbians" were "assuming a role in the educational process." Jack Abramoff, meanwhile, was described as the opposite of all these unmanly characteristics. "Jack, not known for being a squish," stood up for the author's right-wing campus paper when even the local College Republicans had turned against it. J. Michael Waller, "Bare-Fisted Journalism," *New Guard,* Winter 1982–83.
21. "Boring wimp": *Conservative Digest,* September 1984, p. 14.
22. "Fritzbusters" images can be found wherever one digs in the right-wing student literature of those days, and the shirts and stickers can still be found at thrift stores and on eBay. The lyrics of the "Fritzbusters" song appeared in the *Washington Post* on September 20, 1984. An estimate of the number of "Fritzbusters" T-shirts sold appears in James Barron, "Young Fritzbusters Are Reined In," *New York Times,* October 4, 1984.
23. Michael Barone, "A Tale of Two Nations," *U.S. News and World Report,* May 12, 2003. See also Barone's book on the subject, *Hard America, Soft America: Competition vs. Coddling and the Battle for the Nation's Future* (New York: Crown Forum, 2004).
24. "Fighting America's last stand": John Rees, "Collegiate Conservative Jack A. Abramoff: An Exclusive Interview About Young Conservatives On the Campuses With the National Chairman of the College Republicans," *Review of the NEWS,* September 8, 1982, p. 50. "Defund the enemy": Steve Baldwin, director of the CRs' "Project Inform," quoted in Charles Crossfield, "College Republicans Back on the Front Lines," *Conservative Digest,* November 1982.
25. This is J. Michael Waller, the author of the aforementioned article on "Bare-Fisted Journalism" and a "deputy projects director" for the College Republican National Committee in 1982 and '83. The *Sequent* repeatedly attacked Washington-area professors for their "Marxist bias," as the issue of February 8, 1984, put it. The same issue bears the headline "Christmas Break on the Nicaraguan Front Lines" and describes a week Waller spent hobnobbing with the Contras. The issue for March 1984 carries the headline "Spring break in El Salvador" and features an interview with the notorious death squad leader Roberto d'Aubuisson, who "has been repeatedly attacked by the liberal United States media for his strong conservative views and frank words."
26. Abramoff's remark about ending "peaceful coexistence with the Left" appeared in the *1983 Annual Report* of the College Republicans. Like so many of his ideas from those days, this one appears to have originated with the Conservative Caucus leader Howard Phillips, who submitted a memo to President Reagan in 1982 calling on him to abandon his "strategy of consensus or 'detente' with [his] political adversaries in

the Congress, the Washington establishment, and the nationwide liberal support network." Phillips reprinted the memo as appendix B in his book *The New Right at Harvard* (Vienna, Va.: Conservative Caucus, 1983), p. 181.

27. The word "revolution" could even take on the wistful notes of lost youth, as at a 1992 College Republican reunion when Abramoff, by then a producer of wretched movies, hosted an alumni session called "Rejoin the Revolution." See 1992 College Republicans' *Centennial Celebration* (n.p.: n.p., n.d. [1992]).

    Sword and shield: "Message from the Chairman" in the *1983 Annual Report* of the College Republicans, p. 3. The phrase is also used in the 1982 *Review of the NEWS* interview cited above and in a 1995 profile by John W. Moore, "A Lobbyist With a Line to Capitol Hill," *National Journal,* July 29, 1995. "Fighting for the Revolution": *CR Report,* May 14, 1983, p. 5. 1984 Republican Convention: Raleigh E. Milton, ed., *Official Report of the Proceedings of the Thirty-Third Republican National Convention* (Republican National Committee: n.p., 1984), p. 21. What Abramoff said was, "It's the job of all revolutions to make permanent their gains."
28. Both quotations: *Review of the NEWS,* September 8, 1982.
29. This quotation is from Irvine's preface to James Tyson's *Target America: The Influence of Communist Propaganda on U.S. Media* (Chicago: Regnery, 1981), p. viii. *Target America* was one of the books distributed by Abramoff's central office to campus chapters of the College Republicans.
30. Arnaud de Borchgrave and Robert Moss, *The Spike* (New York: Avon, 1981). There were several references on the floor of Congress to *The Spike* as an accurate description of the way the KGB works. Indeed, for the paperback edition, the authors had to change the name and description of the sinister think tank at the center of the conspiracy because it bore too close a resemblance to the real-life Institute for Policy Studies, which was not, after all, a KGB-controlled organization. Edwin McDowell, "Changes Made in Novel After Suit Is Threatened," *New York Times,* May 10, 1981.
31. Ingo Swann, ed., *What Will Happen to You When the Soviets Take Over* (Belmont, Calif.: Starform, 1980). The book includes an essay by Richard Pipes of the Committee on the Present Danger (it's sandwiched between "Furriers" and "Gas and Electric Workers") and lurid illustrations of KGB agents torturing and killing their way through the country. Fall of the United States, p. 3. Betrayal by our leaders, p. 4. Automobile mechanics, p. 58. Bankers, p. 60.
32. Waller first comes up in the Abramoff corpus in the young leader's September 1982 interview with the *Review of the NEWS,* when Abramoff told the Bircher magazine about his colleagues' enthusiasm for the forthcoming *Sequent.* A few months later Waller returned the favor by

writing admiringly of Abramoff in the YAF's magazine *New Guard*. In 1982 Waller came on board Abramoff's College Republican National Committee as "deputy projects director"; in May of 1983 he and some other CRs pulled a prank at a party held by the Institute for Policy Studies, in those days a favorite bogeyman of the right. Like many of Abramoff's CR homies, Waller also took a job at the United Students of America Foundation, where he served as "director of research." The USA Foundation published Waller's report, "CISPES: A Guerrilla Propaganda Network," in November 1983; it was sent out with cover letters signed by Abramoff in which the future supercorruptionist attested to its great significance.

Waller now says he and several others broke with Abramoff in 1983 after they "suspected [Abramoff] of financial improprieties." After an interlude working for other right-wing groups, however, Waller resurfaces in Abramoff-land in 1992 as "director of international security affairs" at the International Freedom Foundation, which Abramoff had founded six years previously. Waller also thanks Abramoff in the acknowledgments of his 1991 book, *The Third Current of Revolution*. Since the breaking of the Abramoff scandal, however, Waller has become a frequent critic of the fallen lobbyist, recounting for other journalists how Abramoff played Washington's right-wing network for his various lobbying clients. (He did not respond to inquiries from me.)

"Deputy projects director": College Republican National Committee, *Forty-Fifth Biennial Convention* (n.p.: n.p., 1983), n.p. YAF magazine: J. Michael Waller, "Bare-Fisted Journalism," *New Guard*, Winter 1982–83, p. 37. Crashing the IPS party: *CR Report*, May 14, 1983, p. 2. USA Foundation: J. Michael Waller, "CISPES: A Guerrilla Propaganda Network," a twenty-one-page report printed on United Students of America Foundation letterhead, with a cover letter signed by Jack Abramoff and dated November 7, 1983, from collections of Political Research Associates. See also the account of Steven Burkholder, "And Why They Let Anyone Be an Informant," *Washington Monthly*, January 1989. Suspected improprieties: According to Waller's entry on his blog, Fourth World War, for January 3, 2006. "Director of international security affairs" at the International Freedom Foundation: According to the foundation's newsletter, *Freedom Bulletin*, for June 1992. Waller as Abramoff critic: Stone, *Heist*, p. 40.

33. "Congress's Red Army" was the title of an article Waller cowrote with Joseph Sobran for *National Review*, July 31, 1987; the quote about voting with the Soviets can be found on p. 27. Carter administration as pro-Castro: Allan C. Brownfeld and J. Michael Waller, *The Revolution Lobby* (Washington, D.C.: Council for Inter-American Security, 1985), p. 55. Classified documents: *The Revolution Lobby*, note, p. 6.
34. In 1987, along with fellow *Dartmouth Review* firebrand Gregory Fossedal, D'Souza cowrote *My Dear Alex*, a novel made up of letters in

which a senior KGB agent instructs a junior KGB agent on how to get the American media to parrot KGB propaganda, along the way revealing his damning fondness for liberal Democrats. This satanic figure is friends—*friends!*—with Norman Lear and Jane Fonda. He applauds the work of liberal newspaper columnists. He reveals as KGB fabrications the connotations of the word *McCarthyism* and the notion that Hitler was a man of the right. He even invents a handy voter guide to show how frequently the libs in Congress take the Kremlin line.

It was brilliant! Here is how *Human Events* covered the book's publication, in its August 15, 1987 issue.

> Pick your issue: Pershing and MX missile deployment, the Strategic Defense Initiative, or aid to freedom fighters in Nicaragua and Angola. Then compare the positions of, say, Ted Kennedy and Mikhail Gorbachev. The same? They usually are.
>
> This alarming affinity is served up with skill and humor in *My Dear Alex,* a new novel by two of the brightest young rising stars in the conservative movement.

35. "Now it's our turn": Sidney Blumenthal, "Jack Wheeler's Adventures with the 'Freedom Fighters': The Indiana Jones of the Right and His Worldwide Crusade Against the Soviets," *Washington Post,* April 16, 1986.

    Wheeler is, incidentally, one of the few friends of Jack Abramoff to stand by the lobbyist in the hour of his downfall. On his Web site, To The Point News, Wheeler insists that Abramoff is simply the victim of evil liberals up to the same tricks as in the old days. In a revealing post from December 2, 2005, Wheeler recalls how, in 1984, Abramoff went to a gym in Beverly Hills to work out and got "strange looks" from all present. He wondered why. "Then he looked in the mirror and remembered he had put on his favorite t-shirt.

    "In large red letters across the front, the t-shirt said: 'I'd Rather Be Killing Communists.'

    "Now you see why the Democrats demonize him."

    On August 16, 2005, Wheeler offered a more detailed explanation. "Jack Abramoff was frogmarched into Railroad City, nationally humiliated in front of his daughter, and has been the target of a left-wing media vendetta, for one and one reason only: to use him to try and get Tom DeLay," Wheeler fulminated. "The Democrats and the [*sic*] their media buddies could care less about Abramoff. That he was close to DeLay is all that matters. So they harped on and ramped up scandals about him—over a dozen front page stories in the Wa[shington] Po[st] alone—until they had the fascist egos of prosecutors sufficiently lathered up."

36. "Coordinating meetings": Charles Moser and Andrew J. Gatsis, "Free Congress Recommendations," in *Combat on Communist Territory,*

ed. Charles Moser, a book copyrighted by the Free Congress Foundation but published by Regnery (Lake Bluff, Ill., 1985), p. 215.

Freedom fighter fanzine: *Freedom Fighter,* edited by Moser and Warren H. Carroll, the founder of the right-wing Christendom College, was issued by the Freedom League, which had the same street address as the Free Congress Foundation. Articles describing the RENAMO group as an ally of Christianity: See *Freedom Fighter* for April 1986, September 1986, and November–December, 1986. The profile of Gulbadin Hakmatyar appeared in *Freedom Fighter* for November 1985.

RENAMO's "brutal holocaust": This was the 1988 assessment of Deputy Assistant Secretary of State Roy Stacey, as reported by (among many other outlets) the Associated Press, "Mozambique Blames Its Civil War on South Africa," April 27, 1988.

37. "What makes UNITA [Savimbi's guerrilla group] unique in a world replete with resistance movements is that this one vehemently espouses its belief in free enterprise, balanced budgets, self-reliance, regular free and secret elections, and decentralization of power and private property." Peter Worthington, "Anti-Communist Guerrillas on the Verge of Success," *Wall Street Journal,* August 20, 1985.
38. Kirkpatrick, wingers: Phil McCombs, "The Salute to Savimbi: Bush, Kirkpatrick Join a Conservative Chorus," *Washington Post,* February 1, 1986. Norquist: As described in Easton, *Gang of Five,* p. 171. Abramoff: The movie was *Red Scorpion.*
39. "Jonas Savimbi: The Real Leader of the Free World": Phillips reprinted this article four times that I know of. It appeared in his *Issues and Strategies Bulletin* for July 15, 1985, his broadsheet *Grassroots* for December 1985/January 1986, his book *Moscow's Challenge to U.S. Vital Interests in Southern Africa* (Vienna, Va: Policy Analysis Inc., 1987), chap. 11, and in his column in *Conservative Digest,* August 1985. "Savimbi is an extraordinary man": from " 'Made in Moscow' State Dept. Policy for Angola Must Be Overturned," Conservative Caucus *Member's Report,* December 1985, p. 1.
40. The ivory-smuggling racket that kept Savimbi funded is described by Hennie van Vuuren in *Apartheid Grand Corruption: Assessing the Scale of Crimes of Profit from 1976 to 1994* (Pretoria: Institute for Security Studies, 2006), chap. 8. On Savimbi generally, see John Prendergast, "Dealing with Savimbi's Hell on Earth," a Special Report of the United States Institute for Peace dated October 12, 1999, and available online at http://www.usip.org/pubs/specialreports/sr991012.html.
41. Speaking of Jamba, Mike Simpfenderfer, a former colleague of Abramoff's, told me that "never before had anybody gotten a rag-tag group of people from around the world together to talk to each other." I replied, it was quite an extraordinary event. "It was just the way Jack

was able to see things," he continued. "You know, the left always got together in the sixties. The ultimate get-together was at Woodstock. Why shouldn't we get together in our own way? So, again, don't try to reinvent the wheel. And that's where he has a highly creative mind." Me: "So that's what the model was." Simpfenderfer: "That's what it was."

42. On South African involvement, see Chester Crocker, quoted in Easton, *Gang of Five,* p. 166. In a memo addressed to Robert McFarlane dated May 21, 1985, Oliver North and others at the National Security Council discussed the upcoming Jamba gathering and worried about "tainting the 'contras' with the South Africans" since "the meeting location virtually assures some form of South African involvement."
43. Abramoff's planning of the Jamba event is described by Nina Easton in *Gang of Five,* p. 166, and by the journalist Mark Hemingway, "My Dinner with Jack: The Jamboree in Jamba, the Making of 'Red Scorpion,' and Other Tales of the Abramoff Era," *Weekly Standard,* April 3, 2006. The text of the Jamba Declaration, also known as the "Declaration of the Democratic International," appeared in the *Washington Times* on June 6. Norquist's authorship of the "Jamba Accord" is referenced in his bio in *The Third Generation,* p. 246.
44. This was the occasion that moved Howard Phillips to crown Savimbi "the Real Leader of the Free World." There is also a pretentious 1986 documentary film of the Jamba proceedings, *Fires of Freedom,* produced for Citizens for America, the group that formally sponsored the event, and directed by Orin Yost and Carolyn Yost.
45. "The jolt of Jamba," *Washington Times,* June 7, 1985.
46. CFA's founder was the potato tycoon Jack Hume; its leader was Lew Lehrman, the onetime president of Rite Aid drugstores; its Founders Committee was a veritable who's who of eighties money, including Dwayne Andreas, Ivan Boesky, Nelson Bunker Hunt, Henry Kravis, Carl Lindner, various Coorses, a Koch, a couple of big-oil CEOs, a sprinkling of Basses, and T. Boone Pickens.

    "Substantial investment": This is Lehrman's own description of Jack Hume's relationship with Reagan, "The Story Behind 'Citizens for America,'" *Human Events,* December 1, 1984. The membership of the group's Founder's Committee is listed in *Citizens for America First Anniversary* report (dated 1984).
47. Abramoff spoke at the College Republicans National Convention, July 25, 2003. The question he was answering came from one of the young conservatives in the audience: "Are we turning into a big government conservative party? If so, what do we do to get out of that trap?"
48. "Gone native" was an expression commonly used to explain Jack Abramoff's misbehavior as a lobbyist in 2005 and 2006. See, for example, George Will's *Newsweek* column for October 17, 2005, or

Robert Novak's syndicated newspaper column for January 17, 2006. "Becoming cozy with Beltway mores" was an alternate formulation used to explain him away by the editorial page of the *Wall Street Journal* on January 6, 2006.

49. "For years, the Washington social circuit has served as an Ellis Island for immigrants arriving from the backwater provinces with outmoded ideas about limited government," Norquist wrote in 1996. "The embassy receptions and Georgetown dinner parties, with their A- and B-list guests, tantalized and disciplined would-be members of the Establishment. Before they could become proper Washington players, they would first have to be deloused." Norquist, "Georgetown Off My Mind," *American Spectator,* March 1996.

    Ironically, the place I met Norquist was at exactly such a "social circuit" event, although it wasn't in Georgetown.

50. The Conservative Caucus leader Howard Phillips, who worked in the Nixon administration at the Office of Economic Opportunity, recounts how he initially believed in Nixon but became disillusioned when Nixon failed to fully dismember that agency. Nixon won a great victory over liberalism in 1968, he writes, "but tragically, Richard Nixon was not a conservative president, and, he failed to take the actions that would have translated that potential historic turning point into a reality." Phillips, *The New Right at Harvard,* p. 10. See also p. viii.

    Richard Viguerie tells essentially the same story in *The New Right: We're Ready to Lead* (Falls Church, Va.: The Viguerie Company, 1981), pp. 51–52.

51. The once-standard libertarian interpretation of the Reagan administration held that since Reagan did not dismantle the welfare state or even substantially reduce the size of government, his vaunted "Reagan Revolution" never occurred. The classic text here is former OMB director David Stockman's 1986 memoir, *The Triumph of Politics,* and its original subtitle, *How the Reagan Revolution Failed.*

    More populist conservatives distrusted Stockman but developed their own sharp differences with Reagan anyway. Richard Viguerie declared in 1983 that "it doesn't matter who wins the presidential election"; that "there is little difference between the Reagan foreign policy and the Carter foreign policy" (*The Establishment vs. The People: Is a New Populist Revolt On the Way?* [Chicago: Regnery, 1983], p. 9). In that same year Viguerie's colleague Howard Phillips accused the Reagan administration of a "conscious policy of seeking *détente*" with the left—a wording that would later be echoed by Phillips's acolyte Jack Abramoff—and of failing to take down the "Big Banks, the Great Society infrastructure, the imperial judiciary, the Pharisaic lawyers, the cultural priesthood of humanism in the media, the corporate socialists, and the twisters of truth who continue to dominate our principal educational institutions." Howard Phillips, "A Message for the President," *Review of the NEWS,* January 12, 1983, pp. 53–56.

For numerous further examples of the right's equivocations about Reagan, see Godfrey Hodgson, *The World Turned Right Side Up: A History of the Conservative Ascendancy in America* (Boston: Houghton Mifflin, 1996), pp. 248–52.

52. As early as August 1996, with the new Republican Congress only a year and a half into its tenure, Paul Weyrich declared that he was ready to give up on the whole enterprise. "Now, I feel as if I have wasted thirty years of my life—I really feel that way," he moaned to the Council on National Policy. "I feel such an utter sense of betrayal that I would have to stand before you and talk about that kind of leadership—never mind Gingrich, he was never trustworthy—but the rest of them, such a sense of betrayal that I would have to stand before you and mention . . . that Trent Lott, in three weeks time, confirmed ten times the number of federal judges that Bob Dole permitted to be confirmed in the first six months of this year. And this is a guy everybody prayed for to get into the Republican leadership. I could go on and on." Weyrich, "Party Loyalty Must Not Demand Too Much," *Policy Counsel,* Fall 1996, p. 59.

    Weyrich is something of a congenital pessimist. But in 1997, when Gingrich gave up his confrontational stance against President Clinton and decided to give a balanced budget priority over tax cuts, a large chunk of the conservative movement joined the rebellion against him. "Who is the most powerful liberal in American politics?" wrote Pete King, a Republican congressman from New York, referring to Gingrich.

    > He has prevented the Republican majority in Congress from addressing affirmative action and race-based quotas. He has forced congressional Republicans to shelve their drive to defund the National Endowment for the Arts. He has stood firm against tax cuts. He is a confidant of Jesse Jackson's. He is a pal to Alec Baldwin. He is a cheerleader for bipartisan cooperation at any cost and a pious opponent of the unspeakable horrors of harsh partisan rhetoric.

    Peter King, "Why I Oppose Newt," *Weekly Standard,* March 31, 1997. Gingrich resigned in 1999.

53. Bruce Bartlett, *Impostor: How George W. Bush Bankrupted America and Betrayed the Reagan Legacy* (New York: Doubleday, 2006). Bartlett begins his assault on Bush by seeking to prove that Dubya has not been true to the traditions of Ronald Reagan, criticisms of which were no longer in fashion among movement conservatives by 2006. But, of course, no one inflated the deficit as grotesquely as Reagan him-

self, and in this respect, as in many others, Bush was merely doing as Reagan taught.

54. The opportunism of most of this criticism is exemplified by the case of Richard Viguerie. In late 2006 Viguerie published a fire-breathing populist manifesto titled *Conservatives Betrayed: How George W. Bush and Other Big Government Republicans Hijacked the Conservative Cause* (Los Angeles: Bonus Books), and then, when Alberto Gonzales stepped down as attorney general the following summer, released an "open letter" to Bush that began, "I know you and I have had our differences in the past" and went on to propose a list of candidates for the position who might mollify the conservative movement. You could read it here as of August 27, 2007: http://www.conservativesbetrayed.com/gw3/articles-latestnews/articles.php?CMSArticleID=2337&CMSCategoryID=19.

Chapter 4: Marketers of Discontent

1. Abramoff uses the phrase "political entrepreneur" in Stacy E. Palmer, "Conservatives Count on Reagan's Popularity with Young Voters," *Chronicle of Higher Education,* October 31, 1984, p. 14.
2. Coin dealers: The relationship between extreme right-wing sentiment and enthusiasm for gold is a subject that awaits its chronicler. Republican congressman Ron Paul, who coauthored *The Case for Gold* with Lew Lehrman, advertised his services as a rare coin dealer in 1986. The pages of *Conservative Digest* and the various Bircher magazines were routinely filled with ads for precious-metals investment advisers.

   Help beleaguered conservatives: The "Life Amendment PAC," as described in Robert Timberg, "Anti-Abortion PAC Gives Aid Where It Isn't Wanted," *Baltimore Sun,* July 17, 1982.

   Anti-union charity: The National Right to Work Committee. Fake anti-union charity: The National *Freedom* to Work Committee, organized by Howard Jarvis, who later became famous as the leader of the California tax revolt, apparently raised some $250,000 in 1965–66 through telephone solicitations but did nothing to fight organized labor. Alan Crawford, *Thunder on the Right: The "New Right" and the Politics of Resentment* (New York: Pantheon, 1980), pp. 102–3.

   Channell: Quoted in Theodore Draper, *A Very Thin Line: The Iran-Contra Affairs* (New York: Simon and Schuster, 1991), p. 55.
3. Crawford, *Thunder on the Right,* p. 51. The person Crawford is quoting is Terry Dolan of NCPAC.
4. A few efforts deserve honorable mention, however. People for the American Way have a sizable collection of right-wing ephemera from the eighties which they kindly allowed me to peruse. The famous Wilcox Collection on Contemporary Political Movements at the

University of Kansas, while less focused, goes back to the sixties. The latter is comprehensively indexed; PFAW's collection is not. The best account of the direct mailers' business practices is found in Crawford, *Thunder on the Right*.

5. Survey of the direct-mail scene: Crawford, *Thunder on the Right*, chap. 2. Viguerie's defense: *The New Right*, pp. 92–95.
6. The "tax revolt" organization was called the "Populist Conservative Tax Coalition, Inc."; it was advertised on the inside front cover of *Conservative Digest* for May 1984. Viguerie's history of the New Right was *The New Right: We're Ready to Lead;* his populist manifesto was *The Establishment vs. The People: Is a New Populist Revolt on the Way?* The former was advertised on the front cover of *Conservative Digest* for October 1980; the latter on the front cover of *Conservative Digest* for November 1983.
7. The Maryland Democrat survived. NCPAC's TV commercials from 1980 are described in "The War of the Wolf PACs," *Newsweek*, June 1, 1981. "Ruin America" letter, quoted by Mark Shields, *Washington Post*, June 11, 1981. Democrat from Maryland: "The War of the Wolf PACs."
8. Terry Dolan, threat to congressman: Larry J. Sabato, *PAC Power—Inside the World of Political Action Committees* (New York: Norton, 1984), pp. 96, 101. "Biggest threat to America": Myra MacPherson, "New Right Brigade," *Washington Post*, August 10, 1980.
9. MacPherson, "The New Right Brigade."
10. Reputation for error: Sabato, *PAC Power*, pp. 100–101. "Groups like ours": MacPherson, "New Right Brigade."
11. On NCPAC finances, see Robert Timberg, "Insiders in NCPAC Operate Group Like a Family Business," *Baltimore Sun*, July 13, 1982. Personal profit scheme: Jerry Knight, "Mythical 'Study' of Market, NCPAC Lobbying Used in Fight to Keep Tax Straddle Legal," *Washington Post*, July 5, 1981. Amway-like scheme: It was to be called the "National Conservative Task Force," and it is described in "State Crushes Pyramid Scheme," *Seattle Times*, May 19, 1985.
12. "Organize discontent": Crawford, *Thunder on the Right*, p. 165. See also Richard Viguerie and David Franke, *America's Right Turn: How Conservatives Used New and Alternative Media to Take Power* (Chicago: Bonus Books, 2004), p. 128.
13. This is how Phillips opened a speech to the YAF in 1979, according to *Conservative Digest*, March 1980, p. 10.
14. An undated fund-raising letter from the Conservative Caucus Research, Analysis & Education Foundation (Jack Abramoff is listed as a trustee on the letterhead) that I found in the files of PFAW accuses the State Department of giving away an Alaskan island to the Soviets, an act of outright "appeasement" toward the hated foe. A description of Phillips's efforts on the canal issue can be found in Viguerie, *The New Right*, p. 70.

Great financial success of the issue: Alan Crawford describes the American Conservative Union's results with the Panama issue in *Thunder on the Right,* p. 8.

15. "Politics is not a battle of the millions": Howard Phillips, *The New Right at Harvard* (Vienna, Va.: Conservative Caucus, 1983), pp. 9, 8.
16. See, for example, Phillips's quarterly publication *Grassroots* for June 1981, where Jefferson's quote is used to kick off an article assailing the Legal Services Corporation, a long-standing Phillips bête noire, or the December 1981 issue of the Conservative Caucus *Member's Report,* where Jefferson's words introduce a general manifesto, "Why Congress Should Defund the Left." See also *The Howard Phillips Issues and Strategy Bulletin* for February 25, 1985, where Jefferson's statement is used to applaud William Bennett's tenure at the National Endowment for the Humanities, where he was "cutting off funds for pro-Sandinista, pro-abortion, and pro-nuclear freeze groups."
17. The "faith-based advocacy" of NEA, AID, DoE, and public health clinics: These are all mentioned in the Conservative Caucus *Member's Report* for December 1981, p. 3.

    Harvard, Yale, Berkeley: *Howard Phillips Issues and Strategy Bulletin,* April 22, 1985, n.p. All quotes are in bold in original, and the first two are in all caps and underlined.
18. The disastrous Anne Gorsuch era at the EPA, for example, met with Howard Phillips's strong approval, because Gorsuch had defunded the left. In *Conservative Manifesto* for May 1983, for example, he commended her for "reducing the amount of Federal funding which [environmental organizations] had received" and then assailed President Reagan for giving her no "air cover" when those environmental organizations criticized her (p. 6).
19. Thanks to Phillips's obsessive chronicling of his daily activities in *Conservative Manifesto,* we can track the two men's relationship with some precision. Jack Abramoff first wanders into its pages when he participates, along with Phillips, in a May 1982 panel discussion on the hated nuclear freeze. In August Phillips was visiting Taiwan and rejoicing that, thanks to the country's dedication to capitalism, "there are no hippies here"; soon thereafter he was meeting with Abramoff and others to figure out how to counter the Reagan administration's apparent sellout of the Taiwanese. A month later there was a second teeth-grinding betrayal to report: Abramoff confided to Phillips that the Republican National Committee had diverted a large chunk of the College Republicans' funds to a campaign to pass a tax increase!

    Now the two men were comrades in wronged righteousness, and before long Phillips had made Abramoff the director of his Conservative Caucus PAC. In January of 1983, they met to discuss Jack's idea for the United Students of America Foundation, and two months later they were scheming to defeat Charles Percy, the liberal Republican senator from Illinois (an odd thing for a College Republican to be doing, regardless of his conservatism). In the spring of 1983 Abramoff was a speaker at the Conservative Caucus's "Leadership Conference"—probably the only occasion in history at which one could attend presentations by both Jack Abramoff and R. J. Rushdoony, the founder of "Reconstructionist" theology. Shortly thereafter Phillips returned the favor by speaking at the College Republican national convention; and at some point in that year the stationery on which Phillips's PAC sent out its three-alarm fund-raising letters began to include the name of "Jack Abramoff, Executive Director."

20. "In the U.S.A. Foundation's headquarters [a spin-off of the CRs] hangs a poster put out by the Conservative Caucus that bluntly states one of the foundation's major objectives—'de-fund the left'—and quotes Thomas Jefferson: 'To compel a man to furnish funds for the propagation of ideas he disbelieves and abhors is sinful and tyrannical.'" Palmer, "Conservatives Count on Reagan's Popularity," p. 14.
21. This period is described by Nina Easton, "Abramoff's Grand Aims Came Early," *Boston Globe,* February 6, 2006.
22. The Student Coalition for Truth is described in *Laissez-Faire,* Fall 1983. The doings of the Committee for Democracy in Grenada are detailed in the *CR Report* for November 1983. *Laissez-Faire* was a four-page bulletin produced by the College Republicans and, according to their own description, circulated on college campuses in numbers upward of 100,000. As far as I can tell, there is only one copy extant in all the libraries of America.
23. This was another fight the CRs inherited from the old YAF. On the YAF's campaign against Nader and the PIRGs, see Nicholas von Hoffman, "Yaffers and Yaffettes," *Washington Post,* August 20, 1973, and "Funding PIRG's," a letter to the editor of the *Wall Street Journal* from Charles L. Orndorff, September 1, 1975.
24. Abramoff himself fulminated that Nader "has set up one of the greatest sinful and tyrannical empires in the history of American college campuses." See "Funding for Nader Group Called Unethical," an interview with Abramoff that appeared in the *Washington Times,* April 11, 1983.
25. These quotations are drawn from an untitled report written by the journalist Allan Nairn in 1986.
26. Ibid., p. 17.
27. Ibid., p. 15.
28. Ibid., p. 18.
29. Rothbard's days as a USAF campus organizer are described in Thomas J. Meyer, "Conservative Student Groups Try to Topple PIRGs," *Chronicle of Higher Education,* March 20, 1985. Energy industry: CFACT fund-raising letter, signed by Norval Carey and dated August 6, 1986, in PIRG files. Funders of CFACT: Foundation Directory On-

line. "Regulators gone wild": This is an essay by one Jefferson G. Edgens that was posted on CFACT's Web site in 2006, truly a wild year for the EPA. See http://www.cfact.org/site/view_article.asp?idCategory=10&idarticle=1082.

30. In retrospect, it seems natural and normal that Jack Abramoff should have received his first real lobbying assignment from Oliver North; after all, they were the central figures in the two biggest political scandals since Watergate. At some point in March 1985, North drew up a "Chronological Event Checklist" orchestrating all the many PR measures that were to sway the Contra vote in Congress. He assigned Abramoff to squire a group of "Central American spokesmen" to strategic congressional districts and "media markets," and then run a "targeted telephone campaign" to persuade Congress to support the Contras. On April 16, Abramoff was to bring his Central Americans to Capitol Hill for some one-on-one lobbying, and the next day to preside over a conference bearing the typically alarmist name "Central America: Resistance or Surrender." President Reagan himself was mentioned as a possible attendee.
31. "The main performance at the briefing was a slide show by North," writes Theodore Draper in *A Very Thin Line,* the authoritative history of the Iran-Contra affair. "Channell described its effect—the people in the room 'were all excited to death.' " North went on to give the slide show presentation for Channell numerous times in 1985 and 1986. Draper, *A Very Thin Line,* pp. 58–59.
32. On Channell, see Christopher Hitchens, "It Dare Not Speak Its Name," *Harper's,* August 1987; David Corn, "The Return of Spitz Channell," *Nation,* April 16, 1988; Thomas Edsall and David Hoffman, "Reagan Ex-Aide Was Channell Go-Between," *Washington Post,* May 1, 1987; Richard L. Berke, "Channell Backers Sad and Dismayed," *New York Times,* May 3, 1987.
33. Draper, *A Very Thin Line,* pp. 57–58, 67. On the friends and lovers, see Hitchens, "It Dare Not Speak Its Name," and Corn, "The Return of Spitz Channell."
34. Channell's epithets for his donors appear in Hitchens, "It Dare Not Speak Its Name."
35. Viguerie, NCPAC: Richard L. Berke, "Col. North Bolstering Fund Effort," *New York Times,* July 15, 1987. An ad for *Telling It Like It Is* appeared in *Human Events,* September 5, 1987.
36. The credits of *Telling It Like It Is* include the line "A Production of the International Freedom Foundation, Jack Abramoff International Chairman." It was written by Jeffrey Pandin, directed by Ken Lisbeth, and the production was supervised by Duncan Sellars, who would succeed Abramoff as chairman of the IFF a short while later.

    North's fund-raising slide show, which makes up the bulk of *Telling It Like It Is,* turns out to be a particularly paranoid bit of cold-war crisis peddling. Central America is important, it tells us; Nicaragua is communist; it has a huge army and "sophisticated" air bases; when Mexico goes communist—no explanation given here—things will get really bad. Here, North's voice continues, is some proof that Nicaragua helps commies in other countries—proof that "you never saw . . . in the American media"; and here is the evil-looking Hind helicopter, "the most deadly airborne platform in the world today," a Soviet weapon on which eighties conservatives dwelled with a mixture of loathing and sweet desire. And here are the Contras, struggling bravely and dying piously. Behold: the simple wooden crosses beneath which they bury their comrades. The end.

37. The problem of fake Ollie North fund-raisers was so acute that North himself acknowledged it in one of his fund-raising letters, writing, "Yes, this letter is from me—Ollie North—and not from any other individual or organization." (Letter in files of PFAW, dated October 24, 1988.) Jerry Falwell: Amy Fried, *Muffled Echoes: Oliver North and the Politics of Public Opinion* (New York: Columbia University Press, 1997), p. 144. Howard Phillips: As quoted in B. Drummond Ayres Jr., "For North, Missions That Have One Goal," *New York Times,* April 21, 1990. Usual round of plunder: Jill Abramson, "Campaign to Pardon North Raises Funds, But Not All for Ollie," *Wall Street Journal,* December 1, 1988. U.S. Senate race: John F. Persinos, "Ollie, Inc.," *Campaigns and Elections,* June 1995.
38. On the Enterprise, see Draper, *A Very Thin Line,* p. 40, and Blumenthal, *Pledging Allegiance: The Last Campaign of the Cold War* (New York: HarperCollins, 1990), pp. 21–22.
39. As Sidney Blumenthal pointed out, these features give Iran-Contra a considerable resemblance to Watergate also. Blumenthal, *Pledging Allegiance,* pp. 30–31.
40. "Quite cynical about government": North's boss, Robert McFarlane, quoted in Draper, *A Very Thin Line,* p. 566.
41. As I write this, for example, the *Washington Times* is on its fifth day of outrage about "Democratic House staffers" who reportedly insisted on getting inoculated against certain diseases before attending a NASCAR race. No other national newspaper is covering the story. But every conservative in the capital knows the details, and precisely how to interpret them. "Republican staffers," of course, "refused the shots," and NASCAR fans are said to be mighty steamed at those Beltway liberals who seem to think red-state values are a communicable disease. Audrey Hudson, "Racing Fans Fire Back at the Hill," *Washington Times,* October 14, 2007.
42. Norquist quoted in Tom Hamburger and Peter Wallsten, *One Party Country: The Republican Plan for Dominance in the 21st Century* (Hoboken, N.J.: John Wiley & Sons, 2006), p. 182.

Chapter 5: From Paranoia to Privatopia, by Way of Pretoria

1. Information technology, Wheeler proclaimed in 1996, was "about to slice open the Ship of Bureaucracy's innards, sending it to the bottom of the sea." This would come to pass when the Internet allowed people to hide their assets more effectively and avoid taxation. Jack Wheeler, "The Technology of Freedom: Why Governments Are Becoming Obsolete," an address to the Council for National Policy, March, 1996, as printed in *Policy Counsel,* Fall 1996, pp. 64, 66, 68.
2. Fortunately for the historian, in 1987 Howard Phillips collected all his writings on southern Africa into a self-published book called *Moscow's Challenge to U.S. Vital Interests in Southern Africa.* These arguments can be found in chap. 4 of that work. The quotations come from p. 60 of *Moscow's Challenge* and from an advertisement for Phillips's 1986 South Africa tour that accompanied the October 2, 1985, issue of his *Issues and Strategy Bulletin.*
3. One South African I spoke to recalled that *The Graduate,* the groundbreaking 1967 movie, was not released in South Africa until 1972, and then it was so heavily censored that its plot was impossible to follow. He himself kept up on countercultural events, he told me, by reading *Time* magazine.
4. In 1995 Bruce Rickerson, a frequent contributor to IFF publications, wrote in a letter to a friend that he suspected "that two competing anti-sanctions groups were assisted in their formation in Washington just prior to Reagan's veto of the sanctions bill in October 1986." The IFF was one of these. Letter to Leo Raditsa, a professor of ancient history at St. John's College, dated July 28, 1995, and included in the Leo Raditsa Papers at Harvard College Library.
5. "All-out war": Martin Feinstein, "The Truce Is Over, Warns Wits Right," *Rand Daily Mail,* July 1, 1981. "Undermining the will": "Campus Politics: Right Claims Foothold," *Star* (Johannesburg), June 27, 1984. Baseball bats: See "Karen Bliksem's" column in the *Sunday Independent,* June 16, 1996. Spent lavishly: Susan Fleming, "Rightwing Student Body Spent Funds of R75,000," *Star* (Johannesburg), November 19, 1984. "Support from the business community": "Student Group to Pay Costs in Legal Settlement," *Star* (Johannesburg), September 9, 1982. See also " 'Moderate Student Group Is Launched,' " *Star* (Johannesburg), April 25, 1984. Publications that borrowed heavily: A 1985 National Student Federation brochure lifted, without attribution, Abramoff's remark that "it's not our job to seek peaceful co-existence with the Left," and reprinted other statements of the maximum leader with slight modifications to make them fit the South African context. Jamba: Claudia Braude, "A Blast from the Past," *Mail & Guardian* (Johannesburg), January 20–26, 2006. On Crystal's connections to South African military intelligence, see Peta Thornycroft, "How Project Babouchka and Gypsy

the Mole Tried to Persuade a Hostile World that the Old SA Was OK," *Sunday Independent* (Johannesburg), July 16, 1995.

6. Others went off to party in Sun City, the casino resort that was at that very moment the target of a high-profile global entertainment boycott. See Hans Pienaar, "Who Pays for This Party?" *Sunday Times* (Johannesburg), July 21, 1985. Almost the only online account of the "Youth for Freedom" conference that you will find online today comes from Howard Phillips's son Brad, today the head of a Christian organization monitoring religious persecution, who remembers the occasion as an idealistic one. See Stephen Goode, "Brad Phillips Answers the Calling in Africa," *Insight on the News,* September 6, 1999.
7. See "Secret SA Plan for Right-Wing Indaba," *Weekly Mail* (Johannesburg), June 21, 1985, p. 1, and Pienaar, "Who Pays for This Party?" Another description can be found in Allan Nairn, op. cit., and Easton, *Gang of Five,* pp. 168–69. Quote from the organizer is from Nairn's untitled report.
8. The only reference to "Liberty and Democracy International" that I have ever seen appears in Vivienne Walt, "Conservative Lobbyists Open S. African Office," *Newsday,* November 9, 1986.
9. The Kemp jet scheme was revealed by Dele Olojede, "Apartheid Front Mulled Funds for Kemp Team," *Newsday,* July 23, 1995. Olojede continues:

   > Kemp, who voted for economic sanctions against the apartheid regime over then-President Ronald Reagan's veto, vehemently denied Friday that he had anything to do with the request for a plane and said that the aide who wrote the letter [requesting the plane from the IFF] acted without authorization.
   >
   > "I've made a lot of mistakes in my life, but that's not one of them, tying myself to South African intelligence," an anguished Kemp said in an interview.

10. This was the case with all other South African propaganda efforts as well. Commenting on the South African front groups exposed during the Information Scandal in 1979, the Toronto *Globe and Mail* columnist Stan McDowell wrote:

    > The beauty of it was that these fronts did not have to do what [onetime head of the Information Department] Dr. [Eschel] Rhoodie called selling the unsellable. They were free to say, I deplore apartheid, but . . .
    >
    > Four little words, but potent as original sin. For taken up by a host of supposedly independent, supposedly multiracial organizations, they made it seem that thousands of South Africans were irresistibly on the move toward change and justice, and thus entitled to tell the rest of us: We're doing our best. And it's

working. But don't push us too hard. Or the Communists will get us. And after they get us they'll get you.

11. Craig Williamson quoted in Phillip Van Niekerk, "How Apartheid Conned the West," *Observer* (London), July 16, 1995.
12. Russel Crystal, the de facto head of the IFF, has not been particularly open about its history. But he is oddly forthright about the transaction behind the group's attacks on the ANC. "The military intelligence, there were certain things they wanted done—tackling the ANC as a terrorist-communist organization," Crystal told *Newsday* in 1995. "The projects we did for them, they paid for." Dele Olojede, "D.C. 'Think Tank' was Front for S. Africa; Foundation Was Funded to Protect Apartheid," *Newsday,* July 17, 1995.
13. The role of the IFF in the House Republican Study Committee's June 25, 1987, hearings is described by Phillip van Niekerk, "Exposed: The SA Front that Sucked in the World," *Sunday Independent* (Johannesburg), July 16, 1995. Among the IFF's many attacks on the ANC were two 1987 reports charging the organization with child abuse, "The Role of Youth in Revolutionary Warfare" and "Suffer the Children: Child Abuse for Revolutionary Ends in South Africa." The ads assailing Mandela are described in Olojede, "D.C. 'Think Tank.' " The war on Ted Kennedy was mainly composed of direct-mail missives claiming that the IFF had discovered a new Kennedy scandal and would make it public with your generous financial assistance.
14. I found two slightly differing versions of the boneheaded IFF manifesto. One is an unsigned pamphlet (probably from 1986) distributed in the United States featuring the photo of Abramoff and Reagan. The other appeared on pp. 3 and 4 of vol. 1, no. 1 (Winter 1987) of *Southern African Freedom Review* and is signed by Abramoff and Russel Crystal. My quotations here are taken from the latter version.
15. Wim J. Booyse, "Getting Beyond the Mandela Smokescreen," *International Freedom Review* [*IFR*] 1, no. 2 (Winter 1988). Henry Kriegel, "Afghanistan: Has Reagan Sold Out the Mujahideen?" *IFR* 1, no. 4 (Summer 1988). James P. Lucier Jr., "Letters from Moscow," *IFR* 1, no. 1 (Fall 1987). (Lucier was an aide to Senator Jesse Helms.) Duncan Sellars, "The Sandinistas' Untold Story," *IFR* 1, no. 2 (Winter 1988). John Lenczowski, "Military *Glasnost* and Strategic Deception," *IFR* 3, no. 2 (Winter 1990).

    Another example: A 1987 IFF publication on the atrocities of the ANC went after the familiar American antiapartheid group TransAfrica for being communist dupes. "All the facts point to TRANSAFRICA being extremely useful to revolutionary causes, if not, indeed, a communist front," the report proclaimed. "Researchers at the eminent Lincoln Institute for Research and Education [another right-wing think tank] say the lobby organization is a spokesman for 'Soviet and Cuban supported terrorist groups.' " *Suffer the Children: Child Abuse for Revolutionary Ends in South Africa: A Report by the International Freedom Foundation* (IFF: Washington, D.C., 1987), p. 21.

16. "Subversion by C.I.A.," *New York Times,* February 20, 1967. See also "Infiltrating the Campus," *New York Times,* February 16, 1967. The scandal was first exposed by *Ramparts* magazine, in its issue for March 1967; you can read the original story online today at http://www.cia-on-campus.org/nsa/nsa.html.
17. According to a *New York Times* story for February 27, 1967, Barry Goldwater "demanded today to know why the Central Intelligence Agency had been financing 'left-wing' organizations but not conservative groups such as the Young Republicans." An editorial in *National Review* for March 7 of that year speculated in its highfalutin way that, "granted the propriety of this field of activity, it might still have seemed to the public and to Congress, if the facts had been openly before them, that some other campus organizations should have shared in the largesse, and that among the young Lochinvars sent to do battle in the international conclaves a few hard anti-Communists and even an occasional enthusiastic pro-American might have been included."

    The explanation for the CIA's blundering, the wingers decided, was liberal bias. As Howard Phillips himself put it in the *Washington Post* for July 3, 1974, the NSA incident revealed the CIA to be "an instrument of establishment liberalism." In addition to Phillips, two other figures who would later play a role in Abramoff's own clandestinely funded youth organization—Donald ("Buz") Lukens and Charles Lichenstein—made similar points. See Steven V. Roberts, "C.I.A. Is Criticized by Conservatives," *New York Times,* February 23, 1967.
18. Williamson's role in the IFF is described in Dele Olojede, "D.C. 'Think Tank' Was Front for S. Africa; Foundation Was Funded to Protect Apartheid," *Newsday,* July 17, 1995; and Phillip Van Niekerk, "How Apartheid Conned the West," *Observer* (London), July 16, 1995.

    For a description of Williamson's career as a "superspy," see Terry Bell with Dumisa Buhle Ntsebeza, *Unfinished Business: South Africa, Apartheid and Truth* (London: Verso, 2003), chapters 7 and 9.
19. As far as I have been able to determine, there was only one media item that guessed the true nature of the IFF during its lifetime: a 1989 article in *CovertAction Information Bulletin.* See David Ivon, "Touting for South Africa: International Freedom Foundation," *CovertAction Information Bulletin* 31 (Winter, 1989).
20. The CIA's in-house magazine was *Studies in Intelligence;* Lichenstein edited it in 1955–56, according to an article on the history of that publication found on the CIA's Web site: https://www.cia.gov/library/center-for-the-study-of-intelligence/csi-publications/csi-studies/studies/vol49no4/Fifty_Years_1.htm. Examples of Lichenstein's later intelligence writing included an afterword to *The CIA and the American*

Ethic: An Unfinished Debate, by Ernest W. Lefever and Roy Godson (Washington, D.C.: Georgetown University Press, 1979), and two book reviews for the *Wall Street Journal* (June 17, 1985, and January 10, 1986) on espionage matters.

21. CIA officials contributing to IFF magazines: One former CIA official who contributed was Donald Jameson, identified as a CIA specialist in eastern Europe and the Soviet Union. He wrote "Covert Activities and New Priorities" for *laissez-faire* 1, no. 3 (Winter 1992). Another example of the organization's ongoing concern with intelligence agencies was the article "Countering Economic Espionage" by Hans-Ulrich Helfer (described in his contributor's note as as a veteran of the "Swiss police, state security and army security services"), *laissez-faire* 1, no. 4 (Summer 1992).

    FBI: The FBI kindly released nine pages having to do with the IFF in response to a FOIA request. Four of these pages are negative or almost-negative responses to previous requests for information from the days when the IFF was first making headlines. The last five consist of correspondence between the IFF and the FBI in 1992 and 1993 regarding what one internal FBI document calls "favorable dealings" between the two organizations concerning the former KGB officials.

    The IFF's Potsdam conference was held at the Schloss Cecilienhof on November 15, 1991; it was advertised in *laissez-faire* 1, no. 2 (Autumn 1991), and described briefly in issue 3. The former CIA director who attended was William Colby; the KGB chief was Oleg Kalugin.

22. Peter Leon, a respected Johannesburg attorney who represented investors in Abramoff's South African film production company, recounted for me the time in the late eighties when he noticed Craig Williamson, even then a notorious figure, at a business meeting of a later Abramoff production. Leon was astonished to see that the two men were acquaintances. He asked Abramoff how he happened to know this blackguard, and received "some excuse that didn't really add up." Wait a second, I said to the lawyer, thinking maybe I hadn't understood. Abramoff was *friends* with Craig Williamson? "Absolutely," Leon replied.

23. Lance Gay, "Group That Opposed Mandela Had Secret South Africa Funds," *Houston Chronicle,* July 30, 1995.

24. The description of *laissez-faire* can be found in the IFF's newsletter, *Freedom Bulletin* 5, no. 4 (April 1991), p. 2. The issue of *terra nova* dedicated to Hayek was vol. 1, no. 3 (Spring 1992). See especially the Hayek memorial (p. 3) written by John Blundell, then president of the Charles G. Koch Foundation and today the vice president of the Mont Pelerin Society. The lucky South African politician who got the autographed copy of *The Road to Serfdom* was Mangosuthu Buthelezi, a perennial IFF favorite. The presentation is depicted in *Freedom Bulletin* 5, no. 5 (May 1991), p. 5. The presentation of the "Freedom Award" to Vaclav Klaus is described in *Freedom Bulletin* 5, no. 1 (January 1991), p. 1.

25. Or, more accurately, advocating "a return to market hunting" of deer. See Ronald Bailey, "North America's Most Dangerous Animal," *Reason,* November 21, 2001.
26. Nicholas von Hoffman, "Yaffers and Yaffettes: Only Leftovers for Heroes," *Washington Post,* August 20, 1973.
27. The most celebrated "scenario planner" was Clem Sunter, an executive at Anglo-American, the gigantic gold-mining concern. His one-man crusade for South Africa's future is described in *Leadership,* the main South African business magazine, vol. 6, no. 3 (1987).

    Patrick Bond also describes this period in *Elite Transition: From Apartheid to Neoliberalism in South Africa* (Pietermaritzburg, SA: University of Natal Press, 2000).
28. Privatization was a special concern of the South African business community, and *Leadership* covered the issue in detail. See its interview with the finance minister Barend du Plessis, vol. 7, no. 1 (1988), and the special issue on privatization ("Breaking the Mould"), vol. 7, no. 3 (1988).
29. Constitution and free enterprise: *Freedom Bulletin* 5, no. 3 (March 1991), p. 2.
30. In 2005 Richard Sincere, an American who edited *terra nova* in 1992, recalled for readers of his blog, "Our overarching aim was to promote liberal democracy and free enterprise as an alternative to both communism and apartheid." Like everyone else associated with the IFF, Sincere says he had no idea that the South African government was behind the foundation, and even characterizes this "overarching aim" as being "typical of conservative and libertarian think tanks and advocacy groups in the closing years of the Cold War." http://ricksincerethoughts.blogspot.com/2005/07/lost-in-stars.html.
31. *Leadership* denounced apartheid nearly constantly in the late eighties, although it remained dubious about the ANC.

    On the relationship between capitalism and apartheid, see Dan O'Meara, *Forty Lost Years: The Apartheid State and the Politics of the National Party, 1948–1994* (Athens, Ohio: Ohio University Press, 1996), pp. 182–89.
32. "Government interference in the workings of the market, whether through regulation or taxation, always has costs that outweigh benefits. When a society has a market free from state intervention, clearly defined rights of individuals to own property and make contracts, and unencumbered operation of basic economic laws (such as supply and demand), its benefits always outweigh costs. This is true in social, political, and cultural terms." From an editorial by Mark A. Franz, *terra nova* 1, no. 2 (Winter 1991–92), p. 1. The quote regarding the lessons of communism can be found on p. 2.
33. "Top-down system of control": Christopher Lingle, "Social Democracy: No Solution for Post-Apartheid South Africa," *terra nova* 1, no. 2

(Winter 1991–92), p. 77. "South Africa's war against capitalism": Richard Sincere, "Ending Apartheid, Ending Socialsim" [*sic*], *International Freedom Review* 3, no. 3 (Spring 1990), p. 67. "Remarkable resemblance": Lingle, "Social Democracy," p. 77. "If black South Africans": Sincere, "Ending Apartheid," p. 76.

34. This is a pull quote that appears on p. 42 of "Freeing Up Southern Africa's Energy Markets," an essay by the South African business professor Frank Vorhies that appeared in *terra nova* 1, no. 2 (Winter 1991–92).
35. Transcript, "The Plight of the Children of South Africa," Hearings before the House Republican Study Committee, June 25, 1987, p. 31.
36. Along with Don McAlvany, Duncan Sellars edited a newsletter called *African Intelligence Digest,* the purpose of which was "to inform Americans on the strategic importance of South and southern Africa and the Soviet bloc strategy for the domination of the African continent." To this end, Sellars printed darkly conspiratorial and even racist material, such as a 1985 letter from a reader ("it makes several very valid points") that declared "the paramount issue is that black Africans are in no way qualified for freedom and self-government, and are altogether unlikely to become qualified soon (if ever). Thus, for South Africa to extend the franchise to include Blacks as political equals is to abandon the country to rapid descent into anarchy and chaos." *African Intelligence Digest,* May 30, 1985, p. 7.
37. See Leslie Alan Glick, "NAFTA: Touchstone for 21st Century Prosperity," *terra nova* 1, no. 3 (Spring 1992); Brian Doherty, "The Fair Trade Brigades: Selling Out Free Enterprise," *terra nova* 1, no. 3 (Spring 1992); and Graciela D. Testa, "Threats to a Liberal Trading Order," *terra nova* 1, no. 1 (Summer 1991).
38. See Richard Miniter, "The Green World Order," *terra nova* 1, no. 2 (Winter 1991–92); and Jonathan H. Adler, "Off Balance," *terra nova* 1, no. 4 (Summer 1992). This last, a review of Al Gore's *Earth in the Balance,* is a particularly memorable piece of work, as it identifies Gore both with the "Cold War worriers" (p. 65) who spread panic about communism *and* with communism itself, opining of Gore's plan that "such massive regulation of society was attempted by the former regimes of the Soviet bloc, and the result was disastrous" (p. 67).
39. The privatization issue was *terra nova* 1, no. 2 (Winter 1991–92). "Privatizing the Oceans" (as it was listed on the magazine's cover) was written by one Kent Jeffreys, a champion think tanker who has held positions at Cato, Heritage, the Competitive Enterprise Institute, *and* the Alexis de Tocqueville Institute.
40. Rod Paschall's article "Privatizing Counterinsurgency" appeared in *terra nova* 2, no. 1, the final edition, which appeared in Autumn 1992.
41. The story of Executive Outcomes and its high-speed victory over Savimbi has been told often. One place to read about it is P. W. Singer, *Corporate*

Warriors: The Rise of the Privatized Military Industry (Ithaca, N.Y.: Cornell University Press, 2003), pp. 101–10. See also the excellent account of Executive Outcomes' intervention in Sierra Leone, "An Army of One's Own" by Elizabeth Rubin in *Harper's,* February 1997.

Chapter 6: "The Best Public Servant Is the Worst One"

1. "People are policy" is the "maxim" contributed to the "folklore of the conservative movement" by Edwin Feulner, one of the founders of the Heritage Foundation, according to Sidney Blumenthal (*The Rise of the Counter-Establishment,* p. 50). "Personnel is Policy" is item 26 on Morton Blackwell's "Laws of the Public Policy Process." See http://www.leadershipinstitute.org/resources/?pageid=speeches&s=11.
2. Blackwell quotes: Phillips, *The New Right at Harvard,* p. 146. Norquist: Hart, *The Third Generation,* p. 160. "Norquist is called by some the Lenin of the Third Generation," wrote Hart admiringly on p. 15.
3. "Farm system": David Shribman, ". . . And Recruit for the Government," *New York Times,* October 12, 1983. Shribman quotes both Morton Blackwell and Phil Gramm on the importance of "credentialing." Bitter battles: Robert S. Greenberger, "Some Conservatives Claim They Blocked Political 'Purge' at the State Department," *Wall Street Journal,* December 28, 1984. See also Blumenthal, *The Rise of the Counter-Establishment,* p. 50.
4. This story is told by Ariana Eunjung Cha, "In Iraq, the Job Opportunity of a Lifetime: Managing a $13 Billion Budget with No Experience," *Washington Post,* May 23, 2004.
5. Of the many stories to appear on the U.S. attorneys scandal and Monica Goodling, see: Eric Lipton, "Colleagues Cite Partisan Focus by Justice Official," *New York Times,* May 12, 2007; Dan Eggen and Amy Goldstein, "Political Appointees No Longer to Pick Justice Interns," *Washington Post,* April 28, 2007; Dana Milbank, "Monica's Own Monica Problem," *Washington Post,* May 24, 2007; and Hanna Rosin, "The New Establishment: How Evangelicals Became Part of Washington's Fabric," *Washington Post,* May 25, 2007. Rosin is the one who uses the term *goodling* to describe the administration's many hires from evangelical universities.
6. "It's clear that the C.I.A. and the State Department have done most of their recruiting from Eastern schools where there is a clear liberal and disarmament orientation," William R. Van Cleave, a cold-war hawk, told the *New York Times* in 1983. "I'm not suggesting that the Government stop hiring people from East Coast schools, but the United States deserves a balance." As quoted in Shribman, ". . . And Recruit for the Government."

7. This is the subject, broadly speaking, of my previous books, *What's the Matter with Kansas?* and *One Market Under God.*
8. Homer Ferguson "as told to Herbert Corey," "A Plea for Inefficiency in Government," *Nation's Business,* November 1928.
9. Marshall Dimock, "Do Business Men Want Good Government?" p. 35.
10. This is "Executive Branch Civilian Employment," according to the *Statistical Abstract of the United States* for 2003. In 1968, the civilian employees of the executive branch numbered some 2,289,000. This figure was only exceeded in 1943, '44, and '45.

    There are numerous other ways to look at the data. If we exclude the Post Office and Defense employees (1968 was, after all, the height of the Vietnam War), federal employment peaked in 1978 (with 1,225,000 people working for civilian agencies), declined during the Reagan years, and then resumed growing and hit its all-time high in 1992 (1,274,000).

    If we measure the federal workforce as a percentage of all U.S. employment, federal employment has been in decline from the midfifties (in 1955 federal employees were 3.9 percent of all employed people) to the present (in 2003 they made up only 1.99 percent). These numbers are from the *Statistical Abstract of the United States,* volumes for 1976 (p. 248, table 406) and 2006 (p. 330, table 481).
11. Doug Bandow, "Let Washington-Bashing Continue," an essay dated January 20, 1987, and included in the appropriately named book *The Politics of Plunder: Misgovernment in Washington* (New Brunswick, N.J.: Transaction, 1990), pp. 43–45.
12. Nofziger quoted in Chester Newland, "A Mid-Term Appraisal—The Reagan Presidency: Limited Government and Political Administration," *Public Administration Review,* January–February 1983, p. 3.
13. Don Feder, "Those Lovable Bureaucrats," *Conservative Digest,* June–July 1985, p. 24.
14. See Ralph de Toledano's book, *The Municipal Doomsday Machine* (Ottawa, Ill.: Green Hill, 1975), which carried on its cover the alarming question, "Will Public Employee Unions Become Our Political Masters?"
15. A slightly different bureaucrat conspiracy theory was promoted by Howard Phillips. "Bureaucrats hold political power," he told an interviewer in 1980. "They have the ability to elect or defeat a congressman who is hostile to them. They can put into his district programs that will publish newspapers which regularly denounce him, organizations which can build constituencies that work against his reelection, that register voters and have access to the media." "Phillips on the New Right," interview published in *Conservative Digest,* March 1980, p. 12.

    The leader of the Prop 13 rebellion was Howard Jarvis. He is quoted in Joseph A. McCartin, "A Wagner Act for Public Employees: Labor's

Deferred Dream and the Rise of Conservatism, 1970–76," *Journal of American History*, vol. 95 (June 2008). AAUCG: From a direct-mail letter signed by Jesse Helms and quoted in Alan Crawford, *Thunder on the Right*, p. 29. The parent of the AAUCG is the Public Service Research Foundation, publisher of *Government Union Review*. Read more about it at http://www.psrf.org/index.jsp.

16. "Permanent government" is Reagan's phrase, as quoted in Rowland Evans and Robert Novak, "Career Diplomats, Moving Up," *Washington Post*, January 11, 1982.

    According to the 1982 profile of the Reagan administration written by Ronald Brownstein and Nina Easton, "political appointees view themselves as the French at Dien Bien Phu." Brownstein and Easton, *Reagan's Ruling Class: Portraits of the President's Top 100 Officials* (Washington, D.C.: Presidential Accountability Group, 1982), p. 708.
17. Donald Devine, *Reagan's Terrible Swift Sword: Reforming and Controlling the Federal Bureaucracy* (Ottawa, Ill.: Jameson Books, 1991), p. 155. Tanks: Devine as quoted in Charles H. Levine, "The Federal Government in the Year 2000: Administrative Legacies of the Reagan Years," *Public Administration Review*, May–June 1986, p. 203.
18. On the many complaints against the federal bureaucracy in the seventies and the many ideas proposed to fix it, see William T. Gormley Jr., *Taming the Bureaucracy: Muscles, Prayers, and Other Strategies* (Princeton, N.J.: Princeton University Press, 1989).
19. This was especially true of Richard Viguerie's *Conservative Digest*, which constantly ran articles in the early eighties examining Reagan appointees' conservative credentials and complaining bitterly whenever moderates were left in positions of power. Eventually one of the magazine's editors, Mark Tapscott, was given a spot in the administration's personnel office. Newland, "A Mid-Term Appraisal," pp. 15–16.
20. Ibid.," pp. 3, 12.
21. Irene S. Rubin, *Shrinking the Federal Government: The Effect of Cutbacks on Five Federal Agencies* (New York: Longman, 1985), p. 28.
22. Levine, "The Federal Government," p. 203.
23. Calculating the "pay gap" was and is notoriously difficult, since the government's surveys of private industry didn't try to price benefits or stock options, and only included large firms. They also didn't weight the results for the numbers of employees in each grade or private-sector job. Then the methodology was entirely changed in 1991, changed again in 1996, and continued to be adjusted right up to the present, making solid statistical comparisons between now and pre-1990 virtually impossible. Given those complications, here is how I arrived at my numbers.

    1975: My figures come from the *National Survey of Professional, Administrative, Technical, and Clerical Pay, March 1975* (U.S. Department of Labor, 1975), appendix D. I took the average of the annual salaries listed by the survey as being equivalent to federal grades GS-1, GS-7, and GS-15 and found a pay gap of 9 percent for GS-1, 12 percent for GS-7, and 13 percent for GS-15.

1987: I did the same with the *National Survey of Professional, Administrative, Technical, and Clerical Pay: Private Service Industries, March 1987* (U.S. Department of Labor, 1987). Here the pay gaps were 13 percent for GS-1, 31 percent for GS-7, and 37 percent for GS-15.

1990: I used "Comparability of the Federal Statutory Pay Systems with Private Enterprise Pay Rates," the annual report of the president's pay agent, which gives the "comparability gap" directly. For GS-1 it was 22.32 percent, for GS-7 it was 25.89 percent, and for GS-15 it was a whopping 39.55 percent.

24. Susan B. Garland, "Beltway Brain Drain: Why Civil Servants Are Making Tracks—Low Pay, Heaps of Abuse, and a Plague of Political Appointees Are Driving Out Top Managers," *Business Week*, January 23, 1989. Paul Lieberman, "Federal Agents Can Earn Less than Grocery Store Clerk," *Los Angeles Times*, November 26, 1989.
25. Terry W. Culler, "Federal Pay Scare's Hidden Agenda," *Wall Street Journal*, August 11, 1989.
26. On Clinton and the pay gap, see the following "Federal Diary" columns by Mike Causey in the *Washington Post*: "Guaranteed Raise a Goner," March 17, 1993; "Clinton's Sector Strategy," April 15, 1993; "Going After the Pay Gap," June 16, 1993; "The Phony Pay Fight," August 28, 1994; "Downsizing Plot Thickens," March 7, 1995; "Filling in the Pay Gaps," August 29, 1997.
27. Osborne and Gaebler, *Reinventing Government*, p. 38.
28. Managerial revolution: President's Management Agenda, p. 11. Heritage plan: Robert E. Moffit, "Taking Charge of Federal Personnel," a Heritage "backgrounder" dated January 10, 2001, and available online at http://www.heritage.org/Research/GovernmentReform/BG1404.cfm.
29. Expert testimony altered: Andrew C. Revkin, "Climate Change Testimony Was Edited by White House," *New York Times*, October 25, 2007.

    Proposed regulations dismissed: See chapter 7.

    Senior scientists overruled: Here the most remarkable story is that of the NASA political appointee George Deutsch, who ordered the department's Web designer to include the word *theory* after every mention of the Big Bang, and who tried to restrict media access to James Hansen, a highly respected climate scientist who speaks often on the subject of global warming. Deutsch resigned from NASA after it was discovered that, contrary to claims he made on his résumé, he had not graduated from college. See Andrew Revkin, "Climate Expert Says NASA Tried to Silence Him," *New York Times*, January 29, 2006; Andrew Revkin, "NASA Chief Backs Agency Openness," *New York Times*, February 4, 2006; Andrew Revkin, "A Young Bush Appointee Resigns His Post at NASA," *New York Times*, February 8, 2006.

30. Starting salaries at big Washington law firms, I was told in 2008, were around $160,000. In that same year, a government employee at the GS-15 grade with the highest allowable amount of seniority earned $149,000.
31. Levine, "The Federal Government," p. 202. These were mainly won by employees of the National Institutes of Health and various Veterans Administration hospitals.
32. This is Martin Rodbell of the National Institute of Environmental Health Sciences, who won the prize in 1994.
33. See Matthew Josephson, *The Robber Barons: The Great American Capitalists, 1861–1901* (New York: Harcourt, Brace, 1934), chap. 3.
34. Grace Commission, *War on Waste,* pp. 149–57.
35. "Cushy deal": Grace as quoted in Peter Ajemian and Joan Claybrook, *Deceiving the Public: the Story Behind J. Peter Grace and His Campaign* (Washington, D.C.: Public Citizen, 1985), p. 25. Disability: Grace, *Burning Money,* pp. 1–3. Poshness, first class: John Rees, "Peter Grace: An Exclusive Interview with the Distinguished Chairman of the Grace Commission on His Proposals to Save Us Trillions," *Review of the NEWS,* May 30, 1984, pp. 51–52. N.b.: On p. 50 of this article is an advertisement for a book by Anastasio Somoza, the late dictator of Nicaragua, bearing the headline "The Terrorists Thought They Had Silenced Somoza . . . but They Were Wrong!"
36. Office of Management and Budget, *The President's Management Agenda* (August 2001), p. 17. Available online at http://www.whitehouse.gov/omb/budget/fy2002/mgmt.pdf.
37. Scott Shane and Ron Nixon, "In Washington, Contractors Take On Biggest Role Ever: Questions of Propriety and Accountability as Outside Workers Flood Agencies," *New York Times,* February 4, 2007.
38. I am thinking of two types of contracts in particular: noncompetitive or "no-bid" contracts, which made up fully 66 percent of contracts awarded during the recovery effort from Hurricane Katrina, and the extremely lousy IDIQ contract, which is being used more, not less, even though it closes off competition in all sorts of ways. The use of these contracts is described in "Dollars, Not Sense: Government Contracting Under the Bush Administration," Minority Staff of the House Committee on Government Reform, June 2006, pp. 10–13.
39. Scott Higham and Robert O'Harrow Jr., "GSA Chief Seeks to Cut Budget for Audits: Contract Oversight Would be Reduced," *Washington Post,* December 2, 2006. According to the *Post*'s account, the Bush appointee in charge of the General Services Administration (GSA) labeled as a "terrorist" an official who criticized her effort to outsource oversight over outsourcing.

    The connection between the blindfolding of the watchdogs and the rising tide of corruption is made by Laton McCartney, "Bribery in the Beltway," *CIO Insight,* April 2, 2007. In another instance of this impulse, Duncan Hunter, a Republican congressman from Southern California, tried to shut down the office of the Special Inspector General for Iraq Reconstruction, which is charged with uncovering waste and fraud amongst the defense-contractor bonanza taking place in that country. His effort failed. See James Glanz, "With Foe's Change of Heart, Iraq Watchdog Is Likely to Survive," *New York Times*, December 8, 2006.

40. The boast is found in a "Letter from the Director" of the Office of Personnel Management dated 2004: http://apps.opm.gov/HumanCapital/stories/2004/Quarter3.cfm. As far as I can tell, the numbers of federal civilian employees are as follows: 1982, 2.8 million; 1994, 2.97 million; 2001, 2.71 million; 2007, 2.67 million. One problem with all these data is that they come from different sources, and it seems to be difficult to find two offices that use precisely the same numbers. The ones I consulted were: 1982, *War on Waste*, p. 230 (which measures only the executive branch); 1994 and 2001, Office of Personnel Management, *Federal Civilian Workforce Statistics: The Fact Book 2005 Edition* (published 2006); 2007, "OPM Employment and Trends, January 2007," table 1, available at http://www.opm.gov/feddata/html/2007/january/table1.asp.

41. "All too often the problem is the public sector," wrote Doug Bandow.

    "Where that is the case, do we want government institutions to operate more efficiently? The federal bureaucracy created energy shortages through price controls and other ill-considered regulations; better-enforced regulations would only have made the crisis worse. . . . More effective execution of the law would cost consumers even more." "Let Washington-Bashing Continue," p. 44.

42. See Rick Perlstein, "E Coli Conservatives," http://commonsense.ourfuture.org/e_coli_conservatives_thebigcon.

43. Norquist: "We must establish a Brezhnev Doctrine for conservative gains." Hart, *Third Generation*, p. 158.

    Goldwater campaign: According to the *New York Times*, Goldwater's adviser Stephen Shadegg, the author of a book called *How to Win an Election*, "took a lesson from Mao Tse-tung and applied his infiltration tactics to American politics." "How to Win at Any Cost," *New York Times*, August 22, 1964. Another Goldwater adviser who systematically copied Communist techniques was Clif White, as described by Rick Perlstein in *Before the Storm: Barry Goldwater and the Unmaking of the American Consensus* (New York: Norton, 2001), pp. 173–74.

44. The Department of Homeland Security, Frank Rich wrote, "isn't really a government agency at all so much as an empty shell, a networking boot camp for future private contractors dreaming of big paydays." Frank Rich, "The Road from K Street to Yusufiya," *New York Times*, June 25, 2006.

45. On FEMA before the hurricane, see Jon Elliston, "A Disaster Waiting to Happen," *Independent Weekly* (Durham, N.C.), September 22, 2004.

The letter from Pleasant Mann, head of the FEMA AFGE local, is dated June 21, 2004. It can be read here: http://www.pogo.org/m/cp/cp-2004-AFGE4060-FEMA.pdf.

46. On Katrina and FEMA more generally, see Eric Klinenberg and Thomas Frank, "Looting Homeland Security," *Rolling Stone*, December 2005.

    On Fluor and Heritage, see Lee Edwards, *The Power of Ideas: The Heritage Foundation at 25 Years* (Ottawa, Ill.: Jameson Books, 1997), p. 27. Bechtel: For example, George Shultz and Caspar Weinberger, secretaries of state and defense in the Reagan administration, were both Bechtel executives. See Saloma, *Ominous Politics*, pp. 33–34.

47. Christine Perez, "HUD Secretary's Blunt Warning," *Dallas Business Journal,* May 5, 2006.

48. The HUD inspector general did not find that Jackson actually fired any contractor for criticizing President Bush, as he had once claimed. He did, however, raise the issue of favoritism in New Orleans. See Edward T. Pound, "Investigators Probe Whether HUD Chief Steered Contract," *National Journal,* October 4, 2007. Virgin Islands: Rebecca Carr, "Atlantan Named in HUD Inquiry," *Atlanta Journal-Constitution,* December 27, 2007. Reluctant city housing authority: Carol D. Leonnig, "HUD Chief Accused of Retaliation: Philadelphia Officials Sue After Land Dispute," *Washington Post,* February 4, 2008.

49. This is according to the Native American Contracting Association, as cited in Kimberly Palmer, "The Alaskan Edge," *Government Executive,* July 15, 2005.

50. I am referring here to a half-billion-dollar no-bid contract won by Chenega Technology Services in 2004 and promptly outsourced to SAIC and AS&E, both of which intended to bid for the contract in the first place. See Robert O'Harrow Jr. and Scott Higham, "Alaska Native Corporations Cash In on Contracting Edge," *Washington Post,* November 25, 2004. According to the news story, Chenega Technology Services is based in Alexandria, Virginia, and counts 33 Alaska natives among its 2,300 employees.

51. This is virtually confessed to in one Alaska Native Corporation's statement of its "unique rights."

    > Tribal and ANC-owned firms have been granted special contracting opportunities under the F[ederal] A[cquisitions] R[egulations] for government contracts in general and for DOD contracts in particular. These include unique 8(a) rights, expedited A-76 authority, and bonuses for DOD contractors that subcontract with Native American-owned firms. However, to fully put these rights to work in order to aggressively attack the extreme poverty that exists on Indian reservations and in Alaska Native Villages, the tribal and ANC-owned firms often need mentoring

> from large established government contracting firms that can help guide them through the intricacies of DOD contracting and provide technical support while the firms are building their in-house capability. Working with tribal and ANC firms to put these unique rights to work provides the DOD contractor with an opportunity to help reduce some of the worst poverty in this country, to meet its SDB goals, to make money, and help further legislative initiatives.

See http://www.goldbeltraven.com/images/ANCownedfirmsSpecialRights2002.pdf.

52. These and many other examples are given by Benjamin Wallace-Wells in "Alaska, GOP Welfare State," *Washington Monthly,* July–August 2005. See also Leslie Wayne, "Security for the Homeland, Made in Alaska," *New York Times,* August 12, 2004 (about the Alaska Native Corporations that subcontracted security work to Wackenhut); and Chuck Neubauer and Richard T. Cooper, "Senator's Way to Wealth Was Paved with Favors," *Los Angeles Times,* December 17, 2003 (about Ted Stevens and the Alaska Native Corporations).
53. Birch Horton Bittner & Cherot, whose clients include Chenega and Nana Pacific: Ronald G. Birch was once chief of staff to Stevens; William H. Bittner is the brother of Stevens's wife.
54. Blank Rome, whose top officers were instrumental in establishing the Department of Homeland Security. (The firm's chairman is Tom Ridge's former fund-raiser David Girard-diCarlo; high-ranking lawyers at Blank Rome include Mark Holman, a former chief of staff to Tom Ridge; and Carl Buchholz, a former special assistant to President Bush.) One of the firm's lawyers was the chairman of the Republican convention in 2004; another lawyer vocally supported the attack on Democratic candidate John Kerry by the Swift Boat Veterans for Truth. On the firm's homeland security practice, see the AP story, "Lobbying Firm Run by Ridge's Former Fund-Raiser Built Long List of Homeland Security Clients," dated January 12, 2005. As of July 2007, the employees of Blank Rome were listed as the largest campaign contributors to the presidential candidacy of John McCain.
55. Van Ness Feldman. The Alaska politicians in question are Frank Murkowski and Don Young.
56. According to the San Diego newspaper, Cunningham justified one of the ADCS contracts with the typical winger idea that "the People's Republic of China might try to take over Panama once U.S. forces left." Dean Calbreath and Jerry Kammer, "Contractor 'Knew How to Grease the Wheels,'" *San Diego Union-Tribune,* December 4, 2005. See also Laton McCartney, "Bribery in the Beltway."
57. David Johnston and David D. Kirkpatrick, "Washington Deal Maker Details Palm Greasing," *New York Times,* August 6, 2006.

58. All of these are described in the grand jury's indictment of Brent Wilkes, United States District Court, Southern District of California, filed February 13, 2007. One of the many places you can read this forty-two-page document is http://www.nctimes.com/pdf/wilkesindictmenta.pdf.
59. Ibid.

Chapter 7: Putting the Train in Reverse

1. John S. Long, "Pentagon 'Revolving Door' Turning Faster," *Cleveland Plain Dealer,* August 17, 1986.
2. A much-noted defense of the "revolving door" was made by *Washington Post* financial columnist Steven Pearlstein, in the issue for July 2, 2003. ("A Revolving Door? So What?") Since every military contractor was playing the revolving-door game, Pearlstein reasoned, none of them enjoyed a competitive advantage over any other, and so it was moot. Besides, he argued, having people who understood the procurement system in the private sector not only brought certain efficiencies but also "produced a military arsenal that, while hardly cheap, is unmatched anywhere else in the world."

   This is absurd. Efficiency and competition are precisely what the revolving door sacrifices, giving us instead the epic wastefulness, failed weapons systems, and unnecessary overbuilding for which the Pentagon has won such reknown (small example: the crappy but unbelievably expensive V-22; large example: the war in Iraq, which is on track to be the second-most expensive war in U.S. history). Besides, the American military was sufficiently powerful to keep us safe long before the age of the revolving door and all the amazing waste-revelations of the eighties, nineties, and the present. The armed forces' greatest moment of all time came while their spending and their relationships with contractors were under the constant scrutiny of the Truman Committee.
3. The law requiring the Department of Defense to keep records of employees who left to work for the defense industry was repealed in 1996. See "The Politics of Contracting," a report issued by the Project on Government Oversight, June 29, 2004, pp. 8–9. The article by John Long mentioned above is included as appendix B in this report.
4. This is, of course, Darleen Druyun, who approved a deal to lease tanker planes from Boeing instead of simply buying them, which would have been cheaper. She herself referred to the deal as a "parting gift to Boeing" and took a job there in January 2003. Read Druyun's confessions at http://www.pogo.org/m/cp/cp-druyun-postpleaadmission-2004.pdf.
5. The public duties of these individuals and their current positions are described in Craig Holman, "The Government-to-Lobbyist Revolving Door," in *A Matter of Trust: How the Revolving Door Undermines Public Confidence in Government—And What to Do About It* (Wash-

ington, D.C.: Revolving Door Working Group, 2005), pp. 40–45. The committee chairman was Billy Tauzin of Louisiana, who reportedly accepted a deal worth $2 million a year from PhRMA less than two months after the prescription drug benefit passed.

6. Eric Lipton, "Former Antiterror Officials Find Industry Pays Better," *New York Times,* June 18, 2006. Frank Rich, "The Road from K Street to Yusufiya," *New York Times,* June 25, 2006.
7. See "Factual Basis for the Plea of Mark Dennis Zachares" attached to Zachares's plea of guilty to one charge of conspiracy, dated March 14, 2007, and available on the Web site of the *St. Petersburg* (Florida) *Times,* http://www.sptimes.com/2007/04/24/images/Zachares_Basis_for_Plea.pdf.
8. Public Citizen, *Congressional Revolving Doors: The Journey from Congress to K Street* (Washington, D.C.: Public Citizen's Congress Watch, 2005), p. 1. Holman, "The Government-to-Lobbyist Revolving Door," p. 44.
9. Kim Eisler, "Hired Guns," *Washingtonian,* June 2007, p. 68.
10. Jonathan Weisman, "Embattled Rep. Ney Won't Seek Reelection," *Washington Post,* August 8, 2006. The quotation is a paraphrase of remarks reportedly made to Ney by then–Majority Leader John Boehner.
11. Reed Hundt, who served as FCC chairman during the Clinton years, wrote in 2005 that he once asked Bennett's assistance securing Internet access for public schools. Bennett "told me he would not help," Hundt wrote, "because he did not want public schools to obtain new funding, new capability, new tools for success. He wanted them, he said, to fail so that they could be replaced with vouchers, charter schools, religious schools, and other forms of private education." Hundt published his essay on Talking Points Memo. You could read it here as of August 2006: http://www.tpmcafe.com/story/2005/10/1/105329/697.
12. " 'They are really trying to undo the laws of the land by administrative and budgetary action,' said Russell W. Peterson, president of the National Audubon Society. 'It is a very serious situation and one that obviously stems from President Reagan himself.' " *New York Times,* December 19, 1981.

    See also the July 3, 1981, essay on Reagan's novel strategy by Howell Raines. "In key Cabinet and regulatory jobs," Raines wrote, "the Reagan transformation amounts to a revolution of attitude involving the appointment of officials who in previous administrations might have been ruled out by concern over possible lack of qualifications or conflict of interest, or open hostility to the mission of the agencies they now lead." Raines, "Reagan Reversing Many U.S. Policies," *New York Times,* July 3, 1981.
13. Purge/YAFers: Jack Anderson, "Howard Phillips' Hit Men at the OEO," *Washington Post,* February 17, 1973; Jack Anderson, "Phillips Hires New Crew to Fire Old," *Washington Post,* March 31, 1973.

Local OEO employees: "OEO Legal Aid Dying in California," *Washington Post,* February 20, 1973; "Legal Unit Killed in Jackson, Miss.," *New York Times,* April 29, 1973. Leaked memo: "OEO: Cato Strikes by Night," *Washington Post,* February 22, 1973. Broder: "Sacrificing Legality for Efficiency," *Washington Post,* February 27, 1973. "Marxist notion": "Acting OEO Chief Discerns Marxism in Poverty Agency," *New York Times,* February 4, 1973.

14. See "OEO: Cato Strikes by Night"; "Contempt for Congress," *New York Times,* April 21, 1973; "Judge Halts Move to Disband O.E.O.," *New York Times,* April 12, 1973. Phillips describes his disillusionment with Nixon on pp. 4–6 of *The New Right at Harvard.*
15. These were, respectively, Robert Burford, James Harris, and John Crowell, all of whom are described in Ronald Brownstein and Nina Easton, *Reagan's Ruling Class: Portraits of the President's Top 100 Officials* (Washington, D.C.: Presidential Accountability Group, 1982).
16. "Leaders selected for their symbolic value rather than their administrative skills predominated in the president's [i.e., Reagan's] first round of regulatory appointments. A number of these appointees were drawn from the industry they had been chosen to regulate; others were identified as critics of the missions of their designated agencies (one, James Watt, had explicitly challenged his agency's mission). Still others were relatively obscure professionals with little or no knowledge of the agencies they were to manage or industries they were to regulate. Appointments of the last type appear to have been intended to broadcast White House indifference to the missions of certain agencies and independent commissions." George C. Eads and Michael Fix, *Relief or Reform? Reagan's Regulatory Dilemma* (Washington, D.C.: Urban Institute Press, 1984), pp. 143–44.
17. Ibid., p. 143.
18. "Environmental Agency: Deep and Persisting Woes," *New York Times,* March 6, 1983.
19. Eads and Fix suggest that "agency paralysis" brought about through conflict between political and career staff was a deliberate goal of "some people in the administration." *Relief or Reform?* p. 143.
20. As it happens, the man they spied on was Hugh Kaufman, the famous EPA whistle-blower, who has crossed swords with just about every presidential administration since Jimmy Carter's. "Briefing," *New York Times,* July 3, 1982; "The House Cites Mrs. Gorsuch," *New York Times,* December 19, 1982; "The Superfund Turned Upside Down," *New York Times,* December 28, 1982.
21. The language of management theory: John Horton, assistant administrator of EPA, quoted in Philip Shabecoff, "U.S. Environmental Agency Making Deep Staffing Cuts," *New York Times,* January 3, 1982. Previous administrator: William Drayton, chief budget officer under the Carter administration, quoted in ibid.

22. Office of Enforcement: Philip Shabecoff, "Ecology Charges Fall Off Sharply," *New York Times,* October 15, 1981. "Peer review": Gorsuch mentions this strategy and many others in John Rees, "The Amazing Anne M. Gorsuch: An Exclusive Interview with the Administrator of the Environmental Protection Agency Reveals Why Radicals Are Attacking Her," *Review of the NEWS,* June 16, 1982, p. 49. Promise of nonenforcement: Philip Shabecoff, "E.P.A. Chief Assailed on Lead Violation," *New York Times,* April 13, 1982. Memo: David Burnham, "Reagan Dismisses High E.P.A. Official," *New York Times,* February 8, 1983.
23. Jo Becker and Barton Gellman, "Leaving No Tracks," *Washington Post,* June 27, 2007.
24. Quoted in Mike Soraghan, "Watt Applauds Bush Energy Strategy," *Denver Post,* May 16, 2001.
25. By using legal loopholes to expand the pollution allowable by coal-burning power plants and by renouncing lawsuits the government had basically won against polluters, wrote one former EPA official, "In a matter of weeks, the Bush administration was able to undo the environmental progress we had worked years to secure." Eric Schaeffer, "Clearing the Air: Why I Quit Bush's EPA," *Washington Monthly,* July–August 2002.
26. See "Restoring Scientific Integrity in Policymaking," a 2004 statement by the Union of Concerned Scientists. http://www.ucsusa.org/scientific_integrity/interference/scientists-signon-statement.html.
27. Eric Pianin, "Proposed Mercury Rules Bear Industry Mark: EPA Language Similar to That in Memos from Law Firm Representing Utilities," *Washington Post,* January 31, 2004.
28. Mines: Ian Urbina and Andrew W. Lehren, "U.S. Easing Fines for Mine Owners on Safety Flaws: Penalties Not Collected," *New York Times,* March 2, 2006.
29. The head of the Consumer Product Safety Commission is Nancy Nord, a former executive with the U.S. Chamber of Commerce. See Dana Milbank's account of her comical performance before a Senate subcommittee, *Washington Post,* September 13, 2007. On Nord's opposition to the bill giving her agency greater funding and authority, see Annys Shin, "CPSC Leader Called On to Resign," *Washington Post,* October 31, 2007. On the free trips enjoyed by Nord and her predecessor, see Elizabeth Williamson, "Industries Paid for Top Regulators' Travel," *Washington Post,* November 2, 2007.
30. Breast-feeding ad: Marc Kaufman and Christopher Lee, "HHS Toned Down Breast-Feeding Ads," *Washington Post,* August 31, 2007.
31. *NOW,* January 7, 2005, transcript available at http://www.pbs.org/now/transcript/transcriptNOW101_full.html.

    Almost identical language was used when an FDA scientist criticized a diabetes drug in 1998. His supervisor, he says, told him, "We have to maintain good relations with the drug companies because they are our customers." Michael Scherer, "The Side Effects of Truth," *Mother Jones,* May–June 2005. Other examples of the FDA's ongoing war with critics of prescription drugs are recounted in Gardiner Harris, "Potentially Incompatible Goals at F.D.A.," *New York Times,* June 11, 2007.

32. This is Emily Stover DeRocco, then the head of the Department's Employment and Training Administration (ETA). The phrase can be found in announcements for a conference called "Workforce Innovation 2002," a get-together the department sponsored for "workforce investment professionals." Emphasis in original. Read it here: http://workforcesecurity.doleta.gov/dmstree/ten/ten2k1/ten_03-01.htm.

    The historical inversion here is worth noting: In the seventies, ETA was on the short list of federal agencies conservatives hated most. It oversaw the program established by the Comprehensive Employment and Training Act (CETA), a full employment scheme that created jobs for otherwise unemployable people, and which had "a marked social service bias," according to a history of the period. "Many of its programs were targeted to the poor; training, counseling, and job placement were seen as a way of reducing poverty." The Reagan administration effectively abolished CETA in 1983. See Irene Rubin, *Shrinking the Federal Government,* p. 77.

33. See Chavez's book *Betrayal: How Union Bosses Shake Down Their Members and Corrupt American Politics* (New York: Crown Forum, 2004), or her many newspaper columns in the nineties.

34. I am referring here to Morgan Reynolds, who was an economist at Texas A&M prior to becoming the Labor Department's chief economist in 2001. Reynolds was the author of a 1987 Cato Institute book titled *Making America Poorer: The Cost of Labor Law;* in the entry for "Labor Unions" in *The Concise Encyclopedia of Economics* he refers to unions as "labor cartels" and pronounces them irredeemably racist and sexist. See http://www.econlib.org/Library/Enc/LaborUnions.html.

    Prisoners, on the other hand, make an ideal workforce in Reynolds's view. In a 1998 paper he drafted for the Heartland Institute, he called for wardens to become "marketers of prison labor" and for the construction of "industrial parks next to prisons" so that convict labor might be harvested more efficiently. However, Reynolds cautioned, it was critical that no minimum-wage laws be considered as we brought prison labor online. http://www.heartland.org/Article.cfm?artId=746.

    Read up on Reynolds's 9/11 theories at his Web site, http://nomoregames.net/.

35. See Tanya Ballard, "Lawmaker Questions Labor Transit Subsidy Dispute," *Government Executive,* September 26, 2003, and "Labor Department and Union Wrangle Over Transit Subsidy," *Government Executive,* July 1, 2003.

36. "Regulatory jungle": Elaine Chao, "A New Culture of Responsibility," a speech given to the National Federation of Independent Businesses,

Washington, D.C., June 14, 2002. "Voluntary compliance": This ought to be the slogan of the Bush administration, but I am deriving it in this case from an unnamed Labor Department document quoted in Stephen Labaton, "OSHA Leaves Worker Safety Largely in Hands of Industry," *New York Times,* April 25, 2007. "Much stronger financial incentives": From Mark Wilson, "How to Close Down the Department of Labor," Heritage Foundation Backgrounder no. 1058, October 19, 1995.

37. Wage and Hour: Kim Bobo, *Wage Theft in America: Why Millions of Working Americans Are Not Getting Paid—and What We Can Do About It* (New York: The New Press, 2009), p. 119. Wal-Mart: Steven Greenhouse, "Wal-Mart Agrees to Pay Fine in Child Labor Cases," *New York Times,* February 12, 2005. OSHA: "Since George W. Bush became president, OSHA has issued the fewest significant standards in its history, public health experts say," reports the *New York Times.* "It has imposed only one major safety rule. The only significant health standard it issued was ordered by a federal court. The agency has killed dozens of existing and proposed regulations and delayed adopting others." Labaton, "OSHA Leaves Worker Safety." Humorous speech: It was called "Adults Do the Darndest [*sic*] Things" and was delivered on May Day, 2006. Read it here: http://www.osha.gov/pls/oshaweb/owadisp.show_document?p_table=SPEECHES&p_id=922.
38. "Project champions": See the Center for the Business of Government's interview with Patrick Pizzella at http://www.businessofgovernment.org/main/interviews/bios/patrick_pizzella_frt.asp. "Create and own their goals": Pizzella, "Shedding Light," *Government Executive,* October 1, 2005.
39. "Star pupil": Kimberly Palmer and Amelia Gruber, "New Initiatives at Labor Department Lead to High Scores," *Government Executive,* December 1, 2004. "Fought [its] way": Maurice McTigue, "The High Performance Government Organization of the Future," a speech delivered to the SES Leadership Training Conference, U.S. Department of Labor, July 28, 2005. McTigue is the director of the Government Accountability Project at the Mercatus Center at George Mason University.
40. McTigue, "The High Performance Government Organization."
41. Examples include Tom DeLay's 1995 "Project Relief," described below, and George W. Bush's suspension of the Clinton administration's ergonomics standard, described above.
42. Eads and Fix, *Relief or Reform?* p. 5. See also Chris Mooney, *The Republican War on Science* (New York: Basic, 2005), p. 105, and Tozzi's own remarks on OIRA, in Dick Kirschten, "The 20 Years War," *National Journal,* June 11, 1983.
43. Graham's trademark idea was to apply cost-benefit accounting to regulations. If done right, this formula can nearly always be made to show that regulations force industry to absorb enormous costs for minuscule public benefits. See the description of his thinking in Greg Anrig, *The*

Conservatives Have No Clothes: Why Right-Wing Ideas Keep Failing (Hoboken, NJ: Wiley, 2007), chap. 6.

The list of companies that supported Graham's work is dazzling: the Internet research operation "SourceWatch" lists over a hundred corporations and trade associations that had donated to the Harvard Center for Risk Analysis as of January 2004.

44. Among the regulations OIRA blocked or muted on Graham's watch were: a rule on air pollution from oceangoing cargo ships, a rule on air pollution from snowmobile motors, a rule on runoff from construction sites, a rule on the incredibly smelly runoff from factory hog farms, and a rule that would have required cars to alert drivers when a tire was low. In each case, Graham sided with industry against the federal agency in question, usually the EPA. For details on each of these stories, see OMB Watch's "Graham Files": http://www.ombwatch.org/regs/grahamfiles.
45. Microsoft and Instinet represent the high-tech money; PhRMA, Pfizer, and Bristol-Myers Squibb make up the Big Pharma brigade; the NYSE, the NASDAQ, Merrill Lynch, and Morgan Stanley bring a taste of Wall Street; BP Amoco, the Kochs, the American Petroleum Institute, and Exxon round out the obligatory big-oil detachment; and bringing up the rear is Philip Morris, the cigarette king, apparently willing to underwrite any operation that promises to damage the regulatory state.
46. Chamber of Commerce: Christine Triano and Gary Bass, "The New Game in Town: Regulation, Secrecy, and the Quayle Council on Competitiveness," *Government Information Quarterly* 9, no. 2 (1992). Unnamed aides to Vice President Dan Quayle, as quoted by Bob Woodward and David S. Broder, "Quayle's Quest: Curb Rules, Leave 'No Fingerprints,'" *Washington Post,* January 9, 1992.
47. According to Triano and Bass, "the Quayle Council invites regulated corporations unhappy about the results of regulation to quietly turn to the White House for relief." They quote Allan Hubbard, a director of the council, as saying, "When they feel like they are being treated unfairly, [industry groups] come to us."

Vice President Dan Quayle was the chairman of the Council on Competitiveness. According to the 1991 Woodward and Broder story cited in the previous note, the council's "'no fingerprints' and 'no appeal' rules make Dan Quayle the man to see in the Bush administration for business people across the country and their Washington lobbyists." Woodward and Broder then describe how Quayle went about the council's business.

> Word quickly spread through the business community that the Competitiveness Council was ready and able to help on regulatory matters, and its agenda filled up.
>
> In almost every city he visits as a campaigner, Quayle holds closed-door round tables with business people who have made sizable contributions to the local or national GOP.

Another example is an EPA air-pollution rule that, on orders from the council, "was revised in line with the demands of industry lobbyists." Michael Weisskopf, "Regulatory Adviser Has Stake in Chemical Firm; Hubbard Has Participated in Pollution-Control Decisions Affecting the Industry," *Washington Post,* November 20, 1991.

48. Quotes from Chris Mooney, "Paralysis by Analysis: Jim Tozzi's Regulation to End All Regulation," *Washington Monthly,* May 2004. See also Rick Weiss, "'Data Quality' Law Is Nemesis of Regulation," *Washington Post,* August 16, 2004, and Mooney, *The Republican War on Science,* chap. 8.
49. Tozzi is "a self-described 'market-based conservative,'" according to Mooney. "Paralysis by Analysis."
50. Tom Geoghegan, *See You in Court* (New York: New Press, 2007), pp. 65, 60, 64.

Chapter 8: City of Bought Men

1. These last few developments are described by Thomas B. Edsall in "Lobbyists' Emergence Reflects Shift in Capital Culture," *Washington Post,* January 12, 2006.
2. Thanks to "the ever-expanding business of lobbying," wrote the lobbying expert Jeffrey Birnbaum in 1992, "Washington became a modern, prosperous city during the 1970s and 1980s." Jeffrey Birnbaum, *The Lobbyists: How Influence Peddlers Get Their Way in Washington* (New York: Times Books, 1992), p. 7.

   "Washington's biggest business," "new Washington aristocracy": From the series of stories called "Citizen K Street" by the *Post* editor Robert Kaiser; the first installment (out of twenty-seven) ran on the front page of the *Washington Post* on March 4, 2007. "How Lobbying Became Washington's Biggest Business" was the subtitle of the series. "A new Washington aristocracy" was a line that appeared in Kaiser's final installment, titled "Conclusion." Read the whole thing here: http://blog.washingtonpost.com/citizen-k-street/.
3. According to the Web site of Gunderlin Limited, the manufacturer of the building's elevators. See http://www.gunderlin.com/projects/commercial-Low/101constitution.htm.
4. 1986: Evan Thomas, "Peddling Influence," *Time,* March 3, 1986; the quote is from Jack Valenti of the Motion Picture Association. 1992: Birnbaum, *The Lobbyists,* p. 5. Political scientist: "80,000 Lobbyists? Probably Not, but Maybe . . . ," *New York Times,* May 12, 1993. The thirty-five-thousand figure is repeated frequently. See, for example, Jeffrey H. Birnbaum, "The Road to Riches Is Called K Street: Lobbying Firms Hire More, Pay More, Charge More to Influence Government," *Washington Post,* June 22, 2005.

5. Birnbaum, "The Road to Riches."
6. Kaiser, "Citizen K Street."
7. "Restless ambition": "Citizen K Street," Chap. 16. "Extract wealth": Ibid., Chap. 12.
8. "Knitting": Chap. 11, "Citizen K Street." "All the parties profited," "blown away": Chap. 4. The goo-goo liberal in question was Joseph Califano, secretary of health, education, and welfare in the Carter administration. Former president of Boston University: Chap. 23.
9. "Conclusion," "Citizen K Street."
10. And "by 1924 the big business, industrial, and financial pressure groups had all but succeeded in their aims," the author continues. Karl Schriftgiesser, *The Lobbyists: The Art and Business of Influencing Lawmakers* (Boston: Little, Brown, 1951), p. 32.
11. The committee's findings and the industry's response as quoted in ibid., pp. 23, 25.
12. The Mulhall story is recounted in Kenneth G. Crawford, *The Pressure Boys: The Inside Story of Lobbying in America* (New York: Julian Messner, 1939), and Schriftgiesser, *The Lobbyists,* chap. 3. Leaders of the NAM, when called to account for Mulhall's doings, proceeded to make essentially the same argument as Abramoff, Gingrich, and the insurance trust. "Their plainly shown attitude," one member of the investigating committee erupted, "was that the American Congress was considered by them as their legislative department and was viewed with the same arrogant manner in which they viewed their other employees, and that those legislators who dared to oppose them would be disciplined in the same manner in which they were accustomed to discipline recalcitrant employees." Quoted in Kenneth G. Crawford, *The Pressure Boys,* pp. 49–50.
13. Both companies describe these services on their Web sites. See http://www.akingump.com/services/ServiceDetail.aspx?service=267 and http://www.burson-marsteller.com/Practices_And_Specialties/Pages/Issues_and_Advocacy.aspx.
14. David Harvey calls this crisis the "wealth crash" of the seventies. Harvey, *A Brief History of Neoliberalism,* pp. 15, 16.
15. "Put simply, takeovers constitute the key solution to the most serious problem inherent in the operation of publicly traded corporations," namely, the failure of corporate mangement to keep the shareholders' interests foremost in their decision making, wrote two experts in corporate law in 1988. With the advent of the leveraged buyout or hostile takeover, this situation was changed: "Thus, to reduce the risk of being swept out of office, managers are constrained to keep stock prices as high as possible by running their companies efficiently and in the interests of the shareholders." Henry G. Manne and Larry E. Ribstein, "The SEC v. The American Shareholder," *National Review,* November 25,

1988. For more on this subject, see Doug Henwood, *Wall Street* (New York: Verso, 1997), chap. 6.

16. Reagan: "Buddy, Beware," *Time,* December 1, 1975. Reagan campaign literature denouncing lobbyists is quoted on p. 1 of Richard Viguerie's populist 1983 book, *The Establishment Vs. The People.* Viguerie went on to include a whole chapter attacking "big business" for being insufficiently capitalist, for trading with the Soviets, and for subsidizing offensive entertainment.

    See also "The 'Iron Triangles,'" an unsigned 1982 article in Viguerie's *Conservative Digest* in which lobbyists are depicted as one leg of the liberal "iron triangles" that were thought to dominate the city (example: lobbyists for the teachers' union gave orders to the House Education Committee, which then ordered the bureaucracy to do the liberal lobbyists' bidding). "The 'Iron Triangles': How Washington's Buddy System Works Against *You,*" *Conservative Digest,* October 1982, pp. 22–23.

17. I already mentioned the power lobbyists gained over the EPA and the Department of the Interior. The eighties were also the heyday of the "Beltway Bandits," the defense contractors, consultants, and lobbyists who worked together to grab slices of the enormous Reagan defense budget—and who kept substantial pieces of the loot for themselves. For an example of the journalism on the subject, see Dave Griffiths, "The Brigadiers of the 'Beltway Bandits,'" *Business Week,* July 4, 1988, p. 33.

    Another classic eighties lobbying moment was the brief flurry of outrage surrounding Michael Deaver, a close adviser to President Reagan, who left the White House in 1985 and became, almost instantly, one of the most powerful lobbyists in town. Deaver also became a symbol of influence-for-sale, even making the cover of *Time* magazine in 1986, posed in limo, with cell phone, Capitol dome visible in the background.

18. Rush Limbaugh used to refer to the Freshmen as "the dittohead caucus." Even their critics professed admiration for their anti-Washington attitude. They "saw themselves as temporary emissaries sent by the voters to Washington on a mission," writes Linda Killian in *The Freshmen: What Happened to the Republican Revolution?* (Boulder, Colo.: Westview Press, 1998), p. x. "They were brash, irrepressible, and passionately committed to the cause of balancing the budget and shrinking the size of the federal government. The freshmen were a new breed, different from the men and women who had preceded them to Congress. They were not polished, cookie-cutter politicians. They were quirky and plainspoken."

    On Limbaugh and for a passionate appreciation of the Freshmen, see Rich Lowry, "The Freshmen," *National Review,* January 23, 1995.

See also Paul Weyrich, "A different class of Freshman," *Washington Times,* December 26, 1994.

19. Gingrich speaking at the Heritage Foundation in 1990, as recounted by Larry Sabato and Glenn R. Simpson in *Dirty Little Secrets: The Persistence of Corruption in American Politics* (New York: Times Books, 1996), pp. 91–92.
20. J. Bradley Keena, "The Freshmen Troops Fight On," *Washington Times,* January 31, 1996.
21. Nina Easton offers the idealistic take on McIntosh's career in *Gang of Five*. See chap. 2 in particular.
22. That McIntosh's bill was designed to "defund the left" was common knowledge among his Republican brethren. See Killian, *The Freshmen,* p. 182.

    The same point is made by David Maraniss and Michael Weisskopf, *"Tell Newt to Shut Up!": Prizewinning* Washington Post *Journalists Reveal How Reality Gagged the Gingrich Revolution* (New York: Touchstone, 1996), p. 89.
23. Others have made the same point. For example, the reason business failed to get its way in the 1986 corporate tax rewrite, according to *Showdown at Gucci Gulch,* a classic study of the industry, was the fragmented approach of the corporate lobbyists. "The total firepower of these special interests was potentially fatal to any piece of legislation, yet they never managed to form an efficient 'killer' coalition." Jeffrey H. Birnbaum and Alan S. Murray, *Showdown at Gucci Gulch: Lawmakers, Lobbyists, and the Unlikely Triumph of Tax Reform* (New York: Random House, 1987), p. 287.
24. "Struggle for the business community's soul": Norquist, *Rock the House,* p. 138.

    Business PACs: The great right-wing prophet of business PACs was Guy Vander Jagt, a congressman from Michigan. His constant agitation on the subject is described by Brooks Jackson on pp. 73–74 of *Honest Graft: Big Money and the American Political Process* (New York: Knopf, 1988); his disappointment at the failure of PACs to bring about the free-market revolution is described on pp. 75 and 87.
25. DeLay aide: John Feehery, quoted in "To the Chagrin of Some Republicans, Lobby Group Hires Former House Democrat," an Associated Press story printed in the *St. Louis Post-Dispatch,* October 14, 1998. Scanlon: Jill Abramson, "Republicans Are Irked at Industry Group's Hiring of Democrat," *New York Times,* October 14, 1998.
26. Norquist tells this story in slightly different form in *Rock the House,* p. 137.
27. Although *Honest Graft* contains little evidence of such crimes, there are numerous cases of legislators shaking down lobbyists, especially at the state legislature level. Norquist quote: Norquist and Stanley Greenberg, "Republicans and Democrats," *The American Enterprise,* January–February 1996.

28. See also the anonymous reference to *Honest Graft* on the Web site of the K Street Project under the headline "The TRUE K Street Project Endorses the Drive to Ban Tony Coelhoism," http://www.kstreetproject.com/index.php?content=TonyCoelho.

    Norquist, "Why I Started the Project," *USA Today,* September 13, 2006.

29. "The system of money-based elections and lobbying rewards those who cater to well-funded interests," Jackson wrote. Jackson, *Honest Graft,* pp. 295, 55.

    Tony Coelho ran the Democratic Congressional Campaign Committee in 1986 and gave the reporter Jackson complete access to his deal making and to the DCCC's papers. This yields a fascinating look at the many howling perversities of the PAC world, but it hardly makes the Democrats out to be an extortion ring.

    I went through Jackson's book fairly carefully, and while the author suggests in the introduction that Coelho "pressures business lobbyists for campaign money in ways that sometimes amount to intimidation" (p. 5), his evidence for this is weak. The first instance of such intimidation comes on p. 70, and it consists entirely of Coelho setting up parties where PAC directors could meet senior Democrats, including two powerful committee chairmen. No threat of any kind is recorded by the author, but merely because these senior congressmen are present Jackson concludes, "The threat was clear. Business would withhold money from these Democrats at its peril." No follow-through is noted, however, and "the response [by business PACs] was disappointing."

    A more direct example is described on pp. 78–79, when Coelho and other senior House Democrats sign a letter to a construction-industry lobby group demanding that they contribute to the campaign of a colleague or see their "relationship" with the Democrats "be damaged." But the lobby did not contribute, and Jackson records no effort by the Democrats to retaliate against them.

    The only really conclusive instance in which Coelho and Co. express displeasure with someone and then act on it is the case of one D. G. Martin, a Democrat who ran for Congress in North Carolina in 1986 on an anti-PAC platform. Coelho's demand that Martin drop his clean-politics idea is described on p. 222; the decision by the DCCC to withhold money from Martin's campaign is described on p. 223. Martin lost.

    On the other hand, Jackson offers hundreds of concrete, undeniable examples of Democrats doing *favors* for PACs and big-money contributors, and sometimes being embarrassed for it because they are supposed to be, after all, the "party of the people."

30. Jeffrey H. Birnbaum, "Going Left on K Street; More Democrats Hired to Lobby Despite GOP Efforts to Shut Them Out," *Washington Post,* July 2, 2004.

31. Juliet Eilperin, "No Democrat Need Apply, House GOP Tells Lobby," *Washington Post,* October 14, 1998.
32. Juliet Eilperin, "Business Group Backs Democrat Whose Hiring Irked GOP Leaders," *Washington Post,* October 15, 1998.
33. DeLay: Maraniss and Weisskopf, *"Tell Newt to Shut Up!"* pp. 110, 117. Santorum, chairman of the RNC: Nick Confessore, "Welcome to the Machine," *Washington Monthly,* July–August 2003.
34. The lobby group was the Indiana Farm Bureau; the freshman who made this remark was Mark Souder of Indiana, a former YAFer. As the *New York Times* told the story, Souder was placated "only after it [the Farm Bureau] bowed to his demand that it replace its lobbyists with people sympathetic to his conservative views." Richard L. Berke, "Congress's New G.O.P. Majority Makes Lobbyists' Life Difficult," *New York Times,* March 20, 1995.
35. In their very first term: Maraniss and Weisskopf, *"Tell Newt to Shut Up!"* p. 114.

    According to a story published by *USA Today* immediately after the election of 2006, thirty-nine of the original seventy-three House Freshmen were still serving in a public office of some kind (thirty-one were still in the House, six were in the Senate, one was a governor, and one was in the Bush administration); Sonny Bono died in office; of the thirty-three remaining, sixteen have worked as lobbyists at some point. http://www.usatoday.com/news/washington/2006-12-07-gop-1994-2006_x.htm.

    The numbers from the seventies are from Craig Holman, "The Government-to-Lobbyist Revolving Door," *A Matter of Trust* (Washington: Revolving Door Working Group, 2005, published online at www.revolvingdoor.info), p. 44.
36. According to Peter Stone, Norquist wrote to Tom DeLay in early 1995 that it "would probably be worthwhile for Jack Abramoff to stop by and brief you on the 'K' Street project," and then proceeded to describe Abramoff as the project's ideal lobbyist. Stone, *Heist,* p. 40.
37. David E. Rosenbaum, "At $500 an Hour, Lobbyist's Influence Rises With G.O.P.," *New York Times,* April 3, 2002.
38. Berke, "Congress's New G.O.P. Majority."
39. Philip Shenon, "In Congress, a Lobbyist's Legal Troubles Turn His Generosity into a Burden," *New York Times,* December 19, 2005.
40. Ridenour made this comment to the Senate Indian Affairs Committee, June 25, 2005. It can be found on p. 30 of the committee's hearings on "Tribal Lobbying Matters," part 1.
41. This is the conclusion of the Minority Staff Report, Senate Finance Committee, "Investigation of Jack Abramoff's Use of Tax-Exempt Organizations," October 2006, p. 26.
42. Maraniss and Weisskopf, *"Tell Newt to Shut Up!"* p. 114.

43. This was Representative Cass Ballenger's "Safety and Health Improvement and Regulatory Reform Act of 1995." See Maraniss and Weisskopf, *"Tell Newt to Shut Up!"* chap. 5, "Revenge of the Business Class."
44. The coverage of this meeting and the Telecom Act that followed furnish a good illustration of how confused reporters can get when they view events through the default libertarian prism of mainstream journalism. Ken Auletta, who covered the first event for the *New Yorker,* spent many of his column inches depicting the media companies as innocent and uninformed victims of political extortionists; the story was even illustrated by a cartoon of an elephant and a donkey (bipartisanship!) each shaking money out of a helpless businessman. But the facts were precisely the opposite: the act itself, as the world now knows, was almost as pro-business as it was possible to be.

    See Jeff Chester, *Digital Destiny: New Media and the Future of Democracy* (New York: New Press, 2007), p. 26, and Ken Auletta, "Pay Per Views," *New Yorker,* June 5, 1995. On the Telecom Act itself, see Robert McChesney, *Rich Media, Poor Democracy* (Urbana: University of Illinois Press, 1999).
45. The story is told in "Let the Lobby Boys In," the second chapter of Maraniss and Weisskopf, *"Tell Newt to Shut Up!"* The quote appears on p. 12.
46. According to the lobbying columnist Jeffrey Birnbaum, the group of companies spent $1.6 million on lobbying and received a tax break that saved them $100 billion. Birnbaum does not give the time frame for the tax cut, so I am assuming the savings all came at once. "Clients' Rewards Keep K Street Lobbyists Thriving," *Washington Post,* February 14, 2006.
47. See Alex Kaplun and Allison A. Freeman, "Coal; In final tally, Appalachian mining counties go solidly for Bush," *Greenwire,* November 5, 2004. Also check out "Mine the Vote's" Web page at http://www.bipac.net/page.asp?g=nma&content=startpage.
48. Tina Seeley, "EPSA's Shelk: True Believer," *Energy Daily,* August 5, 2005.
49. *Times*: Jodi Rudoren and Aron Pilhofer, "Hiring Lobbyist for Federal Aid, Towns Learn That Money Talks," *New York Times,* July 2, 2006. Number-one firm: John Cochran, "Budget Villain, Local Hero," *CQ Weekly,* June 12, 2006, p. 1611.
50. Birnbaum, *The Lobbyists,* pp. 126–27.
51. On Kies, see Jonathan Chait, "Company Man," *New Republic,* June 5, 2000, and also Jeffrey Birnbaum, "Washington's Most Dangerous Bureaucrats," *Fortune,* September 29, 1997.
52. Jeffrey Birnbaum, "GOP Lobbyists Plan Show of Support for DeLay," *Washington Post,* November 12, 2005. Public Citizen compiled a complete list of the fund-raiser's hosts.

53. Union president Douglas McCarron writes that "the revenue generated by the building will go back into the field, organizing a new generation of carpenters." "Building for the Future," *Carpenter*, July–August 2002.
54. See the proud and lengthy explanation of this decision in *Carpenter* magazine, October–December 2004.
55. See Bush's "Remarks to the United Brotherhood of Carpenters and Joiners of America Legislative Conference," June 19, 2002, available at http://www.presidency.ucsb.edu/ws/index.php?pid=73043.

Chapter 9: The Bantustan That Roared

1. Ridenour's words can be found in a National Center for Public Policy Research press release dated November 25, 1996, and headlined "Washington Could Learn a Great Deal from the Commonwealth of the Northern Mariana Islands." Bilbray's remarks were reported by the *Marianas Variety* on December 31, 1996. Both Ridenour and Bilbray took Abramoff-organized trips to Saipan.
2. "America's Hong Kong": Ronald Bailey, "America's Hong Kong," *American Enterprise*, May–June 1997. "Free-market model": An unnamed colleague of Abramoff's quoted in John Moore, "American Dream or Pacific Nightmare," *National Journal*, December 13, 1997. "A vibrantly successful experiment": Peter Ferrara, "Tinkering with the Success of Liberty," *Washington Times*, October 10, 1995.
3. P. F. Kluge, *The Edge of Paradise: America in Micronesia* (New York: Random House, 1991), p. 26.
4. Ibid., p. 127. Yes, I know. It was a StarKist can that Charlie wanted to get into. The image is great anyway.
5. F. Haydn Williams, letter to Representatives Richard Pombo and Nick J. Rahall II, dated February 23, 2004, copy in possession of the author.
6. *Third Annual Report* of the Federal-CNMI Initiative on Labor, Immigration, and Law Enforcement in the Commonwealth of the Northern Mariana Islands, July 1997.
7. "The local immigration policy has no limit; it is wide open, unrestricted," according to a 1996 statement by Juan Babauta, then the CNMI's Washington representative, as quoted in "Economic Miracle or Economic Mirage?" a report of the Democratic staff of the House Committee on Resources, April 24, 1997, p. 3.
8. "CNMI policy permits the staffing of major employers in the territory—garment factories, security companies, the hotel industry—with a permanent floating army of foreign workers who have no opportunity to become permanent members of the community and who, by nature of their status, culture and powerlessness, are extremely vulnerable to exploitation, pressure, and mistreatment." Congressman George Miller and Democratic Staff of the House Committee on Re-

sources, "Beneath the American Flag: Labor and Human Rights Abuses in the CNMI" (n.p.: n.p., March 26, 1998), p. 15.

9. "The fact that an employer can have an alien worker removed from the CNMI on one-day's notice is a powerful incentive for an alien to obey an employer's demands, even though the demands may be illegal or abusive." *Third Annual Report,* p. 11.
10. As of 1997, the minimum wage in Saipan for garment and construction workers was $2.90 per hour; for more exalted occupations it was $3.05 per hour. Domestic workers averaged sixty-four cents per hour. Appendix 2 of the *Third Annual Report* describes various tricks then in widespread use in CNMI garment factories which, through recruitment fees and other mandatory fees, could reduce a worker's net earnings to $3,150 per year for her first two years.
11. The basic tenet of labor law is the right of workers to form unions. As we shall see, however, the CNMI government was vehemently opposed to labor unions.

    Not only could workers on Saipan be confined to their barracks in those days, but they required permission from the islands' labor department to change employers. Numerous other tricks were invented to keep workers from discomfiting their employers. According to a 1997 report by the Democratic staff of the House Committee on Resources, "the CNMI government enacted a law to shorten the time period under which workers are allowed to file claims of unpaid wages or overtime compensation." "Economic Miracle or Economic Mirage?" pp. 5, 9.
12. Ferrara, "Tinkering with the Success of Liberty."
13. Although residents of the CNMI pay the same income taxes as other Americans, the returns go mainly to the local government instead of the U.S. Treasury and can be rebated to the taxpayer by the local government as it sees fit. Additionally, capital gains taxes in the CNMI are considerably lower than in the mainland United States.
14. "Regulatory burdens have been minimized. Licenses and permits for foreign entry, new businesses, construction and development are quickly and easily granted." Ferrara, "Tinkering with the Success of Liberty."
15. This was a provision of the covenant between the CNMI and the United States. See "Economic Miracle or Economic Mirage?" p. 3.
16. In 1998, a congressional report noted that "the CNMI government actively solicits foreign investment to take advantage of its unique trade arrangement with the United States, advertising the litany of special privileges granted to investors in the CNMI." "Beneath the American Flag," pp. 7–8.

    In 2007, the Saipan Chamber of Commerce continued to advertise the same things under the headline "Doing Business Here." http://www.saipanchamber.com/doingbusiness.asp.

17. On the components of the ideal free-market country, or "neoliberal state," see David Harvey's discussion of Iraq under U.S. rule in *A Brief History of Neoliberalism,* pp. 6–7.
18. John Bowe, *Nobodies: Modern American Slave Labor and the Dark Side of the Global Economy* (New York: Random House, 2007), pp. 169, 170.
19. Ibid., p. 171.
20. Terry McCarthy, "Give Me Your Tired, Your Poor . . . ," *Time,* February 2, 1998. See also Miller et al., "Beneath the American Flag," p. 25. The *Third Annual Report* noted in 1997 that there was "one alien domestic worker for every 2.6 local households" (p. 4).
21. For example: http://www.dailykos.com/story/2007/2/11/1734/23082.
22. Bowe, *Nobodies,* pp. 229–30.
23. See ibid., p. 246.
24. Ibid., p. 251.
25. See, for example, Tina Sablan's fiery attack on the island's political leaders: http://www.chamorro.com/community/tsablan_cnmi.html.
26. Robert Collier, "Stalemate in Talks on Saipan Workers," *San Francisco Chronicle,* January 20, 1999.
27. The first big-media story about labor abuse in the CNMI, as far as I have been able to determine, was by William Branigin of the *Washington Post;* it ran in August of 1994 and was titled "U.S. Pacific Paradise Is Hell for Some Foreign Workers; Filipinos Report Beatings, Rapes, Lockups." The Philippine government took action in the early part of 1995, banning workers in certain categories from taking jobs in the CNMI. The ban was lifted later, after CNMI leaders promised reforms, but the threat that it would be reimposed hung over the islands throughout the Abramoff era. See *Pacific Daily News* (Guam), January 7, 1995, and May 23, 1997, and *Marianas Variety* (Saipan) March 30, 1995.
28. Both resolutions took exception to the CNMI's minimum wage system. They were approved in April 1996.
29. In a 2002 "security report" commissioned by Fred Black, the U.S. attorney for Guam, the islands' political corruption is described in a shocking shorthand. The report accuses CNMI Immigration of allowing entry to members of foreign organized crime groups and summarizes political conditions with the following statement: "The political environment on Guam and the C.N.M.I. is largely controlled by a few well placed families and wealthy business people in each location. Nepotism and financial advantage are a distinct part of island politics." *Report on Security in Guam and the C.N.M.I.: A report from the districts of Guam and the Northern Mariana Islands to the U.S. Attorney's Office on security and immigration,* dated June 7, 2002, p. 12, hereafter *2002 Security Report.* The report is available online at http://www.talkingpointsmemo.com/docs/immigration-report/?resultpage=1&.

For colorful detail, see the furious *j'accuse* posted on the Internet under the title saipansucks.com.

30. The man's name was Joaquin S. Torres; the garment company was Willie Tan's L&T Corporation. See Rafael H. Arroyo, "Torres to Speaker: Garment Sector not ready for a 30-cent wage hike," *Marianas Variety,* March 13, 1996.
31. Fitial can be found claiming authorship of the guest worker laws in his testimony to the Senate Committee on Energy and Natural Resources, "United States/CNMI Political Union," July 19, 2007, p. 47.
32. See http://www.commerce.gov.mp/new/economic_development/research_and_development.php.
33. The U.S. Department of Labor was, in fact, a bureau of the U.S. Department of Commerce until 1913. The two were separated because of the obvious contradiction in their missions.
34. Allen Stayman, formerly an Interior Department official overseeing the islands, recounts how he was once told by a frustrated DOLI official tasked with setting up a worker tracking system, "it's just a scam. We're supposed to make it look good for you guys, but we're supposed to continue to meet the needs of the special interests."

    The former attorney general I spoke to also describes what she calls the "rule du jour" system, in which the labor chief would "basically issue oral edicts, and that was the rule of the day. There was nothing in writing, they ignored their own laws, they ignored their own regulations, they chose to accept complaints or deny complaints at will."

    The system persisted until quite recently. In 2007 Stayman, who was on the staff of the Senate Energy Committee, showed me a stack of letters sent by the federal labor ombudsman on Saipan to the local Department of Labor drawing its attention to one egregious bit of worker abuse after another, each one part of a pattern going back years and years. The local department's response: nothing. "The director of labor," Stayman continues, the astonishment plain in his voice, "made a ruling in which workers who file a complaint do not have standing in the adjudicative process regarding their own complaint."
35. The reason Torres thought the NLRA didn't apply on the Marianas was that the CNMI government had the exclusive right to control its own immigration, and unions would probably try to bargain for longer job tenure for their members. "The almost certain efforts by unionized nonresident workers to achieve job security," Torres insisted, "is an example of the application of the Act directly contradicting Commonwealth policy and its right to control its own immigration." Rafael H. Arroyo, "Solons don't like unionized labor," *Marianas Variety,* December 21, 1994.
36. Yes, they really made this argument. See Gaynor Dumat-Ol, "Filipinos Granted Chance to Unionize," *Pacific Daily News,* March 25, 1995.

37. The islands' Employers Council issued a report diagnosing the problem in July of 1995, according to Rafael Arroyo, "Union Activity on Saipan in High Gear, Says Report," *Marianas Variety,* July 20, 1995. "Like a disease": Mar-Vic C. Munar, "Business Leaders on Saipan Unite . . . 'Stop the Unions,' " *Marianas Variety,* September 1, 1995.
38. Torres on the profits unions make: "One More Time Against Unions," Letter to the Editor, *Marianas Variety,* date not visible on my copy (probably 1995). Torres on bigwigs in limousines: "Torres Shuns Unions for Aliens," *Marianas Variety,* August 4, 1995. Persona Non Grata: Ninth Northern Marianas Commonwealth Legislature, HR No. 9-141, December 18, 1995: "A House Resolution to declare Elwood Mott, a resident of the State of Hawaii and a union organizer, a persona non grata in the Commonwealth." One reason cited by the CNMI legislature for its bizarre move was that "the formulation of unions here effectively promotes a division between resident and non-resident employees."
39. Torres's two-year proposal would obviously have been in violation of the nation's labor laws, which prohibit discriminating against union members in such a fashion. On the particulars of the proposal, see Mar-Vic C. Munar, "Torres to Push 2-Year Limit for Alien Workers," *Marianas Variety,* March 18, 1996.

    Torres's blacklist hints were contained in a press release dated March 18, 1996, titled "Union Sneaky and Untruthful," which he had reprinted in a two-page advertisement in the *Marianas Variety,* March 20, 1996.
40. Reyes: "Send Home Displaced Workers," *Marianas Variety,* March 18, 1996.
41. For example, the response of then-Governor Froilan Tenorio to the brewing trouble with the Philippines was literally to blame the victims. "I am getting fed up with complaints about Filipino workers here. . . . I am entertaining the idea of banning them." *Philippine Daily Inquirer,* December 5, 1994.
42. Twenty-nine is the total arrived at by John Bowe, who has written the most insightful account of the Saipan situation. See Bowe, *Nobodies,* p. 178.
43. Specifically, tours offered by the South African Foundation, an association of business leaders. This point is made in what seems to be Abramoff's very first letter to Froilan Tenorio, the CNMI governor who later hired him, dated February 8, 1995.
44. See Bruce Rickerson, "Why Did President Reagan End Up with Sanctions?" *Southern African Freedom Review* 2, no. 1 (Winter 1988). Rickerson attributed Reagan's inability to beat back the sanctions movement to, among other things, South Africa's failure to invest sufficiently in a trips program for American congressional assistants. The ideal trips program was the one run by Taiwan, Rickerson concluded. With only a few modifications, his description of it could pass for a description of what Abramoff proceeded to do eight years later.

> Over the years, many hundreds of [congressional] staff aides have been able to travel to that country. On their return, they have been inducted into an extensive network of ex-travellers, who, in turn, suggest new travellers. Taiwanese diplomatic officers follow-up on these contacts for years. The result of Taiwanese efforts is an extensive network of Congressional staffers who know people from Taiwan and have visited the country (p. 73).

45. Of course, by the time Abramoff was running the Saipan trips, the IFF's role as a South African front group was well known. Apparently that fact did not sour his relationship with these people.

    I counted at least five men who both wrote for an IFF publication and who traveled to the Marianas, including Richard Miniter, Doug Bandow, Bill Pascoe, Milton Copulos, and Dana Rohrabacher.
46. This memo was briefly infamous in 1998. It was discussed in the *Seattle Times* (March 22, 1998), the *Washington Post* (March 31, 1998), and the *Houston Chronicle* (April 1, 1998). At the Senate Energy and Natural Resources Hearings of March 31, 1998, it was discussed at some length, with each of the officers of the CNMI government asked to provide an explanation. None of them could. (See pp. 77–78 of the published version of the hearing.)
47. A less incendiary example of the same phenomenon—the coordination of government and garment industry—can be found in the July 27, 2000, letter from Team Abramoff member Michael O'Neil to the office of Governor Pedro Tenorio in which Abramoff's law firm accepts a contract to lobby for the CNMI. O'Neil discloses that the firm also represents the Western Pacific Economic Council, an organization of garment factory owners, but that this is no big deal because "our representation of the CNMI would be for the purposes consistent with those of the WPEC."
48. "Dirty infestation": "Pop Quiz," March 4, 1997; "Thank You, Willie Tan!" March 6, 1997, both written by Charles P. Reyes Jr., both published in the *Saipan Tribune*.

    "Flaunt the rights of employees": John DelRosario, "The Go for Broke Brigade," *Saipan Tribune*, February 24, 1999. To be fair, DelRosario's writing in this latter column is so confusing that it is impossible to say whether he is advocating this punishment for the D.C. bureaucrats who want to impose the minimum wage on Saipan or for featherbedding local government officials, both of whom are denounced in the course of the piece.
49. Tan's remarks on politicians and the business community appeared in the *Saipan Tribune*, the newspaper he owns, on April 4, 2001. He has spoken elsewhere of the need for "public-private partnership." See Giff Johnson, "Empire in the Sun," *Pacific Magazine*, August 1, 2003.
50. See Charles P. Reyes Jr., "Carpe Diem, Marianas!" *Saipan Tribune*, December 21, 2000. On another occasion, Reyes offered a near-complete

reiteration of Abramoff's old "free market of ideas" theory. "In a liberal democracy, speech is not free," Reyes instructed his countrymen. "We have to pay to get our message across, to tell our side of the story. Our friends in Washington need money to promote liberty and counter the efforts of those who would deprive us of it." Reyes, "Our Freedom Fighter in D.C.," *Saipan Tribune,* Wednesday, July 12, 2000.

51. I am relying here on Peter Stone's account in *Heist,* pp. 61–63. Willie Tan's payment for the trip is discussed in an e-mail from Jack to Willie dated December 17, 1999.
52. "Man of Vision" is the title of an interview with Fitial that ran in the *Saipan Tribune* on December 29, 2000.
53. Frank Rosario, "The 'Economy Governors,'" *Pacific Magazine,* March 1, 2006. http://www.pacificmagazine.net/issue/2006/03/01/the-economy-governors.
54. Greg McDonald, "Mexican Guest-Worker Plan in U.S. Is Pushed by DeLay," *Houston Chronicle,* January 6, 1998.
55. The promotional Web site is http://www.escapeartist.com/e_Books/Andorra_Report/Andorra_Report.html (I accessed it on March 17, 2007). On libertarian New Hampshire, see http://www.freestateproject.org/.
56. For the widespread use of this metaphor in apartheid South Africa, see Joseph Lelyveld, *Move Your Shadow: South Africa, Black and White* (New York: Penguin, 1985), p. 79. State president P. W. Botha made this point for an American audience in an interview with *Conservative Digest,* November, 1987, p. 7.
57. According to Nicholas Haysom, the former chief legal adviser to Nelson Mandela, the Bantustans were "the final solution to South Africa's political problems. In the Apartheid dream, there are no 'blacks' in 'white' South Africa, only foreign nationals who are there at the whim of their hosts, to 'minister to their needs' and to be subject to their discriminatory laws." *Ruling with the Whip: A Report on the Violation of Human Rights in the Ciskei* (Johannesburg: University of the Witwatersrand, 1983), p. 4.
58. The "president for life" of Ciskei was Lennox Sebe. On his corruption, see J. B. Peires, "Ethnicity and Pseudo-Ethnicity in the Ciskei," in *Segregation and Apartheid in Twentieth-Century South Africa,* ed. William Beinart and Saul Dubow (London: Routledge, 1995). The alleged mafia kingpin was Vito Palozollo. The incident is described in van Vuuren, chap. 10.
59. On Sebe's war on labor, see Haysom, *Ruling with the Whip,* and Joseph Lelyveld, "A 'Homeland' Spurs Protests from Blacks," *New York Times,* November 27, 1981.

   Referring to the commander of the Ciskei armed forces and police (and also Sebe's brother), Major General Charles Sebe, Haysom writes, "Poets and playwrights were supposed to apply to him before they could write because 'they have a method of putting across their ideology through poems and plays. I have taken it upon myself that any person who has a gift as a poet or playwright should be scrutinized.'" Haysom, *Ruling with the Whip*, p. 19.

60. Because it seemed to justify the Bantustan scheme, a backhanded support for black nationalism became an official policy of the apartheid government. In his 1985 book on South Africa, *Move Your Shadow*, Joseph Lelyveld observed that "insisting that they belonged in 'their own countries'—even if they had never seen them, even if there was not the remotest chance that they would ever go, even if most of these so-called countries existed only in [Prime Minister Verwoerd's] mind—was actually to champion black nationalism" (p. 15). Ciskei was a hard case, however. As the historian J. B. Peires puts it, Ciskei had "absolutely no basis in any ethnic, cultural or linguistic fact whatsoever." The entire justification for the place had to be invented—and insisted upon constantly. The people of the Ciskei are Xhosas, but by the time of Ciskei's founding, the Xhosas already had an official homeland: Transkei. Therefore, as Peires puts, it, Sebe committed "himself to the invention of a wholly novel and therefore wholly bogus ethnicity." Peires, "Ethnicity and Pseudo-Ethnicity," pp. 256, 279.
61. An example of the conservative fondness for Ciskei is the ten-page homage to the Bantustan's "radicalism" that was published by the libertarian journal *Reason* in 1985. Its author brushed off, one by one, most criticisms of Ciskei as fibs, exaggerations, or a failure to understand indigenous Ciskeian culture (a one-party state, for example, was said merely to reflect the traditional search for consensus within the tribe). He dwelled lovingly on the Bantustan's extreme campaign of tax-cutting, privatization, and deregulation, all of which constituted, as the Ciskeians themselves proudly said, "the removal of white man's law from black business." The place was said to attract even Americans, one of whom told the author, "It's like abolishing OSHA and more back in the States." Ciskei's way was so revolutionary, in fact, it might even be the undoing of apartheid itself. John Blundell, "Ciskei's Independent Way," *Reason*, April 1985, pp. 29, 28, 30, 33.

    See also Leon Louw and Frances Kendall, *South Africa: The Solution* (Bisho, Ciskei: Amagi Publications, 1986), which compares Ciskei to Hong Kong and praises its complete abandonment of pure food regulation. Pp. 51–52, 221.

    Corporate tax, income tax: See the advertisments of the Ciskei Peoples Development Bank Limited, headlined "Chequemate the Taxman in One Beautiful Move," which ran in nearly every issue of *Leadership* in 1986 and 1987.

    Labor peace and concessions to industrialists: *Ciskei: An Old Nation, a New Country* (Ciskei: Department of Foreign Affairs, 1983), p. 14.

62. Lelyveld, *Move Your Shadow,* p. 172. The book from which Lelyveld heard the general quote was *None Dare Call It Treason.*
63. Phillips on Ciskei investment opportunities: October 2, 1985, tour advertisement.
64. Louw's fantasy of "Cisbo" (Ciskei merged with the "Border Region") appears on pp. 221–23 of *The Solution.*
65. The interior secretary was Bruce Babbitt; his assessment appears on p. 18 of the 1998 hearings cited above. The representative of the Saipan Chamber of Commerce was Kerry McKinney; her quotation from Martin Luther King was in her formal statement to the committee, which appears on p. 97 of the hearings.
66. *Seattle Times,* March 22, 1998; *Washington Post,* July 26, 2000.
67. "Trouble in Paradise," an unsigned editorial in the *Journal of Commerce,* March 27, 1998. The magazine's reporting on the CNMI was otherwise excellent. See Paula L. Green, "Marianas a Haven for Asian Makers," September 25, 1997; Paula L. Green, "Apparel Makers Facing More Heat in Marianas," October 7, 1997; and John Maggs, "Saipan in Midst of Textile Conflict," March 6, 1998.
68. America was a land defined by its epic racism, declared the editor of the *Marianas Variety* in 1997, and in their rush to condemn the CNMI it was the liberals and journalists who were now the bearers of the "great tradition" of "waging genocide on non-white people." But the brave people of the Marianas, "aside from refusing to die *en masse,* have refused to surrender control over their own affairs to the do-gooders from the mainland." "Shame Indeed," *Marianas Variety,* May 16, 1997.
69. "Impose their imperialistic will": Charles P. Reyes Jr., "The New Imperialism," *Saipan Tribune,* October 19, 1999. "Racist agenda of economic annihilation": John DelRosario, "Racist Remarks from Former OIA Misfit," *Saipan Tribune,* July 28, 2000. "The rights of the indigenous people": John DelRosario, "The Washington Hearings," *Saipan Tribune,* August 27, 1999. Abramoff as hero to the indigenous: Charles P. Reyes Jr., "Our Freedom Fighter in DC," *Saipan Tribune,* July 12, 2000.

    The suffering of indigenous people being one of the foremost liberal causes of the time, this must have seemed like a foolproof way to confuse the threatening goo-goos. Study as you will the language of the UN Declaration on the Rights of Indigenous Peoples, however, you will find there no affirmation of such peoples' right to reduce *other* peoples, nonindigenous and inauthentic though they might be, to indentured servitude.
70. The three letters can be found in the supporting materials assembled by the Senate Indian Affairs Committee and included in the record for the "Oversight Hearing Regarding Tribal Lobbying Matters," November 2, 2005, part 2, pp. 421–27. They are attached to an e-mail dated Feb-

ruary 24, 2004, and they are written for the signatures of Chief Martin of the Mississippi Band of Choctaw Indians ("Undermining Tribal Self-Determination"), Richard Milanovich of the Agua Caliente ("Dangerous Racism"), and Lovelin Poncho of the Coushatta tribe ("An Attack on Tribal Autonomy").

71. This is PL 15-108. See the critique of the law by the federal labor ombudsman, Jim Benedetto, printed in the *Saipan Tribune* for October 31, 2007, and available at http://www.saipantribune.com/newsstory.aspx?cat=3&newsID=73787.
72. The tribune of indigenous pride is a group called "Taotao Tano" (literally, the people of the land). "To Free the Oppressed," reads one of the banners they parade around Saipan, but addressing the impoverished guest workers on a Web site the group makes the meaning of this noble sentiment starkly clear: "Weren't you all supposed to work and leave?" Other charming slogans: "Taotao Tano's First!" "Just do your job right!" and "Taotao Tano's Are Watching Your Movements!" See http://taotaotanocnmi2.blogspot.com/.

Chapter 10: Win-Win Corruption

1. During a 2001 audit, the CNMI government made available to the public almost all of Jack Abramoff's billing records and correspondence with CNMI authorities. It takes up thousands of pages and describes the day-by-day activities of each member of his team of lobbyists. In them we read about:
    - Grover Norquist's famous Wednesday morning meetings; Paul Weyrich's Stanton Group meetings; CPAC; and the Heritage Foundation's annual Resource Bank conference—all of which were attended by members of the team.
    - Think tanks like Citizens for a Sound Economy, the Competitive Enterprise Institute, and the Adam Smith Institute of London, England.
    - Smaller pressure groups like Americans for a Balanced Budget and Frontiers of Freedom.
    - Numerous journalists, both freelance and employed by publications like the *Wall Street Journal,* the *National Interest,* the *Public Interest,* the *Orange County Register,* the *Providence Journal,* and, of course, the *Washington Times.*
    - A youth-oriented outfit, the Leadership Institute.
    - A national security concern, the National Defense Council Foundation.
    - Antiwaste and anticorruption watchdogs like the National Legal and Policy Center and Citizens Against Government Waste.

2. Burton Pines, as quoted in Gregg Easterbrook, " 'Ideas Move Nations,' " *Atlantic,* January 1986.
3. Ferrara: Eamon Javers, "Op-Eds for Sale," *Business Week,* December 16, 2005. Bandow: "The Lesson Jack Abramoff Taught Me," an article that appeared in the *Los Angeles Times* for January 4, 2006. I found it here: http://www.aei-brookings.org/policy/page.php?id=241.
4. These are all chapter or section titles from *The Politics of Plunder.*
5. Federal Reserve as "legal counterfeiter": Doug Bandow, *The Politics of Plunder,* p. 135. Community Reinvestment Act: ibid., p. 75. Social Security as Ponzi scheme: You can find this metaphor anywhere on the right, but see in particular Peter Ferrara, "The Political Foundations of Social Security," in Ferrara, ed., *Social Security: Prospects for Real Reform* (Washington, D.C.: Cato Institute, 1985), p. 96. Environmental Protection Agency as Gestapo: Tom DeLay, as quoted in Maraniss and Weisskopf, *"Tell Newt to Shut Up!"* p. 13. City governments as looters: Grover Norquist, "Politics," *American Spectator,* April 1999. Taxation and muggers: Grover Norquist, "Let Big Gov Get Off Our Backs, and Let Us Keep the Money We Earn," *Philadelphia Inquirer,* January 20, 1998.
6. To prove his point, Scanlon evaluates a number of cases of misbehaving congressmen from 1798 to 1870, then skips to the Adam Clayton Powell debacle of 1967. Congressmen have been bad throughout our history; therefore there have been no changes worth investigating. Michael P. S. Scanlon, "Ethics, Politics, and Partisanship: An Evaluative History of the House Ethics Process from 1789 to 1967," unpublished MA thesis, Johns Hopkins University, April 2006, p. 3.
7. Ibid., p. 80. In fact, Cunningham was *sentenced* in 2006. He took bribes earlier.

   Scanlon also takes exception to Nancy Pelosi's assertion that the Congress Scanlon had helped to corrupt was the "most closed, corrupt Congress in History." Scanlon's reply: it was worse in the nineteenth century! "This is very strong, well-documented evidence of wide spread corruption in Congress over 137 years ago. The presentation of this research into the public realm at the very least establishes that the statements by the Minority Leader and some in the media, that this Congress is the most corrupt in history is questionable at best" (p. 81).
8. On this delicate matter Scanlon wrote, "Not only do you kick him—you kick him until he passes out—then beat him over the head with a baseball bat—then roll him up in an old rug—and throw him off a cliff into the pound surf below!!!!!"

   A 1998 e-mail from Scanlon to Tony Rudy, as quoted in Brody Mullins, "Behind Unraveling of DeLay's Team, A Jilted Fiancée," *Wall Street Journal,* March 31, 2006.
9. Fred S. McChesney, "Rent Extraction and Rent Creation in the Economic Theory of Regulation," *Journal of Legal Studies* 16 (January

1987), pp. 102, 104. This is an essay-length summary of McChesney's ideas; he later enlarged it into a book called *Money for Nothing: Politicians, Rent Extraction, and Political Extortion* (Cambridge, Mass.: Harvard University Press, 1997).

10. McChesney, "Rent Extraction," pp. 109, 113.
11. Ibid., p. 111.
12. Larry Sabato describes the episode in *PAC Power,* p. 134. He does not describe it as a case of extortion by Congress, however, but just the opposite: a highly convincing demonstration of private money's new-found influence in Washington. On the Reagan-era FTC, see Ronald Brownstein and Nina Easton, *Reagan's Ruling Class: Portraits of the President's Top 100 Officials* (Washington, D.C.: Presidential Accountability Group, 1982), pp. 413–25. In 1982 the chairman of the FTC was James Miller III, a fixture of the right-wing think-tank world.
13. Here are McChesney's words.

    > The history of the FTC's "Used Car Rule" provides an example of the gain to politicians from threatening this type of regulation and later removing the threat for a fee. In 1975, Congress statutorily ordered the FTC to initiate a rulemaking to regulate used-car dealers' warranties. The FTC promulgated a rule imposing costly warranty and auto-defect disclosure requirements, creating the opportunity for legislators to extract concessions from dealers to void the burdensome measures. In the meantime, in fact, Congress had legislated for itself a veto over FTC actions. On promulgation of the rule, used-car dealers and their trade association descended on Congress, spending large sums of money for relief from the proposed rule's costs. When the concessions were forthcoming, Congress vetoed the very rule it had ordered.

    McChesney, "Rent Extraction," p. 114. In a footnote, McChesney acknowledges that the congressional veto was overturned by the Supreme Court, whereupon the Reagan FTC "essentially gutted" its own rule.

    The statute by which Congress "statutorily ordered" the FTC to regulate is the Magnuson-Moss Act; neither Warren Magnuson nor Frank Moss were still in Congress in 1982.
14. Susan Schmidt, "A Jackpot from Indian Gaming Tribes," *Washington Post,* February 22, 2004.
15. "The Real Gas Gougers," May 11, 2006; "Hot Topic: Pains at the Pump," April 26, 2006. See also "Pains at the Pump," May 28, 2007, and "The Gas-Gouging Myth," May 24, 2006, all in the *Wall Street Journal.*
16. Of course, for kickbacks to be beneficial, the specialist to whom the client is referred must do a quality job, and this Scanlon apparently did

not do. See Mark V. Pauly's work on kickbacks in medicine, "The Ethics and Economics of Kickbacks and Fee Splitting," *Bell Journal of Economics* 10, no. 1 (Spring 1979).

17. "Decriminalize Insider Trading," an essay from 1989, was reprinted in Bandow's book *The Politics of Plunder,* p. 264. See also Doug Bandow, "Insider Trading—Where's the Crime?" *National Review,* April 16, 1990, pp. 37–38. On price gouging, see Doug Bandow, "Price Gouging in the Public Interest," an essay dated October 27, 2005, that appeared on the Cato Institute Web site, http://www.cato.org/pub_display.php?pub_id=5150, and Doug Bandow, "Congress All Pumped Up," an essay dated May 14, 2007, that appeared in the *American Spectator,* http://www.spectator.org/dsp_article.asp?art_id=11429.
18. Wheeler, "The Technology of Freedom," p. 66. Addressing a meeting of the Council for National Policy, Wheeler went on to celebrate the democratization of blackmail. First, you "use computer databases to discover what hidden assets and shady deals any politician of your choice (from local to federal) may have." Then

    > you could put it into a plain white envelope which is hand-delivered to your target, together with a note saying all of this will be made public unless its recipient announces his or her retirement.
    >
    > I'm sure there is no truth to the rumor some of you may have heard that there is a group of ex-CIA and ex-NSA computer geniuses called "The Fifth Column" with a Cray supercomputer, and that all these life-long devoted public servants who are suddenly retiring from Congress—such as Patsy Schroeder who already had her re-election materials printed, or Charlie Wilson who had already bought air time, or Charlie Rose or Sam Gibbons—got a plain white envelope just prior to their announcements.
    >
    > Probably just a coincidence.
    >
    > It's also not true, you understand, that I know one of the "Fifth Column" fellows as a personal friend. That's just a rumor.
    >
    > So—I can see the thought balloon above each of your heads: When does Slick Willie get his envelope? (pp. 70–71)

19. See L. Gordon Crovitz, "Milken and His Enemies," October 1, 1990; Henry G. Manne and Larry E. Ribstein, "The SEC v. the American Shareholder," November 25, 1988; "The Milken File," August 31, 1992; and "Meeting with Milken," November 10, 1989, all in *National Review.*
20. Here is a sample of the argument: "To get to the crime of price fixing, three rights are magically transmuted into a wrong. Everyone has the

right to offer the fruit of his labor and investment in the marketplace, the right of assembly, and the right of speech. But as soon as you exercise the first of these, you lose the rest. Say you're a maker of the pig-feed additive lysine: If you assemble with other lysine makers in a hotel room and speak about the price of lysine, you become subject to treble damages and prison time among real felons." Holman Jenkins, "The 'Crime' of Price Fixing Finally Finds a Real Victim," *Wall Street Journal,* February 4, 1997.

21. These thoughts are found in McChesney's meditation on the Abramoff affair, "Indian Givers: Politicians and Tribal Gambling Casinos," an entry dated February 6, 2006, in the online *Library of Economics and Liberty,* http://www.econlib.org/library/Columns/y2006/Mcchesneygambling.html.
22. Norquist interview with *Reason,* February 1997.
23. For example, the National Legal and Policy Center's "Corporate Integrity Project" criticizes the buying of influence by the wealthy but also insists it is "the inevitable result of high levels of government spending and intervention in the marketplace." See http://www.nlpc.org/cip.asp.

    Another example is furnished by Fred McChesney, in the "Indian Givers" essay cited above: "If one does not like what the Jack Abramoffs in Washington do, the only way to stop it is to reduce government control of gambling. On the other hand, if you like bigger government, be prepared for the next Abscam or Keating Five . . . and the next Abramoff."
24. David Margolick, "Washington's Invisible Man," *Vanity Fair,* April 2006, p. 251.
25. *Free marketeer* was a term Abramoff used to describe himself and the CRs in the early days. See the interview with him by John Rees in *Review of the NEWS,* September 8, 1982.
26. Robert Putnam with Robert Leonardi and Raffaella Y. Nanetti, *Making Democracy Work: Civic Traditions in Modern Italy* (Princeton, N.J.: Princeton University Press, 1993), pp. 89, 111.
27. According to the business writer Stephen Baker, soon after Hurricane Katrina hit, Richard Edelman, a public relations exec hired by Wal-Mart, was boasting of "how his company helped Wal-Mart generate good buzz during the Katrina catastrophe. Edelman learned early that Wal-Mart employees were using blogs to communicate logistics. They got the blog URLs to conservative blogs, which then made their way to mainstream media. This all fit nicely into the story line that was taking shape: Government doesn't work, Wal-Mart does." See "Edelman shows Wal-Mart the power of blogs," *Business Week Online,* October 26, 2005, at http://blogs.businessweek.com/the_thread/blogspotting/archives/2005/10/edelman_shows_w.html.

28. "Failure of government": Radley Balko (of Cato, Reason, Foxnews .com, etc.), "When the Catastrophe Is Government," an essay posted on Foxnews.com on September 7, 2005. *Fortune*: Issue of October 3, 2005. Henninger: "Bureaucratic Failure: To understand Katrina's Problems, Read the 9/11 Report," *Wall Street Journal,* September 2, 2005. John Tierney, "From FEMA to WEMA," *New York Times,* September 20, 2005.
29. Lincoln Steffens, *The Shame of the Cities* (1904; reprint, New York: Sagamore Press, 1957), p. 4. Lincoln Steffens, *The Autobiography of Lincoln Steffens* (New York: Harcourt, Brace, 1931), p. 413.
30. "In one place on Earth, the theory would finally be put into practice in its most perfect and uncompromised form," writes Naomi Klein. "A country of 25 million would not be rebuilt as it was before the war; it would be erased, disappeared. In its place would spring forth a gleaming showroom for laissez-faire economics, a utopia such as the world had never seen." Klein, "Baghdad Year Zero: Pillaging Iraq in Pursuit of a Neocon Utopia," *Harper's,* September 2004. "[Paul] Bremer had come to Iraq to build not just a democracy but a free market," writes Rajiv Chandrasekaran, the *Washington Post* reporter, in *Imperial Life in the Emerald City: Inside Iraq's Green Zone* (New York: Knopf, 2006). "He insisted that economic reform and political reform were intertwined. 'If we don't get their economy right, no matter how fancy our political transformation, it won't work,' he said" (p. 62).
31. Chandrasekaran describes the various kids and the preference for politics over expertise on pp. 91–94 of *Imperial Life*. Feith's sandbagging of Jay Garner is reported on p. 31.
32. The *Economist* quoted in Klein, "Baghdad Year Zero." Chandrasekaran, *Imperial Life,* p. 13. Contracting specialist, an anonymous officer of New Bridge Strategies, one of Joe Allbaugh's firms, quoted in Thomas B. Edsall and Juliet Eilperin, "Lobbyists Set Sights on Money-Making Opportunities in Iraq," *Washington Post,* October 2, 2003.
33. The fiasco of the Iraqi army is described by Chandrasekaran, *Imperial Life,* p. 273.
34. Ibid., pp. 115–17. The treatment of Iraqi unions by the occupiers was particularly tragic. As numerous others have noted, unions have played an important role in postwar reconstruction efforts everywhere from South Africa after apartheid to Europe after World War II. Among other reasons, this is because they tend to be secular and class-based, rather than race-based. The American occupiers of Iraq, though, made no effort to cultivate the Iraqi labor movement, even though it had been an enemy of the Saddam Hussein regime, and in fact specifically retained Saddam's anti-union laws while repealing almost everything else. See

Matthew Harwood, "Pinkertons at the CPA," *Washington Monthly,* April 2005.

35. Peter McPherson, quoted in Chandrasekaran, *Imperial Life,* p. 120.
36. Armed entrepreneurs: James Glanz and Stephen Farrell, "Militias Seizing Control of Grid, Starving Baghdad of Electricity," *New York Times,* August 23, 2007. Garden hoses: The *Washington Post* ran an Associated Press photo on August 5, 2007, that carried the following caption: "Abdul Amir Hussein connects a network of water hoses to apartments in a central Baghdad, Iraq complex Saturday, Aug. 4, 2007. The Baghdad water supply has been severely affected by power blackouts and cuts that have affected pumping and filtration stations. Iraq's electricity grid could collapse any day because of insurgent sabotage, rising demand, fuel shortages and provincial officials who are unplugging local power stations from the national system, electricity officials said on Saturday."

Conclusion: Reaching for the Pillars

1. DeLay: Peter Perl, "DeLay's Next Mission from God," *Washington Post,* April 9, 2006.

   Abramoff: "Address by Jack Abramoff, Chairman College Republican National Committee," Raleigh E. Milton, ed., *Official Report of the Proceedings of the Thirty-Third Republican National Convention,* August 20, 1984, p. 21.

   Norquist: "We must do everything we can to institutionalize the conservative revolution and make it permanent in the minds of the people," Norquist said in August 1984. "We must establish a Brezhnev Doctrine for conservative gains. The Brezhnev Doctrine states that once a country becomes communist it can never change. Conservatives must establish their own doctrine and declare their victories permanent, not only in foreign policy, but in domestic policy as well. A revolution is not successful unless it succeeds in preserving itself." Hart, *The Third Generation,* p. 158.
2. On breaking the cycle of nationalization and privatization, see John Burton, "Privatization: The Thatcher Case," *Managerial and Decision Economics,* 8 (1987). On the privatization of housing, see Naomi Klein, *Shock Doctrine: The Rise of Disaster Capitalism* (New York: Metropolitan Books, 2007), p. 135. Eradicating Labor Party socialism: Richard A. Melcher, "Thatcher's Revolution: Act III," *Business Week,* May 25, 1987.
3. The quotes cited here are drawn from the following essays, most of them available on the Web site of Americans for Tax Reform. "Crush the structures": Norquist, "The 2000 Elections Will Decide the Democrats' Future," *American Spectator,* April 1999. Trial lawyers:

Norquist, "Cornered Rats Fight Hard," *American Enterprise,* March, 2004. Labor unions: "Happy Warrior," an interview with Norquist published in *Reason* magazine in February 1997; see also Norquist, "The 2000 Elections." "Mexican truck drivers": Norquist, "Cornered Rats." NEA: Norquist, "The Second Term Diet," *American Spectator,* March 2004. "Big city machines": Norquist, "The 2000 Elections." "Dead man walking": Norquist, "We Raise Taxes, They Cut Spending?" *National Review Online,* June 30, 2006.

4. In the days when labor was strong, "it did not confine itself to bread-and-butter issues for its own members," remembers the columnist David Broder. "It was at the forefront of battles for aid to education, civil rights, housing programs and a host of other social causes important to the whole community." Broder, "The Price of Labor's Decline," *Washington Post,* September 9, 2004.
5. "According to polls, virtually no voters chose Bush on the basis of his support for private accounts." Hacker and Pierson, *Off Center,* pp. 40–41.
6. Klein, *The Shock Doctrine,* chap. 8.
7. Stockman, *The Triumph of Politics,* p. 74.
8. As Stockman himself describes it: "These dramatic changes in both my comprehension of budget estimating and the true fiscal math of the supply-side program occurred almost overnight. That should have been cause for second thoughts and reassessment of the whole proposition. But it didn't happen that way" (*The Triumph of Politics,* p. 74).
9. Ibid., p. 74. Stockman further describes his plans to force the liberals' hand on p. 145 and 147.
10. Shortly after the conclusion of the 1988 presidential campaign, Friedman wrote an op-ed for the *Wall Street Journal* titled "Why the Twin Deficits Are a Blessing." While he disapproved of the spending that built the deficit, he wrote, the deficit itself was a good thing because it "has been the only effective restraint on congressional spending." By blowing all that money on tax cuts and aircraft carriers, in other words, Reagan had prevented liberals in Congress from spending it on *their* pet projects.

    Friedman reiterated his rosy views on deficits again during the George W. Bush years, after the government had worked its way to surplus and fallen back again. "If anything, at the moment, the large deficit has a positive effect of holding down further spending," Friedman said in 2006. "In that sense, it is a good thing. But it is not a good thing if produced by more spending." *New Perspectives Quarterly,* interview with Milton Friedman, Spring 2006, available at http://www.digitalnpq.org/archive/2006_winter/friedman.html.
11. "We didn't invent deficit spending," Reagan growled at New York governor Hugh Carey in 1981. See Stockman, *The Triumph of Politics,* p. 162.

12. President Reagan himself appointed a "Commission on Privatization," and both the Heritage and the Reason foundations issued reports on the subject. All were cast as solutions to the deficit emergency. See David F. Linowes, ed., *Privatization: Toward More Effective Government: Report of the President's Commission on Privatization* (Champaign, Ill.: University of Illinois Press, 1988); Stephen Moore and Stuart M. Butler, eds., *Privatization: A Strategy for Taming the Federal Budget Fiscal Year 1988* (Washington, D.C.: Heritage Foundation, [1987]); Robert W. Poole, ed., *Privatization: Toward Resolving the Deficit Crisis* (Santa Monica, Calif.: Reason Foundation, 1988).
13. The figures I am using here are those given by Robert Reich in *Locked in the Cabinet* (New York: Knopf, 1997), p. 28. They appear to be in current dollars; in constant dollars the numbers were slightly less scary.
14. "Stockman's Revenge": George Stephanopoulos recalls hearing both Bill and Hillary Clinton refer to the deficit in this way during the budget showdown with Congress in 1995. Stephanopoulos, *All Too Human: A Political Education* (Boston: Little, Brown, 1999), p. 387. Greenspan: Bob Woodward, *The Agenda: Inside the Clinton White House* (New York: Simon and Schuster, 1994), p. 106. Clinton: Woodward, *The Agenda,* p. 84.
15. Conrad Burns, a Republican senator from Montana, directed millions of dollars to something called the Northern Rockies Center for Space Privatization. Duncan Hunter, a Republican representative from California, caused tens of millions to flow to a tiny company building a supposedly supersonic plane that never flew.
16. James Burnham, *Suicide of the West: An Essay on the Meaning and Destiny of Liberalism* (1964; reprint, Regnery, 1985), p. 140.
17. For a description and an unsparing dismantling of this idea in its every particular, see Hacker and Pierson, *Off Center*.
18. These quotations all come from Tom Peters's book *The Circle of Innovation: You Can't Shrink Your Way to Greatness* (New York: Knopf, 2000), pp. xvi, 69.
19. From a speech Falwell gave at a September 11, 1983, memorial service for McDonald, as reported in the Birch Society's *Review of the NEWS,* September 21, 1983, p. 46. The first two ellipses are in the original, as is the first set of brackets and the italics.
20. Hacker and Pierson, *Off Center,* p. 112.
21. Representative Steny Hoyer of Maryland, the current House majority leader, is K Street's reigning favorite among the Democratic leadership, although his appeals to lobby-land have fallen far short of Tom DeLay's. See Brody Mullins, "Hoyer's Own 'K St. Project,'" *Roll Call,* May 21, 2003 (an article posted on Hoyer's official majority leader Web site). The party on the tenth floor of 101 Con was held in 2006 to celebrate Hoyer's victory over John Murtha for the majority leader post. See "K Street Happy with Hoyer Victory," *The Hill,* November 21, 2006.

22. The champion Democratic earmarker is John Murtha, who has sent some $2 billion in earmarked funds to Johnstown, Pennsylvania, his hometown. See John R. Wilke, "How Lawmaker Rebuilt Hometown on Earmarks," *Wall Street Journal,* October 30, 2007.
23. The champion in this regard is almost certainly Hillary Clinton, whose massive fund-raising has mysteriously paralleled the even greater fund-raising done by the foundation and presidential library of her husband, former president Bill Clinton. See Don Van Natta Jr., Jo Becker, and Mike McIntire, "In His Charity and Her Politics, Many Clinton Donors Overlap," *New York Times,* December 20, 2007.
24. John Breaux, a Democratic senator from Louisiana, famously said in 1981 that his vote could not be bought, "but it can be rented." When he announced his retirement from public service in 2004, he became the immediate object of a "bidding war" between the city's most prestigious lobbying firms. In 2008 he announced his partnership with Trent Lott, a Republican senator from Mississippi. The Brinks remark is attributed to an anonymous lobbyist and is quoted in Jeanne Cummings, "Lobbying Lucre Awaits Lott," *Politico,* November 26, 2007. The "bidding war" is mentioned in Geoff Earle, "K Street Bidding for Breaux," *The Hill,* October 20, 2004.
25. GNP and industrial production numbers are from the *Economic Report of the President* (Washington, D.C., 1965), p. 3. "A growing abundance, widely shared" appears on p. 31.

    "Rich people once lived in a world apart," wrote Getty; "today almost the only difference between the multimillionaire and the reasonably well-to-do man earning $15,000 to $25,000 a year is that the millionaire works harder, relaxes less, is burdened with greater responsibilities and is exposed to the constant glare of publicity." J. Paul Getty, "The World Is Mean to Millionaires," *Saturday Evening Post,* May 22, 1965, p. 10.

    Getty went on to propose this meek justification for the existence of the rich: "Though our rewards may be small, we [i.e., millionaires] are, if our society is to remain in its present form, essential to the nation's prosperity. We provide others with incentives which would not exist if we were to disappear. As active businessmen, we find it useful to have money simply because a tolerable margin of financial security makes for increased efficiency and competitiveness. If I were not using my fortune usefully, I would have little justification for having it in the first place."
26. "Lost touch with reality": Hofstadter made this remark in a lecture in 1962 and was much abused for it. "A vital blow": This was one of Hofstadter's criticisms of the Goldwater movement in 1964. See David S. Brown, *Richard Hofstadter: An Intellectual Biography* (Chicago: University of Chicago Press, 2006), pp. 152, 157.

Afterword: Götterdämmerung

1. William Black, "Reexamining the Law-and-Economics Theory of Corporate Governance," *Challenge*, March–April 2003.
2. Frank Partnoy, *Infectious Greed: How Deceit and Risk Corrupted the Financial Markets* (New York: Henry Holt, 2003), p. 295.
3. At Washington Mutual, the bank that became most famous for openhanded lending, incentives lined the road to hell, with realtors receiving fees from the bank for bringing in clients, with the shakiest loans bringing mortgage brokers the most lucrative commissions, and with the CEO raking in $88 million from 2001 to 2007, before the outrageous risks of the scheme cratered the entire enterprise. See Peter S. Goodman and Gretchen Morgenson, "By Saying Yes, WaMu Built Empire on Shaky Loans," *New York Times*, December 28, 2008.
4. Preemption of state-level regulation: See Eliot Spitzer, "Predatory Lenders' Partner in Crime," *Washington Post*, February 14, 2008, and Edmund Andrews, "Fed Shrugged as Subprime Crisis Spread," *New York Times*, December 18, 2007.
5. Greg Ip and Damian Paletta, "Lending Oversight: Regulators Scrutinized in Mortgage Meltdown," *Wall Street Journal*, March 22, 2007.
6. Binyamin Appelbaum and Ellen Nakashima, "Banking Regulator Played Advocate over Enforcer," *Washington Post*, November 23, 2008; Binyamin Appelbaum and Ellen Nakashima, "Regulator Let IndyMac Bank Falsify Report," *Washington Post*, December 23, 2008. The phrase "competition in laxity" was originally coined to describe Reagan-era banking regulation. See William K. Black's study of the S&L disaster, *The Best Way to Rob a Bank Is to Own One: How Corporate Executives and Politicians Looted the S&L Industry* (Austin, TX: The University of Texas Press, 2005).
7. On Reagan's SEC chief, John Shad, see Brownstein and Easton, p. 718; and "The Man from Wall Street," the four-part series on Shad by David Vise and Steve Coll that ran in the *Washington Post* in 1989. The quotation from the SEC's chief economist is from part four of that series, dated February 8, 1989.
8. On Harvey Pitt, see Eli Mason, "White Paper or Whitewash?" *Accounting Today*, January 5, 1998; Marcy Gordon, "Consumer Advocates Uneasy About SEC Head Nominee's Statements," the Associated Press, July 20, 2001; and Stephen Labaton, "Government Report Details a Chaotic S.E.C. under Pitt," *New York Times*, December 20, 2002.
9. See the February 28, 2005, speech by Lori Richards, Director of the SEC's Office of Compliance Inspections and Examinations. http://sec.gov/news/speech/spch022805lar.htm.
10. See Walt Bogdanich, "Impartiality of S.E.C. is Questioned," *New York Times*, October 7, 2008.
11. See Adam Zagorin and Michael Weisskopf, "Inside the Breakdown at

the SEC," *Time*, March 9, 2009, and Stephen Labaton, "SEC Concedes Oversight Flaws Fueled Collapse," *New York Times*, September 27, 2008.

12. James D. Cox and Randall Thomas, "SEC Enforcement Actions for Financial Fraud and Private Litigation: An Empirical Inquiry," Vanderbilt Law and Economics Research Paper No. 03-08, May 23, 2003. Eric Lichtblau, "Federal Cases of Stock Fraud Drop Sharply," *New York Times*, December 25, 2008.

Acknowledgments

My first thanks must go to my research assistants, Ben Francis-Fallon and Allison O'Brien, who delivered astonishing results under impossible deadlines. Jim McNeill and Matt Spieler were also very helpful. To all of these do I also apologize for the mountains of direct mail letters, billing records, and awful books that I asked them to read.

The good people at USA PIRG assembled for me an impressive collection of news clips on the eighties campus right. People for the American Way gave me access to their voluminous files of right-wing direct mail. The Wilcox Collection of Contemporary Political Movements at the Spencer Library of the University of Kansas was also helpful in this regard, as was the National Security Archive at George Washington University. Al Ross at the Institute for Democracy Studies followed the career of Jack Abramoff long before that was cool. Chip Berlet and Political Research Associates combed their vast collections of right-wing materials and came up with amazing finds. Research librarians are an admirable breed generally, but those at the National Library of South Africa, the Wisconsin

Historical Society, and the University of Hawaii, Manoa, deserve special mention for their help with this project.

I received valuable guidance on the workings of Washington from Scott Amey, Danielle Brian, and Beth Daley of the Project on Government Oversight; from Gary Bass at OMB Watch; from Joan Claybrook and her colleagues at Public Citizen; and from Deborah Greenfield and others at the AFL-CIO. Larry Sabato talked to me about Northern Virginia. Wendy Doromal, Dennis Greenia, P. F. Kluge, and especially John Bowe, author of the great book *Nobodies*, helped me understand the Northern Mariana Islands. Joe McCartin and Jacque Simon outlined for me the history of federal workforce issues. John Daniel of the School for International Training told me the story of the IFF and the Truth and Reconciliation Commission, while Dan O'Meara guided me through South Africa's unhappy recent history. Patrick Bond and Hennie van Vuuren were also very helpful with my research on that country. Bill Minter provided valuable assistance on Angola-related matters.

I am grateful to Franklin Foer and the people at *The New Republic* for publishing an earlier version of the section on 101 Constitution, as well as for all the help they gave me on the piece. Thanks also to the *New York Times* for giving me the opportunity to work out some of this book's themes in a guest column. *Harper's Magazine* let me use their pages to explore the issues relating to Social Security privatization. Chris Lehmann furnished metaphors with remarkable promptness. And, as always, George Hodak did a superb review in record time.

To Eric Klinenberg goes the credit for opening my eyes to the whole issue of government-by-contractor; to *Rolling Stone* magazine and Eric Bates go my thanks for publishing some of our collective thoughts on that issue. Jonathan Adelstein, Jaron Bourke, Terry Bracy, David Carmen, Kim Eisler, Raj Goyle, Tom Schaller, David Sirota, Chris Strohm, and Jason Vest each helped me understand Washington in their own way. Michael Bracy, Paul Brown,

Ben Edwards, and Conor O'Neil showed me around. Alan Nairn turned up at exactly the right minute. David Miner seemed always to know whom to call and how it all went down.

My most profound thanks to Sara Bershtel and Riva Hocherman at Metropolitan Books—one couldn't ask for a smarter and more dedicated editorial team. Or for a more supportive agent than Joe Spieler, who for years has managed my literary affairs. To Wendy, Maddy, and Theo, my eternal gratitude for their patience and consideration.

Index

About the Author

Thomas Frank is the author of *What's the Matter with Kansas?* and *One Market Under God*. The founding editor of *The Baffler* and a contributing editor at *Harper's*, Frank has received a Lannan award and is a columnist for *The Wall Street Journal*. He lives, of course, in Washington, D.C.